Fort Worth
A FRONTIER TRIUMPH

Fort Worth
A FRONTIER TRIUMPH

Julia Kathryn Garrett

Foreword by Jenkins Garrett

TEXAS CHRISTIAN UNIVERSITY PRESS
FORT WORTH

*I dedicate to the Junior Historians of the 1940s and 1950s,
and to all youths this chronicle of facts and
legends with the hope that it reveals a historical truth:
men should develop an awareness that
world and national events do influence their lives.*

Library of Congress Cataloging-in-Publication Data

Garrett, Julia Kathryn.
  Fort Worth : a frontier triumph / Julia Kathryn Garrett
    p. cm.
  Facsim. of: Austin, Tex. : Encino Press, 1972
  Includes bibliographical references (p. 341) and index
  ISBN 0-87565-155-0
  1. Fort Worth (Tex.) –History. I. Title
F394.F7G37 1996
976.4'5315–dc20

95-38125
CIP

1996 facsimile edition made possible by the generosity of Virginia R. Wagnon.
First edition made possible by the generosity of former students of the author:
Mrs. John M. Griffith, Jr. (Martha Leonard), Mrs. Leleand A. Hodges, Jr. (Ann
Leonard), Miss Miranda Leonard, Mrs. Raymond A. Pittman, Jr. (Sue Rowan),
Mrs. Madelon Leonard Mariotti, Mrs. George B. Vaughan (Dianne Garrett). In
this manner they expressed their appreciation for having had the opportunity of
studying under Miss Garrett at Arlington Heights High School.

The index for the 1996 edition of this volume was compiled by Carol Roark.
Text design: William Wittliff • Jacket design: Margie Adkins.

Preface

Books are written through visionary wisdom of others. They embolden a writer to remain steadfast until his work is completed.

For eleven years my manuscript was reposited on a shelf in the Fort Worth Public Library until Jenkins Garrett, by constant insistence that I complete the work, and through generous guarantees that the manuscript would be published, has brought this chronicle into existence.

The manuscript was written in response to an impelling request by Mary Daggett Lake, now immortal, for a popularized story of Fort Worth. She possessed an intense consciousness of responsibility to nurture the traditions of our city. This awareness of an inherited trust arose from a sensitive perception of the beauties and potential splendors of the bluffs rimming our valley at the forks of the Trinity, and from a knowledge of the historical experiences of America that had taken place here.

Because her insight into the evidence that the splendors of nature and the actions of man are interwoven, she dedicated her life to preserving both the history and nature's glories of this area. She left to posterity trails of beauty in the parks of the city and an archive of Fort Worth history that she spent her life gathering, which is now the property of the Fort Worth Public Library.

As a child she lived with the historymakers of our city and spent days riding in a buggy with her great-uncle Captain Ephraim Merrill Daggett, as he pointed out historical sites and enacted the epoch-making events of Fort Worth which he knew firsthand. As an adult, she spent years visiting the first hundred pioneers, guiding them to write their autobiographies or reminiscences. From these accounts by pioneers along with their scrapbooks and her library of rare books came much of the material for this homespun chronicle.

The Junior Historians of Arlington Heights and Paschal high schools, as chapters of the Texas State Historical Association, were another compelling force. Many Junior Historians were descendants of the pioneers. Their zeal in preparing the biographies of their forebears for publication in the *Junior Historian*, now the *Texas Historian* magazine, was an inspiring directive to me.

In writing this narrative of human experiences, life in our area of the upper Trinity is reviewed from the time of Spanish explorations of this region in the eighteenth century until the closing years of the era of Reconstruction in 1872. At that time, the economy was firmly laid and political rights were restored to veterans and local officials of the former Confederacy, climaxing a period in the birth and blooming of Fort Worth.

An attempt has been made to present the early history of this city not as a record of historical events, but rather an account of men being profoundly affected by them. History is not the bare record of leaders directing events. People's daily living is history—their facing of challenges created by the economic, political and social conditions of their time, the searching of their consciences, and the acceptance with valor of their trials and triumphs.

Hence these stories of the birth and young years of Fort Worth, both legend and historical fact, are descriptive of the great tides of American history as they flowed through the day-by-day living of the first hundred pioneers. This philosophy of history was taught to me by Professor Herbert Eugene Bolton, a historian of renown in Western Europe and the Western Hemisphere, who is now deceased.

I departed from the inflexible limits of Bolton scholarship by divesting the framework of the book of documented footnotes; however, my sources are identified in the bibliography.

I give this chronicle to the city of my birth with the hope that it will reveal to citizens that man in each period of time will be unable to indulge in ignoble ease, but shall be compelled to search his mind and strive for progress in his universe.

My grateful thanks are offered to Doctor W. C. Nunn, Professor of American History at Texas Christian University for reading the manuscript and improving it through constructive deletions. I am also indebted to Doctor Klaude Kendrick, Chairman of the Social Science Division of Texas Wesleyan College for his encouraging words. After reading the manuscript, he said that others would be entertained by the chronicle which had captured the mood of the period.

There are many people to whom I owe an eternal debt. Pioneers gave hours in interviews from which were gleaned historical treasures. The staff of the Southwest History and Genealogy Division of the Fort Worth Public Library extended many courtesies, aiding me in search for data. Abby Moran expended scholarly labor by suggesting revisions of the final manuscript. My friends, especially Edith Deen, gave me strength when vagrant thoughts suggested abandonment of the project. My mother, Lillie Longinotti Garrett, was the high tower of strength during fifteen summer vacations from teaching as I wrote from morning until evening.

JULIA KATHRYN GARRETT

Contents

Prologue

FORT WORTH was planted on a river whose prodigious wealth had been recorded in history since the beginning of the sixteenth century; and like the Biblical tree planted by the rivers of water, would flourish and its leaves would not wither. Río de la Santísima Trinidad, together with the empire of prairies which roll and swell from its wooded banks, has always drawn men to delight in its life-giving abundance. The Trinity suggests a shining target of preoccupation, drawing generations of Spaniards and Americans to press into the mystery that shrouded it. For the Spaniards, the mystery faded into Indian villages and buffalo hides. For American pioneers, the mystery blossomed into homes and wealth.

History broke over the Trinity in 1519. Alonso Álvarez de Piñeda, Spanish explorer from Jamaica, was the first European to sail and map the Gulf coast of North America from Florida to Vera Cruz, Mexico. He was searching for a strait which would lead westward through North America to the Orient. Piñeda did not find a strait; instead, he discovered the outline of the coastlands of the Gulf of Mexico and the rivers of Río Grande, Trinity, and Mississippi. He did not name the Trinity, but drew it on the official map of his exploration for His Majesty, the King of Spain.

Since that day a cavalcade of men has ascended and crisscrossed the Trinity and valley. From the time of its exploration by the helmeted Spaniards in the 1540s, to the coming of the spur-booted frontiersmen of the Texas Republic and the United States Dragoons, the beauty and wonderful fertility of the valley impressed these men. Each in his turn recorded this in his official journal to his government, as related by Don José Antonio Pichardo, a Mexican professor recognized by the Spanish government as the foremost authority of the geography and history of North America in the nineteenth century. Pichardo submitted a survey of the history of the Louisiana-Texas boundary dispute between Spain and France to his country in 1812, in which he included descriptions of the Trinity from the journals of the Spanish explorers: Francisco Vásquez de Coronado, 1541; Luis de Moscoso, 1542; Alonso de León, 1690; Domingo de Terán, 1691; Domingo Ramón, 1716; Marques de San Miguel de Aguayo, 1721; Don Diego Ortiz Parrilla, 1759; Athanase de Mézières, 1778; and José Mares, 1787.

Posterity of Tarrant County is indebted especially to one of these men —de Mézières. His official reports of the land, and of the Indians of the upper Trinity and Brazos valleys north to the Red River, fill a one-volume book, and are the first account of this area in the latter part of the eighteenth century.

Father Juan Agustín de Morfi, before his death in 1783, wrote a monumental history of Texas, *Historia de la Provincia de Texas, 1673–1779*, in which he described the Trinity. The dominant qualities of the river are captured in his description:

The Río de la Santísima Trinidad rises to the north of the pueblo of San Teodoro (whose territory it makes productive) in three springs, which unite into one very large stream, and forms a channel to receive the many arroyos which augment it. In many places its bottom is of very fine flint. It is navigable along a great part of its course, which extends for 150 leagues eastward to the sea, into which it empties. It is subject to terrible floods in the rainy season, or when the snow melts.

These Spaniards spoke of the delightful banks of the Trinity; of the wooded groves which gave shelter to beast and man; of the waters abounding in fish; of the productive lands which rose from the banks to stretch away into flower-spangled prairies and expanses of grass; of fertile fields of wild flax, hemp, and rye, interspersed with woodlands in which there were vines heavy with grapes; and of the incredible number of wild chickens, turkeys, geese, buffaloes, deer, and antelopes.

Like their Spanish predecessors, officers of the army and militia of the

Republic of Texas, in their official reports to the secretary of war during the 1830s and 1840s, were also to use superlatives in describing the lands about the headwaters of the Trinity. Moderns must return in imagination to this wilderness and attempt to recapture the excitement enjoyed by Spanish explorers and American pioneers. League after league, vara by vara, mile by mile, on horse or in covered wagon, they discovered a new world or a new wonder at each bend of the Trinity.

The name Trinity, was given to the river in 1690 by Alonso de León. Leading an expedition to East Texas to found the first Spanish mission, he encamped on the banks of the river on Trinity Sunday and affixed that name on his map as Río de la Santísima Trinidad. Although explorers of the 1540s gave different names to the area, the name Trinity became the accepted term. A poetic, and original interpretation for the name was to be offered two hundred years later by one of the earliest historians of this region, Judge C. C. Cummings, who wrote:

Fort Worth sits on the high bluff at the junction of the two first prongs of the Trinity River, known as the Clear Fork and the West Fork of the Trinity River. The third prong, the Elm Fork, flows thirty miles below, just above the city of Dallas. These make the trine of the Trinity. . . . The Spaniards saw the clear pure waters of the Clear Fork and idealized it as the spirit, the red waters of the West Fork the impurities, representing the soul; thus they thought that the river is a symbol of the body, soul, and spirit.

The Trinity attracted men. Indians knew that villages on its banks would flourish. Spanish explorers discovered them there, and Texas militiamen in the 1830s and 1840s found Indian villages about the headwaters where Indian squaws planted and gleaned crops on the nearby prairie, and warriors hunted on the distant plains. These villages were prosperous in the Indian manner—well-stocked with hides, buffalo robes, dried meat, tallow, and corn.

The first white settlement on this river was a Spanish mission and presidio founded near its mouth in 1756 to exclude French traders. The Spaniards named the presidio San Agustín and the mission, Nuestra Señora de la Luz (Our Lady of Light), a significant name for the first settlement, for like a light, the Trinity River through the centuries has drawn men to its banks.

Ybarbo, a Spanish cattle baron, founded the second settlement in 1774, naming it in honor of the viceroy of New Spain, Nuestra Señora del Pilar de Bucareli. Its life was brief and full of trouble. Floods and Indian raids made it untenable. Nevertheless, this river was to continue to magnetize men.

In 1806, the third and last settlement of the Spaniards was Villa Santísima Trinidad de Salcedo, where the King's Highway crossed the river. By the time of Stephen Fuller Austin's Texas, Anglo-Americans were to build the town of Liberty on the east bank, seventy miles from Galveston Bay. It was to flourish, becoming the third largest port in Texas, and to hold this distinction to the closing days of the future Republic of Texas.

As the Texas frontier advanced slowly from the Gulf coast northward along the Trinity, men founded towns on its luxuriant banks. Two centuries after Spain founded Nuestra Señora de la Luz, Anglo-Americans in 1853 were to raise another beacon of light at the forks near its headwaters in an abandoned fort—Fort Worth—with the vision of attracting adventuring settlers and traders. This faint beacon of civilization in the north Texas wilderness was to entice farmers and cattlemen to nestle around it in the valley and the prairies, and thus it was to grow into a seedling village, provisioning cattlemen, buffalo hunters and homeseekers moving west. By the 1870s, this seedling, deeply rooted on the banks of the Trinity, was to burgeon with the coming of the railroad in 1876.

Foreword to the 1996 Edition

JULIA KATHRYN GARRETT was a unique and most charming Texas lady. So many memories of her swirl around in my mind, but first of all I think of her as a vivacious, inspiring, challenging and driven high school teacher, loved by her students and admired by her colleagues. She often spoke of her conviction that it was imperative that students of the high school level understand the importance and relevance of history–and to this calling she elected to dedicate her academic life.

She organized an after-school history club at Arlington Heights High School in Fort Worth. I recall one evening meeting of the club to which the parents were invited–over 150 students and parents attended. The papers given by the students at this meeting reflected extensive research and direction.

Miss Garrett's approach to history as "a great adventure" undoubtedly flowed from her experiences as a doctoral student of the renowned Professor Herbert E. Bolton of the University of California at Berkeley, whom she described in the acknowledgments of her book, *Green Flag over Texas,* as "master teacher, eminent American historian, explorer and cartographer." This enthusiasm for history was instilled in many of her students.

I am also mindful of Miss Garrett as a scholar. Her avid research activities carried her to the Mexican national library, Biblioteca Nacional de Mexico, and the Mexican national archives, Archivo General Público de la Nación de México, the Library of Congress in Washington, D.C., the Texas State Library, the Bexar Archives of the University of Texas at Austin, and the Bancroft Library of the University of California at Berkeley.

Green Flag over Texas was originally written as her doctoral dissertation under the supervision of Professor Bolton and later published in 1939. This book covers the "Spanish-American Revolution" of 1811-1813, with full footnotes and index, and is considered by scholars one of the classics of this period of contest for the control of Texas.

When the absence of footnotes and index in *Fort Worth: A Frontier Triumph* was mentioned to Miss Garrett, she explained without hesitation that such was a deliberate omission on her part. In this work she wanted to write a reader-friendly, flowing story or chronicle of Fort Worth which young people and laymen alike could read and enjoy, unencumbered by the academic style of *Green Flag*. She best explains it herself in the Preface: "I departed from the inflexible limits of Bolton scholarship by divesting the framework of the book of documented footnotes, however my sources are identified in the bibliography." The dedication of the volume further reflects her purpose in writing the Fort Worth story:

> *I dedicate to the Junior Historians of the 1940s and 1950s,*
> *and to all youths this chronicle of facts and legends*
> *with the hope that it reveals a historical truth:*
> *men should develop an awareness that world*
> *and national events do influence their lives.*

Nevertheless, I deem the addition of an index to this edition as a needed tool for ready access to the text.

It will be noticed that this volume ends with the Amnesty Act of 1872 adopted by the Congress of the United States. In 1971 when Miss Garrett was assured that her work of nineteen years relating to Fort Worth would be published, she, at the outset, was reluctant to attempt the editing of her manuscript for publication because of her failing eyesight. Nevertheless, she began with zeal, but when she had finished the editorial work through 1872, her eyesight would not permit her to proceed further. It was decided to publish what she had completed as a separate work. This volume is the result of that decision. The unedited manuscript which continues the chronicles of Fort Worth from 1872 to 1900 was given by her to the Special Collections of the Library at the University of Texas at Arlington, along with manuscript material relating to the publishing of the original edition of this work.

Miss Garrett was disappointed that she could not continue the editing of the years beyond 1872, but she expressed her feelings that the publication of *Fort Worth: A Frontier Triumph* justified the years she had spent in research and writing about her native city.

Jenkins Garrett
Autumn 1995

FORT WORTH: A Frontier Triumph

Conflict
on the Prairies

THE prairies stretching from the wooded banks of the forks of the Trinity, and sweeping on beyond to the Red River, were sources of nourishment and power to the prairie Indians and to the invading white man; but they were also areas of conflict. The conflict over the land, from the forks of this river and the upper Brazos northeastward to the Red River, lasted from the early years of 1700 until 1845. Spaniards and Frenchmen, Spaniards and Englishmen, Spaniards and Americans, Texans of the Republic and citizens of the United States, each in his day, vied with one another to control the prairie Indians, for the Indian trade provided white men with riches and nations with an empire. This conflict of a century and a half is a part of the robustly romantic history of Fort Worth and Tarrant County.

CHAPTER 1

The Promise
on the Prairies

IT was in the spring of 1778, and the conflict for control of the Texas prairies had already begun. A strong man seated magnificently in a comfortable saddle—one made for an explorer of the big Texas wilderness—rode in the midst of a score of horsemen through the high grass sown with spring flowers. The incredible beauty and sights of the prairie enchanted them.

Their behavior was not that of toiling members of an official expedition of His Majesty, the King of Spain, bent upon serious business. They were skylarking through the Grand Prairie and the valley of the West Fork of the Trinity, where now sprawls the metropolis of Fort Worth. Abundance of buffaloes, deer, antelopes, turkeys, partridges, geese, cranes, rabbits, and hares sported before them. There was so much wildlife that they did not give thought merely to satisfying hunger, but rather to gratifying their luxurious tastes as they practiced their marksmanship.

As the soldiers frolicked along the journey, the leader of the expedition envisioned uses to which the inexpressible richness of the land could be applied to man's welfare. He wrote in his journal for the king that the numerous springs and creeks would encourage the irrigation of the adjacent plains; the woods that beautified their banks would meet man's many needs; the rocks, which made the bottoms of the creeks firm, would facilitate the construction of dams; and further accentuating the value of these lands was a "Grand Forest" (East Cross Timbers), which cut across the rolling prairies. Being very dense but not very wide, the "Grand Forest" would give protection to those going from one Indian village to another, as well as serve as a landmark to even the most inexperienced traveler. Such was the description and analysis of the land which Athanase de Mézières, the leader of this expedition, recorded.

De Mézières, Paris-born, had been in the service of France for forty-five years in Louisiana, winning distinction as the foremost French-Indian agent and diplomat of the Louisiana-Texas frontier. When France lost the French and Indian War of 1763 and was driven from the continent of North America, Great Britain, the victor, took Canada and Louisiana east of the Mississippi. France gave Louisiana west of the Mississippi to Spain, her ally in the war against Great Britain. Now the conflict was no longer a clash between Spain and France on the plains and prairies of North Central Texas, but between Spain and England.

Spain knew how to use talent. De Mézières, the Frenchman, one of the most dangerous threats to Spanish power in Texas, had been directing Indian affairs from Louisiana, to the dismay of Spain and to the commercial glory of France. Nevertheless in 1769, Spain, in need of a genius, employed her former enemy to explore North Texas and the Red River area, to make a survey of the Indians, to draft a program for Spain's control of the Indians, and to devise means of excluding English traders from the territory. Spain was determined that Englishmen should not control the Indians in Spain's Texas as the French had done.

No doubt, as de Mézières rode on his mission, he reviewed the manner in which Frenchmen had dealt with the prairie Indians. Since France had founded the Louisiana trading post of Natchitoches on Red River in 1714, Spain and France had been in headlong conflict—not with massed armies but in clashes with French fur traders and Indian agents. Frenchmen ascended Red River to Indian villages near the present sites of Clarksville and Ringgold, Texas. There they traded trinkets for horses and then rode south to barter goods for pelts, hides, horses, and mules with Indians of the upper Brazos and the forks of the Trinity to Red River. Spain sent military expeditions from San Antonio with treaties to persuade the Indians to give their loyalty to their Great White Father in Spain. Spanish missionaries were sent to found missions on the upper Red River, on the San Gabriel tributary to the Brazos, and on the San Saba tributary of the Colorado. Then Spain tried to convince France, by correspondence, of her violation of Spanish territory; and fumed because French traders continued to prosper on Texas prairies.

World events changed the destiny of man. Leaving San Antonio in March 1778, de Mézières had traveled over the Old San Antonio Road to the settlement of Bucareli on the Trinity near present-day Madisonville. Then he ascended the valley, visiting an Indian village near present-day Grand Saline. From there, he turned west and crossed the Trinity. More riding brought him to a Tawakoni Indian village on the Brazos near Waco. The route thus far he had explored in 1772. From this point near Waco the journey was new adventure. De Mézières ascended the Brazos eight leagues, turned north, followed the western edge of the East Cross Timbers, and forded the West Fork of the Trinity in the environs of today's Fort Worth; and traveling in a northerly direction, reached two Taovayas Indian villages on the Red River near the present town of Ringgold. He found, as he expected, that English guns and ammunition proved that English traders, like French traders, had found Indian trade lucrative. Returning to Natchitoches, he prepared to combat the Indian problem of North Central Texas.

But de Mézières died the next year.

Events of 1778, however, removed Spain's fear of Great Britain in this section of Texas, because Great Britain had her hands full in America with her thirteen rebellious colonies. Spain's surcease from trouble in North Texas was brief. By the close of the American Revolution, Spain was without masterful official servants like de Mézières, and was growing militarily weak. Her problems were greater than her might. American frontiersmen from the newly-born republic of the United States, were now the threat to Spanish power of the Texas prairies.

These Americans were pursuing wild horses across the Grand Prairie. The wild mustangs were driven into the United States, ending their days in the stables of Southern gentlemen, where race horses were bred. The most notorious American horse thief—in the opinion of Spanish soldiers —was Philip Nolan. He made several trips to Texas in the 1790s to catch mustangs. Spanish soldiers killed him in battle in 1801 at his corral near the Brazos above Waco.

Prairie Indians were well armed with American guns and goods which they had purchased with horses, mules, and hides. With these vicious accessories of civilization, the Indians left their villages in the East Cross Timbers to steal more horses and mules for trade and their own need. They swept as far south as San Antonio and other settlements along the Old Spanish Road.

In 1821 Spain lost most of her empire on the North American continent to the new republic of Mexico. While Mexico ruled Texas from 1821 to 1836, the American traders had a heyday in the northern area, corralling horses and buying furs and hides. Too burdened with civil war, the Mexican government was oblivious to events in this section of Texas. More than 20,000 Anglo-American settlers, many with slaves, entered Texas promising fidelity to the Mexican republic in exchange for land grants. However, their heritage of rugged individualism and ideas of freedom were a greater power in their lives than this new pledge to Mexico, which eventually passed into hostile resistance when the Mexican government violated their (the Anglo-Americans') creed for living as they saw it.

After the battle of San Jacinto, the Republic of Texas was a reality. The new nation, however, inherited a portion of the century-old conflict on the northern prairies of Texas—the control of Indians and Indian trade. The Indian was an obstacle to possession of the magnificent empire from the forks of the Trinity to the Red River. For ten years, the Republic wrestled with its Indian problems: the exclusion of American traders, and prevention of Indians crossing over from the United States, as well as the keeping of Texas Indians from bartering at trading posts in the United States.

Regardless of changes in the white man's government, Indians emerged from their villages in the East Cross Timbers, dashing over the prairies on their mustangs to hunt deer and buffalo. They took the products of their hunt to trading posts located in President Jackson's Indian Territory across the Red River, or bartered with traders from the United States. Returning to their Texas villages armed with American goods and guns, they fiercely resisted the surveyors of the Texas republic and the pioneers attempting to build homes beyond the frontier. They thieved and plundered as far south as Bastrop, San Antonio, and Houston. Presidents of the Republic, Sam Houston and Mirabeau B. Lamar, each tried to remove the Indian barrier to settlement of the beautiful lands of the Upper Trinity.

CHAPTER 2

The Barrier
on the Prairies

THE newly-born Republic of Texas was generally spoken of as the "Land of Promise" by citizens of the United States and Europe. Some exuberant optimists spoke of it as the "land of milk and honey." But as one wit said, "Although Texas was the land of milk and of honey, it was necessary to milk the cows and gather the honey."

Pioneers came to escape the poverty in the United States brought by the financial panic of 1837, and to find opportunity as citizens of the Lone Star Republic. The removal of the Indian barrier from the upper valleys of the Trinity and Brazos was the beginning of the history of Fort Worth and Tarrant County.

The north to which Texans referred in the late 1830s and 1840s was the sections which present-day Texans know as North Central Texas. In this area are located the cities of Dallas and Fort Worth, the prosperous municipalities of Denison, Sherman, Waco, Wichita Falls, Vernon, Gainesville, Hillsboro, Jacksboro, Mineral Wells, and Weatherford, as well as other vigorous towns.

The frontier line of settlement was a very thin string of a few cabins daringly erected along the Red River to Fannin and Grayson counties. Westward, beyond this sparse line was the gathering ground of Indian nations in the last period of glory as rulers of Texas wilderness.

Here they took their last stand. These nations were the Comanche; the Wichita, Taovayas, Tawakoni, Kichai, and Iscani tribes of the Wichita Confederacy; the Caddo, Ionie, and Anadarko tribes of the former Caddo and Hasinai Confederacies; and the Deadose and the Bidai who, at the dawn of Texas history lived in the lower middle valleys of the Trinity and Brazos rivers. Disease had reduced the number of these ancient Texas tribes, and the civilization of Spanish and Anglo-American settlements had driven the tribal remnants into this northern section.

Into this area had come also many tribes from the United States, whose expanding frontier line had pushed them into Texas. The great trek from the United States began in the early 1800s. Since 1831, the policy of the United States government had been to remove Indians from the states to the Indian Territory, which they had set aside for this purpose between the Arkansas and Red rivers. Such a policy had plagued Texas by augmenting the numbers already on the northern prairies. These tribes from the United States were the Coushatta, Kickapoo, Delaware, Shawnee, Choctaw, Chickasaw, Cherokee, Creek, and Kiowa.

About 1690, with the beginning of the formal settlement by Spain, North Central Texas had been the empire of the Wichita Confederacy. These were the aborigines of present Tarrant County. As stated earlier, de Mézières in 1772 and 1778, on his expeditions through the Trinity and Brazos river valleys across Tarrant County to the Red River, left a voluminous record of the Wichita tribes. He visited the Yscani and Kichai Indians living in villages near the east bank of the Trinity in present Anderson County.

On the west bank of the Trinity, he discovered two villages—one of the Kichai and the other a Tawakoni—which he named La Tortuga, meaning The Turtle. It was in present Freestone County. And over on the Brazos, he sojourned to two villages of the Tawakoni. One was near present Waco, which became the chief village of the Wacos. The other village was north of it. Far to the north on Red River, where Ringgold now stands, de Mézières found two Taovayas villages. The Taovayas irrigated their fields, raised good crops of tobacco, and grazed fine herds of cattle along the banks of Red River.

Wichita tribes were a semi-agricultural people. The women were most industrious. They planted fields of maize, beans, watermelons, pumpkins; and the Kichais and Iscanis cultivated the sweet potato. They gathered luscious wild grapes, each bunch weighing one to two pounds. The women also harvested the crops and saved the seeds for the next year's planting. They cared for an astounding number of children; tanned, sewed, and painted skins; made clothes and tents of deerskin and buffalo hides; preserved the deer meat with salt obtained from the salt flats near present Grand Saline; and cut buffalo meat into strips, hanging it up to dry. They provided for tribal welfare while men limited their activities to warfare and hunting on the northern prairies. Tallow, lard, and hides of bear, deer and buffalo had a ready market among white traders.

Wichita warriors were well-dressed men. They wore leather jackets, leggings, and moccasins, carried leather shields, and adorned their heads with cap-like helmets ornamented with buffalo horns and the tips of buffalo tails, dyed brilliant colors.

In the early eighteenth century, the Wichitas were forced to share their lands of the Trinity and Brazos river valleys with the Comanches. Apaches pushed the Comanches out of their northern plains eastward, into the country of the Wichita. Comanches moved as far south as Nacogdoches and the Blackland Prairie. Wichitas tolerated the Comanches, who were not always fair in their dealings, because they needed the Comanches as an ally against the Apaches from the west and the Osage from the north. Characteristics and customs of the Wichita tribes in the 1830s had not changed radically since the survey of de Mézières.

In 1837, officials of the Republic were informed that the Wichita tribes —Kichai, Tawakoni, Waco, and Pawnee—500 warriors strong, were hunting and traveling on the prairies around the headwaters of the Trinity, Brazos, and Colorado rivers. They moved with great celerity. All the Indians were well mounted on fine horses and armed with bows and arrows, which were their chief weapons, although they possessed guns obtained from American traders. "These formidable rogues of the prairies" were raiding settlements, carrying away children, and stealing cattle and horses, which they sold to traders in the United States.

To further vex Texas administrators, these Wichitas were friendly with the Comanches numbering about 8,000 according to a report sent to President Andrew Jackson in 1836. With their herds of cattle and horses, the Comanches ranged from the Guadalupe Mountains in the Trans-Pecos country, across northwest Texas rivers to the Red River. In this vast domain, they moved their perfectly organized tent villages of buffalo skins every three days. When a new village site was chosen, the squaws erected the tents in orderly rows in a few hours.

There were other excellent hunters in the north who lived entirely by the chase. They were the Kickapoo, Delaware, and Shawnee tribes numbering 500. Unlike the Comanches, they were friendly to the whites and did not claim their hunting grounds. The Delawares were the friends of all tribes, therefore interpreters and peacemakers. Officials of Texas learned to use them as their chief emissaries. The Kickapoos by 1819 had ceded all their lands in Illinois to the United States government and moved southward. Stephen F. Austin, in one of his many surveys, located them on the upper Trinity and Sabine. In the 1830s they roamed through present Tarrant County, on up the headwaters of the Trinity and thence to the Red River. The Ionies and Anadarkos sought their living in this same area. East of the Trinity lived 350 Coushattas. They were not to be feared, as only eighty warriors were among them.

In the East Cross Timbers and the area of present Tarrant County were many villages of the Caddo Indians. In 1835, Caddoes living in the United States made a treaty with the government, ceding their lands. Keeping their agreement with the United States to move west, many entered Texas, joining their Caddo brothers. These woodlands were miniature forests, not wide, but dense. Sun rays only gently pierced the foliage. Villages of wood huts covered with grass erected in the cool darkness of these woods concealed this tribe from its enemies.

After their thieving expeditions, the Caddoes hid for several weeks in their villages in the woodlands, enjoying their stolen goods: horses, cattle, featherbeds, blacksmith forges, and stoves.

Eight hundred Tonkawas between the Colorado and La Vaca were not such a problem for the Republic. West and north of the Colorado roamed 900 Lipan Apaches, the scourge of Texans. But this northwestern frontier would have to wait.

The young giant Republic of Texas beset with many difficulties, of which 20,000-odd Indians was but one, had only sufficient resources to wrestle with the frontier. The need of the moment was to regulate and control the Indian barrier from the forks of the Trinity to the Red River.

CHAPTER 3

"My Brother's Keeper"

SAM HOUSTON, the first president of the Republic of Texas from October 22, 1836, until December 10, 1838, had a plan for controlling Texas Indians. Upon the Indian policy of the Republic hung the story of the birth of Tarrant County. President Houston believed that if Indians were permitted to live with whites in a brotherhood of faith, most of them would be peaceful inhabitants. Houston planned to accomplish in a six-point program this spirit of brotherhood.

In East Texas, Congress would grant to Cherokees and other Indians the lands which they cultivated, thereby fulfilling the pledge Texans made to the Indians in exchange for their loyalty during the revolution for Texas independence.

In North Texas, the Republic would prevent Indians from the United States roaming the Texas prairies; and exclude traders from the United States (because those traders without thought of the consequences were known to arm Indians with guns which they turned against Texans); and lastly, the Republic would try to lure Texas Indians away from trading posts in the United States. Red men, like their white brothers, needed economic security. Furthermore, the Republic would establish trading houses to which the red men could bring their horses, cattle, buffalo robes, hides, lard, and tallow to barter for goods.

Freed from dependence upon trading posts in the United States and provided with their needs, the red men would cease to raid the farms and towns of Texans. Houston admitted that there were always bad Indians as there were bad white men. Rangers were sufficient to keep the former under surveillance. Treaties made with various tribes, accompanied by frequent councils and distribution of gifts, would bring peace with a minimum of hostilities.

In the spring of 1838, Houston's agents, smoking the pipe of peace with Tonkawas and Comanches of North Texas, made treaties including the usual terms: friendship, trading houses, gifts, and official visits to the capital of the Republic.

Summer followed with heat and trouble. Vicente Córdova, a Mexican agent expelled from East Texas for having incited a rebellion among the Indians and Mexicans in that area, fled to the forks of the Trinity. Throughout the summer he encamped in the woodlands about the Trinity in present-day Dallas and Tarrant counties, and conspired against the Republic of Texas. Three hundred Indians and Mexicans were in correspondence with Matamoros, Mexico. The Kickapoos, Bidais, Wacos, Tawakonis, and Kichais of the upper Trinity and Brazos, were in a conspiracy with Córdova to aid Mexico in driving the whites from the lands of Texas.

The land office of the Texas republic had opened in January 1838. By early spring, surveyors and locators had been marking trees in the upper Trinity and Brazos valleys, miles beyond the settlements. Indians, seeing them at work, believed the words of Mexican agents and, at least in part, they were words of truth: "The buffalo and deer are the Indian's cattle, the turkey and geese his poultry. When white men come to the prairie," the Mexican agents asserted, "they not only will take the Indian's cattle and poultry, but also will drive him from his prairie hunting ground." Anadarkos, Ionies, Wichitas, and Caddoes, usually friendly, became sullen and morose. The Indian reaction was to kill the whites and raid the settlements.

President Houston continued, during 1838, to pursue his policy of brotherhood and to spare no effort to conciliate the Indians. In spite of Córdova's conspiracy at the forks of the Trinity, a treaty was signed with the Wacos, Tawakonis, Kichais, and Pawnees. Settlers of Red River County were displeased with Houston's policy as well as alarmed because of recent raids and rumors of Córdova's conspiracy.

In September, John H. Dyer, brigadier general of the Fourth Brigade, raised a company of volunteers and moved against the Indians on the Trinity. When the expedition approached this river, Captain Henry

~~~~~~

Stout and his brother were sent ahead to reconnoiter. At Elm Fork, they battled with eight Indians, killing one. From there, Captain Stout moved towards the East Cross Timbers. Meeting a band of Kickapoos, he was informed that this whole area was full of Caddoes and that he should leave in haste. He did. After he returned to the main camp with the message, General Dyer ordered most of the men to return home. His reason for this order: the season was so dry and the grass was without nourishment.

Then General Dyer with Captain Stout and a small band, rode to join a group of men from Fannin County, commanded by Daniel Montague. They were camped on Pilot Grove Creek, a headwater tributary of the East Fork of the Trinity. The party, according to Captain Stout, "went high up the Trinity and searched the area for Caddoes, but found none. They rode down the Clear Fork on their return, and finding a small encampment, killed three Indians." The men were destitute of provisions, and returned home with small reward for their venture into the Trinity wilderness.

The cold, dry winter of 1838 bore down on the northern frontier. With winter came hostilities. As early as October, the Wacos murdered citizens in the streets of Bastrop. During the winter, they made frequent raids to steal horses. As cold weather advanced, Indian hostilities increased, along with a growing opposition to President Houston's Indian policy. No one expressed more ably this opposition to Houston's pipe of peace offer than did General Hugh McLeod. A tall, gaunt warrior, weather-beaten by steaming prairie heat and piercing cold winter winds, McLeod had lived and toiled with Indian problems, such as were now harassing Texans.

The vice-president of Texas, Mirabeau Bonaparte Lamar, on December 10, 1838, succeeded Houston as president. From Lamar's campaign speeches, made in the summer of 1838, McLeod no doubt understood that there would be a change in the Republic's Indian policy. In an official report to Lamar, there was little restraint as McLeod poured out his dissatisfaction with the condition of Indian affairs.

Headquarters near Port Caddo
December 1, 1838

Dear General [Lamar]

General Rusk has returned from a campaign against the Caddoes. He disarmed a part of the Caddoes near Red River and returned them to their United States agent at Shreveport, Louisiana. The Caddoes pledged good behavior until the Caddo tribes in Texas also should make peace.

So stands that matter, but you must understand these are not all the

Caddoes. By far the larger portion of the tribe are under Tarshar, the Wolf, camped among the wild Indians of Texas at the three forks of the Trinity.

We start immediately for the three forks of the Trinity and the Cross Timbers. The Fourth Brigade under General Dyer will have 400 men ready as soon as we get to Clarksville. Let us drive these wild tribes off and establish a line of block houses. If the United States will not remove their own Indians (Cherokees, Shawnees, Delawares, Kickapoos, Choctaws, Alabamas and Coshattees [Coushattas]) to say nothing of these Caddoes who they have literally driven into our Country—I say if the United States is faithless enough to refuse to remove them, we must await a more auspicious moment than the present to exterminate them.

The auspicious moment of extermination would come, no doubt, when Lamar's administration was in full sway. McLeod had forsaken the policy of President Houston, the great brother of red men. Rangers, trading houses, gifts, treaties—what had been the harvest of such a policy? In the mood of an Indian fighter, McLeod laid aside his pen and portfolio. He spent the month of December in the saddle as a member of the first large military expedition of Anglo-Americans into the area which a decade later was to become Tarrant County.

In the early days of January 1839, an exhausted McLeod again took out his portfolio and pen.

Red River County, Below Clarksville, 60 miles, Dear General [Lamar], We are recruiting our broken down horses and equally exhausted selves after a march in my opinion, unparalleled since that of de Soto's.

McLeod with General Rusk and a company of soldiers, had ridden from Clarksville to the Clear Fork of the Trinity in the severe cold of December. There they warmed themselves by the campfires of General Dyer. McLeod had left Clarksville on November 24, 1838, with 500 men. No doubt, before the expedition ended, McLeod and the men believed their experience comparable to that of de Soto's men. They were adventuring in a wilderness, inhabited only by wild beasts and Indians. These Texans were ignorant of de Mézières' records.

In December 1838, in the wilderness of the Clear Fork was pitched the first large military camp in what is now Tarrant County. In the next century, on these same prairies would be erected military camps for World Wars I and II.

Leaving a company of men with the baggage at the camp, Generals Dyer and Rusk led the army through the East Cross Timbers. Soldiers found silent, wooded thickets and empty villages. It was evident that Caddo scouts had discovered the approach of the largest military expedition their eyes had ever beheld in this northern section. They deserted their villages in a headlong rush.

After scouring the area which yielded small prizes of blankets, guns, and buffalo hides, the military company burned every Caddo village. With the Cross Timbers cleared of Caddoes, the expedition traveled west across a barren prairie to the Red Fork of the Brazos. Weariness and low rations sent them back to the camp on the Clear Fork.

Here, too, food was a problem. Captain Edward H. Tarrant, whom General Rusk had left at headquarters on Red River with instructions to gather beef cattle and to drive them to the camp on the Clear Fork, had failed to arrive with the beeves. General Rusk waited. The men suffered much weariness, hunger, and the very cold weather. In dire need of food, General Rusk decided to abandon his wagons and eat the oxen.

Strength renewed, the army began the return journey. Leaving the wagons on the banks of the Clear Fork to the ravages of weather, they crossed the Trinity northeast of the present town of Arlington, proceeded eastward to the head of the Neches and Sabine rivers, and rode on to Clarksville.

McLeod's official report of the expedition written to Lamar, reveals how greatly he was impressed with the East Cross Timbers and prairies flanking the Clear Fork. He wrote:

That section of the country and particularly the Cross Timbers, frequently represented as a sterile waste, is the finest portion of Texas as a body— and its bottoms are equally as fine as the Brazos.

We saw large droves of buffalo and wild horses, by the latter I do not mean mustangs, such as are found in western Texas—The Ukraine [Russia] cannot excel these prairies in the beauty, and fleetness of its wild horses. They are said to be derived from various sources, but however derived, the mustangs bear no proportion to them, and they sell when caught, persons follow it as a business, for $300 to $500. The weather was so severe, we could not enjoy the sport [of catching them].

Nine days elapsed between McLeod's first official report and his final report of the expedition to the East Cross Timbers and the Clear Fork of the Trinity. At Nacogdoches, in better spirits after a rest, he was able to analyze the results of the expedition. On January 18, 1839, he wrote Lamar that, in his opinion, the expedition was worth the cost. For the Indians of the upper Trinity Valley

never knew they had an enemy beyond the neighborhood of east Texas, nor did they believe a white man could go to the prairie. And when they find a wide road from Clarksville to the Brazos and learn from the Kickapoos that five hundred men built the road, they will perceive the hopelessness of contesting with the white man for this finest portion of Texas.

McLeod was a militarist, not a prophet. The East Cross Timbers and the lands about the forks of the Trinity were to be purchased for settlements by conflict.

CHAPTER 4

The Sword

"LET the sword do its work," a favorite slogan of David G. Burnet, the provisional president of the Texas republic during its revolution for independence, became the policy of President Lamar in his administration of Indian affairs.

Lamar was not his red brother's keeper. He reversed President Houston's Indian policy. In his inaugural address in December 1838, as the second president of Texas, Lamar called for the following: the total expulsion of United States Indians domiciled in North Texas, the establishment of a line of military posts along the frontier, and the organization of a strong military force.

Congress promptly complied. Laws were passed which provided for the construction of a military road from the Red River to the Nueces River; the creation of more than ten companies of Rangers of fifty-nine men each; and the organization of a mounted regiment of 840 men. Soldiers were to enlist for three years at sixteen dollars a month, and to receive a bounty of thirty dollars and a land certificate.

Provision for the establishment of troop headquarters for this mounted regiment reveals that the center of danger was in North Central Texas and included the present counties of Dallas, Tarrant, Johnson, Hood, Hill, and Bosque. The law provided that the largest number of men, 168, were to be stationed at or near the three forks of the Trinity, and 112 at or near the Brazos. Under the Indian threat, settlers from the Red River to the older settled areas about Bastrop on the Colorado lived in a world of uneasiness. Many people had accepted as facts the surmises which were abroad in Texas. It was estimated that there were some 45,000 warriors concentrated in Indian Territory whom the settlers feared would cross the Red River to make murderous and thieving incursions into Texas. To the fear of these savages was added the dread of the wild tribes of the prairies who, unopposed, were well entrenched in woodlands of the Trinity.

The secretary of war of the Texas republic, Albert Sidney Johnston, had proof that the Cherokees and other agricultural Indians of East Texas were cooperating with the prairie Indians to drive the white men from North Texas. So Lamar, in line with his extermination policy, declared that the Cherokees were not entitled to land in East Texas. He offered to compensate them for the land on which they were living, and ordered them to withdraw from Texas. This, they refused to accept, and ignored the order to leave their homes.

Land titles for the Cherokees became a sharp political issue. In the meantime, the white settlers of East Texas, uncomfortable under the July sun of 1839, were further disturbed by warfare. The Cherokees fought the troops sent by Lamar to expel them. Most of the warriors were slain along with their famous Chief Bowles, the beloved friend of Sam Houston. Survivors of this Cherokee conflict were driven into Arkansas.

Like a volcanic eruption, the so-called "Cherokee War" shook the other Indian camps from the Red River to the Rio Grande. The tribes of North Central Texas feared that, like the Cherokees, they too would be expelled from their homes. They took up their tomahawks. A list of disasterous raids was recorded by the War Department of the Republic during 1839 and 1840. But the settlers from the Red River to the newly founded settlement of Austin were more fortunate than the North Central Anglos, for they lived within easy reach of barricades.

A second incident, the Council House Fight, incited the Indians' anger and increased their fear, for in March 1840, Lamar had invited the Comanches to San Antonio for a peace council to which they were to bring their white prisoners. This terminated in a massacre at the council house. The deaths of twelve chiefs, sixty-five warriors, and several squaws unleashed a torrent of vengeance.

In the summer of 1840, Comanches and Kiowas, 1000 strong, rode in fury from their northern homes to answer Lamar's policy of the sword.

Their anger carried their raids as far as Victoria and Linnville on the Gulf Coast. Settlers were slain, towns were captured, thousands of horses were stolen, and children were carried away. As the Indians retired from their destructive raids, they were pursued by volunteers under General Felix Huston and Edward Burleson. At Plum Creek, near present-day Lockhart, the Indians were defeated. In the fall of 1840, Colonel John H. Moore destroyed a Comanche camp on the Colorado River near present Colorado City. Comanches took refuge in the northern wilderness.

For five years, from 1839 to the latter part of 1843, the northern frontier, in the words of Sam Houston, "bled at every pore with Indian depredations and treachery." In later 1840, the scene in the north of the Republic had not changed since the first boom of settlement in 1838. Clarksville, on the Red River, remained the only town of note. There were scattered settlements in Lamar and Fannin counties. A few cabins stood bravely around Fort English near present-day Bonham. The most westerly settlement was at Preston's Bend, known as Coffee's Trading House. Between this thin line of settlements along the Red River and the sparse one north of Austin stood an unyielding wilderness.

In order to penetrate this area about the forks of the Trinity, Captain Jonathan Bird organized a company of Rangers from Bowie and Red River counties. Men enlisted for three months. In late winter of 1840, they went to the upper Trinity to erect a military post to encourage settlement. Such forts had a way of attracting settlers until the land was won from the Indians. About twenty miles below the junction of the Clear and West forks of the Trinity, and northeast of the main stream on the military road which led from the Red River to Austin, Captain Bird and his men selected the site of a fort.

The woods soon rang with the sharp staccato of axes as the Rangers hewed trees for the first settlement in Tarrant County. On the northeast bank of a lake, a block house was erected. The outer walls were made of logs set on end in picket form. Then a deep entrenchment was dug around this. It was an excellent earthwork. Seventy-odd years later Fort Worth businessmen were to seek refuge from city strain, using the same trenches in constructing the Calloway Lake Country Club.

From the vantage point on the bank of the lake, the Rangers were guaranteed a water supply for their horses and an observatory from which to watch for Indians who likewise might be drawn to the lake to water their stock. Fresh water for man bubbled from a spring at the edge of the lake about forty feet from the block house. For concealment, a shield of oak woods made a semicircle about the military post.

The Rangers' sojourn was brief in spite of their labor and care in erecting the fort. Three months' term of service passed quickly. Life perhaps was uneventful although hunting was good and Indians were hostile. But spring plowing and home may have beckoned the Rangers to return to their civilization. The fort was abandoned.

Soon a party of prospectors led by Captain Robert Sloan arrived to enjoy the fruit of the Rangers' labor. Their stay at Bird's Fort also was brief and marked with trouble. The Indians killed a distinguished member of the party, David Club from Illinois, a hero of the Black Hawk War of 1832. The party returned south. Perhaps the unknown grave at Bird's Fort today is that of David Club, the Indian fighter. Lamar's policy of the sword was paying dividends in bloody tomahawks.

A few years later, Captain Bird petitioned the government of Texas to compensate him for his effort in building the fort. This was not granted. President Houston, in vetoing the appropriation for Bird's relief, gave his reasons:

Relief for Jonathan Bird 1844
To the House of Representatives

Executive Department, Washington
[on the Brazos]
January 29, 1844

To the Honorable, the House of Representatives:

The bill for the relief of Jonathan Bird has received the consideration of the Executive; and for reasons which he deems sufficient he returns the same to the House without approval.

The total inability of the nation to pay these claims at this time and sustain its government, must be apparent to all who have examined into our present financial condition. There are numerous claims which the country would willingly discharge, were it able to do so; but which must be deferred from the force of necessity to some future period. Many other citizens of the Republic have expended their means in erecting forts and block houses for the protection of themselves, their families, and neighbors.

CHAPTER 5

Minutemen

INDIAN hostilities almost depopulated North Texas after 1839. It dwindled to less than half. Those men courageous enough to remain, rarely experienced the joyful excitement of welcoming the arrival of new settlers. They joined companies of minutemen, the title given the volunteers authorized for frontier defense in the session of the Fifth Congress of the Republic of Texas. The act was signed in February 1841.

The act authorized the settlers in the frontier counties to organize companies of not less than twenty nor more than fifty-six minutemen, rank and file. Each company elected its own officers. The Republic's Congress had made extravagant provisions for the military, according to the amount of money in the national treasury, but the number of troops was inadequate for the immensity of the northern wilderness. Texas was financially embarrassed. The creation of companies of minutemen therefore was a provident measure for frontier defense.

Prime essentials for a minuteman were not only character, but also the means to provide himself with a horse, saddle, and a gun with 100 rounds of ammunition, besides furnishing his food rations in the amount which his captain deemed prudent for the expedition. The sternest requirement was that he must at all times be prepared to ride promptly when the summons came.

Compensation for such rigid demands was ample. Minutemen were exempt from performing any other kind of military service, from working on the public road, and from paying taxes: state, county, corporation, poll; also on saddle horses. Then there was financial compensation of one dollar a day for not more than fifteen days of service for one expedition; and during one year their service on expeditions was not to exceed four months.

Word had come to the minutemen of Fannin and Red River counties to ride promptly to Choctaw Bayou in what was then Fannin County, but later became Grayson. It was May 4, 1841, the busy season for plowing and planting, when the men began to rendezvous at the bayou. Early arrivals relieved the tediousness of waiting for others by talking of crops, cattle, trade and Indian raids.

A recent atrocity had called these men from their plows. In March Captain Yeary and his wife had been wounded when ten Indians stormed their home in southeast Fannin County. Captain Yeary became an eager member of the minutemen at Choctaw Bayou. Indian raids were becoming not only more frequent, but more daring. Kickapoos were driving herds of horses from the Red River Valley settlements. Scouts had reported that the villages of these Indians were at the headwaters of the Trinity.

Henry Stout, the famous scout of General Dyer's Fourth Brigade, who had gone with him in 1838 as related earlier, became informer of the massacre details perpetrated upon the Ripley family in Red River County, later Titus County. His story was a bloody one. Mr. Ripley had been absent from home. Young Ripley, twenty years of age, had been entrusted with the care of the family and the plowing. A band of Indians found the lone plowman in the field. The family heard a shot. Looking out they saw their brother dead in the furrow, and the Indians rushing upon the house. The family fled from their home toward a thicket. On the way the eldest daughter, sixteen, was shot and killed. Two younger daughters reached the thicket and survived to relate the tragedy. Mrs. Ripley, with her smaller children running to hide in a canebrake, were overtaken and beaten to death with clubs. After raiding the house, the Indians applied the torch. Ripley's infant child, asleep in his crib, was consumed in the flames.

Raids upon the Yeary and Ripley families, horse thieving by the Kickapoos, the vaunting boldness of the Indians, and a report that the villages of the marauders were on the headwaters of the Trinity prompted the assembling of the minutemen in Chocktaw Bayou.

Sunrise of May 5 stirred the camp of volunteers in Chocktaw Bayou to action. Since most of the citizen soldiers had arrived, the first order of the day was to organize into a military company and elect officers. They elected James Bourland, captain, William C. Young, lieutenant, and Doctor Lemuel M. Cochran, orderly-sergeant. John B. Denton and Henry Stout were placed in charge of a few men as scouts. Edward H. Tarrant, General of the Fourth Brigade, Texas Militia, was a member of the group, but was not elected to a command. However, respected as a senior officer, he was consulted on every measure, and before the expedition ended, was in command. When members of the expedition wrote their memoirs forty years later, they recorded the event as Tarrant's expedition. Historians also have so credited him.

Soon after the plowmen and cattlemen of the Red River Valley had been strengthened with military organization, they rode west to the abandoned Fort Johnson near the present town of Denison. This fort had been erected the year before by Colonel William Cooke of the regular army of the Republic. There the company spent several days in barracks waiting for volunteers who had been detained.

On May 14, 1841, sixty-nine men mounted their horses and rode from Fort Johnson. The second large military expedition to enter the area of future Tarrant County under the authority of the Republic was off to rout the Indians. (Tarrant County was to receive its name from this expedition.)

The minutemen believed that the villages of the hostile "Keechies" (Kichais) were on the upper banks of the West Fork of the Trinity near the present town of Bridgeport in Wise County. Five days of riding brought them to this place. They found two deserted villages of seventy lodges near fields desolate with last season's corn stalks. General Tarrant deemed it imprudent to burn the villages, situated on a high hill, for the smoke could be seen for miles. Axes slashed enough destruction to make the villages uninhabitable. The first blow in the war of retaliation had been struck. With rising spirits, the minutemen moved on. In the words of Tarrant:

We changed our course southeast following the course for some distance from the main western branch of the Trinity; and on the twenty-first we crossed the high divide; and that night camped on the eastern branch of the Brazos.

Two days of riding to the Brazos produced no results. No Indians or signs of their habitation appeared. The company decided to return to the Trinity to search the western branch to its mouth. Two days' journey brought them to the Trinity toward the north. As they traveled down its valley in late afternoon, a new interest on the high prairie near the river aroused them from their weariness. A lone Indian was sighted. Tarrant gave the command. The company divided, cut off escape, and captured the savage.

It was time to end a day of hard riding. A high open prairie was no place to spend the night. They returned to the wooded shelter of the river and made camp at the fork of Fossil Creek which flowed from the north into the Trinity about eleven miles from present-day Fort Worth.

At sunset preparation was made to kill the Indian prisoner because he had been sullen and would not reveal the location of the Indian village. For the description of this incident, we have the words of Andrew Davis. At Fort Johnson, the minutemen had urged Andrew, a youth of thirteen, to return home. He had refused and had doggedly ridden his mule, though he was never able to gain a place among the company except in the last column of riders. This evening, Andrew stood at the front of the semicircle of men. To the youth, according to his own words, "The scene was awful in its solemnity. The Indian was placed with his back to an elm tree, his hands were drawn around the tree and tied, and his feet, bound together, were firmly fastened to the tree. Twelve men stood before him. The order rang out to present arms. The Indian cried aloud, his words were not distinct but his cry seemed to say, 'Oh man!, Oh man!' Tarrant sent Captain Yeary with an interpreter to the prisoner. 'We be friends,' he mumbled, and made a full revelation of the location of the Indian village."

Darkness came. Tarrant sent Stout with ten men to find the village, to select a point of attack, and to return by four o'clock in the morning.

CHAPTER 6

Minutemen at Village Creek

MEN hurried about in the darkness preparing to break camp. Stout's scouting expedition had returned in the night with information and plans. Stout led the men east into the rising sun of May 24, 1841. They were silent. No doubt they knew one another's thought: the time of revenge was at hand, and there would be bloodshed. Thus they arrived at the ford of the Trinity where, in the words of General Edward H. Tarrant:

> Generals Rusk and Dyer charged a Kickapoo camp in 1838, in sight of the lower cross-timbers. Here we recrossed the Trinity from the eastern side to the western side and came upon the high prairies one mile from the ford; we found very fresh signs of Indians.

On a buffalo trail, fresh horse tracks were discovered. In good scouting spirit, Henry Stout with six other scouts spurred their horses to follow the trail. They returned to report that a village was three miles beyond on a creek. The men arrived by nine o'clock within 400 yards of the village and took up a position behind a thicket. From their hiding place, they could see Indians moving about in their village. Orders were given in muffled tones, to divest themselves of blankets, packs, and all encumbrances; to mount their horses, to form lines and, when the word came, to charge into the village. In five minutes, the men were prepared. Tarrant spoke.

"Are you ready? Now, my brave men, we will never all meet on earth again; there is great confusion and death ahead. I shall expect every man to fill his place and do his duty. Charge!"

General Tarrant, Captain John B. Denton, aide to Tarrant, and Captain Bourland led the charge. Four hundred yards of land lay between Tarrant's command and the Indian village. The space was covered in a flash. The onslaught was fierce, and the surprise complete. The sudden burst of bullets, like thunder over their huts, brought terror-stricken Indians running from their homes, some falling in death as they fled. The air was full of bullets. The village was captured. Indians fled along a wide trail leading down the bank of the creek. Hastily a few men were detailed to stand guard at the village, while the other horsemen galloped in pursuit. Within two miles, they rode upon a second village. The work of death was fearful.

Young Andrew Davis was the last horseman to arrive at the village, for his mule was slow. Soon this was shot from under him, and he took shelter behind a tree. A feeling of desolation swept his being. He felt, in the death of the animal, as though he had parted from his best friend. Other riders lost their mounts, too, but they fought on. Andrew, seeing this, left the tree and joined in the fight. Thus this second village was quickly taken. There was another village in sight towards which the horsemen dashed, and many men, now unmounted, ran on foot.

Indians of the third village, having had time to prepare their guns and ammunition, fired rapidly. The minutemen drove them away. From this point, there was no distinction between villages. For a mile and a half the huts stretched along the creek. Soon the minutemen became so scattered, General Tarrant, fearing the various groups would be cut off and destroyed, ordered the men to rally at the second village, to which the rear guard had now come with the packs from the first village.

Minutemen in tattered clothes, covered with dust, wet with sweat, and famished for food and water, assembled for roll call. The men quenched their thirst at a spring where Tarrant had taken his position for roll call. All the men answered "Here," for which Tarrant gave Divine thanks. Only ten were slightly wounded. He then ordered them to go to the nearest huts where they should satisfy their hunger with dried buffalo meat; and to be ready, after a brief rest, for further advance.

Denton and Bourland, each with a company of ten men, having promised Tarrant that they would not allow themselves to be ambushed, rode off in different directions to scout the woods. To their surprise, they met about one mile and a half from the second village, where the separate trails joined. At the junction of these paths, they discovered the largest trail they had yet seen. One end led over a mountain to the west; the other extended eastward toward the Trinity, crossing a creek upon which the villages stood. Looking across this stream through the timber, they saw a village which appeared to them larger than any other they had attacked. Words were exchanged as to the wisdom of entering the thicket and crossing the creek to it.

Stout and Denton challenged one another's bravery. This was against both wisdom and caution. But regardless, Denton, Stout and Captain John Griffin rode forward at a gallop, and the others followed.

Upon reaching the creek, they reined their horses to cross. As the hoofs of the horses of the first riders splashed in the water, bullets whizzed from the woods. Denton was killed and Stout was severely wounded, while Griffin suffered only a slight wound. Bullets came from all directions. The clothes of the men were pierced. They could not see the enemy; and being few in number, they did not attempt to rush into the wooded thicket. Instead, they dismounted, began to yell, and to make demonstrations as if to charge the creek. Soon the yells and bullets of the Indians ceased, and they suddenly left their grounds. Unable to hold its position, the scouting party hastily fled to the second village where Tarrant had made headquarters.

In the absence of the scouting party, Tarrant, with his men, had been making survey of the situation. After inspecting the villages and questioning the prisoners, they were in possession of disturbing information. The villages were inhabited by a thousand warriors, more than half of whom were away hunting on the distant prairie. The minutemen counted 225 lodges and there were more in the large village which they had glimpsed through the thicket but did not dare approach. They saw 300 acres in corn. There may have been more fields beyond the large village.

Being farmers, the Indians had an eye for farm tools when they went on their marauding expeditions, and had collected a large stockpile of every type except plows. In the huts, the minutemen found a huge supply of ammunition: guns, sergeants' swords, musket flints, musket powder, pig lead, and musket balls. Each lodge had two or three bags of powder and lead tied in equal portions. Some lodges had featherbeds and bedsteads.

One lodge was a blacksmith shop with an excellent set of blacksmith's tools. Recently the Indians had been molding bullets. These villages, they also learned, were depositories for the stolen horses from the Red River Valley and homes of the murderers of the Red River pioneers as well. They were members of many tribes: Cherokees, Creeks, Seminoles, Wacos, Caddoes, Kickapoos, Anadarkos, Kichais, Ionies, and others.

The sun indicated that it was mid-afternoon, and plans for the night should be made. A conference was held, for the Texan leaders were convinced that if the Indians discovered the smallness of their number, they would attack them as they crossed the Trinity, because they could easily be separated from one another in the woods on either bank and quickly overpowered. On the other hand, if they remained at the village all night, the Indians would have time to concentrate their forces, surround the village and annihilate them. It was decided to take up their march, to cross the Trinity, and to spend the night on the high prairie.

Before departing the village, a squad of men volunteered to return to the scene of Denton's death and recover his body. They feared that the Indians might have scalped him. However, their anxiety vanished when they found Denton's body unmolested where they had laid it. Carefully wrapping it, they tied it on a gentle horse, and returned to camp.

Upon their arrival, they found the company prepared for the return journey. The enemy's cattle and booty, which the minutemen had captured in the villages on the creek, had been made ready for the trip. This war prize consisted of six head of cattle, thirty-seven horses, 300 pounds of lead, thirty pounds of powder, twenty brass kettles, twenty-one axes, seventy-three buffalo robes, fifteen guns, thirteen packsaddles, three swords, and shovels, besides other sundries. Tarrant had not wished to take prisoners and had permitted them to escape, with the exception of a little Indian boy who became Tarrant's charge for the next two years.

Tarrant gave the order to start at five o'clock. Weary men spurred their horses' flanks and rode from the creek which was henceforth to be clothed in historic glory. For this small creek, rising in present-day Johnson County, flowing northeasterly for twenty-six miles and emptying into the Trinity about three miles from Arlington, was to be known as Village Creek.

The minutemen followed the route by which they had come that same day at sunrise. They jogged twelve miles, crossed the Trinity where the timber was thin, and camped for the night on the prairie; which in 1849 was to be incorporated into a county named for Edward H. Tarrant, the hero of the Village Creek Fight.

Next sunrise they were riding northeast. When the Indian villages were twenty-five miles behind them, the company halted to bury their friend, Denton. On a high elevation near Oliver Creek, they dug a grave of good depth with tools they had brought from the Indian villages. They lined the grave with rocks, placed another stone over the body and filled

in the grave. Because of such precaution, Indians would not find the resting place of Denton. In sorrowful silence the company again took up
their march. They would remember this man and his sacrifice, but
would posterity?

Five years later, in 1846, the prairie land where the minutemen had
buried their friend was to be organized into Denton County, and much
later, the deceased scout's body was to be reinterred in the public square
of the city of Denton.

May was drawing to a close. It was warm; the Indian fighters were
weary. The horses jogged, then trotted, as the riders talked of the good
lands in the Grand Prairie, the many springs, the good pastures, and the
well-timbered banks of the Trinity. Some of the minutemen declared
that the country at the forks was better land for homes than the Red
River Valley, if only men could be free of Indians.

They rode along the west side of the East Cross Timbers and the Elm
Fork through the area which was to be Denton and Cooke counties, and
crossed Elm Fork where later Gainesville was to be founded. They then
took the trail northward toward Fort Johnson, the point from which
they had originally set out on May 14, 1841. After six days of arduous
riding from the camp on the Trinity, they reached their destination.
Safely within the barracks of Fort Johnson, they divided the booty seized
from their enemy. They disbanded in June and hurried home, for they
were late with their spring planting.

CHAPTER 7

Frustrated Effort

GENERAL TARRANT was an unhappy warrior since his return from the Village Creek expedition. He could not be content with an incomplete campaign—not such a soldier as he. In his youth, he had served with Andrew Jackson in several Indian campaigns; had marched off with "Old Hickory" to the war of 1812; and had passed through the blistering battle at New Orleans—General Jackson's immortal victory.

Born in 1792 in North Carolina, he was only a youth of sixteen when he left his Tennessee home for the War of 1812. Wars for liberty had been his life. He then left Tennessee for Texas, arriving in 1835 to fight in the army of the Republic in its struggle for independence from Mexico. He joined the newly organized Texas Rangers. In 1838, he had tried his talent in the role of congressman of the Republic of Texas, only to find it displeasing. Trained in the school of General Jackson, he had the spirit of the frontier warrior. Soon he returned to his Ranger duties in North Central Texas.

Tarrant was restless. He could not forget the fact that, with a band of minutemen, he had fled from an unfinished battle because the Indians outnumbered them. Early in June, he began measures to raise a large expedition for a second campaign to the upper Trinity. Volunteers were recruited by letters and by word.

He persuaded General James Smith of Nacogdoches, commander of
the militia in that district, and a former soldier of Old Hickory's in the
Creek war, to join him in the expedition. Smith agreed to raise a company of minutemen in East Texas and meet Tarrant with them somewhere in the East Cross Timbers. These two military units would clear
Indians from the Cross Timbers and the forks of the Trinity. Then the
promise of homes in this fertile region could be realized.

In mid-July, hundreds of men were riding in groups converging upon
Fort English, near present-day Bonham. There they organized a regiment with General Tarrant as supreme commander. By July 20, 1841,
more than 300 men departed from Fort English. Tarrant led them southwest with speedy directness. On the west bank of the Trinity, they
pitched camp, probably on the site of one of their former camps in present Tarrant County.

From this camp, scouting parties penetrated the woodland thickets to
locate the Indians. For several weeks, minutemen lived in the saddle,
persistently tracking down every sign of Indians, to find no enemy at the
end of the trail. Fatigue and discouragement ruled their spirits. Neither
the Indians nor General Smith's company from East Texas was discovered. Tarrant laid aside his well-planned attack, led the men back to
Fort English, and disbanded the regiment—a frustrated effort.

Tarrant had failed to find General Smith in the Cross Timbers, but
Smith had kept his word. Leaving the Nacogdoches district with a company, he moved northwest. On the way, he halted at King's Fort, now
the town of Kaufman. The settlers related to him their experience of
the previous evening when they repulsed a severe Indian attack.

Next sunrise, Smith was following the trail of these Indians which led
him to the Trinity where Dallas now stands. On Spring Branch, a mile
on the west side of the Trinity, Smith made camp near a spring. The
water was so delicious that the men named it Honey Spring. On the
same campsite, a few months later in 1841, the father of Dallas, John
Neely Bryan, was to pitch tent.

From Honey Spring camp, Smith sent out twelve scouts under the
leadership of Captain John L. Hall to seek the location of the Indian village of the famous Village Creek Fight. The scouting party crossed
Mountain Creek, traversed the prairie on the west side of the Trinity,
entered the East Cross Timbers, and came within a short distance of
Village Creek, where they halted. There were many trails converging
upon the creek which they decided was evidence that the Indian village
was near. The area and the location was as it had been described to
them, and they felt they were now on dangerous ground.

Captain Hall chose from his scouts two of the most skilled in wood-craft—John H. Reagan, a buckskin-attired surveyor, and Isaac Bean, an Indian trader. A half-day of spying brought reward. These men found the village occupied with Indians and discovered that the place was approachable at both the upper and lower ends. After memorizing the lay of the land, they returned to Captain Hall, who was hiding in an oak thicket. When darkness came, Hall with his scouts reported to General Smith, who had moved camp to Mountain Creek.

The following day at noon, Smith was at Village Creek. He divided the men into two battalions. Reagan, as guide, conducted General Smith's men to the upper end of the village. Bean guided Lieutenant Colonel Elliot's to the lower end of the village. The men successfully reached the positions, and as they waited for the signal of attack, their eagerness mounted. At length the word came, and they charged the village. To their dismay, the place was deserted. The enemy had fled, leaving their supplies and camp fixtures. Smith concluded that the Indians had discovered Tarrant's force and had departed barely in time to elude his regiment.

Failing to find Tarrant, he returned to Nacogdoches. The third expedition to enter the future Tarrant County in the year 1841 terminated in a bloodless adventure.

The minutemen's efforts were not lost, however, for their expeditions bore good fruit later. No doubt the Indians, without being seen by either Tarrant or Smith, discovered these large military forces and fled. The frequent appearance of companies of armed pioneers—they had seen three companies within the year 1841—forewarned them that the East Cross Timbers and the forks of the Trinity were no longer a retreat unknown to white men. Many of the more warlike accepted the warning. They moved into the upper Brazos Valley and into present Parker and Palo Pinto counties.

Furthermore, they were prepared to accept the treaty which Sam Houston was to offer them in 1843. All things were working together for the clearing of the upper Trinity Valley for settlement. Like real estate land boomers, the minutemen of the campaigns of Tarrant and Smith made known the fertility of the soil, the many fine springs, the excellent timber, and the bountiful game. Living in the Red River Valley and East Texas, they were in a position to give advice to the homeseekers arriving in that section.

Some of the minutemen heeded their own advice and moved into the area. One, Hamp Rattan, enchanted with the country, prepared without delay to move his family there. From official reports, it may be concluded that this man was with Jonathan Bird at the founding of Bird's Fort, also with General Tarrant at Village Creek. Knowing of the location of this fort, Rattan thought that it would be a ready-made home. In September 1841 he wrote from Paris, Lamar County, to Captain Bird that he was gathering supplies for the return. In the fall of that year, with other homeseekers, Rattan set out. Deserted Bird's Fort lost its desolation when Rattan, Captain M. Gilbert, James J. Beeman, and Beeman's half-brother reined their horses to a halt, and their families promptly climbed from their wagons to make the fort their home.

Disappointment was the lot of these first settlers of future Tarrant County, for the Indians had burned off the grass, and no game of any kind was to be found. Having relied upon the reports of previous adventurers, telling of an abundance of game, the party had brought only scant provisions. Late November did not improve matters. Winter was at hand, so a wagon was sent to the Red River for supplies. Christmas came. It was not a merry one. The wagon of supplies was overdue, and starvation was fast approaching reality. Rattan, Solomon Silkwood, and Alex W. Webb left the fort in search of the relief wagon.

Anxiety rode with the three horsemen, as their mounts trudged through six inches of snow. The severe cold numbed their hands and faces. One mile and a half southeast of the present town of Carrolton in Dallas County, nature offered aid to their food problem. Discovering a heavily laden bee tree, they dismounted to cut it down. Intently at work, they were surprised when a shot rang out, and Rattan slumped to the earth dead. Silkwood and Webb returned the fire, killing one Indian of a small band, and then fled to Bird's Fort.

An unmarried man from the fort set out alone to find help. He met the relief wagon, and on December 30, 1841, the party reached the place where Rattan was killed. Rattan's faithful dog was guarding the body. The party carried the remains to Bird's Fort and, making a crude coffin of an old wagon, buried Rattan in the oak grove near the fort.

After Silkwood had returned to Bird's Fort, he died from exposure and exhaustion caused by hard riding through the severe weather to escape the Indian murderers of Rattan. He was laid to rest beside his former comrade. These graves, among the first in Tarrant County, were those of men who not only had faith in opportunity, but also had courage to dare to seek it beyond the frontier line. The surviving homeseekers remained a little longer at Bird's Fort, trying to make it home. However, adversity conquered, and they left the next year.

The immediate reason for their departure appeared in the person of John Neely Bryan. Early in 1842 he visited them and told the men of a fertile area abounding in all the riches frontiersmen could enjoy, situated in the vicinity of his cabin on the Trinity. Drawn by this new hope, Gilbert and Beeman led their band from Bird's Fort to join their fortunes with Bryan; thereby terminating the first settlement in Tarrant County.

Although forsaken, this fort had not completed its historic destiny. In the summer of 1843, it would give refuge to the remnant of the tragic Snively Expedition in its retreat southward to the Texas capital. In August and September of 1843, sheltering President Houston, it would be adequate setting for his Indian powwow and treaty of 1843. After this event, Bird's Fort would disappear from the record of the pioneers, only to reappear in the name of the settlement, Birdville, present-day Haltom City, which would arise in the vicinity of the military post, Fort Worth.

CHAPTER 8

The Hand of Friendship

WOULD the north of the Republic be a promise of homes for men or a stark wilderness? That depended upon peace between red and white men. To continue the war with the Indians begun by Lamar's policy would make the north a forbidden land where men's hope would end in the war whoop. To restore peace to Indian camps would cause the upper valleys of the Trinity and Brazos to blossom with farms and towns, while stagecoaches and ox freighters would etch roads across the prairies. The north of the Republic should be the "Land of Promise" for immigrants from the United States and Europe.

Such was the reasoning of President Sam Houston. He took up his quill and wrote in bold strokes to Tod Robinson, chairman of the finance committee in the house of Congress:

I should have the means of procuring peace with the Indians on our borders. . . . I should be gratified to have an appropriation of fifteen or twenty thousand dollars as an Indian fund.

Procrastination had no place in Houston's affairs. It was January 5, 1842, less than a month since his second inauguration as the third president of the Republic of Texas. This brief note revealed that Houston intended to fulfill his campaign promises made in the summer of 1841, and to carry out the policy which he had explained to Congress shortly after his inauguration in December. He had promised to end the war with the Indians and to practice rigid economy. He needed funds for immediate use. A request for $20,000 for Indian affairs was rigid economy in comparison with Lamar's expenditure which had amounted to $2.5 million. Lamar's extravagant spending in dealing with Indians had produced war and closed the northern area to settlement.

It was imperative that Houston be frugal. Texas, in 1842, faced bankruptcy with a debt of about $7 million with currency unacceptable in world markets and without credit among nations. Houston had spent less than $100,000 on Indian affairs during his first administration. And in his opinion and that of his friends, he had produced satisfactory relations with the red man by frequent councils, peace treaties, trading houses, and gifts. Now faced with an empty treasury, Houston planned to pursue the same inexpensive Indian policy in his second term as president, and to promote the colonization of the northern border. Houston carried out his policy and made another chapter in the history of Fort Worth and Tarrant County.

The campaign to prevent the north from remaining uncolonized was underway by the spring of 1842. Houston explained his plan in official correspondence written from the Executive Department, Houston, April 14, 1842: "Indian trade from the headwaters of the Trinity to the Rio Grande" should be controlled by the Republic. Texas Indians should be lured from the Mexican trading post at Santa Fé, New Mexico, and from Coffee's trading house on Red River. Without delay, a trading post should be established on the upper Brazos beyond the frontier line, as well as other posts. Indians would discover that trade in the Republic was as profitable as at Santa Fé and at Coffee's.

When trade flourished, war would end. It was believed Indians would cease stealing people and horses, and Texas could reclaim her captive individuals. Houston, however, was a realist. He planned protection for the trading posts. He ordered good pickets and cabins placed at these business places with good lots enclosed with stout rails. To strengthen the new bond of friendship, he announced that peace treaties would be signed, and after these pacts were concluded a guard of from ten to twenty men would be sufficient at each trading post. A policy of trade and treaties, Houston declared, would cost the government one dollar to $100, which in the past had been expended to keep up the mockery of war with the red man.

Indians should know that a new "White Father" offering peace and trade now guided Texas. In the words of Houston, "The sun is again shining upon us. . . . Sorrow will no longer fill our hearts." Agents were made ready to go to the border chiefs to inform them of this fact. In May, Houston had requested Attorney General George W. Terrell to see and induce Joseph Durst and Colonel Leonard Williams to visit the border braves. Houston wanted master hands for this undertaking and Durst had a reputation as a time-seasoned Indian agent. Living on the west bank of the Angelina, he had served the Republic as special agent for critical missions. Colonel Williams, likewise an expert, had lived as a resident agent at trading posts and understood the mood of the Indian when at trade. Terrell succeeded in fulfilling Houston's request. On July 5, 1842, Colonel Williams, Joseph Durst, Colonel Henry E. Scott, and Ethan Stroud were commissioned by President Houston "to treat with any and all Indians on the frontiers of Texas."

Next day, Houston wrote a "Talk to the Chiefs of the Border Tribes," which the newly appointed agents were to deliver. He understood the fiber of the red man's mind and heart, knew the modes of expression which could woo them from the warpath. He had an appealing literary style. Sharpening his quill he pleaded:

My Friends: The path between us has been red, and the blood of our people remains on the ground. Trouble has been upon us. . . . I learn that our red friends want peace; and our hand is now white, and shall not be stained with blood. Let our red brothers say this, and we will smoke the pipe of peace.

You shall come to our council-house in peace; and no one shall raise a hand against you. Let the tomahawk be buried, and let the pipe of peace be handed around the council of friends. I will not forget this talk—nor my people.

Interspersed among the beautiful phrases were three specific requests. Houston invited the chiefs to a peace council to be held on the Brazos at the Waco village on October 26, 1842. To this council Houston instructed the chiefs to bring their white prisoners who, he understood, were held in suffering; and there the Texans would exchange with them the Indian women and children whom they held as prisoners. He also promised that the new trading houses would be opened to the Indians.

On September 4, the commissioners returned from their mission to report their success: the Indians were eager to make peace. Good news was followed by disappointment. Fall rains were heavy and rivers flooded, which kept Indians away from the appointed council on the Brazos in October, 1842.

Thwarted plans did not deter the Texas Congress with carrying through the promised trading posts. The first of these was to be located on, or near, the south fork of the Trinity somewhere between the lower and upper East Cross Timbers in present Tarrant County. The second was to be constructed at, or near, Comanche Peak, and the third near the old Spanish fort on the San Saba. A Bureau of Indian Affairs was organized to function under the War Department.

The spring of 1843 came, and Houston supported by Congress moved again to bring red and white men together in a peace council. The last day of March was crowned with success. Commissioner Terrell and two others passed the pipe of peace around the council on Tawakoni Creek, near the present city of Waco. Talk ended in an agreement with representatives from the Delawares, Caddoes, Wacos, Shawnees, Ionies, Anadarkos, Towakonis, Wichitas and Kichais that their tribes would attend a grand council at Bird's Fort on the Trinity at the full moon of August, with representatives from all tribes in Texas and from those living north of Red River.

Indians departed from the council comforted with new promises. In the meantime, while waiting for the August meeting, hostilities were to cease, Indians could trade at Torrey's new trading house on the Brazos and could plant corn north of this post.

Events were moving toward Houston's goal. As early as March, correspondence had ensued between Houston and Governor Butler of Indian Territory. Houston wished to identify his Indian policy with that of the United States and to impress upon the red man that the two Great White Fathers—the president of the United States and himself as president of the Republic of Texas—were working together; and that Lamar's policy no longer prevailed.

On May 13 from the capital, Washington-on-the-Brazos, Houston sent to G. W. Hill a commission, instructions, and a "talk." Hill was to attend the Grand Indian Council to meet at some place near the Wichita River in United States territory, and to communicate Houston's "talk" to the Indians residing in that nation through the approval of an officer of the United States.

Hill had another specific responsibility. He must give the Indians a definite understanding of the August full-moon meeting at Bird's Fort; and since the fort was removed so far beyond the settlements that white men could not haul food there, they must take along their own provisions.

Houston, the writer of diplomatic notes, was stirring the northern prairies to a new day. Before Hill was commissioned, a party of horsemen with packhorses of supplies was slogging into the wilderness carrying gifts and a "talk" from the Great White Father, President Houston, to Comanche Chief Pa-hah-yuca. These men-at-arms were Colonel Joseph C. Eldridge, General Superintendent of Indian Affairs; Thomas S. Torrey, Indian agent; Hamilton P. Bee, a comrade of Eldridge in former talks; three Indian interpreters; several Delawares as hunters, helpers and traders; and A-cah-quash, the Waco head chief called "Old Squash."

A seasoned monarch in Indian relations, Houston, in his "talk" to Comanche Chief Pa-hah-yuca and his instructions to Eldridge—both written at Washington-on-the-Brazos May 4, 1843—were documents that evidenced imagination and wariness. Indians were to understand that the gifts were offerings of friendship, not of fear, and that no more would be made until a firm peace was established. Eldridge was to make sure that the Indian interpreters, Shaw and Conner, should strongly impress the Comanches that a new chief with a pacific policy now ruled Texas and that former President Lamar, responsible for the massacre of Comanches at the Council House in San Antonio, had left Texas, never to return. Comanches, Houston promised, "will never again be told falsehoods. . . . There is room enough for the Comanches in the prairies . . . I will always be their friend and never forget them. Nor shall the winds scatter my words."

Furthermore, Eldridge was to tell Pa-hah-yuca that Houston expected him to send runners with talks to all the tribes of the Comanche, and that he wished the head chief of each band to attend the council at Bird's Fort in early August when the moon would be full. The Comanches were to bring all the white prisoners to this place where they would be exchanged for their own people held prisoners by the whites. Houston was giving evidence of his faith by sending with Eldridge two Comanche children captured at the Council House Fight—a small boy named William Hockley and Maria, a little girl. These were being returned to their own people well attired, showing proof of the white man's good care of his prisoners.

Success rode with Eldridge's party on the first lap of his journey. He traveled up the Brazos Valley, passed Fort Milam near present Marlin, the last settlement on the frontier, and reached the extreme northern outpost, the Torrey brothers' trading house on Tawakoni Creek. Here they found a large party of Delawares. After a day and night celebration, followed by two days of slumber required to recover from the frolic, the party moved on.

A few days riding brought them to a point above the forks of the Trinity, probably in present Wise or Jack County. Beside the bank of the West Fork, they made camp for a few days, while Delaware messengers made excursions to the rim of the rolling prairies, seeking any tribes which they might invite to visit them. Delegations from eleven small tribes heeded the invitation: Wacos, Anadarkos, Toweaches, Caddoes, Kichais, Tehucacanos, Delawares, Bidais, Biloxis, Ionies, and one or two others.

They came with alert ears and eager appetites for gifts. Eldridge did not permit this outburst of Indian vitality to vanish in the prairie winds. He staged a powwow, magnifying the glory and importance of the new path offered the red man. He appeared in dress uniform. Bee performed the duties of secretary. The council was made solemn by embracing, smoking, and wordy exchanges. In fact, a day was spent in parleys. On the second day, Eldridge delivered a talk which won from these tribes promises to be at Bird's Fort in August.

It was July. The party pushed forward. A-cah-quash, with two Waco girls, former prisoners who were now to serve as proof of the new friendship policy, rode ahead to the Wacos. Finding his friends, "Old Squash" was embraced with affection, thus assuring a friendly reception for the party following him. Eldridge made camp three miles from the Wacos, and sent runners to find the Comanches. Day after day they waited. Late in July, Eldridge, without provisions and dependent upon wild meat and fruits, rode westerly across the plains.

In early August, they found the long sought after Comanches. An old chief, gathering plums a few miles out from the camp, returned to the Comanche tents with the news. Five hundred warriors rode out to meet Eldridge's party and escorted them into the town. This was a climax worthy of their three months of zealous searching. Chief Pa-hah-yuca being away, his wives received Eldridge.

The commissioners waited a week for the head chief. During this time the Comanches moved twice. The white party accompanied them. A week of difficult waiting passed before Pa-hah-yuca arrived. He courteously received Eldridge; but the next day started badly. A council of 100 warriors was called. The white commissioners were excluded, but not A-cah-quash and the three interpreters. The warriors deliberated until sundown. Anger mounted. These white men, they argued, represented the government that had killed their kinsmen in the Council House at San Antonio. Afraid of more treachery, they would not go to the Grand Council at Bird's Fort. They called for the death of the commissioners. A-cah-quash wept and pleaded for his friends' lives. Houston's three interpreters tried to convince the warriors that Eldridge was a peace messenger with a white flag. Torrey, Bee and Eldridge alone in their tent listened to the angry jargon, knowing that the Comanches were demanding their lives. With the last rays of the sun, Pa-hah-yuca spoke. The day ended with the message that the white messengers would be spared.

That night, to assure the safety of the commissioners, Pa-hah-yuca's warriors guarded the visitors' tent, and they awakened to a more auspicious day. Pa-hah-yuca invited Eldridge and his companions to a council.

In the meantime, on August 9, 1843, the Grand Council at Bird's Fort was getting under way. Many moons had waxed and waned since Eldridge left Washington-on-the-Brazos. He wondered if the indefatigable Houston, waiting at Bird's Fort, would understand his failure to bring the Comanches to the powwow.

Entering the council with Pa-hah-yuca, Eldridge was determined to turn failure into a measure of success. Since the boy prisoner had already been given to the chiefs, he now carried the little Comanche girl, Maria, dressed in white man's finery, and ceremoniously presented her to Pa-hah-yuca. He delivered Houston's message and said that, since it was now too late to meet the prearranged Grand Council, another would be arranged, if they would come to meet the Great White Father. This talk was followed by a distribution of gifts. Pa-hah-yuca signed an agreement that hostilities and horse stealing would cease until the president could send a commission higher up on the prairies to meet the Comanches, but that they would not go to Bird's Fort.

Miles of plains had to be crossed before the returning party reached the Red River. Eldridge made haste knowing of Houston's impatience. In late September, 1843, they rode into Bird's Fort. G. W. Terrell and Edward Tarrant greeted them. Houston had returned to Washington-on-the-Brazos. But that is another story.

CHAPTER 9

The Treaty of 1843

The red brothers all know that my words to them have never been forgotten by me. They have never been swallowed up by darkness; nor has the light of the Sun consumed them. Truth cannot perish, but the words of a liar are as nothing. I wish you to come and we will again shake hands and counsel together.

A promise written in the firm strokes of Sam Houston and confirmed by the seal of the Texas republic had been carried to and fro through the north by Indian commissioners from early March to August, 1843. This promise had passed through the Indian camps from the forks of the Trinity and upper Brazos northward, and beyond into Indian Territory in the United States. Houston's correspondence in preparation for the council at Bird's Fort would fill a volume. Even small details for the Indians' comfort had not escaped his expansive sympathy for the red man. In one of his last letters of instructions before the Grand Council should meet, he ordered Benjamin Bryant, an Indian agent, on July 8, 1843, to gather all Indian prisoners held by the government, as well as those in possession of the Lipan and Tonkawa Indians, and take them to Bird's Fort. Before setting out with the Indians, Bryant was to take care "to clad comfortably the Indians, to procure moccasins or some other covering for their feet," and on the journey to the council to spare them "as little physical distress as possible." Houston's fatherly tenderness did not overreach his sense of thrift. He reminded Bryant that comforts were to be purchased with an eye for economy. Four captains of the Lipans were to join Bryant's caravan of prisoners. Representatives of the fierce Lipans indicated that the council at Bird's Fort was not to be a mere powwow.

While Colonel Eldridge was on his mission, Houston was preparing for his part in the Bird's Fort Council. On July 28, 1843, the door of the crude executive office at Washington-on-the-Brazos was closed on the problems of the Texas republic: debts, revenue, Mexico's hostility, foreign relations with Britain and France, and the question of Texas' annexation to the United States. Houston was turning his insatiable mind to the Indian problem. He was off to Bird's Fort and did not plan to return to the capital until September first. John H. Reagan, the young surveyor, was guide for the president's party. He knew the country of the upper Trinity, for he was surveying the area which would become Dallas County. Reagan was both guide and companion to Houston, who admired the politically astute mind which was to make Reagan years later both an eminent congressman and the first chairman of the Railroad Commission of Texas.

Houston was a good traveler. On July 30, the president's party was at Montgomery City, and on August 3, they reached Crockett in present Houston County. He advanced into the Trinity Valley of which he had heard much; and each mile unfolded a world that surpassed his dream. The first week in August found the president encamped at Bird's Fort. Many tribes had gathered, and as each day brought the joyful sight of other tribes arriving, voices and camp noises swelled from cadence to turbulence. The different tribes had varying dialects but communicated with each other by embellishing their jargon with sign language.

The full moon of August came and spent its brilliance while Houston waited. The Comanches and Wichitas did not come to pitch their tents. Eldridge, Hamilton, and Bee did not return from the north. Almost a month passed. Finally, he decided to speak with those tribes that had abided by his word. He called a council. Indian pomp, a fidelity of Houston's youth, was easily summoned to dramatize his action. He clothed his giant frame in a purple velvet suit embossed with embroideries of foxes' heads. An extraordinary bowie knife of giant size, conspicuously thrust in his belt, armed him with the might of the superior hunter. A well-folded Indian blanket thrown in debonair manner over one shoulder proclaimed, in brilliant hues, his brotherhood with the red man. With silver eagle spurs clanking, resplendent as the Great White

Chief, he walked into the solemn council of Indian chiefs who were dressed in their best feathers and their most riotous colors.

The Indians understood and believed his words. "We are willing to make a line with you, beyond which our people will not hunt. Then in red man's land beyond the treaty line unmolested by white men, the hunter can kill the buffaloes and the squaws can make corn."

Houston's irresistible power carried Indians with him to the climax of his speech, where he was able to turn the temporary defeat into victory. His words called his red brothers to share his burdens. He told them that since the full moon had waned and all the tribes had not come to the council, and also because many duties of the Great White Father called him to return to serve his people at Washington-on-the-Brazos, he could wait no longer for the coming of the other tribes. Therefore, they should receive two of his trusted friends to make a treaty when all the tribes gathered.

Houston's words drew his audience unto himself. They agreed to abide by his promises; also to receive G. W. Terrell and Edward H. Tarrant as they had received him; to make peace with them knowing that a treaty with them was the same as with him, for Terrell and Tarrant were his mouthpieces. On September 2, Houston was back at his desk in the executive office: a man who had spent much of himself both physically and spiritually to bring peace to the northern wilderness of the Republic, and to open the land about the forks of the Trinity to colonization.

Terrell and Tarrant found it tedious waiting for late arrivals to the Grand Council. Their task, as stated before, was to make the final treaty ending the four-years' war with the red man. Some new event was bound to change the days of delayed hope. It came when Eldridge and Bee rode into Bird's Fort. Terrell and Tarrant received them with the joy of men welcoming comrades whom they believed had died in the uncertain country of the enemy. Eldridge's message was that the Comanches would not come to Bird's Fort. This changed the course of Indian diplomacy from waiting to writing a treaty of tremendous consequences.

A Treaty of Peace and Friendship between the Republic of Texas and the Delaware, Chickasaw, Waco, Tiwocano [Tawakoni], Keachi [Kichai], Caddo, Anadah-kah [Anadarko], Ionie, Biloxi, and Cherokee tribes of Indians, concluded and signed at Bird's Fort on the Trinity River the 29th day of September, 1843.

This treaty embodied all of Houston's peace policy and arranged conditions which would last a quarter of a century. Today, this document reposes in the archives of the State Library of Texas. A seal of the Republic mounted upon white, blue, and green ribbons makes the signatures of President Houston, Indian Commissioners Terrell and Tarrant, and the marks of the unlettered chiefs an authentic and binding law. In fading ink one can read the twenty articles which opened the wilderness about the forks of the Trinity.

Nearly half of the articles dealt with war. Both parties agreed and declared that they would forever live in peace and always meet as friends and brothers; and that it was the duty of warriors to protect women and children. The treaty further stipulated that if Indians went to war, they would neither kill women and children nor take them prisoners. Furthermore, these red men would never unite with enemies of Texas or make treaties with them. Too, if the Indians learned that Texas was at war with any people, a chief was to go to an Indian agent and be conducted to the president of the Republic for counsel. It was presumed that trouble then would vanish; and both parties would deliver all prisoners held at that time. These were not evasive terms which might lead to serious bickering; these were provisions struck in clear reasoning within the reach of the red man's day-by-day living.

What is safety in peace unless accompanied by security, and how would the Indians find that security unless guaranteed a red man's land in which to hunt and raise corn, as well as trade with white men? The treaty answered that question through ten articles based upon the rock of Indian economy. Texas was to be divided into two parts—red man's hunting grounds and white man's farmlands. When the treaty line was determined, there would be built a line of trading houses to which Indians could bring hides, pelts, buffalo robes, and tallow to barter for needed goods. Beyond the line of trading houses no white persons should pass without special permission of the president. No person would go among the Indians to trade except licensed traders, and they could not furnish Indians with war equipment except with consent of the president. No man living under the laws of Texas could sell intoxicating liquors to Indians; nor could anyone except licensed traders purchase the goods of Indians. Any property found among whites belonging to Indians, or property belonging to whites found among Indians, would be restored to their owners.

The treaty provided that each year the president would call a council, would present gifts when he deemed it proper, and would make arrangements with Indians which he considered necessary to their happiness. The president would send blacksmiths and other mechanics, men to work mines, and schoolmasters with their families to instruct Indians in the English language and the Christian religion. Indians would receive the men whom the president sent and treat them kindly. No harshness, only tenderness, kindness, love, and friendship were written into each clause of the treaty except one. The one clause bound both red and white men by the terms that any person violating peace was subject to punishment.

In the senate chamber of the Texas Congress on January 31, 1844, the treaty concluded at Bird's Fort was ratified and three days later, Houston affixed his signature. In February 1844, citizens and Indians learned from the president's proclamation and through Indian agents that the Treaty of 1843 had become law.

In early March, twenty chiefs and head men—signers of the treaty at Bird's Fort—assembled at the capital. Houston received them, presented gifts, and told them to go forth to tell the Comanches and other wild tribes to come in and make peace. He reaffirmed that trading houses would be provided on the Trinity and the Brazos.

By December 1, 1844, A. G. Kimbell and Lewis G. Greer had been granted the right to establish a trading house on or near the Trinity between the upper and lower Cross Timbers. And on the fourteenth of that month, Houston instructed two agents to go to the Comanches and other Indians on the frontier of the Republic of Texas and to carry gifts to the head chief of the Comanches, Pa-hah-yuca. They were to reiterate the terms of the treaty, e.g., that the government had made arrangement for the establishment of trading houses; that numerous benefits would be derived by carrying on traffic with these traders; and that when peace was established blacksmiths would come to their camp to mend their guns.

This 1843 treaty was to be the means by which the lands about the upper Trinity emerged from wilderness to habitation. It became the pattern for three future treaties of the Republic signed with the Indians, bringing to the frontier as much order as reasonable white men could expect. As stated previously, it divided the Republic of Texas into two parts—red man's hunting grounds and white man's country. It was reaffirmed that the red man's land began north of a line drawn roughly from the present town of Fort Worth to Menard, and from Menard to San Antonio. The promised trading houses were to be established at the juncture of the Clear Fork of the Trinity at the present site of Fort Worth, at Comanche Peak near Granbury, and on the San Saba River near the old Spanish mission in Menard County.

Most Indians moved north of the treaty line. There were Indians who broke the treaty, crossing into the white man's country; and there were white traders who would never acknowledge that there was a red man's land into which they should not venture. Nevertheless, the Indians moved farther west, and the pioneers whipped their horses into the upper Trinity and Brazos valleys. The frontier line did move forward.

Traders and trappers formed the vanguard of settlement, since the treaty promised trading posts on the upper Trinity. Three astute men with goods possessing Indian appeal had ventured about sixteen miles west beyond Bird's Fort. In chill November, they pitched camp in a live oak grove near the Clear Fork of the Trinity in the area of the present southeast corner of 11th Avenue and Cooper Street, Fort Worth, though this has been disputed. Another pioneer locates the camp in present-day Botanic Garden.

From winter until spring of 1844, Ed Terrell and John P. Lusk, the first businessmen for this future city, traded trinkets for pelts. However, their business psychology was discordant with the rhythm of the Indian mind, which was to boil into hostility. That spring, Terrell and Lusk cut logs for their trading house and stacked them in orderly piles. But it takes many arms to raise logs in place, and the nearest to help them were two traders at White Rock in present Dallas County. They journeyed to ask help of these neighbors.

On the return, not far from the site of what would have been the first house-raising in Fort Worth, hostile Indians captured the riders, holding them as prisoners. Terrell was expert at escaping from bad situations. By promising that the white men would obtain corn for Indians and return with it, they freed themselves, but now they were not so dauntless. Instead of returning to the house-raising, they rode northeast into the settled country of Bonham. Thus the first business house of future Fort Worth closed in the spring of 1844.

The license for another trading post in this area was granted by President Anson Jones to Mathias Travis, March 6, 1845, to be on the South Fork of the Trinity. By September 1845, a house and several sheds, all fenced with pickets, opened for business. The location was three miles from the West Fork at Marrow Bone Springs, known later as Johnson's Station, three miles south of the present town of Arlington.

The 1843 treaty was not only a boon to traders, but also sent surveyors farther up the Trinity Valley. They camped among the trees near the forks. One outfit of surveyors thus temporarily occupied the present location of Forest Park in Fort Worth near the Clear Fork in 1845. Two large bur oak trees were marked as "witness trees" for the southwest corner of the E. S. Harris survey. These two witness trees, calculated to be about 250 years old in the 1940s, are among the few remaining south-

east of the bridge over the Trinity River on University Drive. Another
party of surveyors sent by the Peters Land Company were killed by Indians in the vicinity of the Trinity forks in 1845. Within the decade following, surveyors would drive the stakes of Tarrant, Dallas, Denton,
Ellis, Collin, Kaufman, Navarro, Bell, and Limestone counties. The
Treaty of 1843 would establish a line of demarcation which would
achieve national significance in 1849.

Texas became a state of the United States on December 29, 1845,
sending the United States and Mexico to war in 1846. When the war
ended two years later, the government of the United States assumed the
centuries-old problem of Indian defense, adopting as the frontier line
the demarcation fixed by the Treaty of 1843 which would give the future city of Fort Worth the slogan "Where the West Begins." To wagon-
sheltered pioneers and buffalo hunters, Fort Worth was to be the last
outpost of civilization to replenish supplies before hazarding into the
perilous west. To the pioneers in the late 1870s and 1880s, Fort Worth
still would be on the margin of civilization; for it was to be the last town
of note when the Texas and Pacific Railroad puffed its way West. To
modern motorists, speeding westward over the silver-ribboned highways
from "Fort Worth, the Queen City of the Prairies," the topography of
the countryside would sing, "I am the beginning of the West."

BOOK II

Home-builders and
a Fort on the Prairies

GENERAL TARRANT and the minutemen's fight at Village Creek
in 1841; Houston's plighted word at Bird's Fort in 1843; Rangers', surveyors', and trappers' intrepid advances into the wilderness of the Trinity; the Congress of the Republic with its legal arm; and the annexation
of Texas by the United States in December, 1845—all had gone before,
opening the way for families in covered wagons to roll into the prairie
country in the last half of the eighteen-forties.

Then the final event opening the upper Trinity to settlement came
after the Mexican War. The United States, fulfilling its treaty obligation
to prevent Indian incursions into the Republic of Mexico, prepared to
erect a chain of outposts, which led to the establishment of the fort at the
forks of the Trinity on June 6, 1849. And home-builders came to settle
under the protective arm of the military post.

CHAPTER 10

Luring Land Laws

In its eager desire to settle its empire of more than 18,000,000 acres of unclaimed land, the Republic in 1841 and 1842 granted contracts to immigrant agents much like the Mexican empresario agreements under which Stephen F. Austin had brought in colonists. The area, which was to be organized as Tarrant County in December 1849, was a small portion of an enormous grant covering the whole or a large part of twenty-six present-day counties. This grant, as large as a kingdom, was extended by the then President Lamar, to W. S. Peters and nineteen associates, nearly all of whom resided in Kentucky. The Republic retained alternate sections in the contract and all unappropriated public land was closed to settlement until proprietors completed contracts. In the expectation of a land boom, this contract required the introduction of six hundred families within a period of three years.

The boom fizzled temporarily because Mexico had refused to acknowledge the independence of Texas won at San Jacinto. Twice during the year 1842, Mexican troops invaded Texas. In January 1843 the Congress of the Republic gave Peters Land Company and all other colonizing companies an extension of time until July 1, 1848, to introduce the required number of colonists, but altered the terms of the former contract. Each year, contractors were to settle two hundred families within their grants. These terms conjured visions of a quick realization of the American dream: ownership of virgin lands.

Land grants direct from the Republic to individual settlers were called headrights. Each head of a family who settled in a colony was to be allowed 640 acres of land of his own choosing, and each single man who was over the age of seventeen years was entitled to 320 acres. The settler was to be required to build a house and reside in it, to cultivate at least ten acres of land, and to remain on his land for at least three years.

The Peters Land Company planned bountiful remuneration. Without stint it advertised the wealth of the prairie lands in the states of Missouri, Kentucky, Tennessee, Illinois, Indiana, and even in Europe. With each hundred families settled, the company would receive ten premium sections of lands, as well as secure additional compensation from the colonists in the form of fees for surveying the land, erecting cabins, moving colonists to Texas, or supplying necessities.

The year 1843 reached a low mark in immigration, but the year 1844 brought new stimuli to the colonization. Among these incentives was the vanishment of fear of further Mexican invasions. Then, too, James K. Polk campaigned in the United States and was elected president on the slogan "Re-annexation of Texas, Re-occupation of Oregon." While talk of annexing Texas was widespread in the United States, the policy of granting citizenship and suffrage to immigrants after six months' residence in the Republic was appealing to homeseekers.

Another stimulus for settlement was the Texas Homestead Act of 1839. This guaranteed man's shelter, for by law no man's home or tools of trade could be seized or sold for debt. And Congress, in 1844, granted 320 acres of free land in the vacant public domain to settlers fulfilling specific conditions.

Newspapers in the United States carried enthusiastic columns about Texas that whetted the desires of Europeans as well as Americans to obtain Texas scrip that would procure land for fifty cents an acre. By 1845, squatters who had settled on land without deeds were given pre-emptive rights to buy 320 acres at that price. Since acreage in the public domain of the United States sold for $1.25 an acre, Texas had more allure. Land-hungry men reasoned that Texas would soon be under the stars and stripes.

In the fall of 1844, immigration revived. Covered wagons bound for the upper Trinity Valley had signs of "Polk," "Dallas," "Oregon," and "Texas" printed on the covers. These slogans revealed loyalty to James K. Polk of Tennessee, and to George Mifflin Dallas of Pennsylvania, who was candidate for vice-president.

Peters Colony headquarters was at Farmers Branch near the three forks of the Trinity, where a settlement was taking form. There was rivalry with another group of settlers, those gathering around John Neely Bryan's cabin nearby. By 1845 wagon trains were increasing in numbers to the extent that they had to wait their turn to be ferried across Red River. On the banks of the river colonists looked across into "the promised land of Texas," impatient with delay which stretched into hours, sometimes a day. Some crossed at Preston, then followed the Preston-Austin road southward, left that road in southwestern Collin County and entered Tarrant. Another route brought them by way of Jonesboro and over the National Road of the Republic to the village at Elm Fork. This settlement in the mid-fifties was named Dallas in honor of the man who had become vice-president of the United States.

At Elm Fork, the settlers could be ferried over the Trinity at Bryan's crossing, just below the present site of the Union Station in Dallas; or at the other ferry at Cedar Springs two or three miles upstream. A man called Collins operated this rival business. Those entering by way of Nacogdoches, also settlers from East Texas, came to Tarrant County by way of the Comanche Road and the Caddo Trace to Dallas. Ferrying across the Trinity, they struck out over the trackless prairie which, according to an early traveler, was more desirable than the straggling wagon ruts called roads. From Dallas there was a trail leading to the trading house of Mathias Travis at Marrow Bone Springs, as related in chapter nine.

A fourth gateway into Texas was by way of Jefferson on the Red River. By this route settlers followed the trails known as Caddo Trace and Jefferson Road into Dallas and thence across the Grand Prairie into the future Tarrant County. The Shreveport gateway was used by the colonists who had traveled a large part of the way by water. Placing their wagons on riverboats, they descended the Mississippi, then transferred their wagons to a riverboat ascending the Red River to Shreveport, thence overland to the Grand Prairie.

Some of these men from Missouri, Kentucky, Indiana, Illinois, Tennessee, Georgia and other states preferred to act under legal contracts; therefore fastened in their pockets or in a strongbox tucked safely away on the driver's seat were papers from the Peters Land Company which would make their settling legal. But there were others with lean and hard lines about their faces for whom contracts held little significance. Legal procedures would not keep land from their reach. As squatters, they would settle upon the land of their choice, and somehow legal possession would follow. So wagons with masters carrying deeds from the

Peters Land Company, wagons with masters holding land scrip of the Republic of Texas, and wagons with masters without legal papers but with much fortitude converged upon future Tarrant County to build the first permanent settlement.

A change was coming over things in 1847. Texas by then was safely in the Union with all the blessings that such a union brought. Furthermore, Texas was twice blessed, for she was the only one of the twenty-eight states to retain her public lands. As a state, her land policy remained as liberal as when a republic; thereby retaining her allure for newcomers. In 1847, the United States was in the midst of a war with Mexico, the annexation of Texas being one of the causes. Americans were fighting from Santa Fé to California and besieging the ancient cities of Mexico. Nevertheless, in 1847, wagons and more wagons, driven by men who believed that America's "Manifest Destiny" lay in the Texas frontiers, were assembling on the prairies of future Tarrant County.

The Mexican War ended in 1848, and the Peters Land Company contract expired that year. More wagons unhitched about the forks of the Trinity in 1849 and the 1850s. Some of these land seekers were veterans of the recent war. There was much confusion over titles. The Peters company had met with almost every conceivable difficulty and could not fulfill its contract.

After the failure of the company, all unclaimed lands were opened under Texas land laws. In 1850, the state issued certificates to those Peters colonists who had received land prior to 1848, in order to settle contradictory claims arising with the influx of the many newcomers. In 1852, the Peters Land Company was reorganized under the name of the Texas Emigration and Land Company. It was aided by the fact that it had settled 2,205 families in their western empire during 1841 to 1848.

The new company relinquished all its claim to the original colony. In return, it was to receive certificates to seventeen hundred sections of land of the former colony, provided the land had not already been settled. Persons who had claimed land between the years 1848 and 1852 with land scrip, headrights or bounty warrants of Texas, were not displaced. In August 1854, the contract of the Texas Emigration and Land Company was terminated. An episode in the land history of Tarrant County and Fort Worth ended with it.

CHAPTER 11

A Lonesome Dove

THE PIONEERS who arrived in 1845 and 1846 settled in the area of present Grapevine, forming a community which was first known as Lonesome Dove, thus winning the distinction of being the first permanent settlement in Tarrant County.

In time to do a little planting in 1845, Missourian householders in a wagon train ended their journey on the "Grapevine Prairie." With headrights from the Peters Land Company, the Missourians scouted the area and chose their land. Scattered over this region and along the present Denton County line were the log homes of B. F. and Hiram Crowley, Zeb and Eli Jenkins, Dr. J. C. Dunn, Ambrose Foster, Archie Franklin Leonard, James P. Hallford, Jimmy West and many others. Though not clustered close, they yet could see each other's chimneys, or reach each other by short riding. For a time these homesteaders comprised the "Hallford Prairie Settlement."

Upon their arrival here in 1845, they had worked from dawn to sunset to carry them through their first winter on the Grand Prairie. January's coldness in 1846 bound them to their firesides temporarily. However, spiritual contemplation was not neglected. One of their number, Joshua Hodges, a minister, encouraged by his neighbor, James Gibson, called his devout members of Hallford Prairie Settlement to assemble for the reading of the Divine Word in Gibson's cabin, it being well suited for the purpose. In its long room of log walls with earthen floor, warmed by burning timber in a large fireplace, men and women praised their Lord.

Among these worshippers, a newcomer of a few weeks, the Reverend John Allen Freeman, was called upon to preach. He and his wife had entered Texas by way of the Red River the previous November, seeking the East Fork of the Trinity. On the way, Freeman encountered a company of Rangers, the first men he had seen in Texas. In the words of Reverend Freeman:

At that time they were a wild, rough looking set of men, some of them dressed in buckskin, and some of them wore coon-skin caps; some of them were drinking bad whiskey and some of them were playing cards. In this way they spent their time when not in pursuit of Indians, who came in now and then to commit depredations on the settlers.

In a spirit of thankfulness for his safe arrival and for the well-being of these settlers who sheltered him, Freeman began his sermon with the text: I Peter 3:12, "For the eyes of the Lord are over the righteous, and His ears are open unto their prayers." The congregation was visibly moved. At this service, a committee was appointed to consider forming a Baptist church.

On the third Saturday of February 1846, in the log cabin of Charles Throop on the north side of Denton Creek, and on the edge of future Tarrant County, twelve faithful worshippers organized the Lonesome Dove Baptist Church, Cross Timbers. The congregation was to meet every two weeks in the homes of the people. A lengthy statute of the church was written, declaring the faith and prescribing a way of conduct. On a firm foundation was man to act, for it was written,

If any Brother being hurt with another and not applying to him for satisfaction nor the church but proceeds to make remarks before the world and the Brethren he shall be deemed in disorder and shall be dealt with accordingly.

When the organization was completed, the hand of fellowship was given by "Hall Medline, Nancy Freeman, John Freeman, Mary Anderson, Felix Muligan, Henry Atkinson, Lucinda Throop, Maryan Leonard, Susanah Foster, Henry Suggs, Seleta Suggs, Rachel Muligan." It was a significant moment. Author D. D. Tidwell, in his *A History of the West Fork Baptist Association*, states that "not a protestant church stood between the Lonesome Dove church and the Pacific Ocean."

The following Sunday ten more members were added: "Deacon James Gibson, Nancy Gibson, James P. Halford, Sarah Halford, John N. Halford, Malissa Halford, Ordained Minister, Joshua Hodges, James W. Anderson, Elisha Clary, Mary James."

The isolated call of a dove at dusk vividly described this little band's feeble step in the wilderness. By 1849 the ranks of the Lonesome Dove Baptist Church had increased to sixty-six members, and among those gathered into the fold were four colored women. In 1847, the members chose a permanent site for this first church organized in Tarrant County. It was located three miles from the site of its organization in 1846, and a few miles west of the small town of Grapevine.

More and more wagons pulled to a halt as their owners decided on homesites in present Tarrant County in late 1845 and 1846. Patrick A. Watson from North Carolina and Macajah Goodwin from Georgia located their headrights from Peters Land Company in the eastern part of present Tarrant County. Watson's home was north of the present location of Six Flags in the area of the south end of the regional airport and Highway 360, formerly known as Watson's Road.

Goodwin's joy of pioneering was turned into sorrow in the loss of his wife. A few months after his arrival in February of 1846, he built a coffin from the bed of the wagon which had brought his family from Georgia and buried his wife while his son stood guard at a distance to be certain that Indians would not see. With tender strokes the grave was smoothed over, brush lightly piled upon it; then fire crackled until the brush became ashes like a campfire in order that Indians would not know where she was laid to rest. Her grave was on the land of Watson, the Goodwins' neighbor; and in 1846, Watson donated the land for what is said to be the oldest cemetery in present-day Tarrant County.

Unafraid, some men and their families searched for good lands beyond the sight and sound of neighbors. One such man was named Bennett. He took up a claim on Bear Creek far to the south from Watson's. John Hust was another who had weathered the dust of days in his regulation oxteam prairie schooner from Council Bluff, Iowa, ending the journey on a lake near the Trinity River, nine miles east of present-day Fort Worth. This lake was called Hust; and when population increased and cornfields expanded, a mill was built near it by Archibald Leonard.

Although Tarrant County was included in the territory of the old Peters Land Company, not a great number of Tarrant pioneers settled under a headright from that company. The map shows only 150 such claims. This land company, however, is worthy of a salute—a loud and respectful one—for it brought to Tarrant County the first permanent homes, the first grist mill, the first cemetery, and the first church—the Lonesome Dove.

CHAPTER 12

Bubbling Springs

Tıme, changes in nature, and man's progress often obliterate sites of former sources of earth's prolific bounty and centers of man's prosperous living. In the late 1940s, three miles south of the town of Arlington, now a metropolis, were remnants of such a place—small boulders and a hollow of muddy water. A century earlier, bubbling springs of refreshing waters rippled into a creek, Mills Branch, which ultimately flowed into the Trinity. These springs had sustained life through much time, and the boulders embedded about the banks spoke of much history.

Pioneers said the large rocks were ancient bones of a huge prehistoric animal. Other rocks, containing fossil seashells, tumbled about to tell of time—if there were men with knowledge to read them. These stones gave the springs three of the many names by which the area was known: Fossil Springs, Big Bone Springs, and Marrow Bone Springs.

This natural source of water had been home to the Indians, for arrowheads and other artifacts have been found, as well as a huge stone that, by the hollowed-out markings, must have been used to grind corn. Mathias Travis was wise to have built his trading post here where his customers, among whom were hunters, other tradesmen, and Indians could find water and shelter.

Later, this area became the headquarters of Colonel Middleton Tate

Johnson's Company of Mounted Texas Volunteers in federal service guarding the northern frontier against Mexican agents and unfriendly Indians during the Mexican War. Early accounts state that Johnson arrived here in 1847—a most likely date. A colony from Indiana, which came in the winter of 1847, was entertained by him and settled near the springs.

A companion in the service with Johnson, Captain Charles Turner, leaves behind a record which states that upon his return from the Battle of Monterrey, "Johnson immediately made up a company of frontier guards, and after several changes of location, was stationed at Marrow Bone Springs, where he was living at the close of the war between the United States and Mexico." This statement is verified by records in the office of the Adjutant General, War Department, Washington, D.C. From this source it is learned that Johnson served as captain in a company designated "Captain Johnson's Company, Bell's Regiment, Texas Mounted Volunteers." He had entered the service April 5, 1847, at Cartwright Mill, Shelby County (Texas). The next year in July, he was appointed lieutenant colonel. He was mustered out February 3, 1849, at Conner's Station.

Though this was the end of his Mexican War service, Johnson without delay, joined the Texas Rangers, becoming commander of a company for the northern frontier with headquarters at the springs, as stated above. A man of vision, he recognized the value of this beautiful part of the country, and straightway fashioned a dream into material substance. First he staked out land to which he could claim a right under the land system of Texas, and to which he was entitled. His claims were extensive, including portions which comprise the present city of Fort Worth. Then, according to his grandson, Johnson returned to Shelby County, disposed of his property there, and moved his family to the springs in 1849.

No doubt it was Johnson who changed Marrow Bone to Mary le Bone, by reaching back to his English ancestors with whom he had spent imaginative hours in the described beauty of Marylebone Borough in London, made charming by the lighter moments of history. Since the days of Queen Elizabeth, royalty and nobility had sported on Marylebone Hunting Grounds. *Black's Guide to London* (1911 edition) tells us the original name was St. Mary of the Bourne, a bourne being one of several streams, and pronounced in England, "bone"; and that Londoners pronounce the district "Marrybone." The beauty of England, Johnson knew, could not surpass the majestic verdure of his principality in the Trinity Valley. Here was a hunting ground well timbered with massive oaks and rife with deer, antelope, and fowl. Here in this country, beside these springs, nature had placed a garden very much like Maryle-bone Garden in London. Only, at this earliest period, a road, church and fine homes were missing from the scene. But not for long.

By the spring of 1849, a large house, cabins, stables, a gristmill, sorghum mill, sawmill, and blacksmith shop all were in evidence. Stretching away from this prosperous complex were fields of corn, other grain, sorghum and cotton. This plantation displayed careful tending by slaves. Close by the main house were gardens in which vines of beans, peas, and tomatoes heavy with harvest were entwined about neat trellises; while a bountiful crop of squash and melons gleamed beneath their foliage. The pastures were grazed by sleek-coated cows. These thousands of acres proclaimed the fertility of the Trinity Valley. The United States census of 1850 gave the 1849 production of Johnson's horse-powered sawmill as 300,000 feet of post oak plank, and 3,000 feet of oak and cedar scantling. Johnson's mill was well patronized in the 1850s, supplying the mudsills for buildings in Dallas and Fort Worth.

During the fifties, the caravans of settlers multiplied. The colonel's plantation became known as Johnson's Station. It was on the only trail leading from Dallas to the west. Over this trail, a good day's journey from Dallas, wagons swayed and creaked until, in late afternoon, they came to a halt at Johnson's place. Here was ample feed for horses, plenty of slaves to do one's bidding, and a mercantile store to replenish supplies. This outpost in the stretch of the Texas Cross Timbers must have been a heartening sight to men who had traveled through the sparsely inhabited Texas empire; and here made ready to ride again into the stillness of uninhabited prairies.

Colonel Johnson was well endowed to preside over his outpost. A giant of a man over six feet tall, weighing about two hundred and twenty-five pounds, with an erect carriage, he possessed the courage of a warrior. His young manhood had been spent in warfare and adventuring. Born in South Carolina in 1802, he was a staunch Democrat and a friend of Andrew Jackson and Sam Houston, both of whom he imitated. About 1839, he came to Shelby County, Texas, from Alabama, where he had been a legislator of that state. In East Texas, he headed a cavalry of twenty-eight men who fought for the Regulators in the Regulator-Moderator feud. This was a merciless and bloody strife in this section of the Republic from 1842 to 1844. People of Shelby County elected Johnson in 1844 to represent their district in the Congress of the Texas republic.

Vienna, the colonel's wife, had also spent a few years in dangerous activities. She had been a spy for the Regulators. Now as mistress at Mary le Bone Springs, her steady courage and controlled mind were an influence of no mean degree. She comforted the weary women of the wagon caravans and sent them on their way with new strength. She created a home which expressed a sense of well-being, an atmosphere conducive to discussion and to the planning for future progress. It was in this home that her husband and other pioneers mapped the direction of events which shaped the destiny of Tarrant County and the northern frontier of Texas. It was here that a party of United States dragoons found rest in the spring of 1849; and from here departed to search for a location of a military post which became Fort Worth.

In his *Reminiscences of the Early Days of Fort Worth,* page 15, Captain J. C. Terrell wrote: "M. T. Johnson was the father of Tarrant County as E. M. Daggett was the father of Fort Worth, his face being on our city seal. Both were grand men physically, morally and mentally. Johnson was physically the strongest man I ever knew. Neither of them was exemplary or saintly, yet both were to us old settlers veritable heroes. We loved them for the manifold good they did. . . . Both were good Masons."

CHAPTER 13

A Fort and a General

Wɪᴛʜ ᴛʜᴇ Mexican War over, the Federal government turned its attention to Texas, the new state annexed on the eve of the war. The treaty of annexation stated that the United States would assume control of Indian defense in Texas. In the Treaty of Guadalupe Hidalgo, which had concluded the Mexican War, the United States had agreed to prevent American Indians from marauding into Mexico. To comply with these agreements Uncle Sam ordered, in 1849, a cordon of eight forts to be erected in Texas beyond the line of settlement, and to be garrisoned by regular troops of the United States Army.

The projected line of defense was to enter Texas to the north and east of the 98th parallel and proceed in a southwesterly direction to the Colorado and Guadalupe rivers and thence west to the Rio Grande. Assigned to the duty of locating these forts was General William Jenkins Worth, stationed in San Antonio in command of the Eighth and Ninth departments of the army, which included the vast areas of Texas and New Mexico.

In February, 1849, General Worth had commissioned Major Ripley A. Arnold to use companies F and I of the Second United States Dragoons to found two of the forts in the chain. The eastern end of the cordon of forts was to begin, in the words of official instructions, "somewhere near the confluence of the Clear and West forks of the Trinity River," and extend southwestward to the Rio Grande.

By April 17, 1849, Major Arnold had established one of the forts—Fort Graham, one mile east of the Brazos in Hill County. Now he was ready for the next post, which must have a strong, strategic, and healthful site. So with a detachment of dragoons, he proceeded to Mary le Bone Springs with a letter addressed to Colonel Johnson from General Worth. The general wanted assistance, and Johnson was the man he knew could best advise Major Arnold for the new site. Johnson in a masterful and lengthy letter to the supreme military authority in Washington, D.C., had voiced the discontent of settlers because of lack of defense and the gravity of the situation on the frontier.

Projects are outlined and men act. From Mary le Bone Springs on an early May morning of 1849, men of good will rode together to find a site for a fort "somewhere near the confluence of the Clear and West forks of the Trinity River." The party was comprised of Major Arnold's escort of blue uniformed dragoons and Colonel Johnson in command of Rangers: Henry Clay Daggett, W. B. Echols, Simon B. Farrar, and Charles Turner.

A controversy has disturbed historians. Was Major Arnold in that party which selected the location of the post? Peak stated that "Colonel Johnson and four of his rangers accompanied the Major to the camp site," and Simon Farrar, who accompanied Colonel Johnson wrote in 1893, "We started in company with Major Arnold's command up the Trinity River in search of a place to locate the regular troops." Who could better describe the epoch-making event than Farrar since he was there and the only one who has left a written record?

. . . It is out of my power to describe the grandeur of the wild and beautiful scenery of the place where the grand city now stands. . . . After staying about a week at Johnson's Station, we started in company with Major Arnold's command up the Trinity River. . . . We passed through and across timbers, crossing the different creeks as best we could, through a wild, beautiful country inhabited only by Indians, wild mustang horses, innumerable deer, wolves and wild turkey.

About three o'clock in the evening we halted in the valley east of where Fort Worth now stands and killed a deer for supper. We could have killed many more but did not wish to be encumbered with them. We passed our first night near Terry Springs east of Fort Worth later to be known as Cold Springs where we enjoyed ourselves with jokes, etc., indifferent to Indians, wolves, and all the wild enemies of white men.

Next morning Col. Johnson, Major Arnold . . . started to locate the barracks. We went west until we reached the point where the Court House now

stands, there halted and reviewed the scenery from all points and I thought
it the most beautiful and grand country that the sun ever shone on and
while we were at that place in view of all advantages of a natural point of
defense, and our late experience at Monterrey, wherein the strategic action
of General Worth had so terribly defeated the Mexicans, we there, in honor
of that grand old hero, named the point Fort Worth.

This chosen site was on the property of Colonel Johnson and his partner, Archibald Robinson. There was no quibbling about price. Johnson
and Robinson were settling a frontier. They gave the land to the United
States government for use until the post should be abandoned; at which
time, it was to revert to the owners. The post was to have the military
rating of a camp, not a fort. However, five months after the founding of
the camp, it was awarded the title of a fort.

Dragoons and Rangers had completed a momentous mission. Surely
that day, as the small band stood there in the stillness, someone captured the significance. Their action meant something—it was a beginning, a break with a period of uninhabited wilderness, an opening of a
prairie empire; it would unloosen forces from which would be born a
great city.

Under fire and smell of gunpowder, men learn of one another's value.
So it was between General Worth and Colonel Johnson. At the Battle of
Monterrey, Mexico, Johnson's company had served under the general.
There was mutual admiration between these warriors. Many of the
companies of Texas Volunteers had also served under him. His storming
of the Bishop's Palace was imprinted upon their minds. To these Texans,
it was not General Zachary Taylor, supreme commander, but Worth
who was the hero of the Battle of Monterrey. His tactics, they felt, won
the American victory with comparatively little loss of life while General
Taylor had caused a terrible loss in attempting to march up the streets
and storm the city. That was the opinion of Texas veterans. Worth verified his soldiers' admiration for him in a letter to his daughter written
from Headquarters, Second Division, Monterrey, October 2, 1846:

My cup of distinction and happiness is full. My duty, my whole duty, and
more has been done in respect to my operations, and the brilliant results,
there is but one voice, and that is stunning acclaim. . . . My soldiers and
volunteers throng my quarters and huzza me in the streets.

Thank God I have escaped. In a long service I have never been under such
a dreadful fire. I have almost lost my hearing on one side caused by several
consecutive shots that passed so near me as to stagger me almost out of the

saddle. In the street fight I was in uniform and the malignant scoundrels frequently brought their volleys to bear upon me, but all is safe.

General Worth was not frontier born. In 1794, his life began in Hudson City, Hudson River Valley, New York State, an area significant to American history since 1609 when Henry Hudson, the explorer, gave the Dutch claim to the territory. William Jenkins Worth, in his youth was a clerk in a hotel in Hudson City, later Albany. He abandoned his clerkship at the age of eighteen for the army. Warfare became his life. With honor he fought through the War of 1812. On the Canadian frontier, he began with the rank of lieutenant. As aide to General Lewis, his prowess was noted in the capture of Fort George and was followed by commendable action at Chrysler Farm on the St. Lawrence. From these early victories, he went to Buffalo to study in General Winfield Scott's celebrated Camp of Instruction. Equipped with new knowledge, he went to New York to become a member of the military staff of General Lewis. Under the guidance of this officer, he hoped that the application of his tactical theories would help bring the unpopular War of 1812 to a conclusion. Heroism in the Battle of Chippewa won him the rank of captain. The battles of Niagra and Lundy's Lane brought him wounds, an invalid's bed, and the title of Major Worth.

On his recovery, he was made commandant at West Point and served many years at the academy as instructor of tactics. In 1838, as colonel on the Niagra frontier, he allayed an insurrection begun by Bill Johnson, known as the "Patriot War." In 1840, he was in Florida to bring to a successful end the Seminole Indian wars. Several generals had preceded Colonel Worth at various times, but had been unable to subdue the savages. Within two years, Worth crushed all resistance and declared peace. His Florida record was another triumph. He had established a military reputation as a tactician. President Tyler thanked him for his meritorious service; the title of brigadier general was awarded in 1842, and he was retained in command of the Florida Department.

Foreign affairs of the United States in 1845 were moving toward decisive events which gave Brigadier General Worth more opportunities to prove his military genius. In March, James K. Polk entered the White House on the promise that he would settle the Texas and Oregon issues with Mexico and Britain respectively. In February 1845, Congress of the United States by joint resolution had provided for the annexation of Texas and had agreed to settle the boundary dispute between Texas and Mexico. General Zachary Taylor was ordered with an army to establish headquarters at the mouth of the Nueces River in Texas. In 1846,

trouble threatened on the Texas-Mexico border. Worth was sent to Texas
to join General Taylor. Early in March 1845, Worth received orders to
begin the advance toward the Rio Grande. In a letter to his daughter, a
Mrs. Sprague, written April 2, 1846, from a camp opposite Matamoros,
he related:

... have this moment sent in the resignation of my commission and shall, I
trust, in six weeks cease to belong to that beloved service and profession
which I have idolized for thirty-three years. I can no longer remain in it
with honor or self-respect.

I led the advance of the army across the desert from Corpus Christi, and
four days since planted the first American standard on the left bank of the
Rio Grande within 600 yards of the bristling cannon of Matamoros. There
may it ever wave until further advanced in glory.

While he was moving with Taylor toward the occupation of the Rio
Grande, agitation over a point of etiquette led him to the resignation of
his commission. News, however, of the declaration of war on Mexico on
May 13, so stirred his soldierly spirit that he withdrew his resignation
and returned speedily to the field. Many know of his triumph in the
Battle of Monterrey, which earned for him the rank of major general.

After Monterrey, the campaign shifted to central Mexico. Worth,
under Colonel Winfield Scott's command, fought from one triumph to
another: the capture of Vera Cruz, the taking of Cerro Gordo Pass which
led to Mexico City; and the battles of Cherabusco, Molino del Rey, and
Chapultepec, which hoisted the Stars and Stripes over Mexico City. Some
evidence indicates it was Worth's tactics which won Mexico City, but
Scott accepted the credit. A bitter feud arose between Scott and Worth,
his one-time favorite colleague. Scott placed the headstrong Worth under
arrest when Worth preferred charges against him. President Polk inter-
vened and freed Worth. Both Scott and Worth withdrew their charges.
After the peace treaty was signed ending the Mexican War, Worth
remained in Mexico City until June 12, 1848, when he embarked for
home and a long leave.

After a well-merited rest the general, in January 1849, assumed
supreme command of the Eighth and Ninth Departments of the Army
charged with defense of the frontier states of Texas and New Mexico.
Unlike his life of strenuous action, death came to General Worth in the
quiet orderliness of headquarters at San Antonio on May 7, 1849. The
fifty-four-year-old warrior was sick but twenty-four hours, a victim of
the deadly cholera. His obituary in the *Weekly Columbia Republican*
newspaper of New York, stated that his wife and all their children ex-

cept one, were with him at the time of his death. The councilmen of New York City requested Mrs. Worth to ship the remains to their metropolis. General Worth, in part responsible for winning the Mexican War and once considered as a candidate for president of the United States, lies buried today beneath a fifty-foot granite spire where Fifth Avenue meets Broadway in New York City.

It could be safely concluded that when the dragoons and Rangers looked from the high bluff of the Trinity that early spring day and named the new camp to be built there in General Worth's honor, his death had not become a fact to sadden them.

Fort Worth, like the man for whom it was named, had a modest beginning. This fort in the wilderness was the only post founded in Texas by Anglo-Americans which would pass from a collection of log cabins to a metropolis of steel skyscrapers with more than three-hundred thousand population. The fort in the wilderness would be abandoned by soldiers, but settlers would build around it; and some making homes within its walls, would convert it to a fort town. Never would it lose its military character. When it should become a city, it would twice become a military center—in World Wars I and II. After World War II, it would remain an important airbase for national defense, as well as a factory for production of strategic aircraft.

CHAPTER 14

The Lone Fort
on the Prairie

RIFLE SHOTS clapped with ear-piercing sharpness cutting through the heavy silence on June 6, 1849, to climax the raising of the United States flag of thirty stars at the forks of the Trinity. A military ceremony in good form for the records of the War Department in Washington had taken place. The Second Dragoons, Company F, United States Cavalry under the command of Major Ripley Allen Arnold had formally begun the establishment of the military post called Camp Worth.

Tired but happy soldiers, amazed by the beauty of the country, were pleased with the location for their new camp. In the coolness of a live oak grove northeast of the present courthouse square and near what is known as Pioneer Rest Cemetery, the dragoons found that nature had met man's every need. Three-quarters of a mile away cold water gushed from the south bank of the Trinity, which never lost its coolness under the thick shade of great oaks and giant pecan trees. They called it Cold Springs. Throughout all seasons the supply of cold water never failed even when the streams of the Clear and West Forks were reduced to stagnant pools during the hot, slow summers.

This spring was to provide the source of drinking water later when settlers moved in, and until they could dig wells. Later still, it served as a recreation resort for picnics and Fourth of July celebrations up through the turn of the twentieth century. By 1949, a hundred years from their discovery by the dragoons, only a faint bubbly trickle remained due to the south bank being denuded of trees. A road and a bridge leading to this location still bear the name Cold Springs.

Weary, worn soldiers, on that evening of historic June 6, made their beds almost as early as the thousands of wild chickens that came to roost in the nearby trees. Dragoons would sleep away their exhaustion. From June 4 to 6 they had been on the road from Fort Graham, over fifty miles away. Many creeks had been a problem to cross with mule-drawn vehicles loaded with twelve-pound brass field guns, six-pound brass field guns, Springfield smooth-bore muskets, Harper's Ferry sharpshooter rifles, army smooth-bore percussion pistols, one six-pound howitzer, a small mill, carpenter and blacksmith tools, camp equipment, food rations, and medical supplies.

It did not require a bugle to awaken the dragoons at sunrise on June 7. The squawking of a thousand wild chickens as they left their roost in the trees at the break of day, brought the dragoons from their sleep to begin months of unremitting labor. Major Arnold, the only officer with the company that June, had to bear over much. There was the duty of operating efficiently a military post with the problem of keeping the soldiers well; for this camp, though in a beautiful location, was not in a healthful one. Situated in the lowlands and heavily timbered, mosquitoes swarmed, causing illness. This in turn contributed to meager manpower to construct the necessary buildings.

Nine days after camp had been made, Major Arnold revealed his discontent. The post was not taking form rapidly enough in his eager vision. He needed help. From the archives of the War Department, we learn that he wrote to Major General Roger Jones, the adjutant general of the United States, on June 15, in a testy mood and underlined words for emphasis.

General
I have the honor to ask you to look over the enclosed Roll of my Company and to request that if there are any *Drilled* Recruits at the Cavalry Depot that my Company may be filled up—(those assigned me from Detachment brought out by Lt. Smith in November last with one exception had not been drilled at the Carbine Manual or Saber Exercises—or at least knew nothing of either).
I am building a new Post at this Place (the extreme Northern Frontier yet occupied) and my Company is so small that I cannot keep up my Scouting Parties. I have represented this matter to the Col. of the Regiment, and have asked that I might at least have a subaltern officer—I require a Bugler the Boy I have is sickly and his time will expire in November next.

The muster roll that accompanied the letter paraded more vexations: "No First or Second Lieutenant since January last." One of the four corporals, Joseph Noland, was on sick furlough from May 12, 1849, for three months; Thomas Noland, musician, was sick in the hospital; Anthony Kemp, the farrier, was away on extra duty with the War Department; two privates, Stephen Moser and William Dilcher, were away on extra duty with Brigadier General Harney since last April; one private was "perfectly worthless—cannot trust him with horse or equipment"; four privates were sick in the hospital; one had been ill since December 1848; another private of the company had been left behind in the hospital at Austin since December 1, 1848, and had not done a day's service since he joined the company. Since a doctor was not assigned to the company, the major had employed Doctor Jesse Marshall Standifer "to act as Assistant Surgeon for this Post." On the margin of the report, the major made a notation crackling with anger:

But Twenty-five Privates for Duty—building Post, Scouting etc. this not a mere morning Report but the Roll of my entire Company.
R.A. Arnold, Bvt.Maj. 2nd Dragoons Commanding.

If there were a few weak men, there was strength in strong ones—a fact the major made known in return under the title, "Remarks." He wrote, "Frank Knaar, Saddler and always at work at old equipment; John Wagner, driving the company teams; Augustus Helmering, Hospital Steward, and William Zeckler on extra duty as clerk in Quartermaster and Company Department." Then there was faithful Alphonso Freeman. During the first year of the Mexican War in the battle at Contreras, Mexico, Freeman saw Major Arnold in action. He made a decision to follow this warrior. He transferred from the artillery to Major Arnold's cavalry company. Freeman had companionship in another steadfast soldier, Louis Wetmore. Under Major Arnold, they had helped to capture Vera Cruz and Mexico City. The Mexican War over, they remained loyal troopers. We learn of their long trail of faithfulness from the West Point record of Major Arnold. In February 1848, Brevet Major Arnold as Captain of Second Dragoons was assigned to frontier duty; his company was "on March from the Rio Grande to Fort Graham, 1848–1849," and in service at "Fort Worth, 1849–51."

The major's June report did not bring immediate relief. Mail was slow. The nearest post office was "Dallas, thirty-five miles to the east, more than a full day's journey." In mid-August, the War Department received the major's testy report.

Lack of manpower was not the only trouble, but the problem of rations. In another letter, the major informed the adjutant general on July 30, 1849:

> ... Now permit me to say, that this being a Frontier Post, near sixty miles from any other Post; and a considerable distance from settlements that all entertainment necessarily falls upon the officers of the Post. Many Citizen Gentlemen are traveling through this Country, who cannot always provide themselves with all that they need; and whose gentility and necessities call loudly for our Hospitality.
>
> I think that I may safely assert that the Comdt. Officer of this Post will be obliged to entertain more Persons, than the Comdt. Officer of any Atlantic Station.

Double rations were granted Camp Worth by the War Department.

Mosquitoes and malaria had assaulted the health of the small band. Doctor Standifer and the major decided that erection of barracks on the high bluff southwest of their present low situation must be hastened. The summer of 1849 was one of toil and endurance. Never again would the pall of quietness hang over the area. Voices echoed through the little forest along the Trinity beneath the bluff. Scouts called out to comrades, "Here are some sturdy ones," as they marked the straight, tall cottonwood trees for the axmen. Many noises joined the voices in the woods—the pounding of the axes in rhythmic swing as they cut into the beautifully rounded trunks; the splintering death wrenches as the trees crashed; the "gee-de-ap" to the horses to move in place in order that the felled trees could be fastened to ropes; then the intoning words of the teamster coaxing the horses to move off dragging tree trunks up a steep, winding trail to the bluff where the sawmill driven by horsepower buzzed with accurate whirr. Men chanted, "Swing one, two, three—up—down," as logs were lifted into place forming walls for barracks. All day long in the heat of summer, the voices and noises rose and swelled with the incessant work of the dragoons. By August their camp was moved from the grove to the bluff, and the health of the men improved.

Fall came. On October 6, there was excitement in Camp Worth. Company F, Eighth Infantry, two officers and thirty-nine men under the command of Captain Robert P. Maclay and Second Lieutenant John Bold, joined Major Arnold's garrison. Lonely dragoons welcomed the arrival of much needed help, as well as men with new stories. And the infantrymen had good stories to tell. They had come from inhabited country "on the Steamboat Jack Hays up the Trinity as far as it was navigable," then overland through the Trinity Valley to relax in the pleasurable abundance of Colonel Johnson's plantation.

A new burst of energy took hold of the men. Building of the fort went

forward. More trees were cut in the little forest on the banks of the
Trinity. Sergeant Abe Harris, a veteran of the Mexican War with a good
record, commanded the group of infantrymen cutting the trees. Talented
as a cabinetmaker, he knew good wood. His skill was pressed into service in building the officer's quarters. By late fall, the handiwork of the
dragoons and infantrymen was established.

Camp Worth was a sight to gladden the wayfarers as they rode into
the West—an assemblage of log buildings with their ever freshly whit-
ened walls in regular lines rising from the knee-high grass. Over all,
floated the Stars and Stripes. A fort and the American flag in an ocean
of prairie were heartening.

The buildings were erected about a quadrangle bounded by the present
streets of Bluff and Weatherford, Houston and Throckmorton. One
pioneer said that the quadrangle was enclosed by a rope fence which
served as a cattle guard. "Quarters for the soldiers with shops for the
smiths and other artisans in a double row of buildings, made of logs or
of pickets, and all neatly whitewashed," were near the brink of the bluff,
and "composed the North line." Soldiers from their quarters on the
north edge, rather than the officers in their houses on the "South line of
the fort," had the most magnificent view.

In early spring, the redbud of the woods flaunted its pink blooms
among the somber trees yet unleafed. Then spring in its fullness placed
lacy green hats on the little forest. Soon flowering vines lent of their
fragrance to feed the bees. "The harvest was the sweetest honey ever
tasted." In and out of the woods darted antelope and deer; also black
bears and panthers were frequently seen. Birds of many species made
their habitat on the slopes of the bluff. Beyond the trees a valley of knee-
high grasses was riotously sown with wild flowers, spreading miles of
brilliant colors toward the skyline where, in the twentieth century to
come, would be the stockyards, the meat-packing plants of Armour and
Swift, Meacham's Airfield, and several oil refineries. Also near the rim
of the northern horizon like a mystic phantom arose a great mound with
a bluish cast. Soldiers called it "Blue Mound" and it became their barom-
eter. "Blue northers" seemed to gather behind it.

Looking west, the soldiers saw the West Fork of the Trinity meander-
ing toward them to join the Clear Fork beneath the fort where the waters
ran almost bank full, clear as crystal and swarming with fish. On the
west and north horizons "buffalo herds grazed but did not come near the
timber" which outlined the rivers. Soldiers off duty, if good fishermen
and hunters, were not at a loss for amusement.

Facing the soldiers' barracks and distant some two hundred and fifty feet south, were the officers' quarters, consisting of three houses. Arnold occupied the center building. Each house had two rooms separated by a runway or porch. Officers, facing the south, looked out across the Grand Prairie where today are the busy streets of Main, Houston, and Throckmorton. To the southwest they looked where now are Trinity and Forest parks and saw the Clear Fork cutting through the prairies in a winding path heavily outlined by trees. Gazing eastward, they beheld the East Cross Timbers interlaced with the creeks called Village and Sycamore.

The eastern boundary of the quadrangle consisted of long lines of stables with their backs to the present Tarrant County Courthouse. The hospital, quartermaster, and commissary offices completed the enclosure on the west facing out upon what is today the Ripley Arnold Housing Center. An ample parade ground in the center of the quadrangle covered the space now called Belknap Street. East of the center stood the flagstaff which Abe Harris had made by joining two of the tallest cottonwoods he could find with an iron band. This flagpole stood where today, on the Tarrant County Criminal Courthouse grounds, stands a granite monument marking the site of this military post.

Outside the quadrangle, warehouses containing quartermaster commissary stores were on a line with, and west of, the officers' quarters. Supplies in these warehouses were freighted by oxteams of the post from San Antonio, headquarters of the United States Eighth Military District. Still west and north of the commissary warehouse on present-day West Belknap, was a sutler's store—a shop licensed by the government to operate on the premises of military posts or nearby, in order to provide the soldiers with extra frills. George Press Farmer, the first sutler, opened for business two months after the garrison was established.

The Trinity River, Cold Springs, and a well dug by the soldiers under Major Arnold's direction, provided the fort with water. This first well was ninety feet deep and was located in the center of present Houston Street opposite the west entrance of the Tarrant County Courthouse.

In the winter of 1849 Camp Worth was completed, the last in the chain of eight federal forts. It stood a lone sentinel fifty-four miles above Fort Graham in a somewhat northerly direction. By 1850, an excellent road skirting the western edge of the lower Cross Timbers was etched by travel between the two military posts.

On November 14, 1849, there was an event over which to rejoice. The War Department lifted the military post from the rank of a camp to that of a fort. And the city of today cherishes this award by continuous use of the name and by jealously preserving its military heritage. That year closed auspiciously. Christmas day was the climax. Second Lieutenant

Samuel H. Starr of the Second Dragoons arrived with a detachment of recruits and remained at the post the following year. Another officer, First Lieutenant W. F. Street, Eighth Infantry, had already joined Company F the previous October. These troops of dragoons and infantrymen constituted the garrison from that date until April 6, 1851.

Troubles existed in the midst of beauty. "Fever and ague prevailed through the whole year" caused by the "heavy growth of trees and underwood" in the valley below the fort, also by "the great mass of half-rotted vegetable matter and half-dried mud" left along the riverbanks. On the high prairie they were "exposed all winter to the northers and sleets of the country and in summer the scorching heats." Such was the disparaging description of Fort Worth made by Lieutenant W. H. C. Whiting of the Engineer Corps sent by the War Department on an inspection tour of the outer chain of forts. Beginning his tour in October 1849, he completed his report in 1851. Besides disapproving of the vegetation which contributed to the sicknesses, Lieutenant Whiting objected to the location of the stables. These were too near the quarters of both soldiers and officers. The fort was not wholly bad, however. He reported several commendable aspects:

A mill worked by horsepower, hard by the post, and the thickly wooded bottom of the Trinity furnished cheap and ample supplies of lumber and fuel; coarse grained marble making excellent building material and plenty of lime and sand are abundant. No post is so plentifully supplied as to forage and subsistence. Within forty miles are the little villages of Dallas and Alton and numerous hamlets are found through the 'Cross Timbers' which afford nearly all that is needed for consumption by the troops.

CHAPTER 15

The Major

MAJOR ARNOLD commanded the outpost of Fort Worth at the age of thirty-two. Six feet tall, slender, graceful, gray eyes, a dominant forehead topped with auburn hair, a good chin and a mouth set in purposeful lines—he had the bearing of youth. Youthful strength with power drive, he was symbolic of the trait that would dominate Fort Worth's city pioneering.

He began his career at West Point on July 1, 1834. On that date the West Point register shows the name of the new cadet, gives his age as seventeen, birthplace as Pearlington, Hancock County, Mississippi, and date in April 1817. Four years of training, then a new entry on July 1, 1838: "Ripley Allen Arnold, age twenty-one, graduated, commissioned second lieutenant and assigned to First Dragoons, a cavalry unit on duty in the Indian War in Florida." He had graduated thirty-third in his class of forty-five. Perhaps his extra-curricular activities may account for this rating.

A mile from West Point, Benny Havens' saloon was a favorite resort for illegal escapades among the cadets. Here, after their rigid examinations, Cadet Arnold with some classmates indulged in sprees. Probably it was an affair which arose in this place that led to his fighting a duel, an event vaguely mentioned in his record. He was also given to singing and the writing of songs, one of which was sung for many years at the Point.

In Florida, his superior officers observed his military ability, and decided that he should not be wasted at the present in the Florida swamps fighting Indians, when recruits were needed if the Seminole War was to be terminated. Thus his first experience as a warrior was brief. Arnold was transferred to recruiting duty and given a furlough—which meant home and a girl.

In Bay St. Louis, Mississippi, with pretty blue-eyed, brown-haired Catherine Bryant, he arranged a marriage. When her father, a United States marshal, refused to give his consent because of her tender years, Arnold and Catherine eloped. They took a boat across the bay from Bay St. Louis and were married at Pass Christian on Catherine's fourteenth birthday, August 26, 1839. The couple honeymooned in Washington—a strikingly handsome pair.

Completing his recruiting assignment, Arnold returned to spend several years in the semitropical wilds of Florida. He was promoted to first lieutenant on February 1, 1841, for his creditable service against the Seminoles. The inspiration of his superior officer, Colonel (later General) William Jenkins Worth, guided him to hard study in order that he too, might become an expert strategist. He did. In April, 1842, with conspicuous valor, he routed Halleck Tustenuggee's band. Colonel Worth recommended Arnold's promotion to captain. In the report to the adjutant general of the United States:

First Lieutenant Arnold . . . in recent combat with the enemy . . . this young officer in the heat of pursuit, became separated from his company with eight men and found himself in the presence of a superior and well posted force of the enemy, against whom he sustained himself with great gallantry, even when his small force was reduced by one killed and two wounded.

In 1842, peace was declared in the Seminole War. Captain Arnold was sent first to Baton Rouge (then Fort Jessup), Louisiana. From there he was again assigned to recruiting duty.

The tide of international events in 1845 sent Captain Arnold to General Zachary Taylor's forces stationed at the mouth of the Nueces River in Texas. He was fortunate in all of his military tours, but especially in being placed with the Second Dragoons, the regiment of General Worth. In April of 1846, Taylor ordered his army across the Nueces. The Mexican War had begun. Then followed the battles of Palo Alto and Resaca de la Palma. These engagements were Arnold's opportunity. He directed hammering blows putting to rout the Mexican army in the Battle of Resaca de la Palma. One historian said that Arnold led "one of the finest cavalry charges ever made in America." His action did not go unnoticed. When the American army moved across the Rio Grande into Mexico, Arnold was a brevet major. He fought under General Worth at both Monterrey and at Buena Vista. From northern Mexico, he was transferred with General Worth's regiment, to General Winfield Scott's command, where he remained until the peace at Guadalupe Hidalgo in February, 1848.

There was no need of debating what to do with an Indian fighter with a meritorious record for frontier defense. Major Arnold was ordered to return to the Rio Grande. It was set down in the military annals, "Brevet Major Ripley A. Arnold, captain of Company F, Second Dragoons on march from the Rio Grande to Fort Graham 1848–49." There at this fort on the Brazos, the assignment came which was to make him a historic personage. He was to build a military post on the upper Trinity in the uninhabited region of the Grand Prairie and the Eastern Cross Timbers. When the year 1849 came to a close, the United States flag floated over the new post of Fort Worth.

His talent shifted from building a fort to drilling men. A precedent of well-drilled soldiers, thoroughly versed in the manual, was established. He was too positive a character to permit a disorderly soldiery. His discipline was stern, sometimes with a humorous twist. One soldier's appetite for pork caused him to steal a pig from one of the few settlers who had come to nestle under the protection of the fort. Half of the pig was found in the culprit's quarters. Wherefore, in the burning sun of July, he stood for hours with arms uplifted, hands tied together and the pork swung around his neck. He broiled in the July heat and the fat of the pork melted to trickle down his body. The soldiery at Camp Worth was an orderly lot.

The major had learned wise ways with Indians. He understood that they were human beings, and extended kindness. Sometimes, though, kindness was not the solution to a situation: force was needed; and this the major also knew how to display without a bloody conflict. The most amicable relations were preserved with the Indians, who were frequent visitors to the garrison. During the four-year occupancy of the fort by United States troops, there were few incidents to interrupt the perfect accord. After the Village Creek Fight and the Treaty of 1843, most warlike tribes had retreated into present Parker and Palo Pinto counties and far into West Texas. Yet there were remnants of a few tribes in the vicinity: the Kiowa, Waco, Ionie, Delaware, Tonkawa, Towash, and Caddo. In addition there were always predatory bands of Comanches wandering about to make trouble.

Hostilities of course occurred. There was the day that a party of Tonkawa Indians took refuge in the fort. They were never fighters. Centuries ago the Spaniards said the Tonkawas would rather surrender than fight. This day a Towash chief and his tribe had determined to put an end to the Tonkawas who had a few good horses and marketable pelts. The Towash pursued the Tonkawas to the fort and demanded that the major release the Tonkawas to them. Major Arnold ingeniously answered. He had a wooden door set up as a target about a hundred yards distant. He had the fort's only cannon, a six-pound howitzer fired at it. The door was splintered into pieces. Dismayed and frightened, the belligerent attitude vanished. Later, with fear gone, hunger transformed them from warriors into beggars. To their begging Major Arnold replied that he "would just as soon fight them as feed them." Nevertheless, he had three beeves driven out to the chattering group of Tonkawas. Straightway the hungry Indians rode away, happy with their prize of beef.

Another day in 1849, the Comanches from their village in present Palo Pinto made a visit to obliterate the post. Leader of the plan was giant Chief Jim Ned. The white man's fort, according to his thinking, was too close to his hunting ground; and Arnold's scouts had taken one of his ill-gotten horses. Following plans of a war council, two bands of one hundred Comanches each, traveling different paths, were to converge upon the fort. Chief Feathertail with his band took the southeast trail; Chief Ned took the northeast. The second night out from their village, Chief Ned camped to await Chief Feathertail in the valley at the foot of the bluff where a hundred years later, would be the All Church Home for Children and the E. B. Harrold Park.

On top of the bluff, a camping fur trader with good ears, heard many voices arising from the lowlands. Going to the edge of the bluff he looked down upon a band of warriors. It did not take much time for him to cover the distance between his camp and the fort. Within an hour, wagons, infantry and cavalry were ready. Scouts, led by the fur trader, were soon peering over the bluff. As there was a full moon, what they saw made it easy to plan the attack. The Indians were then asleep. The troops were to be divided and attack from three directions. The reliable six-pound howitzer was rolled into place on the bluff. The cavalry galloped down upon the unsuspecting victims. The three units fired into the sleeping camp. Bright moonlight helped the infantrymen to make every shot count. Not a man of the garrison was seriously hurt. Chief Ned fled; met Chief Feathertail's band, and together they retreated to the hills of Palo Pinto. Today, a small concrete shaft located on the property of the All Church Home marks this site of the last large-scale Indian battle in the environs of Fort Worth.

To be fair to the major and the record, the story must be completed. Next morning, the troops were in pursuit of the Indians. Two days later in a Palo Pinto canyon, they engaged these Comanches in a battle of several hours. Chief Ned was killed, and the leaderless Indians fled. Thanks to the major, there were no more hostilities on a large scale in Tarrant County, only petty annoyances.

Life in an army post has its amenities. Major Arnold decided that his men needed to renew their spiritual strength, so he dispatched a dragoon to Lonesome Dove community twenty-odd miles away, with a request that the Reverend John Allen Freeman visit the fort. In April 1850, Freeman's voice intoned the Scriptures to the military personnel. He returned several times to preach between his missions of organizing Baptist churches in Tarrant County, ministering to the many cabins rising on the prairies.

It was not all work at the post; there was some play. In leisure hours, men saw another Major Arnold of geniality, gallantry, and warmth of affection. His companion during such times was a Frenchman, Doctor Adolphus Gouhenant, whose name the frontiersmen simplified and spelled Gounah. The doctor, a man of erudition, "brave, gallant, and a high Mason," was so distinctive a figure in Fort Worth that he was a topic of much conversation. His many accomplishments—clever discourse, music, learning, philosophy, geology, and painting—banished the deadening dreariness of the backwoods. His superior swordsmanship made the off-duty hours fleeting for officers of the garrison. He engaged them in fencing, teaching them many of his dexterous tricks with the sword.

Doctor Gounah's presence at the fort was alleged to have been the result of a blasted dream. He had come from France with the 150 Frenchmen as an advance guard to found a French colony to be known as New Icaria. Under a Peters Colony grant, 500 Frenchmen were to settle in present Denton County. Malaria, crop failures, and difficulties with the agent of the Peters Land Company caused them to abandon their enterprise in 1849. Some moved to new areas, about half of them returned to France, while three men, including Gounah, remained. Shortly afterwards, the doctor went to the fort. Four years later in 1852, he received title to his land grant under the Peters Colony. In the meantime, he had also acquired title to other lands in the Trinity Valley from which timber was cut for the building of the fort. The bill for this timber, amounting to about $4,000 was never paid, though the claim was approved by Major Arnold.

It is not to be denied that Fort Worth was a wilderness outpost. But the major, the Frenchman, and the soldiery made it a vibrant center with the niceties enjoyed by affluent city dwellers. There were dinners when gentlemen of means came to see the country; or when officers of the United States Army came on tour of inspection. And during Fort Worth's existence as an army post, military men of distinction were visitors: "Lieutenant Colonels Wm. J. Hardee, George H. Thomas, Robert E. Lee, Earl Van Dorn, John B. Hood and Fitzhugh Lee." There were times when the entire garrison gave festive parties, inviting the settlers.

By 1850, according to Margaret Ann Loving, there were about a half-dozen double log cabins near the fort, pioneers who had arrived in December of 1849. These families were headed by Archibald Robinson, Archibald Franklin Leonard, Press Farmer, W. R. and Samuel Loving, and Henry Daggett. Within riding distance were a few other families; and in the words of a young non-commissioned officer, Abe Harris, some of these families had pretty daughters who made him sigh, referring especially to the girls in the Wright Conner and Elijah Farmer cabins, west of the fort.

For the parties, tables in the commissary quarters were heaped with the best that the military larder could provide. The guests ate and danced their way through the evening. If it were summer, Mrs. Arnold was in residence and acted as hostess. It was said that she was a beauty with a queenly carriage, a well-educated mind, and possessed a voice unusually winning, impressing those whom she met. Since her husband was frequently called to Washington, Mrs. Arnold made homes both in the capital and in frontier posts. In winter, Mrs. Arnold, with a Negro maid, usually remained in Washington for the schooling of the five children: Sophie, Willis, Catherine, Nannie, and Flora. In summer, they joined the major at his military post.

The Arnold children discovered that their sojourn at Fort Worth was equally as educational as at the national capital. There were nature lessons, even to the domestication of the wild animals, one of which was the pet antelope of Kate. When he strayed away, he was rounded up by the jovial Sergeant Major Harris. Doctor Gounah taught them music, language, and how a gentlewoman sat a horse and rode with grace. There were playmates. And like all pioneer children on the frontier, they played within sight of their parents and under certain restrictions, one of them being "they were never to cross the parade ground of the fort." These playmates were Margaret Ann Loving and the three daughters of the "post surgeon" Standifer—Castera, Eliza, and Julia Caroline.

When the dragoons came to build Fort Worth, Doctor Standifer had left his wife and three daughters in the home of Colonel Johnson at Johnson's Station until he completed a home close-by the colonel's in which he established his family with four trusted slaves. On most Fridays, he journeyed to Johnson's Station to spend weekends with them. Mrs. Standifer died at Johnson's Station in January 1851; after which time, the doctor resigned his post at the fort.

A fort, like a house which knows great joys, does not escape its share of sorrow. In the first summer of 1850, Sophie and Willis Arnold were stricken in death. About a mile northeast, the children were laid to rest in land donated by the major's friend, Doctor Gounah. The two small graves were walled up with rock and capped with a sandstone slab bearing the date 1850. Time has made slight inroad against this tribute of the major's love. Today, one may find this tomb in the extreme southeastern portion of Pioneer Rest Cemetery, skirting the main driveway. Nearby are two graves of unknown soldiers who had also died in the year 1850.

Change placed a heavy hand on Fort Worth in the spring and summer of 1851. There were unhappy hearts among settlers and soldiers alike, because in April, Company F, Eighth Infantry, left the fort which they had helped to build, for a new assignment at Fort Gates. Sergeant Abe Harris of the infantry, mustered out and became a settler. On June 17, Major Arnold, with his Company F of the Second Dragoons, road away to Fort Graham. With them went memories of two years well spiced with labor, achievement, and fun. Louis Wetmore, the loyal trooper, and Frank Knaar, the faithful saddler, remained behind. Their terms of service had expired. They had seen the land, filed claim to some of it, and joined the home-builders.

Captain J. V. Bomford of New York with companies F and H of the Eighth Infantry, assumed command of the post on June 17, 1851. He was a good army man. Later he rose to the rank of brigadier general, and served in the Civil War in the United States Army. Captain Bomford and the two companies remained only seven months.

On January 8, 1852, Major Arnold returned with his dragoons, constituting the sole garrison. They, too, remained but seven months, leaving for the last time August 13, 1852, to again serve at Fort Graham. Soon afterwards, the young major had respite from frontier duty. Called to Washington, he remained there "1852–53 on detached duty." The

year of his tragic fate came in 1853. He returned to his command at Fort
Graham, where on September 6, he was shot to death by Doctor Joseph
M. Steiner, the post surgeon, whom he had ordered arrested for "drunk-
enness and falsifying." In the burial plot at Fort Graham, Arnold was
buried. Thus the builder of the military post from which the great city
of Fort Worth would grow, died by violence at the age of thirty-six years.

When Major Arnold and his dragoons left Fort Worth the year before,
August 13, 1852, the last military detachment for the fort arrived:
Brevet Major Hamilton W. Merrill of New York, captain of Company B,
Second Dragoons. He and his sixty men garrisoned Fort Worth one year
and a few weeks, until it was abandoned as a military post, September
17, 1853.

The day after Major Arnold had been killed at Fort Graham, Brevet
Lieutenant Colonel William Grigsby Freeman, assistant adjutant general, paid an inspection visit to Fort Worth while Major Merrill was
still there. Dated September 7, 1853, the report follows:

The company had only fatigue clothing of the old pattern, but some of the
men wore sky blue, instead of the dark blue jackets. They were armed . . .
with musketoons, sabres, and Colt's revolver pistols. They were reviewed as
foot, but inspected and required to exercise both as horse and foot. The clothing, though not new, was in good order and generally well fitted; the arms
and accoutrements clean and, except the musketoons, serviceable. . . . The
horses (60) are all serviceable, and in finer condition than those of any
mounted troops in Texas. Their equipments were also neat and well
preserved.
In the manual, marching and sword exercises, dismounted the company
showed a fair degree of proficiency. In the saddle they acquitted themselves
very handsomely, marching with accuracy by twos, fours and company front
at a walk, trot, and gallop; skirmishing as dragoons on foot and as mounted
foragers; and leaping the bar and ditch with great spirit and a perfect mas-
tery of their horses. It was evident that much attention had been given to
this part of their instruction.
I was gratified to find it was the solitary exception throughout my tour . . .
the guardhouse . . . without a prisoner. But Major Merrill informs me that
most of his men belong to the temperance society and that he has rarely occasion to confine any one of them . . . I found the discipline and police of
the post excellent. A fine garden of eight acres is cultivated by the men. . . .
No Indians have visited the post since last autumn, except a small party
of Caddoes and Ionies.

The report was not all praise: there was also place for progress. He
did not approve of the mail service. Waco was the post office for Forts
Worth and Graham; therefore, each week a wagon express travelled
fifty-six miles to Fort Graham for the mail. "The nearest towns or

villages are Dallas with 350 inhabitants, thirty-eight miles east; and
Birdville and Alton with a population of fifty each, distant nine and
thirty-five miles respectively." And his next remark did not commend
the fort for good business. The post was located "on a disputed tract of
land," for which "nothing had been paid either for rent or the timber cut
for fuel." This was the last military report on Fort Worth. Nine days
later the dragoons moved out.

In dusty, dry September, the dragoons headed north across the sun-
browned prairies, while wagons heavy with artillery and all the equipment of Fort Worth trailed behind. They were moving to Fort Belknap.
It was September 17, 1853. The history of Fort Worth as a military post
had ended for a time. Colonel Middleton Tate Johnson and Archibald
Robinson were again proprietors of the land.

There are always reasons for change. Lieutenant Colonel Freeman's
report of 1853 was more laudatory than Lieutenant Colonel Whiting's
of 1851 in which he gave an unfavorable picture of Fort Worth from the
standpoint of health. Some said that this 1851 report contributed to the
abandonment of this fort. But that is not the whole truth. Fort Worth
was abandoned because the United States government pushed its line of
frontier defense farther north and west. The red man had by then found
his best hunting ground in West Texas and the Panhandle. So the
federal forts were moved west with the Indians. Then, too, streams of
settlers moving to the Pacific coast made it necessary for our government
to provide roads and furnish protection. The army engineers went exploring in 1849 and 1851, visiting West and Northwest Texas. One of
these engineers was Lieutenant Colonel Whiting.

As a result of Whiting's survey of 1849–1851, the imaginary line, that
in 1843 had been defined at Bird's Fort, was then moved westward; and
Forts Marvin Scott, Croghan, Gates, and Worth were ordered abandoned. Another army engineer, Captain R. B. Marcy in 1849, made a
pathfinding expedition from Arkansas through Oklahoma and the Texas
Panhandle to Santa Fé. Upon his return, he logged the Marcy Trail
from El Paso to Preston on Red River. A new chain of forts from Northeast Texas across Northwest Texas to El Paso was recommended. It was
done and not too soon. There were three specific reasons new forts were
needed during the middle fifties: wagon caravans were ranging across
Indian lands of Northwest Texas, the Butterfield Stage Coach Line was
operating across Texas between St. Louis and California from 1858 to
1861, and the San Antonio-San Diego Stage Line was in service between
1857 and 1862.

Fort Worth had served its purpose from 1849 to 1853. The flag, sound

of bugle, clatter of cavalry, click of guns, and boom of cannon were
gone; but the abandoned army post did not become a ghost fort on the
prairies. Home-builders were gathering about it, while a few families
found shelter within its walls. They were the inheritors of General
Worth's and Major Arnold's good design for living. With labor, care,
and faith Fort Worth would make a victorious transition from a military
post to a "Fort Town."

BOOK III

Fort Town
on the Prairies

THE WORLD was far-reaching in the 1850s; oceans and wilderness separated Americans from fantastic empires in Asia and from the ruling classes in Europe who were disdainful of the strange political experiment in America which admitted frontier rustics to public offices, even to the presidency—and managed government according to the popular will. However, the frontiersman, with his rifles, axes and plows knew what he was about; he wanted land and a cabin on the Texas prairies. To own land was the way to economic and political freedom.

Ignoring events which upset men's lives in Europe and Asia, and the slavery controversy which was dividing men in the older sections of the United States into antagonists (spiteful foes), he hitched his oxteam, also a carriage or buggy if he had one, packed the wagon or wagons if he had slaves, lifted his children into their places, and with his wife rode into the wilderness until he found the good land on the Grand Prairie at the forks of the Trinity. Still he read with interest the headline news in well-known national newspapers, weeks or months old, which he either subscribed to or perused, in the general mercantile store at a crossroads.

News in the decade of the 1850s, the prairie frontiersman read sometimes with perplexity, other times with understanding. In 1850, Nathaniel Hawthorne published a great American novel, *The Scarlet Letter*. In the same year Congress passed the Compromise of 1850 which admitted California to the Union as a free state and settled the western boundary of Texas, by paying Texas $10 million for one-third of her territory—the New Mexico Territory. In 1852, Harriet Beecher Stowe published *Uncle Tom's Cabin*, and the South broke out in blazing oratory against the author, "a muddle-headed abolitionist." In 1853, Congress, considering the building of a railroad to the Pacific and seeking an easy route through the mountains by way of Texas and the Southwest, approved of Mr. Gadsden's $10 million purchase of land from Mexico. In 1854, Commodore Matthew Perry, with a few United States Navy ships, forced Japan to open certain ports to merchants from America and Europe, and to give aid to shipwrecked sailors. That same year the Kansas-Nebraska Act provided for the enforcement of the squatter sovereignty doctrine. The Crimean War opened in Europe when Britain and France joined Turkey in a war against Russia. The news of 1855 was "Bleeding Kansas" due to the civil strife caused by the act the year before. In 1856, attention was riveted on the presidential campaign. The new Republican party entered their first presidential candidate, John C. Fremont, on the slogan "Free labor, free speech, free man, free Kansas, and Fremont." The Know-Nothing party and the Whig party united to elect former President Fillmore. The Democrats won, electing James Buchanan as president. A by-line in the news was the closing of the Crimean War. In 1857, the Supreme Court of the United States handed down a victorious decision for the South in the Dred Scott case deepening the rift between North and South. In 1858, Abe Lincoln campaigning in Illinois for election to the United States Senate debated with Stephen Douglas. Lincoln's direct phrases against the spread of slavery vibrated alarm even in the Texas prairies. In 1859, Oregon was admitted to the Union; John Brown raided Harper's Ferry in an attempt to free the slaves; and the South again flamed into frenzied denunciation of abolitionists.

These events did not make the prairie frontiersman at the forks of the Trinity enviously unhappy because he was not in the thick of affairs. He read the news and returned to ploughing, concentrating all the more on building his world beyond the strong vexatious currents of events that were only ripples amounting to nothing more serious than hearsay. But the frontiersman would discover his error in 1859 when the "ripples" began to churn his prairie world into commotion.

CHAPTER 16

Cabins
on the Fort's Horizon

Sons of pioneers rarely sought security on the settled frontiers. It was the belief and the faith of Americans in those days that their fate was their responsibility; that the western wilderness gave them opportunity; and what they did with that opportunity was up to them. Such was the pioneering spirit which brought one wagon, several wagons, a caravan of wagons, young lonely riders, and even a few on foot from Virginia, Alabama, Georgia, Kentucky, Tennessee, Missouri, and East Texas to the country around the military post of Fort Worth. This spirit of individual responsibility was one of the many forces accumulating to settle the region which was to become Tarrant County and the future Fort Town.

The Mexican War was another force. Men had gone to Texas, then crossed into Mexico. There were many Texans in every camp; and many of them spoke with pride of the advantages frontier Texas offered. Soldiers from other Southern states and Texans from the settled areas of East Texas heard of the opportunity in North Texas. One group of soldiers listened well and placed their "horizon of hope" on that area. These were inhabitants of Shelby County and other parts of East Texas. Those from Shelby were formerly fighters in the Regulator-Moderator War. When the call to arms came, their feud was forgotten. They joined the same company becoming brothers in arms; and their combined fighting ability helped to turn the battles of the Mexican War into victories. War over, they directed their energies to molding the region at the forks of the Trinity.

Of course their way had been prepared for them as we have seen by the land laws of the Republic of Texas, as well as those of the state, the foresight of President Houston's Treaty of 1843, and the military expeditions of General Tarrant and others into North Texas. So much for the why and wherefore of the accumulating forces; but what about the picture that these forces etched on the geography of the Grand Prairie in the Eastern Cross Timbers?

In the score of cabins on the horizon north, south, east, and west of the fort were spirited pioneer dwellers. One at a time, sometimes two at a time, the outline of new log houses with their narrow rock chimneys, which sharply punctured the stark spaces, appeared on the horizon around the fort. With the appearance of each new chimney sending up its curl of smoke to announce the heartbeat of a new home, horsemen rode to welcome the newcomers; and the new neighbors became the conversation of the month. In the first decade of Fort Town's history, either the arrival of a new family or the appearance of a new home was an event to all the residents within a twenty-mile radius. Joy prevailed according to one cabin dweller, "Then life out here in northern Texas was one long dream of sensuous existence. No locks, no bolts and bars, free game, free grass and free men."

North Horizon

Three miles north of the fort in 1849 were two log cabin homes, those of John B. York from Missouri and Seburn Gilmore from Tennessee. York and Gilmore were both men of courage. They came alone with their families and unhitched their oxteams in 1848, a year before the fort was founded. York's first hardship was tragic. Six months after his arrival, he buried his six-year-old son near their new home in the present area of Niles City. Sorrow did not move York and Gilmore to pull up stake and join the caravans of California gold-seekers. They liked wilderness, because to their way of thinking, land was gold. Gilmore, the son-in-law of York, built his home near York's cabin. When Tarrant County was organized, Gilmore became the first county judge of Tarrant, and York, the second county sheriff.

In July 1849, Will York was born, the first boy in the environs of Fort Worth; and in August, Martha Gilmore came into the world with the distinction of being the first girl. At an early age, Martha was an industrious child, and throughout her life, an outspoken feminist. Whenever occasion presented opportunity for boasting, she would remark, "And the men? What would they have done without us girls? We carded the wool, wove the cloth, and made their garments, even though there was not a variety of clothing."

On the same north horizon of the fort, a third log cabin in 1850 cut its silhouette against the background of wilderness. It was the home of "Milt" Robinson, who had driven with eagerness into the upper Trinity Valley with his wife Ann Madison Robinson and their little daughter, Medora. They settled on a section of land, the future site of the Armour and Swift packing plants. "The Robinsons were among the first six families to come here about the time the old fort was established." "Milt" Robinson, as he was affectionately called, became a large landowner donating land for the first school in Fort Worth. When Medora became of school age, she rode horseback each day from her home to school in Fort Town. Later in the fifties, Milt moved his family to Fort Town, building a home "in the western part on what was called Robinson's Branch," an area upon which the Rotary Park was located in more recent times on the southeast corner of Summit and West Seventh streets.

Two more houses were built north of the fort in 1852. From Kentucky came two families in wagons and carriages. William Bonaparte Tucker and his brother-in-law, Abraham Anderson, settled four miles north of the fort in present Jarvis addition. Tucker, who became known as "Bony" turned to politics and moved into Fort Town in 1856. Abraham prospered as a stock farmer, his lands extending from Jarvis addition to the Trinity. Today, just east of Samuels Avenue bridge is a small stream called Anderson Branch, which flows through Trail Drivers Park.

Cattle sold in Shreveport brought Abe Anderson ample cash, which in the 1860s he invested in a large two-story house near his log cabin. A most pretentious house of its day, his new home remained a social center for thirty years. The cowboys liked the Anderson's parlor because it was wide and thirty feet long, making it unnecessary to cramp their style when they swung their partners. The Anderson home was called the dance hall because it lent itself to dancing, which differed in kind and degree from the stately minuet, the quadrille, and the Virginia reel. Mrs. Anderson was a thoughtful interior decorator, for she had placed a long table in the parlor where the men could quickly place their spurs and guns, and upon their departure, could easily find them without an extensive search.

On the horizon north of the fort two other homes which made history for Tarrant County and Fort Worth, raised their walls and roofs. Three brothers—Charles Biggers Daggett, Henry Clay Daggett, and Captain Ephraim Merrill Daggett, veterans of the Mexican War, ventured from Shelby County to the newly established military post of Fort Worth in 1849. Charles staked out a land claim and, in 1854 moved his family to a home on a plot of ground, which is now part of Mount Olivet Cemetery.

Henry, a trader, formed a partnership with Archibald Franklin Leonard, who as mentioned, had arrived in 1845 from Missouri by oxteam settling in what is now Grapevine. In the summer of 1849, they opened the Daggett-Leonard store over a mile from the fort, as Federal law forbade merchants to operate stores within a mile of a military post. In the log cabin mercantile store shaded by giant live oaks and a spring nearby, located today at the foot of Samuels Avenue, these astute merchants engaged in both barter and sale, knowing that pleased customers produced profits. Volume of business was large. Indians and hunters traded dressed buckskins and pelts for merchandise, while the soldiers and settlers, although bartering also, bought goods with money. The small amount of hard money in the community exchanged hands there.

Daggett and Leonard worked to get ahead and did; their revenue being increased by their contract to supply the fort with beef until its evacuation in September 1853. Others engaged in this business of supplying beef for United States troops at Fort Worth, were Press Farmer and Ed Terrell.

In 1851, Henry Daggett married Sarah Ellen Marsh in Dallas and brought his bride to live with the Leonards whose home was near the store. Home, church, and school formed the pattern of the American settlement line as it advanced from the Atlantic to the Pacific, and it was rigidly followed by these newcomers north of the fort.

Martha Ellen Gilmore related that a school "in the early fifties was placed on a hill now known as Diamond Hill." It was built of logs and had a dirt floor. Seats were long logs split in half. Windows were just openings in the walls.

One of our first teachers was an old, old man. He smoked a corn cob pipe constantly, was very absent-minded, and talked to himself all the time. We girls followed him around to see if we could find out what he said. Frequently when smoking, the old man would thoughtlessly stick his lighted pipe into his coat pocket and often set fire to his clothing.

Boys laughed; girls giggled, and lessons were stopped until the fire was extinguished.

West Horizon

On the horizon west of the fort, the first two homes appeared in 1849, those of Wright Conner and Lemuel Edwards. Formerly from Tennessee, Wright Conner settled in Dallas County in 1847. He came to Tarrant County two years later, building his log cabin two and a half miles from the fort on the later site of Camp Bowie in World War I. He was thus the first resident of present Arlington Heights, and headrighted on 640 acres of land under the Peters Land Company. He acquired additional acreage until his land extended from the Clear Fork west to the area of his homestead. Another boundary line was the so-called Bailey property, which included a part of the present Greenwood Cemetery. Conner's family consisted of his wife, one daughter Margaret, and four sons.

To keep the wild animals and Indians from the door of his home, Conner fenced it about with poles and built a stile over the poles for an entrance to his yard. Sons of Conner, in order to catch the many deer jumping over their fence, sharpened thousands of stobs and set them deep in the ground five or six feet apart inside the fence. The Conners never lacked deer meat. In regard to the Indians, the fence did not work. Tonkawas were afraid to cross stiles, but they were high jumpers; and over the pole fence they vaulted to beg, to barter, to steal, or to stare at the Conners.

Farther west on the Clear Fork Lemuel Edwards settled in 1849. He built boats to cross the swollen streams and accumulated one thousand acres of land. On January 29, 1851, near present Benbrook, his son Cass Edwards was born. As soon as Cass could sit on a horse, he learned to manage cattle. Riding over the prairies which today extend southward and west from Highway 80, where is now located Arlington Heights High School and Ridglea Addition, Cass guarded his ranging herd and found companionship with the Tonkawa Indian boys who wandered on the hills. With boyish affection, Cass spoke of them as his chums. "I spoke the Indian language, that is—a language they understood." To the Lemuel Edwards family goes the distinction of having established the first cattle ranch west of Fort Worth. Edwards' lone chimney conveyed the message that homes could be made on the far horizon west of the fort. Others followed, and there were enough men to organize under the inspired word of the Reverend John Rowland in 1857, the Old Rawhide Methodist Church known today as the Benbrook Methodist.

In 1851, Frank M. Burke with his widowed mother, formerly from Missouri, settled on a large tract of land on the Clear Fork farther west.

The Burkes were spoken of as an "outside family" since there were no settlers west of them for two years.

The same year a fourth log cabin appeared on the west horizon. Abe Harris, the faithful and skilled craftsman, whose adroitness had figured largely in constructing the fort, mustered out in December. From Wright Conner he acquired land on which later a part of Camp Bowie was built. When his log house was finished near the Conners' home, he married their daughter Margaret, one of the pretty girls who had attended the parties at the fort. So in the early months of 1852 there were two log houses two and a half miles west of the fort in present Arlington Heights.

Other first residents who joined Wright Conner and Abe Harris were Isaac and Pete Schoonover, who located farms across from Conner's; and Isaac Thomas, whose farm comprised the present street called Thomas Place. By the close of 1856, there were added the homes of Michael and John Baugh and others. Henry Kinder came from Illinois in 1856, settled on land where River Crest Country Club is located, and acquired a reputation of being Tarrant County's best marksman. He amused men on Fort Town's square when they had shooting matches. It was alleged that he could "hit the bull's eye every time with his old-fashioned long-barrel rifle." Even though old-fashioned, Kinder's rifle was "a beauty with a stock of highly polished maple adorned with silver mountings."

Old-timers told this story to illustrate his skill. A buzzard was sailing over the old army post. A tenderfoot wagered Uncle Henry that he could not kill the bird. Never refusing a challenge, Uncle Henry lifted his gun, took aim and replied, "It is contrary to the law of Fort Town to kill a scavenger bird, but I will clip a feather from the right wing when it sails around again." The buzzard circled. A feather floated down from the right wing. "Now, when the buzzard flies around a second time, I'll clip a feather from the left wing so as to even matters up." The buzzard sailed around; a feather floated down from the left wing. A native of Fort Town did not make wagers with Henry Kinder.

On the horizon west and northwest of the fort, an area known to early Fort Worthians as White Settlement also began to take form in 1849. World War II transformed the northwest skyline of Fort Worth and brought new names. The area along White Settlement Road northwest from the courthouse to east of Crystal Springs was incorporated in the city, losing its identity as the White Settlement. The area beyond Crystal Springs where Elijah Farmer settled became West Worth; and on the western edge arose a new city of White Settlement.

Elijah Ward Farmer, his brother Joseph B. Farmer, and Charles

Turner built the first log houses in this area. Turner, like most young men in 1846, had heeded the call to arms and left his home in Shelby County to march across the Rio Grande to the battles which led him to Mexico City. With the war's end, he joined Colonel Middleton Tate Johnson's Ranger force on the northern frontier. He was one of the five Rangers who accompanied Major Arnold to the forks of the Trinity to choose a site for a fort. Shortly after the military post was established, he brought his family from Shelby County, settling on a farm of 640 acres, a part of which is now Greenwood Cemetery. Wheat, cotton, and stock farming brought him wealth. His farm became a plantation, and at the opening of the Civil War, 150 slaves worked his fields.

Turner's log house home was replaced in the mid-fifties by a residence built of finished lumber. The large oak tree that still stands in the center of the entrance to Greenwood was near the Turner home, another social center of the community. Around a large fireplace, men gathered to discuss the price of cattle on the Shreveport and New Orleans markets, to talk Texas politics, and to argue about the Lincoln-Douglas debates; while the ladies discussed the merchandise displayed in Fort Town's stores. The young people danced until past midnight until the evening's supply of great logs burned from a bright flame to a smoldering flicker. These logs were unusually large. There was a reason for this. Turner would promise to give the slave bringing in the largest log a holiday lasting as long as the log would burn. Of course the slaves would vie with each other to see who could bring into the house the largest, longest log. Frequently it would take several slaves to bring in one. Turner was a good master; and at Christmas there was celebration in the Negro quarters with a gift for each slave.

On Fort Town's square, Turner in the mid 1850s became a merchant, the business partner of Henry Clay Daggett, replacing Leonard. Their trade and credit on the outside markets were so extensive that they were merchant princes on the Southwestern frontier. His five daughters and one son, W. M. Turner, made life gay for the second generation of Fort Town's first hundred families.

Land, fertile for wheat and corn, with a bountiful supply of timber for houses and fuel, and a plentiful supply of fresh water were the requisites for a man's kingdom in North Texas in the 1850s. In search of such a kingdom, three Farmer brothers, Joseph, Elijah, and David, originally from Tennessee, left their homes in Fannin County, Texas, where they had settled in 1846. They came to Tarrant County in 1849, and settled on land which today includes the approaches to Carswell Air Force Base.

Elijah Farmer preempted 320 acres under the Texas state land law, six miles west of Fort Town on the present White Settlement Road. To-day the residence of the commanding general of this base is on the for-mer site of Elijah's home, a part of which remained on the land when owned by Raymond Buck in the nineteen-forties. Near Elijah's home was a stream with bubbling springs flowing for a century. The road lead-ing to the gates of Carswell Air Force Base crosses the creek named Farmer's Branch.

One mile north of Elijah's farm, his brother Joseph preempted 320 acres extending north to present Knight's Lake and east to the West Fork. The Farmer brothers' joy at finding such an excellent estate was saddened shortly after their houses were built. David's wife died and was buried in a field on the Farmers' land. Life was not good for David, and his brothers soon laid him to rest beside his wife. These two graves were the beginning of the first cemetery in the White Settlement, which today is in a bleak field east of Grant Lane and south of the North-South run-way of the airfield. There may be found the graves of the first pilgrims who settled in the valley of the West Fork, west of Fort Town. Graves of faithful slaves are also to be found. One is that of John Hickman, who lived to be more than a hundred years old.

The Farmer brothers worked hard, soon acquiring a reputation as able grain farmers. They milled their harvests of corn and wheat at Doctor Wood's mill which was established in the mid-fifties. Indians who had remained in Tarrant County knew where to go to obtain cornmeal. When they went to Elijah's home begging for meal, Mrs. Farmer asked, "Where will you put it?" Whereupon the Indians stripped off both buck-skin leggins, holding them up to be filled; and went away hugging their ingenious sacks closely to their bodies. In a few weeks, they returned for another supply.

Pilgrims of the White Settlement and settlers at the fort were invited to a wedding supper on July 13, 1851, the first wedding west of the fort. Elijah Farmer's daughter Millie was married to James Ventioner, an ambitious young man who owned a large tract of land in the valley of the West Fork. Ventioner's log house was three miles west of the fort on horseshoe bend of the West Fork just west of the present Ohio Garden Road in Brookside Addition. Ventioner's farm extended from the present campus of Northside High School on the Jacksboro Highway west, be-yond the Ohio Garden Road and spread northward across the site of River Oaks to Roberts Cut-off.

Through wise practices, Ventioner seemed to escape many of the dis-asters which overtook some of the farmers. His stock was not often cap-tured by the Indians because he kept his cattle hidden in a live oak grove. He always had cattle to sell on the Shreveport market. He was a good grain farmer as well, arousing a bit of envy. Ventioner was a Frenchman and had all of the abilities of the thrifty farmer of that country. It was said that his crops were never affected by drouths. During the trying years when the question was asked, "Where can I get a little corn for bread?" the answer was, "At James Ventioner's."

In 1851, the fifth rock chimney could be seen above the trees in the White Settlement area. It was Jud Rowland's log home. In search of good corn land and 320 acres of free land, Rowland had driven his ox-drawn wagon from Warren County, Tennessee. He wanted to give his wife, four children, and his wife's widowed sister and her two children a more favorable life. Since his youth he had heard that Texas was the "Land of Promise." He first unhitched his two covered wagons in the present area of Diamond Hill and made camp. Soon he preempted 320 acres in the White Settlement, and for one yoke of oxen obtained two hundred more acres of good farmland.

In 1852, Rowland took his son Jeff with him to see the sights at the voting poll at the Daggett-Leonard store. This was the second election to be held in Tarrant County. Jeff Rowland later declared that near the polling place, "Pa introduced me to important men, among them were Siburn Gilmore, Lemuel Edwards, John York, Ed Terrell, Milt Robinson, Mike Dean and Silas Dean."

Jud Rowland had industrious boys. When they wanted buckskin trousers they gathered a wagonload of pecans from Silver Creek bottom, now covered by Lake Worth. In November 1854, they could not sell the pecans for money, but on the barter market they realized a good bargain. The wagonload of pecans was traded for Indian-dressed buckskin at the Daggett-Turner store, which the tailor in Fort Town made into trousers. Then the Rowland boys were in style.

1854 was a big year for the White Settlement area as well as the entire community surrounding the fort. A caravan from Kentucky arrived, composed of ten wagons drawn by four-horse teams, transporting household supplies; while two-seated hacks drawn by two horses carried the families. At night the hacks were easily converted into beds. This well-equipped train set out from Todd County, Kentucky, in November of 1854. In a mood of eagerness, the families left for Texas and enjoyed each turn of the wheels. The families were those of J. K. Allen, Stephen Terry, John Wims, Nat Coleman, Bob Slaughter, Dick King, a part of Alfred Johnson's family, and two young men, Theodore Petty and Tom Hagood.

It was a good season to travel. Frosty days of November and December renewed their vigor and increased their speed, so that the trip was made in less than a month. They crossed the Red River entering Texas at Clarksville; traveled over the old Military Road of the Republic to Dallas; ferried across the Trinity; and spent the night in that village. Boosters of Dallas looked upon the caravan as desirable immigrants and coveted them for settlers. One promoter approached Stephen Terry whose slaves and fine equipage caused him to conclude that Terry was a cautious man who would be unwilling to risk his wealth in too uncertain adventures; and could be easily convinced that this town offered the most certain future. His words to Terry were disparaging of Fort Town. "Indians will scalp you if you go to Fort Worth." Here his immigrant-snatching propaganda abruptly ended, for the usually gentle Mrs. Frances Caroline Terry, angered by the intimidating threat, spiritedly answered,

I'd just as soon be scalped by Indians as stay here and be eaten up by mosquitoes. Besides, if wild Indians were thirty miles away you wouldn't be here.

Terry ordered his slaves to hitch the oxen to the wagon, also the horse to the buggy. Leaving Dallas, the Kentucky caravan rolled down the hills across the fertile Grand Prairie to Johnson's Station, arriving there December 11. Colonel Johnson celebrated their arrival with an evening of feasting and dancing. He had many questions to ask from these people. With them he discussed the captivating news of the year 1854—ships of the United States Navy commanded by Commodore Matthew Perry were steaming into Yokohama and opening Japan to the western world. The Kansas-Nebraska Act produced an argument. One man asserted that Stephen Douglas had no right to rekindle the slavery controversy by forcing through Congress the act providing for the enforcement of the squatter sovereignty doctrine. Now there would be strife between slave owners and abolitionists in the western territories. The argument ended with the cheerful remark that thanks should be offered to Divine Providence for having guided them to choose Texas for their homes.

Next morning Colonel and Mrs. Johnson presided at a cheerful breakfast, and the caravan in happy spirits set out on the last leg of their journey. A horseman galloped ahead toward Fort Town to notify Alfred Johnson that the friends he had been urging to come to Texas would arrive that afternoon, December 12. Alfred and his wife had come from Tennessee in 1853 and built their log house, a very substantial one, on Cold Spring Road east of the present Pioneer Rest Cemetery.

When the ten-wagon caravan arrived at the Alfred Johnson home, the oak and pecan grove resounded with affectionate greetings unrestrained by grateful cheering. The Johnsons, with short notice, had prepared a welcoming feast. There was a huge pot steaming with savory venison, while a variety of game was roasting on spits over the outdoor fire. Only one luxury was lacking, and it was quickly supplied from the heavily loaded wagons—sugar, a priceless commodity in Tarrant County in the 1850s. The wagons were filled with other luxuries which Mrs. Johnson had instructed the ladies to bring: mirrors, clocks, cooking utensils, cutlery, dishes, bedding, and clothing, for these were rare articles in North Texas. Nor had feminine vanity been ignored in packing. A small hair trunk was a part of every wagon, in which each woman brought a poke bonnet and one or two "best" dresses wrapped in paper to prevent wrinkling. There would be a few occasions when a frontier lady wore silk.

Feasting over, Alfred Johnson took a wagon at sundown and drove to Fort Town inviting "Mrs. Peak and six other ladies" residing in the town to return with him for a welcoming party. Though Mollie Allen King, who told of this event many years later, did not name them, we may surmise from records "the other ladies" were Madames Archibald Robinson, M. T. Brinson, Julian Feild, Henry Daggett, Ephraim Daggett, and Press Farmer. They were pleased to have the Kentuckians join them, for great was the need of more feminine hands to provide food and clothing, and to nurse the sick. From telling the newcomers easy approaches to the problems of housekeeping on the Texas prairies, Fort Town's ladies guided the conversation into gossip about the most currently famous woman—Harriet Beecher Stowe. They had read about her in their husbands' newspapers but had not read her book, *Uncle Tom's Cabin*. They wanted news about the book and people's reaction to it "back home in Kentucky." They complained because traveling book merchants with a yearly almanac, a collection of Bibles, and a novel or two had not yet begun yearly journeys to the forks of the Trinity. They learned that many Southerners said that Harriet Beecher Stowe was not a lady because her story was a colossal prevarication. When they returned to their homes that night, one of them had a worn copy of the controversial novel, and another had Hawthorne's *Scarlet Letter*, borrowed from the newcomers.

Men of the Kentucky caravan rested a few days in Johnson's oak grove, then made a trip or two to the village of Fort Town to "sound out" the old-timers' knowledge of the country. They rode over the area a few more days. With so much fertile earth to choose from, it did not take too long to ponder the selection for purchase. J. K. Allen and Stephen Terry bought land from Wright Conner, who also shared his log home with the newcomers. The three families lived together the first winter. One cabin could be, indeed, a shelter for so many during an Indian raid for which

Conner was prepared. Port holes were made in the log walls through which to shoot. Since Allen and Terry had many horses, they were frequently visited by Indians. Six miles from the fort these Kentuckians built their homes near present White Settlement Road. Their lands increased with their slaves. Terry later turned from farming, buying an interest in a brickyard. Moving to Fort Town, he built a brick house on present-day Pecan Street between Fourth and Fifth streets.

The two unattached young men in the caravan, Theodore Petty and Tom Hagood, lived for three years with the Allens. Tom Hagood's parents and entire family followed the Allens to Texas, preempting land seven miles west of the Allen farm on Silver Creek. Today, the Hagood heirs own the land near Lake Worth.

The songs of slaves vibrated through the timber during the fall and winter of 1854. They made a clearing, built a commodious log house for the master, and cabins for themselves. Later they built a mill on a creek known today as Wood's Creek which flows into the West Fork. It was Dr. M. L. Wood's place which spread over a part of the present site of General Dynamics. The doctor had come with his family from Jefferson on Red River in 1853, settling in one of the vacant buildings of the fort. During his residence in Fort Town, he had concluded that a doctor could not accumulate sufficient wealth practicing medicine where the population was so scant and most of the people healthy. The practice of medicine would be his avocation, while farming would be his vocation.

A successful farmer, Dr. Wood purchased the newest inventions. Crowds came to his farm from distant places to see the first thrasher and first gang plow in Tarrant County. He was also successful in a new venture, the raising of potatoes; while his mill attracted new settlers to the community, increasing the prosperity of the farmers as the fields of wheat, oats and corn increased. The doctor's "safety box" became heavy with hard money. Emma Sarah Woods, one of the daughters, was a pretty sunbonnet girl in the White Settlement school, while the older daughter, Susanna, married Baldwin Samuels, who gave part of the land for Pioneer Rest Cemetery when it was organized in 1870, and for whom Samuels Avenue was named.

The land in Kentucky was wearing out. Men with slaves were moving to Texas. There was land "out there" to be cleared. Slaves were needed. Texas would be a good slave market for decades to come. There were several reasons: Texas was slave soil, and unlike "Bleeding Kansas" and other territories in the "Far West," would escape the bitter wrangle of Americans over the question whether the land would be free or slave. Another factor to consider was the information given in the best immigrant maps and guide books praising the future agricultural empire which awaited men in the Grand Prairie and North Texas. Men were acting upon advice given in J. De Cordover's book and other guides for immigrants. A man of wits did not stay in one place where he could not produce wealth.

Such reasoning resulted in the erection of another home in the White Settlement in 1856. Paul Isbell, his wife and two sons, Ruben Melville and George Rufus Isbell, had left Todd County, Kentucky, with a pretentious caravan and an impressively large "string of slaves." He was a farmer and a trader in slaves. He was looking for good timberland; and camped near Fort Town's square until he found blackland, good timber, and water. Today Carswell Air Force Base occupies the site of the Isbell farm. The Isbells' home, first a log house, later covered with concrete and made commodious by adding several rooms of rock and concrete, was destroyed to make way for the air base in the 1940s, after the United States entered World War II. In Castleberry Addition, a north-south road leading from White Settlement Road to Ohio Garden Road, bears the name Isbell Road.

Paul Isbell became a man of influence. First, he turned Indian fighter. Thieving Indians driving off horses and cattle were cutting too deeply into the profits of the farmers in the White Settlement area. A volunteer guard was formed by John A. Mitchell, Will Allen, George Grant, Paul Isbell, Paul Tyler, Tom, Bob, and Jim Hagood, Charles Mitchell and Joseph and Elijah Farmer. These guardsmen were so fiercely alert that they finally cleared the western section of Tarrant County of hostile Indians until marauding expeditions were infrequent events. Isbell also turned his attention to education for the children. He gave land for the first school in the White Settlement, which stood on Farmers Branch in a field adjoining the Isbell and Grant farms. Today, it would be located at the south end of Carswell Air Force Base.

With Isbell, George Grant had brought his family in the Kentucky caravan of 1856, locating on a farm bordering Isbell's land, and prospered as a landowner and slaveholder. Today the road leading to the General Dynamics plant bears his name—Grant's Lane.

By the close of 1859, settlers had driven deeply the stakes of the White Settlement. Others had come. Prominent among them were C. G. Payne, John Ingraham, Paul Tannehill, John Adams Mitchell and Paul Tyler. The arrival of Paul Tyler with his dog, "Sounder," increased the effectiveness of the volunteer guard. The dog's name befitted the reputation of this big Virginia deer hound loved by the settlers of Fort Town, who mourned his loss when his master moved to the White Settlement. A keen hunter, Sounder trailed deer and bear, making easy the acquisition of a meat supply. Sounder would bay. Men hearing the dog would grab their guns and ride off in the direction of the baying. Before reaching the scene, they knew whether the prey would be deer or bear. Sounder had "one call for a treed bear; another for deer, and he never made a mistake." He was considered a famous Fort Town inhabitant, helping to usher in important events in the village. Barking a cheerful welcome, he accompanied all stagecoaches across Fort Town's square to Steele's Tavern. When Sounder moved from Fort Town, he did not lose character but soon was recognized in the White Settlement.

Both animals and men in the White Settlement, it seemed, were endowed with unique traits which seasoned life with interest so that the settlers had much about which to converse. They talked about the unusual dog, Sounder. They talked about the fastidious lady from Virginia, named Mary. She was known as the wife of John Adams Mitchell, who had earlier settled in Fort Town where Mary became a teacher in 1856. Upon moving to the White Settlement she had become the first teacher in that area. The "Co-eds" in Mary Mitchell's school, she insisted, must be fair ladies. At recess, she would not permit the girls to play outdoors without their sunbonnets and gloves, a habit they followed in their daily routine. In May, Mrs. Mitchell gave a school festival. Only white flowers were gathered from the prairies for decoration; and the girls of unusual fairness were dressed in white. Guests who came to hear the recitations and the singing saw a symphony of white.

The beauty of the program convinced Joe Terrell, a young lawyer in Fort Town, that the event was worth writing about. Citizens of the rival town of Dallas should know about such things. He wrote an article which was published in the *Dallas Herald*. In the closing paragraph of the article, Terrell stated that the area should be called White Settlement. At least, this was one of the several stories giving reason for the name White Settlement. Another version in the early eighteen-fifties was that White Settlement derived its name from being the last outpost of white settlers on the northwestern frontier of the state.

Cemeteries of the White Settlement still exist. In the one located east of the Carswell Air Force Base runway are found the graves of the patriarchs of the Farmer family, George Grant, James Ventioner and his wife, Millie Farmer Ventioner. The other cemetery, known as the Thompson burial ground, is located in a field on Highway 183 one block southwest of the traffic circle leading to the General Dynamics aircraft factory. In this cemetery, some of the tombstones are marble, while others are made from common field stones. Each tombstone silently tells the degree of prosperity achieved by the pioneers beneath. A marble monument, scarcely altered by age, marks the graves of Paul Isbell, his wife, his two sons, and their wives.

South Horizon

On the horizon south of the fort in 1853, log houses were few. There was a reason. Land was fertile but timber, creeks, and springs were not so plentiful as in other areas. One of the first homes built on the uninhabited south horizon was that of George ("Press") Farmer. Coming from Roane County, Tennessee, in 1847, he had first settled in East Texas. That land of pine woodlands he forsook for prairie country in 1849, settling in the big timber along the Clear Fork shortly before the arrival of Major Arnold and the dragoons. Press and Jane Farmer, alone in the wilderness, cut timber and lifted the logs into place for their home. It has been said it was the first house built on the present site of Fort Worth. One of the Farmer descendants identified the location on the Clear Fork one-half mile from the forks of the Trinity in the area known today as West Weatherford Street; while another states that it was two miles south of the public square on the Clear Fork.

Each evening, Press and Jane surveyed with pride the day's work. Their house was almost completed when Indians attacked them. They fled on horseback. Next day returning to the new home into which had gone a month of labor, they found it burned. Heartbroken and afraid, they decided to pitch a tent on the high bluff overlooking the river. Security came to the Farmers three weeks later with the arrival of the dragoons. Press turned from farming to make his living as a sutler and freighting supplies for the soldiers. He won distinction by becoming the father of the first child born in the original limits of old Fort Town. Sue Farmer was born in a cabin of Archibald Robinson, part owner of the land on which the fort was built. In the mid-fifties, Press returned to farming and headrighted on land about ten miles from the fort in the vicinity of the present-day United States Public Health Center Hospital.

Another cabin on the south horizon was that of Louis Wetmore, a soldier who had served under Major Arnold through the Mexican War, and had come with him from Mexico City to serve in frontier defense for Texas. While in the service at Fort Worth, he filed claim to land seven miles south of the fort, and later when mustered out in 1851, he settled on this land. He proved to be a valuable addition to the community. His father, as mayor of Rodenburg, Germany, had educated Louis in the best schools of that country. But the thought of compulsory military service was so displeasing to Louis that he ran away to America, arriving in time to join a company in New York bound for the Mexican War. "A magnetic personality, proficient in many languages, and possessed of many cultural attainments," Louis had much to contribute to the home he established with Hulda Ellis whom he married on January 8, 1853.

In 1854, several more cabins were added to those of Wetmore and Press Farmer. Edward Willburn and Nancy Overton Willburn, formerly from Wisconsin, came to Texas, locating in Dallas in 1843. Well supplied with equipment for farming, Edward Willburn and some of his brothers-in-law secured large tracts of land extending from the limits of Fort Town to Bear Creek about ten miles from the present heart of the city. These men developed fine farms, and several sons engaged in stock raising. When Fort Worth established schools, Willburn built a house in town, where he moved to educate his family of eleven children. However, he did not give up his farm. One of his sons, E. C. D. Willburn, became a trail driver and a rancher in the Benbrook area, and "there are hundreds of Willburn descendants in Texas and California."

A missionary minister of historic interest came to shepherd the settlers south of the fort. He was the Right Reverend Noah T. Byars in whose blacksmith shop, in the village of Washington-on-the-Brazos on March 2, 1836, was signed the Texas Declaration of Independence, and who was General Sam Houston's armorer in the Battle of San Jacinto. In 1855, three miles south of Fort Worth, he founded the Liberty Baptist Church and later, the Ashland Baptist Church in the northwest corner of Tarrant County in 1857.

East Horizon

On the horizon east of the fort, three log houses were erected on Sycamore Creek in 1849. This was the beginning of the present area of Polytechnic. From Tennessee came Samuel and Elizabeth Loving with their daughter, Margaret Ann. In December, they built their home on Sycamore Creek, four miles southeast of the fort. Another member of the family was their orphaned nephew, Merida Ellis, whose parents had died in Denton County in 1847, leaving eight children. Samuel's brother, W. R. Loving, with his family, staked claim on adjoining land along the creek.

A third cabin on the Sycamore was that of Benjamin Ayers. A veteran of the Mexican War, he brought his family from Shelby County, settling first near Birdville. In 1849, he moved to this location, three miles from the fort. In 1850, he was elected Tarrant County's first clerk. Other first-comers to the Polytechnic area were R. J. Tandy and his family. Between the present Lancaster Street and Texas Wesleyan College, Tandy obtained land and became a thrifty farmer. He constructed Tandy's Lake, famous for hunting, fishing and dancing in the 1880s. With Tandy lived his brother, W. L., the county's famous turkey hunter in that decade.

Another home-builder on the east horizon was Captain John M. Durrett. He was to become a figure in Fort Town. He was a Tennessean and brother-in-law of Alfred Johnson who had settled nearer the fort. The two men had married the Fortson sisters, and had come together to Tarrant County in 1853. Durrett established a retreat five miles from the fort in a wooded grove on the road which led from Johnson's Station, and there welcomed travelers. It was said that he was thrice blessed, for his handsome face glowed with kindness and crinkled with merriment. His "kindly nature and bright spirit" reached out to touch everyone he met. With his "melodious voice and violin," Durrett played and sang away the frontier sorrows, and also made music for parties. Politically a conservative, he assumed his share of frontier hardships, and accepted the welfare and government of the community as being among his responsibilities.

Farmers on this east side needed a gristmill. Nine miles northeast of Fort Worth in 1856, a three-story frame structure towered above the tree tops. A turbine churned the water of the Trinity, grinding the farmers' grain. Archibald Franklin Leonard, the miller, was given a share of the grain for the milling. This was the same man who, in 1849, was a partner of Henry Daggett, the trader. Late in 1853, he left Fort Worth, returning to his former home on the Grapevine prairie where he had settled in 1845. There he opened a general mercantile business. The settlement at that place became known as Leonardville. When later he sold out to a Doctor Dunn, the settlement became known as Dunnville; and in 1854, was given a post office. Then the name was changed once more, this time to Grapevine.

Leonard's Mill became a clearing house for news and politics where men piled up words, then acted. A large oak tree just outside the mill had a record for lynchings. Two white men were "strung up" there, paying the price for horse stealing, and several Negroes were hanged. When the farmers of Tarrant, Denton, Wise, and Hood counties brought their grain to this mill, they camped in the timber nearby, trading for their bread in real estate, crops, and livestock. On the eve of the Civil War in 1860, the mill burned; it was rebuilt and owned respectively by one Alverson, John Wheeler, and R. A. Randol. During the last half of its life, the mill was known as Randol Mill, remaining faithful to its duty until 1916.

The first resident of Riverside, Frank Adams, arrived at the fort in 1850. He had followed his friends Colonel Middleton Tate Johnson, Charles Turner, Benjamin Ayers, Captain Eph Daggett (and the other Daggett brothers), from Shelby County to the unclaimed empire at the forks of the Trinity. Frank Adams, a real frontiersman, wore a coonskin cap, coonskin coat, and trousers throughout his life, which ended in 1881. A mile and a half northeast of the fort in present Sylvania Addition, he surveyed his claim and cleared the timbered valley. Later, he returned to Rusk County long enough to find and then bring back a wife, Mary Richardson ("Molly"), the daughter of a wealthy physician. On his cleared land in Riverside, he constructed a large house. A man of many enterprises, Adams did freighting of importance to West Texas and the Indian Territory. On this side of town, he established a brick manufacturing plant, probably making the bricks for Fort Town's buildings. He acquired extensive land interests, among them a beautiful section on Sycamore Creek in Riverside, a stock farm on Blue Mound, and a large ranch in the Panhandle. His cattle were sold in eastern markets as well as Europe.

Boyhood life in the fifties in Fort Town and its environs was like a chapter from *Robinson Crusoe*; that is, according to the reminiscences of Merida Ellis, who spent his boyhood on Sycamore Creek beginning in 1849. With exalting freedom they rode the prairies, swung on the grapevine swings, rowed on the creeks, gigged the fish, which were in such swarms that it was impractical to use a fishing line. When a fellow walked "from his house to his barn, two hundred yards away he had time for pranks by tying a piece of red cloth around his neck, and by the time he reached the barn about a hundred antelopes would be following him." These animals liked the color red. Prairie chickens were alarm clocks, and when the boys awoke, the fields were black with wild turkeys.

Sure there was work to do. The inner bark of the oak trees along with berries had to be gathered for mother to use in dyeing the wool and cotton for cloth. There were gourds to be propped up on the vines so they would grow into dippers. One prop was placed to make the gourd grow long with a round bulb at the bottom. Another prop was placed near the stem so it would grow with a curved neck to make dipper handles. Other gourds—the big ones when ripened—were made into bowls. There were pails and other utensils to be carved from wood. There were pits to be dug where the potatoes were kept through the winter, and candle tallow through the summer. There was a large flat rock to be found, and grooves chiseled in it for the family washboard. There was corn to raise, wild meat to cure, venison hams to be prepared, leather to be tanned, shoes to be made, and buckskin to be dressed and fashioned into clothes. In winter, a few boys consented to wear shoes. "Then they crammed their feet into red russet shoes made of leather as thick as your finger. The longer they wore them the harder they got and the more they hurt." Most boys resisted civilization's shackles, tramping through the prairies in "barefeet as tough as leather."

One job, which was not so much fun for boys, was the grinding of corn. A log was hollowed out, and above the hollow, a pestle made of a block of wood was suspended on a rope fastened to a sapling tree which would bend easily. Then the boys would pull the rope, making the pestle twirl rapidly up and down until the corn was mashed into meal. Wheat flour was made in the same way. "We had to eat chaff and all." On Sunday mornings children enjoyed the luxury of hot biscuits. They were made more delicious by the syrup their mother made from watermelons, which in those days grew in abundance, large and sugar-sweet. Boys hunted poke berries, crushed them to make an excellent ink. Their writing pens were sharpened from choice quills collected and kept in a tidy basket.

Sometimes the fruits of their hard labor vanished in a brief moment. The Tonkawa Indians, mostly friendly, many times grew hungry, appeared at these homes scattered in the timber, cleared the cupboards of food, and departed. The families dared not object. Peace and security had its price. One pioneer, living near the timber east of Fort Worth in the early fifties, said that a settler could make an Indian his friend for life if he gave him a cup of coffee with a slice of broiled ham cut from one of the semi-wild hogs of which the woods abounded. These porkers grazing in the timber fed upon the acorns from a variety of oak trees, pecans, hickory nuts, wild persimmons, grapes, and red and black haws. In the opinion of this pioneer there was nothing finer than the hams from these hogs cured in hickory smoke. He further claimed that these hams were so rich that the mere odor emitted when broiling satisfied one's hunger.

A favorite sport of the small boys was rabbit hunting. One such hunt resulted upon a winter day in 1852 in a serious prairie fire. Boys with their dogs were hunting in the area of present I. M. Terrell High School, which stands on a bluff between East Lancaster and the Trinity and west of Riverside Drive. The boys' dogs drove a rabbit into the ruins of an Indian hut. Afraid to go into the hut, the boys decided to drive the cotton-tailed animal out by burning the grass which was waist high in most places over the countryside. It was winter, and the grass was dry. A northwest wind spread the blaze rapidly. Soldiers from the fort with the few men in the vicinity fought the fire furiously, turning the flames from the fort. But before they brought the fire under control, it had swept almost to present Lake Worth.

Fire prevention lessons were taught the boys, not from printed pages but by execution. Boys spent long hours working to keep a wide space around their homes cleared of brush. They were taught, when they sighted flames on the horizon, to plow a fire lane with speed. A fellow had to be on the alert because of the high grass. The growth of grass was so tall and thick that tender green sprouts grew under it as in a hothouse throughout the most severe winter, attracting countless geese, ducks, and pigeons which swelled the winter's abundant food supply. The old high grass was nutritious for the horses and cattle, but when over-grazed, died out. Therefore, the Indians often fired the prairies in order to give the young grass a chance to grow tall in the spring and make rich pasture for their ponies.

Pioneers on the north, the south, the east, and the west horizons of Fort Worth combined their powers, pushing the frontier farther westward. The roster of pioneers in the country surrounding the fort in 1856 is not complete. But enough information has been gathered from the lips of the first newcomers to give a fairly accurate picture of the settlers at the fort and of those in the country around it.

CHAPTER 17

Birth of Tarrant County

BEYOND eye-view, east of the military post of Fort Worth in 1850, were two settled communities. One was in the present area of Grapevine where the Missouri colony began building in 1845. For a time the community was known as Leonardville and Dunnville respectively, and after 1854, as Grapevine. The second community was around Birdville, not on the site of old Bird's Fort but to the northwest, where in 1848 and 1849 men began to gather.

Settlers assembling in sufficient numbers gave men of political minds a new purpose. Their cups were being filled economically, now they reached for political power which would solidify their community ambition.

Early in the year of 1849 Colonel Johnson had begun to work in Austin to organize into a county the Grand Prairie and East Cross Timbers around the forks of the Trinity. The future county, Johnson and others thought, should be named in honor of the Indian fighter, General Edward H. Tarrant, who had cleared the area for settlement. General Tarrant's heroism in the Village Creek Fight, and his service at Bird's Fort as one of President Houston's representatives in completing the Treaty of 1843 dividing the Texas republic between white and red men, had removed the Indians' headquarters from the little forests about the forks and nearby streams of the Trinity to present Palo Pinto and Parker counties. Colonel Johnson's effort was rewarded on December 20, 1849; and he became known as the Father of Tarrant County. On that day, the Texas Legislature authorized the creation of Tarrant County from Navarro County, and provided that an election be held to choose not only the county seat, but county officers as well.

On August 5, 1850, men in cheerful spirits rode to the polling places. Those of political bent, no doubt, galloped over the prairies in their eagerness to exercise their American prerogative of voting; this time to vote for the creation of their own political district in this newly chosen homeland. They elected Tarrant County's first officials: Seburn Gilmore, county judge; Benjamin P. Ayers, county clerk; Francis Jordan, sheriff; Henry Suggs, treasurer; John A. Hust, tax assessor and collector; and James P. Hallford (sometimes spelled Halford), Daniel Barcroft, Hamilton Bennett, and a Mr. Wilson as county commissioners.

John Hust, county tax assessor, conducted his business by horseback. He rode the county, visited the citizens, assessed the taxes, and collected them at the same time. If a man lacked money with which to pay, he merely promised to bring the money to the courthouse at a certain date. Hust boasted, "A man's word was as good as his bond." When the appointed day came, the taxpayer appeared at the courthouse, not with an excuse, but with the tax money.

The ordinance creating Tarrant County stated that the future county seat should be located in or near the center of the county. Birdville claimed to have that location, and also laid claim to having the most numerous population in and around her environs—about thirty families. Thus Birdville won the election in the summer of 1850, becoming the county seat. This displeased the voters in and near Fort Worth, who preferred a location closer to their landholdings. Their polling booth had been set up in front of the Daggett-Leonard store under a giant oak. This gnarled tree still shades the grounds at the foot of Samuels Avenue, preserved for posterity as a small park with a historical marker.

Organization of Tarrant County was completed by August 26, 1850, with an area of 877 square miles and a population of 664 people, of which 599 were white, and sixty-five were slaves. The state government, however, before the county election was held, went into action immediately after the legislature authorized the creation of Tarrant out of Navarro. In the department of State Comptroller at Austin, is the record of the first tax bill collected in 1850 by W. B. McCabe, assessor-collector of Navarro County "for Tarrant County on property rendered by citizens thereof and situated therein." There were ninety-five taxpayers in Tarrant County and total sum of state taxes paid was $80.78. The tax levy on slaves was higher than on land and cattle. "Thirty-two slaves were valued for tax purposes at $13,600 while 10,384 acres of land were valued at $9845, and 10,214 cattle were valued at $4220." The entire property valuation of Tarrant County in 1850 was $30,190 including "money at interest, $400; and miscellaneous, $850." Colonel M. T. Johnson rendered for taxes that year 1,476 acres of land, 16 slaves, 3 horses and 100 head of cattle.

Statistics are disconcerting. Figures given in the first federal census of Tarrant County in 1850, compiled by the assistant marshal, William Hogan, are inconsistent with the figures of the state tax report and those on record at Austin upon the completion of the county's organization. Of course the time element of several months enters into the variation as well as the fact that each week the wagons of settlers unhitching in Tarrant County brought changes. According to the federal census, there were eighty-two dwellings in the county, 689 white men, women and children, including 113 of the military establishment with their wives and children. There were two physicians, a blacksmith, two ministers, two saddlers, a carpenter, two schoolteachers and one merchant.

Apparently there are omissions. According to records of pioneers who enacted the drama of settling the county, there were more than one blacksmith and one merchant. There were blacksmiths at Grapevine and Birdville. The federal census, like that of the state's tax report, listed Colonel Johnson as the richest man in the county; however, there was a difference in the number of slaves listed for him and those in the county. That is plausible: a difference in time. In spite of the few variations, official records give a rather accurate picture of Tarrant County in 1850. When the organization was completed in August, there were 599 whites and sixty-five slaves—a difference of only twenty-three white persons as given in the federal census, and a difference of only twenty-four slaves.

New settlers with realtors' judgment seeking real estate knew that lands located in the area of the county seat increased in value more rapidly than land on the fringes of the county. Therefore Birdville in 1853 continued daily to attract settlers. There was Albert Gallatin Walker, one of the first surveyors in the upper Trinity Valley, who laid out Tarrant County by surveying the southern, eastern and northern boundaries. There was also John Wesley Elliston from Kentucky. In 1849, one mile west of Birdville near Little Fossil Creek, he established his family, farmed, did blacksmithing, and wrote to his Kentucky friends, "Come out to Texas, it is a greater country than advertised."

In 1853 came a rugged frontiersman, Isaac Parker from Navasota

County. He settled two and a half miles east of Birdville. Years earlier, Parker had served as an Indian fighter, having fought under Andrew Jackson in the Creek War. In 1833, he had come to Texas with eight families led by his father, John Parker, a Baptist minister. Locating on the Navasota River near present-day Groesbeck, the settlement called Fort Parker, was bludgeoned by 300 Comanches and Kiowas May 19, 1836. Elder Parker was killed, so were two of his sons, three small children, and Samuel Frost and his son, Robert. Several women were wounded. Two women and three children were taken away by the Indians. Two of these children were Cynthia Ann and her brother, whose father, Silas Parker, was killed. Isaac tenaciously carried on his father's task of homemaking on the frontier, along with serving in the Congress of the Texas republic, 1837–1845; and in the state legislature for nine years. He was author of the bill giving to Texas counties the right to relocate their county seats by a majority vote instead of a two-thirds vote. Out of this act grew the political fight between Birdville and Fort Worth in 1856 and 1860. To honor Isaac Parker's more than twenty years of service in the Congress of the Republic and the state legislature, Parker County was named for him.

Another arrival of note in 1853 was Edward Hovenkamp from Kentucky. Hovenkamp, a descendant of Dutch settlers of New Jersey, was educated as a lawyer. On a prospecting tour of Texas, he bought a large tract of fertile prairie at Birdville, returned to Kentucky, and in 1854 with his wife and small son James, drove into Birdville in an oxteam wagon. He became Judge Hovenkamp and a leader in legal affairs of the state. By mid-year of 1853, at the county seat of Tarrant, cabins could be counted beyond two-score. The Reverend John Allen Freeman rode from the Grapevine settlement and founded the Birdville Baptist Church. It was dissolved in 1856, but a new church would appear in August 1864.

Personalities of interest were not lacking at Birdville. There was John Boone, a descendant of Daniel Boone of Kentucky, who settled on Little Fossil Creek near Birdville; and, like Daniel, was a hustling, energetic man. The first physician moved to Birdville in 1855 as a result of Hovenkamp's urging—Doctor B. F. Barkley of Kentucky, who soon considered the political welfare of Birdville as serious as the practice of medicine. It was not long before he became the self-appointed director of Birdville's charitable activities, soliciting supplies for the needy when frontier hardships felled a family in want.

The Daggett-Leonard store was so well known that the first term of district court ever held in Tarrant County began its session in the live oak grove at the foot of Samuels Avenue on November 4, 1850. Oran M.

Roberts, then a resident of East Texas, later governor of Texas, presided as judge. The court continued in session two days. Six indictments were found by the grand jury, three for assault and battery, two for firing the prairie, and one for house burning, while one civil case was called and continued. Besides Roberts, the following officers present were Nat M. Burford, district attorney; Sanders Elliot, clerk; and Francis Jordon, sheriff. Of this first court session Judge Roberts wrote in 1896:

I as district judge of the old fifth judicial district, in the exchange of districts with Bennett H. Martin, district judge (of the ninth district which embraced Tarrant County), held the court at Fort Worth in November 1850.

It was held in the end of a little frame store house down upon the bank of the river, kept by Henry Daggett. The district attorney was Nat Burford and the attorneys present were General Tarrant, John H. Reagan and John Cravens, that I now recollect.

While [at Fort Worth] we were invited to dine with Major Arnold who was then quartered with his wife in a hewed log cedar house upon the hill where the city of Fort Worth stands. Just before sitting down to dinner it was discovered that a norther was coming up. We all ran out of the house, mounted our horses, and with rapid speed crossed the river with a chilling wind blowing furiously, and in about a mile reached the house of a Mr. Robertson [Robinson?] where we were boarding, nearly frozen, where we remained shut up two days, sheltered from the worst norther that I was ever in. There was only one house west of us this side of the Rio Grande.

Although Miss Jenkins identified the person in this portrait as Brigadier General William Jenkins Worth, it is not Worth but another unidentified officer. (Worth died in 1849 – early in the history of photography – and there are few authenticated photographs of him.) Worth served creditably under Generals Zachary Taylor and Winfield Scott in the Mexican War.

Tarrant County's first courthouse at Birdville. (From the collection of Ruby Snow Reynolds of Birdville, 1949.)

Captain Julian Feild, one of the first
five settlers in Fort Worth, built the
first gristmill in the area in 1856.

Mrs. Julian Feild, a pioneer, arrived
with her husband at Fort Worth in 1853.

E. M. Daggett, a foremost leader in
building the military post of Fort
Worth into a town.

Mrs. Paul Isbell and her husband were among the first fifty families of the old White Settlement area in the 1850's.

Dr. C. M. Peak, frontier physician and leader.

Mary Victoria Lawrence, scholar and teacher, became the wife of Joseph C. Terrell in 1871.

John Peter Smith. Able as a soldier, a humanitarian, and a civic leader.

Joseph Christopher
Terrell. The civic leader
and able lawyer as he appeared
when he established the first attorney's
office in Fort Worth.

Stephen Terry was a member of the committee that removed the county records from Birdville to Fort Worth in 1856. He was chief justice of Tarrant County during the era of the Confederacy, and was appointed county judge by Governor Hamilton in 1865.

Captain M. B. Loyd, banker of early Fort Worth. He helped organize the First National Bank in 1876.

CHAPTER 18

Vision and Tussle, Then Fort Town

THE forsaken military post Fort Worth was not transformed in a magic flash into a fort town when the United States troops departed in September, 1853. The deserted fort stood on the high bluff with not more than six cabins near it. On the north, south, and west horizons of early Fort Town there were less than a hundred cabins rising from the prairie grasses.

On the eastern horizon was flourishing Birdville, the county seat. There was no current trade at the fort. There were no roads, no cattle trails, only a sea of grass occasionally crossed by a supply train. It was not a picture to assure one that deserted Fort Worth would not easily go the way of other abandoned posts to become a prairie phantom. Hardy individuals in the cabins around about had a different plan. They had not come to the outskirts of the wilderness for an easier world, but one of unlimited opportunity.

Men with vision and tussle would change the abandoned Fort Worth into a town that they would affectionately call Fort Town for two decades. Troops moved out and civilians rushed in. Not even a ghostly shadow had time to permeate the empty buildings. No, it would not become a shadowy apparition to remind homeseekers of the brevity of life and inescapable change. As rapidly as Daggett and Leonard could pack their stock they moved their mercantile store from the live oak grove to the deserted military barracks on the bluff. And Henry Daggett added a new home to the skyline above the fort.

The Daggett neighbors were the Archibald Robinsons, who lived in one of the six log houses near the fort. Robinson and Colonel Johnson, owners of the land, took possession of the premises. Now that the military no longer needed the land, Robinson turned his mind and energy to building Fort Town, disbursing hospitality and generosity, thus winning the title of "Uncle Archie." Many years later, he sold his property and settled on a farm in Denton County.

Captain Julian B. Feild arrived in time to make his home in one of the officers' quarters—the house southwest of Major Arnold's former quarters. Feild, being a trader, had brought a stock of goods: hammers, picks, oxen yokes, harness, huge chunks of solidified sugar for children; and for women, there were coffee grinders, and thread and bolts of cloth for festive clothes. Homespun served for daily wear. On the southwest corner of the present courthouse square, he built a frame store. Now Daggett had competition. Captain Feild's haste to establish himself and a frontier fever sent him to bed. There was no doctor. A friend rode to "Three Forks," the present city of Dallas, for medical aid. Late the next day, the friend returned with a young physician. Feild liked the doctor and his medicine; and as he swallowed pills and tonic, he did a bit of town promoting. Fort Worth would not remain an abandoned fort, but would become a future city and would be a bonanza for a doctor.

What the young medical man heard and saw at the fort and the panorama from the bluff won a new citizen. Doctor Carroll M. Peak returned to "Three Forks," where in the previous spring he had established his bride, Florence Chalfant of Kentucky. Eagerly they prepared to move to Fort Worth. In the fall of 1853 the young physician and his wife made the two-day buggy trip. On their way, they spent the night at the home of Colonel Johnson. The bride won the Johnsons for "life-long friends." The Peaks moved into the vacant officers' quarters southeast of Major Arnold's. Doctor Peak had the distinction of being Fort Worth's first civilian doctor. Mrs. Julian Feild welcomed the bride, taught her artful methods in frontier housekeeping, especially the curing of fresh meats; and later instructed her in the care of infants.

Doctor Peak's education had been obtained at the Louisville Medical College in Kentucky. Serving as physician, surgeon, and dentist, he practiced within a thirty-mile radius of the fort. He said his zone of practice was "bounded on the west by the setting sun." Every day he rode the fenceless country regardless of weather. Many cold nights, called from his bed by a breathless horseman pounding his door and excitedly chanting, "Hurry, doctor," he would don his great coat, put his six-shooter in the holster, mount his horse Gray Eagle, cover his legs with a Mexican blanket, and, perhaps, ride to Johnson's Station or Robinson's Mill, about sixteen miles southwest of Fort Town on the Clear Fork. Returning home at dawn, passing houses, he called aloud to the occupants the good news: "The Smiths have a new baby"—or sorrowful news which sent pioneers scurrying to the aid of their neighbors. An orderly person, a quality which made for his efficiency, Peak equipped himself for every emergency. To his saddle was attached a hollowed-out gourd well stoppered at the handle, to assure drinking water. In a pair of saddle pockets back of his saddle, he carried his equipment. In one was an amputating knife, saw, forceps, and other instruments, while in the other were medicines—the usual of that day: quinine, blue mass, ipecac, and rhubarb.

Lieutenant Holiday, left behind at the fort to recuperate from a fever, lodged in Major Arnold's former quarters. He was there in the autumn of 1853 to welcome Dr. Peak and bride. After autumn rains, cool weather came. Then the lieutenant reported for duty, and M. J. Brinson with his family moved into the evacuated quarters. Young Matthew Brinson was born there that year, the grandson of Colonel M. T. Johnson. (Louisa Brinson was one of the colonel's five daughters.) Brinson engaged in farming and merchandising, and so thrifty was he that in partnership with Bob Slaughter, he was able to build the first brick store building in Fort Town in 1856. This new place of business was located at the southwest corner of Weatherford and Houston streets.

A physician, M. L. Woods, has already been mentioned as the gentleman farmer of the White Settlement addicted to new inventions. He followed Doctor Peak into Fort Town in December of 1853, and took up residence with his family in the vacant commissary building. His ox-teams had pulled a heavy load of furniture from the Woods' former home at Jefferson on Red River. One wagon was quite weighty for the oxen, for it carried a piano, the first such instrument to be brought to Fort Worth. It came in time to play carols for the civilian families who spent their first Christmas in the abandoned fort in 1853. Music of the piano resounded on the square causing excitement. The Indians who came to Fort Town to trade or to beg were frightened at first. They stood far off gazing at the Woods' home. Upon each trip to town, the Indians ventured nearer the house until finally they were brave enough to enter to see the strange object. They decided that the piano keys were teeth of strange animals making a song. After their fear vanished, they came often pleading, "Peck, gals, peck." Mrs. Woods and her daughters graciously complied to the accompaniment of the gleeful grunts of these red men peering through the window and door.

The last person of note to become a citizen of Fort Town in 1853 arrived in crisp December—a capable youth who would make pages in the history of Fort Town. John Peter Smith, Kentucky-born, was a June graduate in that year from Bethany College, Virginia. He was a scholar of classics and proficient in Greek and Latin. After graduation, he returned to his home in Frankfort, Kentucky, and read law. But visions of the much talked of Texas diverted his attention. In November, he took a boat at Louisville, reached New Orleans in the midst of a cholera epidemic, and hurriedly took a boat to Shreveport, where he joined a wagon train bound for Dallas. Here there were too many settlers for a young fellow without money to get an advantageous start in life. He chose Fort Town for his home.

On foot, John Peter Smith left Dallas. He walked for two days through groves and prairies until his feet were sore. Five miles from Fort Town, he came upon the home of Captain Durrett, the frontier music maker. Here he found rest and a friend. Captain Durrett urged young Smith to wait and to ride with him when he made his weekly trip to take a supply of venison to Fort Town. Durrett in later life always boasted, "I brought Peter Smith to Fort Worth." The Peaks gave their fellow Kentuckian a home; and in January 1854, Smith opened the first school in the community in the building formerly used by the soldiers as a hospital. Pupils were few in a settlement of thirty people—twelve youngsters, in fact. After three months as a pedagogue ill health sent Smith from the school room to join a surveying party operating in Jack and Palo Pinto counties. Health restored, he was back in Fort Town in January 1855, clerking in Daggett's store. He continued to survey and meanwhile studied law under A. Y. Fowler, a Fort Town attorney. He was also accumulating large tracts of land in the vicinity. In the 1860s and 1870s he would play an important part in the growth of the town.

Doctor, lawyer, merchant, and artisan were infusing business life into an abandoned fort. Frank Knaar, formerly the faithful saddler of Major Arnold, who had mustered out of service in 1852, made a home near the fort with his wife. She had one luxury—a stove—among the first that was brought to Fort Worth. Bending over his workbench long hours, Knaar mended harness and saddles to such perfection that men said they were as good as new. Some men needed new saddles, while others could afford an extra one. There were not enough hours in a day for Fort Town's first saddler to fill the orders. Major Arnold had verified the dedication of this artisan in his report to the war department July 19,

1849, stating that "Knaar, the saddler was always at work on the equipment." From strength to strength, Fort Town advanced with citizens like Knaar. But life did not spare him sorrows. Today in Pioneer Rest Cemetery one may find a tombstone, marking the grave of his child: "Francis Knaar died July 1, 1867. Aged 17 years."

Charles A. Harper, Fort Town's first lawyer, and John J. Courtney, the town's first notary public, were in demand, because real estate rapidly changed hands, and slaves were being bought and sold. Lawyer Harper came from New Hampshire in 1849. It is evident that this New Englander, on a raw frontier, was reticent. Posterity has only a few facts about his life along with a tintype from which to tell his story. His discerning eyes indicate that he saw much, divulged little, and was capable of deliberate calculations. In Fort Town, he became a God-fearing man. In the Blue Hole of the Clear Fork, he was baptized by Parson A. N. Dean. His record closes with the fact that he was a citizen as late as 1860. Perhaps the Civil War drew him back to the North or the Far West beckoned him.

1854

The year 1854 brought as many unusual men as 1853, men blessed with the talent to build. They were Captain Ephraim Merrell Daggett, Lawrence Steele, Colonel Nathaniel Terry, and the men already mentioned who arrived in the Kentucky caravan, most of whom settled on farms in the White Settlement. Others made their home in Fort Town. Among them, Bob Slaughter, who became the merchant forming the mercantile house of Brinson and Slaughter; Dick King, who opened Fort Town's first civilian blacksmith shop on the present northeast corner of Weatherford and Commerce streets; and Tom Hagood who, in connection with King's smithy, opened a carpenter and cabinet shop. They mended vehicles, made square nails and metal goods, shod the horses, and manufactured hobbles for horses so that they would not stray or be stolen by the Indians.

Captain Ephraim Merrell Daggett, called by his friends, "Captain Eph," was a giant of a man both in body and spirit. An Indian introduced to him, grunted and said, "Too big for a man, not big enough for a horse." With impelling drive, this man made plans and molded events and men to his design of things. As a youth, he had left his father's home at Terre Haute, Indiana, in 1833. Daggett heard that the log cabin village at Fort Dearborn had become a thriving trading post. There he witnessed Fort Dearborn grow into the lusty town of Chicago. He had been a part of its growth for six years, trading with the Indians. Then rheumatism attacked his giant frame, forcing him to seek the warm south. Daggett convinced his father and the remainder of the family to accompany him to Texas, where they settled in Shelby County. Since 1849, Captain Daggett had been a frequent visitor to Fort Worth, acquiring large tracts of land for himself and friends. While here he foresaw a bright future for the area. Like Chicago had been, Fort Worth was a log cabin fort in a wilderness of farming and cattle lands. It could become a thriving trading center, then a vigorous town. He, with his brothers, Henry Clay, the merchant, and Charles Biggers, the farmer, and other pioneers who would capture his vision, would work their "life long through" to make Fort Worth a second Chicago.

From 1848 to 1853 Captain Daggett, turning forty, was one of the gentlemen who made bright conversation at the dinners in the fort. Major Arnold and the captain had become friends during the Mexican War. As a Regulator in the Regulator-Moderator feud in East Texas, he proved his leadership; and it became well known that he had an instinctive sense of honor but was quick to resent insult. When the Mexican War came, he enlisted for six months and marched away as a second lieutenant in one of the two companies raised in Shelby County. When this brief period of service expired, he rejoined for twelve months. This time he left home as first lieutenant in Colonel Jack Hays' noted regiment of Texas Rangers. Soon a company of Rangers was addressing him as captain.

His war record was spectacular. In a bloody three-day siege of Monterrey, he distinguished himself under the command of General Worth who became his exemplar for life. At Monterrey, Daggett also won a friend, Major Arnold. At the Battle of Buena Vista, his company struck deadly blows which aided in bringing about General Santa Anna's defeat, thereby giving the United States control of northern Mexico. After the battle, he pursued Santa Anna, almost capturing him in his tent. Santa Anna fled, wooden leg and all; but Daggett seized the general's gold-braided coat, fine feathered hat, gold epaulets, a cane, and silver washbowl made of 5000 Mexican silver dollars, silver spoons and a saddle. Santa Anna sent a messenger offering a thousand pesos for the return of his uniform. Having failed to capture the general, Daggett was too piqued to comply, and kept his souvenirs.

Outside of Mexico City at San Carlos in 1847, he saved his company of sleeping Texas Rangers who were unexpectedly attacked by guerillas led by Padre Taranta. A light sleeper, Captain Daggett looked up to see the enemy coming upon them. He began to roar with fury in his leonine voice. Every Ranger came to his feet, and the guerillas were soundly beaten. Chief Taranta said he lost the battle because "a big devil screamed terrifically that handled a six shooter so well."

After the conquest of Mexico City, while on a final scouting mission, Captain Daggett climaxed his Mexican adventures by capturing General Valencia, second in command of the Mexican Army. With the Mexican War over, he went to the Grand Prairie in 1849; voted in the first Tarrant County election in 1850; and moved his family and slaves to Fort Town in 1854.

When Daggett's caravan arrived in Fort Town it was an entire day of excitement, because it came in relays. First came the carriage with Mrs. Daggett, and then a two-seated buggy driven by Captain Daggett close behind. There were several wagons with slaves, household goods and tools. In late afternoon, a few slaves appeared driving a herd of dairy cows. Following them were young Negro boys with flocks of turkeys, geese and ducks. Later came slaves driving a few horses and mules. And at dusk trudged forward the plodding oxteams. Just as "a feast is made for laughter," so the arrival of a new homemaker was an event for rejoicing. The evening before the arrival of Daggett's caravan a horseman brought news of what to expect on the morrow, and the wives in the community made extensive preparations for a welcoming party.

Captain Daggett installed his equipment on a farm three quarters of a mile south of the fort's buildings. His fields extended south and east over what is today East Lancaster, South Main, and lower Houston and Main streets. He established Mrs. Daggett in a home located today on the block bounded by Main, Houston, Tenth and Eleventh streets. She was formerly Caroline Nored of Charleston, South Carolina, and was said to have been a beauty. She was the widow of Lemuel Adams, a plantation and slave owner of eastern Louisiana near the Texas boundary, and the mother of his three children. Her daughter Amanda Adams became the wife of Charles Turner, and her two sons, Lemuel Junior, familiarly known as "Bunk" Adams, and William Francis Adams, joined their stepfather Daggett in building Fort Town. And one of the captain's most cherished aides was a lad of thirteen, his only son, Ephraim B. Daggett, whose mother Faribo Hayes, daughter of Captain Hayes, had died in the child's infancy.

With Captain Daggett as a permanent citizen, Fort Town never wanted for amusement, or a driving power in affairs of business or politics. He created business where there was none, and directed men and events in the community. In East Texas and in Austin, Fort Worth became better known than Birdville—he saw to that on his many trips from home.

His relaxation was equally robust. He had a passionate fondness for fun and frolic. Wrestling was a favorite sport; but very seldom could he be matched; and at "pulling stakes" his equal was never found. His excellent marksmanship with rifle and six-shooter was never questioned. Being fond of music, and being a graceful dancer, his home was always open for music and dancing.

At the fort from 1849 to 1853, Daggett had seen people come and go without lodging to ease their weariness. Therefore, in 1853 he bought the cavalry stables of the fort and converted them into Fort Worth's first hostelry. Although it had dirt floors, the place served its purpose. This first hotel was on the corner of Bluff and Houston streets, where the present County Welfare Office is located. It had another distinction. Across its front and covering half the height of the building was the town's first commercial sign—the like of it Fort Worth was never again to see. It amused the inhabitants and startled the travelers. The sign painter was Doctor Gounah, famous friend of Major Arnold. While Captain Daggett was away, Doctor Gounah decided to stimulate trade for his devoted friend. On the canvas he had pictured as gracing the captain's festive board, life-size wild game lusciously cooked to inveigle the appetite of the itinerant travelers; also he had deer running full tilt and bears rampant, as well as many other lesser game. It was said that this sign was such a drawing card that the stranger needed no other invitation.

Lawrence Steele walked under the sign into Daggett's hotel in 1854. He found that the sign was honest advertising, for the table was as crowded as pictured. He ate with enjoyment, looked at the country from the bluff, and listened to the prophecies of the town boosters. Fort Town was the place for his industrious nature; the place where his education, which he had received at the academy in Mecklenburg County, Virginia, could be turned to profit. Son of an Episcopal minister, he was reared in a home of refinement, which he hoped to duplicate for his young family accompanying him. His father, in search of a better living, had moved his family from Virginia to Tennessee, then to Texas in 1839, settling in Harrison County. Now Steele was thirty-four. Fort Town would be his opportunity. He entered the mercantile business with Captain Julian Feild.

The populace of Fort Town had been alerted in time to assemble on the square. A half hour before, a citizen had seen a caravan moving across the prairie towards Fort Worth. This promised to be another event of 1854. It was. Through the tall grass came the greatest array of carriages, wagons, and strings of riding horses, the like of which Fort

Town had never seen: two wagons of thirty-six slaves, wagons of farm tools, wagons of fine furniture well packed, carriages with two pretty girls and their mammies, a carriage with two young men tailored in high fashion, a carriage with a lady of both beauty and aristocratic bearing, and a buggy with Colonel Nathaniel Terry and his neatly dressed body servant, Uncle Daniel. What a magnificent sight the master was in his impeccable clothes, topped with a stovepipe beaver hat. This unique hat and the immaculate clothes would always attract attention among the weather-worn hats of the cowmen and farmers in the classless society of Fort Town—planters with their slaves, small farmers, and cowmen working together pushing open a door into a new economy of the Southwest.

Another center of interest in the caravan was the string of riding horses. One was a beauty. This animal, the gossips learned, was named Ringgold, valued at $3000. Ringgold had a past worth relating. The colonel had been one of the highest flyers in the Union. When it was safe for a Southern man to travel with his slaves through the North without John Brown's interference, he had taken Ringgold to Saratoga, New York, where Daniel, riding Ringgold, won a great race on the Saratoga race track. The colonel, with his high-topped hat and accompanied by Daniel, would be seen riding Ringgold many times a week on Fort Town's square, creating good conversation for the cowboys.

Colonel Terry had turned toward Texas in 1854 as a place where a man could build with less risks and more tangible prospects of a prosperous tomorrow. Cuba, as a future slave territory of the United States, he had despaired of, because there was too much opposition in Congress and in the North; and the filibustering expedition financed by slaveholders of the South to take Cuba had failed in 1851. Then too, Congress in December of 1853 had accepted the Gadsden Purchase that acquired land from Mexico, adjoining Texas and extending along the southern borders of New Mexico and Arizona, in order to provide a railroad to the Pacific Ocean through the less difficult section of the Rocky Mountain chain. This act of Congress would certainly bring iron rails across Texas.

From Colonel Johnson, Terry purchased land at the north end of present Samuels Avenue in the live oak grove. From the grove, the river bottom lands extended toward the present meat-packing plants of Armour and Swift. The best description of the location of Terry's plantation is found in the words of one of his ex-slaves, Lou Skelton, given in the 1930s:

Twas all de valley at de bottom ob de slope from Samuels Avenue to de river, and twas in a sorta ha'f moon shape. De road f'om Samuels Avenue split de old slave qua'tahs on its way to de packin' plants.

A century later, on the site of the former slave quarters, one finds a small community of Negro dwellings, no doubt the probable descendants of Terry's slaves living there.

In the black soil of the river valley, Colonel Terry planted fields of corn, wheat, and oats. He raised many watermelons, which the slaves carried to the Cold Springs nearby. The Terrys were always ready for a watermelon party. They "lived in all the magnificence that money of the time could provide." Their plantation home faced south, fronted with a long porch, which was laid in a well-designed stone floor.

There were other newcomers to Fort Town in 1854. In January, Clara, the first child of Doctor and Mrs. Peak, was born in the officers' quarters. Jake, the son of Press Farmer, was born in the Farmers' home near the square. The community was acquiring a much needed juvenile population.

There is a time to plant, to reap, to rejoice, and to mourn. The year 1854 had been big with events for rejoicing; but there came a day that year when tears were shed again for a friend. Leaders of Fort Worth arranged to bring the body of Major Arnold from Fort Graham. Alphonse Freeman, the trooper who had followed the major since the Mexican War, and had not been separated from him until his death in 1853, except during Arnold's detailed duty in Washington, was in command of the funeral cortege. Arnold's body was placed in Dick King's blacksmith shop the evening it arrived; and late into the night, King and Tom Hagood worked making a new coffin. In the watch that night were his former comrades in arms, now citizens of the town: Freeman, Abe Harris, Frank Knaar, and Louis Wetmore. Next day, the Fort Towners placed the major in his final resting place beside his two children, with Masonic rites—the first Masonic funeral conducted in Fort Worth.

Doctor Gounah knew it was vain to place trust only in the memory of man to safeguard the resting place of the deceased, for he knew how remorseless time obliterates graves. But he did not want an unmarked grave for his friend. His love for the major sustained and controlled his hands, unaccustomed to toil as he cut limestone into slabs and walled in the grave, marking it with an unpolished stone slab. In 1936, the Pioneer Cemetery Association erected a monument at Major Arnold's grave beside the crude sandstone slabs of Gounah's handiwork marking the graves of the Arnold children laid to rest in 1850.

1855

The ghost of an abandoned fort which had come sometimes to haunt the first settlers, retreated before the vigorous village which was taking form in 1855. A public square was shaping around the former military parade ground extending eastward. A new world was teeming into shape for merchants, ox-freighters, farmers, cowmen, who seemed to feel their power and to say, what can stop us? That was the spirit of 1855 in Fort Town.

With a tremendous whiz an ox whip cracked over a long line of oxen. The heavily loaded wagon of pecans and pelts lunged with a screech into ponderous motion. The crowd yelled, "A good trip, John." A man of brawny frame and Celtic extraction retorted, "I guarantee you—no bad luck—I'll make the voyage inside of six weeks." The crowd always gathered on the square to give John White, "knight of the ox goad," the proper send-off on his six-hundred-mile trip to Houston.

John's load was for Brinson, Slaughter, and Daggett, the leading merchants, who had acquired the articles in barter and trade and now were sending them to the Houston market. In return, John's load would be just as heavy with sugar, salt, coffee, flour, dried fruit and fish, garden seeds, shoes, cloth and other merchandise to delight the ladies. Fort Town men would start gathering on the square about thirty-five days after John White's departure, awaiting his arrival to see if he would be on time as promised. They watched "until a lone horseman appeared to the east of Captain Daggett's farm, then all eyes strained until it was ascertained that the rider was old John who preceded his freighter." Then Uncle Jack Durrett tuned up his fiddle to celebrate the end of the "whiskey drouth." John arrived to announce that the freighter would be in shortly. Men cheered their special hurrah for "punctual John." Then when the wagon arrived, all helped to unload it. They wrestled to obtain the desirable sundries for which John managed to always find a place in his crowded freighter. In a very short time these little luxuries which cheered the families were gone. They fought to purchase salt, varying from ten to twenty dollars a hundred-pound, as soon as it was rolled into the stores. Without salt, their smokehouses would be empty.

Sometimes John could not arrive before sundown. Then Fort Towners built a bonfire to welcome him to the square, for one had to be on hand to have a choice of the items so needed and craved. It was a first come, first served situation. Houston was a supply base for Fort Worth. The journey there and back was difficult and tedious. John, an expert navigator of the prairies, traveled alone, improvised bridges, and cut his own

trail. He dared, prospered, and nurtured Fort Town through the fifties
and sixties. After that, John White disappeared in legend.

There was another freighter, but not in competition, for this one was
to the northeast to Jefferson on the Red River. Sam Parks, slave of William Parks, drove to obtain supplies for the Parks' Mercantile Store.
Sam, like John, traveled alone; but Sam went through Indian territory
through which he bought his way by giving Indians merchandise in exchange for safe passage. At night he threw meat to the howling wolves
to keep them from his camp. His master had brought him with another
slave to Fort Town when the Parks family, composed of Elizabeth the
wife, and small son, Thomas, had migrated there.

This other slave was Frances, the faithful family cook. Even when
one hundred and eight years old, she continued to entertain the Parks'
grandchildren with her experiences in Fort Town during the eighteen-
fifties. One day while Frances was busy with the baking, an old squaw
slipped away with baby Thomas, and was making rapid headway over
the bluff toward the Trinity, when Mrs. Parks saw what was happening.
Picking up a butcher knife and calling Frances to follow her, they overtook the squaw, who gave up the baby. Indians loved the white babies.
When in town for trade, they visited the homes in order to gaze at the
infants. The squaws were made happy if they were permitted to cuddle
the little ones in their arms. Sometimes, overruled by their enchantment,
they would try to kidnap. Mrs. Parks had to protect her son especially,
for he had red hair, and according to Indian belief, a red-haired baby
brought good fortune.

Lazy Indians, Frances said, made her chores difficult. If they had no
goods with which to barter, they would try to steal chickens and rob
warehouses of meal, flour and fresh meat. She thought, on the other hand,
that civilized Indians compensated for the bad ones, because they were
pretty in their beads, feathers, and buckskin. And in Parks' store they
brought a variety of baskets finely woven of the willows and reeds, dyed
in many colors—products of the woods thereabouts. Dried pumpkin, a
white people's product, the Indians considered a delicacy for which they
would gladly trade their handiwork. The frontier housewives, in need of
utensils, were delighted to trade meal, sugar, flour, coffee, and such com-
modities, for these beautiful and useful baskets. The Indians' beadwork
brought better prices. A popular design among Parks' customers was a
beaded belt with a pocket suspended from one side and a strap which
went over the shoulder. Parks gave the Indians a bill of groceries for one
of these purses. He also bartered calico for wild flowers, venison, and
wild fowl. Parks was kind to the Indians and found their trade profit-

able. By keeping a gun over the door, he avoided trouble with the hostile ones. When they entered the store, he took the "American fire-and-thunder" off the hook, and trouble fled through the door. Toward the close of the fifties, Fort Worth lost Parks, for upon his father's death, he returned to Red River County to manage the family estate.

What Fort Town lost commercially, it gained musically. Too gregarious and fun-loving to remain on his farm five miles from town, John Durrett moved his family to a home on Fort Town's bluff. The music he made with his voice and fiddle, as one pioneer expressed it, was "the very cream of our simple and somewhat limited enjoyment." On the square during dull hours of business or at parties, "Uncle Jack," as he was called, reeled off among the tunes then popular: "Forked Deer," "Billy in the Low Ground," "Dilcey Hawkins," "Buffalo Gals," and "Black Jack Grove."

And Uncle Jack had more listeners on the square as the weekly market days advanced into the year 1855. The population of Tarrant County was increasing. That meant more business around the public square. There were 280 men subject to jury duty in the county. In the 1855 election for state land commissioner, there were 684 votes cast in Tarrant. This was sixty-five more votes than the total white population in the county in 1850. The slave population had also increased since 1850 from sixty-five to 280. That meant more grain and cotton fields for Tarrant and more trade for Fort Town. And on the public square, two fathers treated their friends to a celebration for increases in their families. In January, Thomas Harrison Daggett was born to Henry Daggett, and Rowan Tucker was born four miles north of the square.

Religious life in Fort Town was shaping into denominational groups by the year 1855. Early in the fifties, a few citizens had formed a Methodist Society so that they could worship in the homes of the members when the Reverends Lewis J. Wright and William Bates, circuit riders, came from Denton. By 1854, Reverend John Wesley Chalk, upon whom the Masonic Lodge 148 conferred the first initial degree of Masonry, became the first more or less permanent preacher, alternating at services with the Reverend Walter South, a circuit rider. The steps in faith taken by the Methodist Society was the beginning of the First Methodist Church. The Baptists met in the home of Press Farmer and other residents, to hear the zealous Noah T. Byars. His followers were enthusiastic as he rode through the county organizing churches.

In the home of Dr. Peak, Mrs. Peak organized the Union Sunday School. In the summer of that year, the First Christian Church was organized in this residence, with the aid of a wandering harvest hand—the

Reverend A. M. Dean. He toiled by day in Colonel Terry's wheat field, and after sundown rode to Fort Town to labor for his faith, bringing together the first church of that denomination. Later he moved on to new conversions, and the pulpit was filled by a succession of ministers.

1855 was the year that men of the town formed beef clubs in order to supply their needs for beef without waste, since there was neither ice nor a butcher shop. Once a week, first one club member then another would supply a beef. The one providing the beef of the week would claim the hide, while the steaks and roasts would be served to the members as they wished. Everyone kept several hogs which were fattened; and when winter came, were slaughtered. The hams and middlings were smoked and hung in the smokehouses with the highly seasoned sausages stuffed into improvised casings.

On an April evening in 1854, ten Masons "by virtue of a dispensation" by the Most Worshipful Grand Master William M. Taylor, met to organize the first Blue Lodge in Fort Worth. John M. Crockett, member of Tannehill Lodge in Dallas, presided. Meetings were held in a room above the store run by Julian Feild and Lawrence Steele. First officers installed were: Julian Feild, Worshipful Master; W. K. Masten, Senior Warden; A. M. Keen, Junior Warden; M. J. Brinson, Treasurer; Lawrence Steele, Senior Deacon; J. W. Smith, Junior Deacon; John Peter Smith, Secretary; and W. B. Tucker, Tiler. Among the first Masons other than the officers listed were Middleton Tate Johnson, W. P. Burts, George Newman, the three Daggetts, Sam Sealy, Joe Snider, W. H. Overton, John J. Purvis, W. T. Ferguson, H. C. Johnson, J. W. Chalk, and J. C. Terrell. On January 18, 1855, the first Masonic lodge in Tarrant County, Lodge 148, was granted its charter. There was not another within a radius of thirty miles, and this Fort Worth Lodge was the last outpost of the Masonic Order on the West Texas frontier in January of 1855.

1856

Fort Town's skyline underwent its greatest alteration during the first decade of its existence this year of 1856.

The first Tarrant County jail was erected on the southeast corner of present Belknap and Jones streets. Colonel Johnson gave the land for it, it being a part of the M. Baugh survey which he owned, and on which later the courthouse and public square were located. Captain Daggett paid for the construction of the jail. Johnson and Daggett made these contributions as inducements to make Fort Town the county seat. The jail was built during the term of office of John York, the second man to serve as county sheriff, an achievement of which he was proud.

A startling change was the construction of the first two-story brick building. A brick mercantile store with the sign of Brinson and Slaughter across its façade, lifted the town from the category of a mere collection of log cabins. It was located on the southwest corner of Weatherford and Houston streets. Sam Sealy had supplied the bricks. He had come in 1854, joined the Masonic lodge, and opened Fort Worth's first brickyard. His adobe bricks had the appearance of crude concrete blocks. They would further promote the aspirations of the log cabin village to reach the true status of a town. People rode into town to see the new brick building of Brinson and Slaughter. On the second floor, they attended the county and state district courts. Famous attorneys who tried cases here were John C. McCoy, Nat M. Burford and J. K. P. Record of Dallas, Judges Ferris and A. Mazi Bradshaw of Waxahachie, John H. Reagan, Judge G. A. Evarts and Thomas J. Jennings.

Julian Feild established the first flour mill at the extreme end of Mill Street on the bank of the Trinity in 1856, and nearby was his sawmill. Leonard's parking lot occupies the area today. No longer did Fort Towners have to go miles to have their grain ground; nor were they required to pound by hand with their stone mortars. John White's ox freighter could not carry enough flour for all the inhabitants. Some did not have the dollars for "store-bought flour." Later, Archibald Leonard's mill nine miles northeast of Fort Town, and Dr. Woods' mill in the far western portion of White Settlement, increased the community's facilities for easier living.

Feild's mill became the crossroads for the trader who wanted to know the latest market prices in barter or hard money. The place teemed with both local and national news for settlers from the southern and eastern sections of the United States moving to Parker and Palo Pinto counties, or farther west. They stopped at Feild's mill before fording the Clear Fork and heading into the wilderness; also the White Settlement inhabitants stopped on their way to Fort Town. Captain J. C. Terrell, in his book *Early Days of Fort Worth*, quotes Uncle Jack Durrett giving directions for the way to Weatherford to one stranger leaving Steele's Tavern. With a bow and expectorating preface, Durrett said:

Weatherford was the county seat of Parker County, which was just thirty miles square and twenty-eight miles due west of Fort Worth; to leave R. H. and William King's blacksmith shop to the left, and also Feild's mill where Judge Seaborne [Seburn] Gilmore licked the miller who was charged with over-tolling; then to cross Clear Fork below the Blue Hole, where Parson

A. N. Dean baptized C. A. Harper, and where Larry Steele's steers and negro were drowned; rising the bank on the other side he'd see a log cabin with a wagon road on both sides, where Squire Stephen Terry married a couple. . . . Take either road, for they come together in 300 yards; proceeding due west he would leave the first house to his left; that Uncle John Kinder lived there, concededly the best offhand rifle shot in Texas, though Judge Gilmore, C. G. Payne and Paul Tyler were good seconds. . . . The fact is, Stranger, there is but one plainly traveled road from here west, and it leads directly to Weatherford.

In 1856, merchandising had lost its venturing thrill for Lawrence Steele. He sold his interest in the store, and built an impressive two-story concrete hotel building on the northwest corner of the public square between present Belknap and Bluff streets. He opened for business under the name Steele's Tavern, and prided himself on its modern accommodations. On the lower floor, the west room was the office and lounging room for men. In this room, Steele provided a stagecoach office in 1856, the first office to sell passenger transportation in Fort Worth. The east room was a parlor and sitting room for ladies. Bedrooms were on the second floor. In front of the hotel on a scaffold, Steele hung a bell which arrived in 1855. It was the town's greatest social asset for children and adults alike.

In 1782, six years after the Liberty Bell rang in Philadelphia, this bell was being made in London; and mellowed by seventy-three years of ringing, it came to Fort Town as the property of Lawrence Steele. Placed on the northwest corner of the public square, it rang to the rhythm of the town's everyday life, keyed to freedom in the frontier of America's new Southwest. And although from faraway London, it seemed to sense that it was a part of every inhabitant's life. It belonged. It clanged with insistence when fire visited the town; it rang with joy for weddings; it called a command to the children at school time; it announced breakfast, dinner, and supper to hungry frontiersmen; it pleaded with the families on Sunday to attend church, and it tolled the funeral dirge as though it wept. The citizens loved it.

Today it is known as the Masonic bell. In 1871, Oscar J. Lawrence and his sister, Miss Mary Victoria Lawrence, teaching school in the first Masonic Lodge building, raised money by public subscription to purchase the bell for lodge and school purposes. It was then hung in the belfry over the Masonic Hall. Each time the Masonic Lodge 148 built a new building, the bell was fondly installed. It was moved from the first lodge building to a new one on Second and Main streets. It is now preserved with care in the Masonic Temple located on the corner of Henderson and Lancaster; and it is rung only on state occasions.

Just off the square on present Main Street, Noel Burton opened Fort Town's first saloon in 1856—First and Last Chance Saloon. This was a literally correct trade name, for it did not matter from which direction one entered the town it was the first and only chance a fellow had to buy Robertson County Kentucky whiskey, local moonshine, or peach brandy. Burton's brandy was popular. He had driven his oxteam in the Kentucky caravan in 1856. Since he was a young bachelor, his wagon was not loaded with household goods. Instead, it creaked with a load of hogsheads which held from 100 to 140 gallons of liquid. Some of these had peach brandy. Many were filled with dried fruits which made Fort Town's famous local brandy. Others contained empty pint bottles packed in cottonseed to be filled when he opened his saloon.

After a year of robust and rugged trading, Burton decided that he did not have the necessary physique requisite for a saloonkeeper in this town. The law forbade the selling of more than one pint at a time over the counter; to which, it was alleged, some fellows questioned, "What's the law? I want more, and aint I got the power to git it?" Brawls followed. Burton was neither a wrestler nor a fighter girded with iron muscles. Brawls became more frequent as he tried to operate under the law. When one became almost a disaster, he decided he was too young to die. He sold the First and Last Chance Saloon and became a farmer. Captain Daggett had always liked young Noel Burton, and to help him out of his difficulty, gave Burton one hundred acres east of Fort Worth. The cottonseed brought as packing was now planted. Potatoes, people said, would not grow here. Burton obtained seed potatoes from Dallas and became a successful potato farmer.

A new building that year was Fort Worth's first post office—a one-story wooden structure on the west side of present Main Street between Second and Third streets. The doors opened to the public on February 28, 1856. Julian Feild, appointed by President Franklin Pierce, was the first postmaster. Perhaps the job was merely a civic responsibility which men added to their serious business of making a living, and may explain the rapid succession of postmasters during the 1850s, for there were four more of them within as many years. Finally, in June 1860, George Boon was appointed and held the post throughout the Civil War. At least, it may be said that it was a demanding job, for a man was forced to keep irregular hours. He must be on hand when the stagecoaches arrived in order to receive and to distribute the mail. Stagecoaches did not operate on a time schedule. The timetable gave only approximate times of arrival. Weather, ruts, and bridgeless streams made the stagecoach schedules, sometimes delaying arrival from one day to a week.

The opening of the post office coincided with the first stagecoach licensed to carry the United States mail. Both events were strides in the town's progress. Formerly, the only means of receiving mail was by rider once a week from Dallas, which was the end of the stagecoach lines licensed to carry the mail. Hence national and state news were days or weeks old when the *St. Louis Missouri Republican* or *Globe-Democrat*, *New York Tribune*, *New Orleans Picayune*, *Austin State Gazette*, *Dallas Herald*, and the *Daily News of Galveston* arrived by mail. In 1856 the United States Mail Line, given a contract to operate from Dallas to Fort Belknap, connected Dallas and Fort Worth with the army posts in North Texas.

July 18, 1856, was the epoch-making day for Fort Towners when the first licensed stage arrived. The townspeople did not behave normally on that occasion, for this event was like another spike nailing down their village on the prairies. When the waiting crowd, watching in the direction of Birdville, saw the first signs of prairie dust rising, hats were thrown in the air, pistols were fired, and some men rode out on a gallop to meet the United States Mail Line. Tonkawa Indians in town to trade stood amazed by the exuberance manifested by the white braves. Amidst deafening hurrahs, the stagecoach rumbled to a stop in front of Steele's Tavern. After the passengers alighted, the crowd followed the stagecoach as it slowly rolled to the new post office where Julian Feild ceremoniously received the first mail packets.

Next morning, early risers gathered to see the stagecoach off. The horses nosed west under the snapping whip of the driver, determined to reach Fort Belknap in record-breaking time. Hence the street running east and west on the north side of the county courthouse is called Belknap in honor of this fort, the largest frontier federal post in Texas for many years. It was built near the Brazos in present-day Young County in 1851.

The first brick residence built by Mr. Slaughter from Sealy's brickyard was another contribution to the change from log cabin village to a realistic town. This "modern" gabled home was built in 1855, according to Captain Joseph Terrell, and was located on the site known today as the southeast corner of West Seventh and Taylor streets. Mr. Slaughter sold it to Mr. M. J. Brinson, who in turn sold it to Mr. George Smith, a shoemaker and a merchant.

Dr. and Mrs. Peak were the next to build a nice house. In 1856 they bought a parcel of land from Colonel M. T. Johnson situated on the Dallas road, which is now the south part of the block bounded by Houston, Throckmorton, Weatherford and First streets. Mrs. Peak planted trees and flowers which she nurtured with water drawn daily from the river and hauled in. A room was added on where the doctor prepared his medicines and opened the town's first drug store under the name of Maitland and Peak.

This title, "drug store," had multiple meanings. There teeth were pulled, broken bones set, and medicine, shockingly unpalatable, was compounded and dispensed. Doctor Peak left records of his prescriptions. His pain-killer was a mixture of alcohol, pepper, mustard, sassafras root, ammonia, and camphor gum. For coughs with "expectoration and night sweats," the remedy was a compound of honey, diluted sulphuric acid, and tincture of opium. "Cholera infantum and summer complaints" were cured with a mixture of charcoal, rhubarb, and ipecac. "To sweat out a cold or ache," a compound of quinine, camphor gum, opium and nitrate of silver was prescribed. Among the trials of youth were being forced by threats or enticed by a sugary reward to swallow Peak's "blue mass," a mercury preparation; and in winter, to wear a lump of his asafetida in a sack suspended around the neck to ward off diseases. Eye ointment was another youthful horror to be born, for it temporarily disfigured the face, being composed of red oxide of mercury, sulphate of zinc, and lard. And turpentine was used both externally and internally.

But all things dispensed at Maitland and Peak's store were not bitter to contemplate. There were colognes, writing paper, laundry soap, ink at twenty cents a bottle, thermometers at $1.25 each, brandy, tobacco, beef, and mustang liniment. In an account book indicative of Doctor Peak's expert bookkeeping is listed in fine penmanship the prices of his goods along with his medical fees. Sometimes he sold beef for three cents a pound and a hindquarter for four cents a pound. Quinine was sold for three cents a grain, sixty cents a drachm and $4.80 an ounce; and it was in demand to combat the constant enemy—malaria fever. His fees were reasonable in frontier terms: $1.00 for each tooth pulled, $1.50 to $2.00 for medical calls "unless detention occurred," when $5 was the usual fee.

The Maitland and Peak Drug Store did not operate many months without competition. William T. Ferguson brought his wife and three small daughters to Fort Town in 1856, built a home in which is now the 400 block of East Weatherford, and established a drug store on the northwest corner of Second and Commerce streets, the site of W. C. Stripling's Parking Garage. Thirty-six-year-old Ferguson had heard from his companions of the Mexican War, and from those of his father, of the high, healthy, and rich Grand Prairie. Born in Illinois, he had married in Kentucky in 1844, and brought his bride to East Texas. His father, Isaac Powell Ferguson, followed him to Texas in 1846; and shortly thereafter, marched with the Texans to the Mexican War. Serving under General

Worth until after the capture of Mexico City, he died and was buried with military honors by the Masons, in the Mexican capital. Bonds of friendship of the Fergusons with the Daggetts, Turners, and other Mexican War veterans drew young William Ferguson to Fort Town in their wake.

Other new buildings and more newcomers continued to appear. But the contents of all wagons coming in were not the same. One prairie schooner brought John Adams Mitchell, a carpenter, his wife Mary, and their infant son, Charles. Shortly after Mr. Mitchell had alighted, the town boosters found a residence for him, and had obtained his promise to cast a favorable vote for Fort Town as the county seat in the upcoming election. The Mitchell family would make a difference to the community. From Danville, Virginia, they had come part of the way by boat via Shreveport. From there, they had been on the road three months because of their precious load: Mary's piano, the second such instrument to grace the town. Mrs. Mitchell became the first music teacher. In the evenings, as a pianist, she entertained the inhabitants. In 1856, she opened the first girls' school in the county, and later became the first teacher in the White Settlement and the famous instructor of the "sunbonnet girls."

Fort Town being "on the make," its population growth was conversation. The accuracy of its census was jealously maintained, as is illustrated by one pioneer's story. On the afternoon of June 14, 1856, a traveler stopped at King's blacksmith shop. While his horse was being shod he inquired of the smithy as to the size of the town. The answer was sixty-seven people.

A lad, the smith's helper, made a correction. "They's sixty-eight, mister." An argument followed, and the lad made a wager with Dick King that for twenty-five cents, he could prove his point. The blacksmith then began to enumerate the citizens, while the traveler, with pencil and paper, kept score. When the smithy finished, the enumeration was sixty-seven. "Now, see?" said the smithy.

The lad retorted, "Yes, but you left out Doc Peak's boy what was born last night!" This favorite pioneer story does not tally, however, with the United States census, which gave the estimated figure of 350 population in 1856. The federal census probably included not only the people in the village on the bluff, but also the outlying settlements of the county. Dick King was counting only the inhabitants on the bluff.

Though Fort Town had only sixty-eight persons in June, 1856, life was nonetheless spirited. Men worked, hunted, and engaged in a little betting. In Doctor Peak's Betting Book, which he kept like an orderly diary, he recorded his bets of 1856. On June twenty-first, he bet Paul Tyler "a pair of boots valued at $10, that Kentucky would cast her next electorial vote for Fillmore for president." On August fourth, he "bet Abe Harris an elegant toilet table (or its price), to be worth at least $25," that C. C. Lacy "would win the election over A. G. Walker for district surveyor." Harris took the negative. On August seventeenth, Peak bet two pairs of boots valued at $20 to one pair valued at $10 that James Buchanan would be the next president if he ran as a Democrat. Theo Petty took the negative.

Fort Town men were also good fathers concerned with the education of their children. From the record we learn:

Pursuant to the expressed will of the citizens of Fort Worth in election, the following gentlemen met in session on Tuesday, September 2, 1856 for the purpose of organizing the Board of Trustees for the government and the control of the Male and Female Schools about to be initiated at this place: Colonel Nat Terry, A. D. Johnson, M. J. Brinson, Thomas O. Moody, William Moseley, Julian Feild, and C. M. Peak.

Officers elected for the school board were Mosely, president; Feild, vice-president; Doctor Peak, secretary; Brinson, treasurer. They provided for a "Male Department of the Institute" which would begin session on September 8, 1856, and continue for ten months under the direction of Professor M. D. Kennedy. The "Female Department" was to be in charge of Mrs. John A. Mitchell. They fixed tuition prices for ten months as follows: Primary Department $16, Senior, $24, all other classes $25.

No sooner had the meeting adjourned than these citizens, no doubt, turned from local government to national politics. It was 1856, a presidential election year. They were Democrats voting for James Buchanan of Pennsylvania; but the effects of the summer campaigns of the candidates made them anxious. The Know-Nothing party and the Whigs, supporting former President Fillmore, were not to be feared. But John C. Fremont of California, the first presidential nominee of the new Republican party, was the candidate to watch because his popularity was gaining in the north and west. His slogan, "Free labor, free speech, free men, free Kansas and Fremont," was too much of a vote catcher, they decided. And the question was asked, "Why doesn't the Democratic party get an ensnaring slogan to aid Buchanan?" In November, they would vote for Buchanan and impatiently await the news to learn who was to be inaugurated the following March.

The local political election, however, exceeded in interest the national one. A Tarrant County election was not an ordinary affair, but one in-

flated with hydrogen sulphide. Since the election of 1850 making Birdville the county seat, ambition churned in the minds of Fort Town leaders, especially Captain Daggett. These leaders, fertile in plans and sharp
in political strategy—or shall we say diplomacy—had nurtured the development of a local pride which eventually surged through every Tarrant citizen, and broke bonds in November 1856.

Fort Town had friends in the Texas legislature and Tarrant County's
representative in the house, Captain Daggett, a resolute statesman. After
much of Daggett's political maneuvering on August 26, 1856, the legislature provided for a second election in which the citizens of Tarrant
County were again to decide the location of their county seat. The election was to be held in November. Preparations had been extensive. In
fact, since the 1850 election, every male newcomer "after partaking of a
little hospitality" was solicited for his vote. Now the maneuvering was
being secret and wary. No ruse would rob Fort Worthians of victory. On
election day, the square was bustling earlier than usual. Captain Daggett, Peter Smith, Jack Brinson, Julian Feild, Max Dunn, John York,
Tom Johnson, and Doctor Peak were stirring. In front of the two mercantile stores were placed barrels of whiskey with new dippers attached;
and beside each barrel was a bucket of sugar for those who liked their
whiskey sweet. Birdville had no persuasive liquid. It was not their fault.
Birdville had purchased a barrel of whiskey, and for safekeeping, hid it
in an oak grove. This was a political war. In order to disarm the enemy,
Fort Worth warriors in the darkness of election eve, went to the grove,
siphoned Birdville's whiskey into their barrel, and returned to Fort
Worth with more ammunition.

The county possessed seven or eight polling places, the chief ones being Birdville, Fort Worth, Simcoe Popplewell's place a few miles southeast of Fort Worth, Leonard's Mill, Robinson's Mill, and Johnson's Station. Fort Town leaders established their private counting house in
Doctor Peak's office. From there all day they circulated back and forth
to the square, encouraging voters, and keeping a score sheet, for they
had hired riders to bring them reports during the day concerning the
balloting in the other voting places. It was said that an Irishman, as he
moved from barrel to barrel, then circled the square before another
round, rolled up votes with his jokes and with this chant: "Fort Worth
water tastes like whiskey, Fort Worth salt tastes like sugar, hur-rah for
Fort Worth."

When afternoon came, votes were getting scarce, and hours were few.
It was time for some more explosive politics. Brinson jumped on a box in
the square and shouted, "Something has to happen d—— quick!" Some-

thing did. The crowd cheered as Julian Feild and Max Dunn with running jumps mounted their horses, and one of them called, "We will dig out some more votes!" They galloped their steeds to Popplewell's polling place, knowing that Simcoe, a prosperous farmer with influence, and a Birdville supporter, might sway votes. Telling nearby dwellers of the need of more ballots for Fort Town, they coaxed a few farmers to Popplewell's.

Sam Woody and his boys swung the tide in favor of Fort Worth. Woody had come from Tennessee, joining his daughter, Mrs. Press Farmer, in 1849. He became, and remained, a spirited Fort Town booster, even while acquiring a sizable tract of good land across Tarrant County's line, making him a citizen of Wise County, and giving him the distinction of building the first log home in that county. Sam forgot Wise County citizenship in his eagerness to help his old friends of Fort Town win their desire of six-years standing.

On election day, Woody took fourteen of his Wise County neighbors and went to Fort Worth. They were not a prohibitionist crowd, but Sam convinced them that they should not imbibe the hospitality offered on the square. In Woody's words: "Boys, we've got to stay sober till this election is over. I must see that each of you votes, so we must hold till we get home. It is a penitentiary offense, and if they find us defrauding the ballot, we will have to leave home for several years."

They followed his counsel. Soberly milling around in the crowd, they joined the pranksters in their fun. Birdville people thought they were citizens from the far western part of Tarrant County. In mid-afternoon, Woody decided it was time to act. He corralled his fourteen neighbors and led them to the poll. Pretending to be in a rush, he pushed forward toward the judges saying, "Come on, boys, let's vote, for we've got a long way to go and must get home before dark." Fifteen votes were cast for Fort Worth as the county seat. These voters were not challenged.

At dusk, two galloping horsemen from Birdville came clattering and whooping to the square, yelling, "Hell's afloat and no pitch hot! Fort Worth has won!" Later in the evening two Fort Worthians came from Birdville with the authentic word. Fort Worth had edged to victory by thirteen votes. Some say it was seven; some say it was was three. Whether thirteen, seven or three, Sam Woody claimed that he turned the tide; and this he did with his fifteen Wise County votes.

Birdville citizens declared that "Fort Worth voted every man as far west as the Rio Grande," and by an expert survey, "They were not able to find as many male citizens in the entire county as voted that day." Birdville had reason to doubt. Statistics should count for something.

There were more settlers in Tarrant County east of the West Fork and Clear Fork of the Trinity than west of these streams, statistics which Birdville could not reconcile with election results.

The day ended with victory. The night was spent in celebration. From somewhere came a barrel of pitch; axes rapidly chunked it; threw it on to the roaring bonfire. The skies were lighted summoning the outlying laggards to the fun. New kegs of whiskey were rolled out of Burton's First and Last Chance Saloon, placed about the square, and opened. From the mercantile stores came packing boxes to make a platform, from which victorious leaders made speeches. Each speech ended in a thunder of whoops, as the speaker was lifted on the backs of men and taken for a jostling ride around the blazing bonfires.

Done with speech-making, Uncle Jack Durrett was lifted on high by the crowd, placed upon the packing boxes, and cheered into music. His exuberance that night, as great as the merriest cowboy, was poured into music-making. His head bobbed; his feet patted to emphasize the rhythm of his fiddling. Until many hours past midnight, Uncle Jack fiddled as the crowd danced again and again through his repertoire: "Billy in the Low Grounds," "Money Musk," "Sally Gooden," "Jenny Put the Kettle On," "Dog in the Rye Straw," "The Campbells Are Coming," "Forked Deer" and "Pop Goes the Weasel." Toward morning, the callers were hoarse, Uncle Jack exhausted, and the dancers tired. Nevertheless, the political victory was worth the celebration because Fort Worth, as the county seat of Tarrant, was on its way to becoming a permanent town in the West.

Such an explosion of human vitality had repercussions which were both tragic and amusing. Political feuding between men of Birdville and Fort Worth mounted after the county seat election and continued into the eighteen-sixties. One pistol battle followed another. Even a new lexicon—"mixed crowd"—was added to the vocabulary of Tarrant County citizens. "Mixed crowds" meant the people consisting of both Fort Worth and Birdville supporters. During the 1860s a mixed crowd gathered at the Cold Springs for a barbecue. Loud censorious words of A. Y. Fowler, Fort Worth lawyer, and Hiram Calloway dispelled the merry-making. The incident was climaxed by Calloway pushing Fowler over a cliff. In the fall Fowler broke his arm. Sheriff John B. York defended Calloway, stating that Fowler's fall was accidental. Both body and pride hurt, Fowler went home to sulk. A few days of smoldering resentment became a flame. When Fowler met Sheriff York in Fort Town west of the courthouse, "as if by signal, both men drew pistols and fired. Each died."

Gunfire and death did not teach the warring communities the error of their ways. Increment of anger and arguments produced disturbing news. Jack Brinson, George Slaughter, and Tom Johnson had an argument in 1856 with a man named Tucker—a Birdville supporter. Tucker was killed. Brinson, Slaughter, and Johnson were tried at the new Tarrant County Courthouse and acquitted. That, however, did not end the feud. To the county seat dispute which divided men there came another political problem to sharpen the division which passed into the realm of an editorial war. John J. Courtney, editor of Tarrant County's first newspaper, the *Birdville Western Express* founded in 1855, supported the moving of the county seat to Fort Worth, and was a resolute secessionist, believing that only by secession from the Union could slavery be preserved. Editor of Birdville's other weekly paper, the *Birdville Union*, founded in 1857, was A. G. Walker, "who laid out the county," was a Birdville supporter and a Union man—two causes for which he fought in caustic diatribes through the pages of his paper. Violent exchange of weekly editorials between Courtney and Walker finally involved personal affronts ending in a pistol battle. Walker, the quicker on the trigger, killed Courtney. Not giving up the fight to return the county seat to Birdville, Walker lived to become the thorn in the flesh of Fort Worth supporters and secessionists during the Civil War.

Children of the two towns took up the feud of their elders. Boys from both localities, after calling one another names, resorted to fighting. Birdville youths were taught that the people of Fort Worth were robbers, and they addressed them as such. Fort Town boys taunted their opponents with the invective, "weaklings," only to learn frequently by bloody noses that this was not so.

After Fort Worth won the county seat election, Charles Turner was appointed chairman of the committee of men responsible for transferring the official records from Birdville to Fort Worth. The committee rode in the night to Birdville and under cover of darkness silently and secretly removed to Fort Worth the records and furniture consisting of a desk, an old table, and a few chairs. This is what happened according to Elizabeth Terry Chapman, whose father, Stephen Terry, was a member of the party. She refutes the dramatized tale of horsemen escorting from Birdville a wagon loaded with records and furniture on top of which perched three fiddlers making gay music as the citizens painfully witnessed the proceedings.

For Birdville citizens their heartbreaks changed into bitterness, as "Court Monday" had become like any other day. Long lines of buggies and wagons were gone from the hitching posts. Spectacled lawyers, farmers, cowboys, merchants were not to be seen about the Birdville courthouse. When the bell of the town's hostelry rang at noon, there was no rush for a center position at the table, the most desired place where platters of meat and bowls of vegetables from each end of the table of necessity crossed. Aisles of the Birdville stores were deserted where previously were heard haggling battles among horsetraders. No longer did Birdville's mart resound with keen bargaining in cattle, grain, and real estate, for now on court Monday, men who had something to sell, or were looking for bargains, went to Fort Worth. As business declined, and stores failed, wagons of citizens began leaving town. Birdville dwindled into a hamlet. A few of Birdville's leaders—Edward Hovenkamp, Dr. B. F. Barkley, and Walker—remained, struggling to fuse new life into the place, and all the while asserting that Fort Worth won the election by fraud. By their agitation, they succeeded later in bringing the controversy before the legislature.

1857

The bell on Fort Town's square rang out the exuberant year of 1856, and pealed in the less tempestuous year of 1857. Nature would require a period of calm after such an outburst of energy and achievement as marked previous year. Now that the town was the county seat, it wore its distinction uneasily because Birdville continued to dispute the election and worked for the return of the seat.

Without a courthouse, Captain Daggett mused, there would be no tangible victory. So the next morning after the night-long victory celebration, he prepared to send A. L. Harris, Luntz Joplin, and Charles Daggett with wagons and oxteams to Cherokee County to buy lumber from the "Rough and Ready Mill." The three men made a quick haul with the lumber. Hammers and saws powered with frenzied wills rushed headlong to build a small three-room structure, the assured way to anchor their new importance.

This courthouse, a gift of Captain Daggett, had a wide hall running through the center. Like the Romans' Temple of Janus whose doors were always open in time of peace, so were the doors of the new Tarrant County Courthouse. Consequently, the town's inebriates who did not want to go home, as well as the stray hogs, had a haven for the night in the courthouse hall. It was located on the present west lawn of today's building, near the curb on Houston Street. The county and district clerks had their offices there; and it served the people of Tarrant County until 1866.

In step with the tune of progress, the town continued the building boom. Masonic Lodge 148 contributed to the beauty of the growing town. Chartered since January 1855, the lodge was sufficiently prosperous to erect an imposing lodge building. It stood on the block now surrounded by East Belknap, Grove, East Bluff, and Jones streets. A two-story brick structure, facing west, it had distinctive features. On two sides of each floor, there were eight windows, four on a side; and on the second floor, there was a window across the front. There were double doors for entrance, and a belfry without a bell until 1871, when the Steele's Tavern bell was purchased. This building served not for just lodge meetings, but was used for church, communal gatherings, and school.

The Christian Church joined the building boom in 1857. The membership had outgrown Dr. Peak's home, and was now ready to erect a two-room concrete structure for church and school purposes, on the present site of West Belknap and Lamar streets. During the week, a teacher challenged Fort Town's youths to take up the long task of learning, and sometimes with peppery discipline. On Sunday, these reluctant scholars returned with their parents to hear the circuit-riding ministers, whose sermons were as sobering as the teacher's lectures. The double-serving function of school and church continued until the Civil War caused Professor J. T. Turner to lay aside his books and paddle. (In the east section of the village—present-day 502 East Belknap—another school was maintained by Miss Mary Armstead.)

The *Dallas Herald* announced further progress for Fort Town that summer. The Federal government had issued a new contract for a mail and stagecoach line from Dallas via Birdville, Fort Worth and Weatherford to Fort Belknap. The contract read in part:

Contract Number 8083 accepted on April 23, 1857, was let to Robert A. Burney and Calvin J. Fuller to convey the mail 145 once a week and back over the following route:

From Dallas
Via Buck and Breck. Estb. 9/18, 1857
  " Estill's Station.   " 7/16/57
  " Birdville
  " Fort Worth
  " Delphine (west part of Tarrant Co.) Estb. 3/15/57
  " Newburg (Parker Co.) Estb. 6/20/57
  " Weatherford
  " Copper Hill (Parker Co.) Estb. 8/8/57
  " Pleasant Valley (Palo Pinto Co.) Estab. 8/8/57
  " Russell's Store (Palo Pinto Co.)   "   "
  " Brazos Agency

This same year, Fort Town lost one of its first citizens. Julian Feild resigned as postmaster, and sold his store and mill. He went with a Mr. Mann to about sixteen miles south of the village, and erected the first steam-run mill in the county. Through farmers' trade and federal contracts to supply flour to Indian reservations and army posts in West Texas as well as Indian Territory and New Mexico, the mill grew to the rating of finest in the Southwest. A town developed around this mill, named Mansfield in honor of the two men.

David Mauck became sole owner of Feild's water mill, which operated as a blessing to the settlers because the other mills in the county were too far away. These other mills were "Witt's southeast of Birdville, Johnson's at Johnson's Station, and John Robinson's about sixteen miles southwest of the Clear Fork." There were also Leonard's mill about nine miles northeast of Fort Worth, and Wood's mill of small capacity in the extreme western area of the White Settlement.

Though Fort Town lost one distinguished citizen, it gained another— Joseph Christopher Terrell, known as Captain Terrell after the Civil War. A lawyer, who would write some of the chapters in the history of Fort Worth, Terrell was seeking a life packed with action. He found it here. His twenty-six years of life had not been prosaic. His people were Virginians of Quaker descent. He had been born in Tennessee while his family was en route to Missouri, where his father, Dr. C. J. Terrell, died one year after they established a home at Boonville. He studied law under his brother, Alexander W. Terrell, in St. Joseph, Missouri. At the age of twenty, he joined the gold seekers on the Pacific Coast and lived in California and Oregon awhile. In 1856 he returned home to see his mother. In 1857 he set out again for California, going by way of Austin, Texas, where his brother Alexander had become a prominent Texas statesman.

Leaving Austin for Fort Worth from whence he was to take the Butterfield Stage from Jacksboro on out to California, he had as traveling companions Colonel Middle Tate Johnson, James Throckmorton, and Charley De Morse of the newspaper *Clarksville Standard.* As the stagecoach rolled along, these companions no doubt attempted to detract him from his goal by tantalizing the young man with talk about the marvels of Texas. They were successful. His plans for California began to lose their attractiveness. Then when the stagecoach stopped at Steele's Tavern in Fort Worth, he saw, to his surprise, his schoolmate Dabney C. Dade of Springfield, Missouri, who had arrived in 1856. Terrell's California dream vanished. Dade and he formed a law partnership. But "a law office could not be found for money on any man's terms." They bought a lot on what is now the northwest corner of First and Main streets, rented a whipsaw, hired a man named John Branon, and within a few weeks had built their own law office.

In search of furniture, they went to Abe Harris, the cabinetmaker. In a shop on East Belknap near the square, Harris made furniture of excellent craftsmanship and artistic design. He selected the choice black walnut trees which were plentiful in the little forests along the Trinity, sawed them into planks, and polished the wood to a beautiful luster.

The day came for the opening of the law firm of J. C. Terrell and Dabney C. Dade. They were proud possessors of Fort Town's new office building. It was a two-room structure with chimneys at each end and an open passageway. The young lawyers, both bachelors, slept in one room and practiced law in the other. They were not tidy housekeepers. Saddles, bridles, hunting and fishing equipment cluttered the passageway. Papers and law books were strewn around, and "hospitality was only 30¢ per gallon with corncob stoppers." The law office of Dade and Terrell was a popular place. However, the bachelors made no progress with the girls.

It was an exclusive society. Even church on Sunday failed to offer opportunity for acquaintance since "the sexes were divided in church meeting sitting on opposite sides of the house, the women with heads covered, but with no chicken or bird feathers on their bonnets." Sundays were long and intolerable. The bachelors were weary of fishing, hunting, and of *Oldham's and White's Digest*. Terrell decided upon an avenue of escape from Sunday loneliness and a means of meeting the girls. He and Dade organized a Sunday School. It proved so successful that there were tears in the eyes of pretty girls when Terrell marched away to the Civil War, and Dade returned to Missouri in 1861 because he opposed secession of Texas from the Union.

An able lawyer arriving in Fort Town in January of 1857 was Junius W. Smith, a North Carolinian by birth. He had moved with his parents to Alabama, but at fifteen, was sent back to Franklin Academy in North Carolina, where he graduated. Returning to Alabama, he read law, and in 1847 was admitted to the bar in Montgomery. Entering politics, he expressed his political theories in editorials in the *Advertiser and State Gazette*. In 1856, he campaigned for the election of James Buchanan to the presidency. After the election he came to Texas seeking recovery of his failing health which he hoped to retrieve in the Fort Worth climate.

1857 was charged with political tension. Sam Houston arrived in Fort Worth, adding excitement. Fort Worthians took their politics seriously. This was the year to vote for a governor, lieutenant governor, and land commissioner. The Texas Democratic convention, representing one hundred and seven counties, met in Waco to nominate candidates for governor and other state officials. Colonel M. T. Johnson was a candidate for nomination of governor. Disturbing the politics of the state convention was the quarrel between Fort Worth and Birdville. There was a contested delegation from Tarrant County—one from Fort Worth, the other from Birdville. The Fort Worth delegation, led by Captain Daggett, was seated. The Birdville delegation, led by J. R. Wallace, was given a seat by courtesy.

The Waco convention failed to give Colonel Johnson the nomination, and instead, Hardin R. Runnels, a wealthy planter, was named the party candidate for the governorship. Sam Houston, United States senator from Texas, announced his candidacy for governor on an independent ticket, running on his record as a Jackson Democrat or Unionist. Many Texans rallied behind the "Old Hero of San Jacinto." The proslavery men supported Runnels because Houston's record on the slavery issue in the United States Senate displeased them. Houston had voted in 1848 to create the free-soil territory of Oregon, refused to sign "John C. Calhoun's protest against what he termed the aggression of free states"; and in 1854, cast his ballot against the Kansas-Nebraska Bill which opened that territory to slavery. This last vote was considered treason by the South. Proslave Texans also had not forgiven Houston for presenting to the senate the "petition of ten thousand vice-regents of Heaven for the abolition of slavery in the District of Columbia and in the ports, arsenals and dock yards of the United States." These alleged celestial agents were known to their local communities as preachers.

Citizens of Fort Worth and Tarrant County were sharply divided. Colonel Nat Terry, Charles Turner, Captain Daggett and Paul Isbell were the largest slave owners in the area, and with certain others were leaders of the proslavery group supporting Runnels. Houston stumped the state often times debating with the extreme exponent of slavery, Louis T. Wigfall, who was campaigning for Runnels. Houston and Wigfall debated at Birdville. Fort Worthians went in a mass. That was the only time Fort Town was a deserted village. It was a sharp political fray. When the debate was over Colonel Terry invited both debaters to pass the night at his plantation. Political emotions that evening were too strong for Houston to accept the hospitality. However, Wigfall became the colonel's guest.

Although Captain Daggett was a proslavery man and was determined to vote for Runnels, his friendship for Houston cut through the thick of his political allegiance. From the debate at Birdville, Houston and Daggett rode together as old friends to Fort Worth. Houston spent the night in Daggett's home, located on block six between present Main, Houston, Tenth and Eleventh streets. That evening, Houston was dispirited. The proslavery issue had alienated the political support of old friends. To add to his discomfort, the wound he had received at San Jacinto was paining him. It was an open wound and had to be dressed frequently. To climax the evening of friendship, Daggett brought out Santa Anna's silver washbowl which he had captured after the Battle of Buena Vista during the Mexican War. Using the silver washbowl, Daggett, with his own hands, bathed and dressed Houston's wound—an action symbolic of the affection of all Texans for this hero of San Jacinto. He was asserting for the people of his state and himself that, regardless of political differences which were growing bitter, Houston always would remain the hero of Texas, always would be the great general who conquered Santa Anna, the self-styled "Napoleon of the West."

Houston understood. Daggett voted to make Runnels governor. Houston lost the election, his first political defeat.

1858

The year 1858 would be one of increase.

The new stage route licensed to carry mail began to operate from Fort Worth in 1858. It was the Fort Worth-Jacksboro Stage Line. Business increased at Steele's Tavern, the stagecoach terminal. People bound for California from the eastern seaboard or from the states of the South or from South and East Texas came by stage to Fort Worth, rested a day or two at Steele's Tavern, then departed for Jacksboro, where they took the Butterfield Overland Stage, whose route made possible transportation connection between the Atlantic and Pacific coasts. It entered Texas across the Red River, proceeded to Jacksboro, one of the few stops on its route through Texas. Leaving Jacksboro, the stage crossed West Texas along the chain of United States forts to El Paso and on to Yuma and San Diego. Fort Town boosters had great sport with the travelers. They took them to the edge of the bluff, showed them the beauties of the Trinity Valley, and tried to make them forget California. They succeeded with a few. Fort Worth was to grow in importance as a stagecoach terminal until in the late 1870s it was to be the largest stagecoach terminal in the Southwest.

More newcomers built homes in the county, or passed through to counties west. Weighted with settlers, sturdy wagons would increase with each month of 1858 in spite of the fact that the discovery of the

Comstock Lode—the greatest silver strike in American history—was putting more wagons on the Oregon and California trails. In Illinois in this year, Abe Lincoln and Stephen Douglas, campaigning for election to the United States Senate, were locked in debate. Lincoln's opposition to the spread of slavery in the western territories, and Douglas' theory of squatter sovereignty doubtless caused the pioneers of that era to slap the reins over their teams and mutter a determined "gid-de-yap," to move into Texas free of this controversy.

In 1858, the population of Tarrant County had reached 4,362. More slaves cultivated more fields of grain. There was an estimated 16,431 acres in cultivation. More sheep and cattle grazed on the rolling prairies. Colonel Johnson was making more progress in promoting a trans-continental railroad route through Texas to the Pacific. And Fort Town merchants made greater profits as well as displaying a larger variety of merchandise.

A frequent visitor to the stores was Press Farmer, the freighter, and business partner of Ed Terrell, formerly supplying the fort with beef, and the father of the first child born in Fort Town in 1849. Press came from his farm south of the village to gaze at the increase and variety of merchandise. He had known and seen scarcities since 1849; and the splurge of goods made him dubious. When the clerks asked Press if he wanted something, he would reply, "No sir, I buy things for their durability, not their flashalarity."

Lucky for the merchants of Fort Worth, sheepmen west of town were either more prone to spend than Press, or had a larger amount of hard money with which to buy the "goods of flashalarity." Perhaps their hard money was easily earned. Sheepmen squatted on land that is now Arlington Heights and White Settlement, letting their sheep roam at will. These men liked this area, and sometimes under the state land law, each filed a homestead claim to 320 acres which would become his three years after applying for the patent—if in the meantime, he had lived on the land, had had it surveyed, and improved it. Today, this same land is valuable, but in the 1850s a surveyor's fee and ten dollars for registration in the State Land Office was all it cost.

When there was a good wool year, these sheepmen sought a large market. After shearing season, ox-drawn wagons filled with wool drudgingly pulled their way across North Texas to Jefferson on Red River, which had water transportation to the big wool and cattle market in New Orleans. Cattlemen also drove their cattle to Jefferson and Shreveport. Outlets for Fort Town in the 1850s to the nation's large commercial markets as well as those of Europe were Houston, Galveston, Shreveport and Jefferson. These cattle markets connected with New Orleans, which in that time was the cattle market of the nation, shipping livestock to Europe and to the eastern seaboard of the United States. Fort Town, by the route of the oxteam freighters during this period, was separated from Houston and Galveston by "six hundred miles." Jefferson and Shreveport were closer for markets to the outside world. There were approximately four hundred miles of railroad track in Texas in the late 1850s. These railroad lines radiating from Houston were decidedly not for cattle freight; and as for passenger service, it was irregular because of weather and the locomotive's habit of jumping the tracks. By 1860, the nearest railroad to Fort Town was at Millican, in the Brazos Valley below present-day College Station, the home of the Texas State Agricultural and Mechanical College.

Cattle to be driven to Jefferson and Shreveport were plentiful according to Colonel W. W. Dunn. From his saddle as his horse trotted toward Fort Town for the first time, the view of the area impressed him with its ranching potentialities. He wrote:

November 2, 1858. I crossed the Trinity on horseback. . . . When first I landed here the grass was tall, thick, and green. . . . Cows almost without number could be seen, and calves sleek and fat were all around for men to look at. I entered Fort Worth about 12 A.M.

Colonel Dunn, Virginia-born, had been a frontier trader in Kentucky, where, at the age of twenty-four, he enlisted and left for the Mexican War. Dunn understood frontier arithmetic. Grubbing, multiplied by wisdom, equaled real estate. Real estate, plus a business which served frontiersmen, equaled profits. In time, Dunn acquired real estate around Fort Town and erected in the early seventies the Mansion Hotel, which Texas newspapers reported was "one of the finest in the State at the time of its construction." It was built on Rusk Street, now Commerce, and covered the block between Fourth and Fifth streets. Later an annex was added, giving the hotel an entrance on Main Street, which was becoming the chief thoroughfare. In addition to business pursuits, Colonel Dunn turned to writing. One article, "Thirty Years in the West," was dedicated to Fort Worth. In 1889, he published a book, *Evolution and the True Light*.

A man who would give Fort Worth land for a fire hall, serve as its first mayor, and would become a competitor of Dr. Peak, was Dr. William Paxton Burts. He arrived in Fort Worth in '58. Born in Washington County, Tennessee, in 1827, Burts had graduated from Martin Academy and Washington Academy in his state and had learned to practice medicine at Geneva Medical College in New York. Near the square, on the northeast corner of Second Street and Rusk, he built his home. Dr. Burts, then thirty-five years of age, began to practice with the most recent medical knowledge. But in spite of his modern methods, it was alleged that superstition was his weakness. When riding to an important case, if a jackrabbit leaped before his horse, miles did not matter. He reined his horse, turned him around and rode home; then took a fresh start.

If the doctor indulged in a superstition, he pursued an important crusade—a water supply for the community. His favorite topic of conversation with men on the public square was the source of their water supply at home. He advocated digging deep cisterns with special care for cleanliness as a guarantee for health. Dr. Burt's efforts in this direction were not lost. In the late fifties and early sixties, several wells were dug, among them the Frenchman's well. Mr. Barbier had been a member of the French colony near Dallas. A financial fiasco made him a citizen of Fort Town, where opportunity was more easily grasped. He bought a lot for a residence on the corner of Bluff and Taylor. With a Frenchman's ingenuity for good living and a Frenchman's eye for good architecture, he built a neat house and dug a deep well. To guarantee sanitation, he constructed over the well a cone-shaped arch made of small field stones, giving it the appearance of a honeybee's hive. The charming appearance of the well might have inspired verse, but the hustling people of Fort Town were more concerned with its cool water than the beauty of design. By the close of the fifties, sixteen cisterns had been dug: four on the square and twelve within two blocks of it in the radius of present Main, Houston, Throckmorton, Commerce, and between First and Second streets. The cisterns for watering the horses were dug in the middle of the streets for three purposes: to furnish drink for those animals, to provide drainage for the streets, and to make quickly accessible a water supply for the bucket brigade in case of fire.

Fort Worth has always had its share of residents who are connected with persons of international repute. The year 1858 brought the first one of such residents, Louis H. Brown, with "an accomplished family" and a few slaves, settled in the environs of Fort Town on Marine Creek, which runs through present North Fort Worth. Mr. and Mrs. Brown reared five children whom J. C. Terrell described as "Misses Lou and Ruth, pretty and accomplished young women, and Horatio, George and Harry, boys of honor and integrity." Mrs. Brown was definitely an asset to the social life of Fort Town. Formerly a Miss Patterson of the wealthy and socially elite family of Maryland, Mrs. Brown's sister had married

Jerome Bonaparte, brother of the great Napoleon Bonaparte, Emperor of the Second French Empire.

New settlers ran the gamut of American society from aristocrats, like the Louis Browns, to the unschooled frontiersmen with natural wisdom. Ed Terrell, who had been making his living through frontier fur trapping and hunting since 1840 when he established the first Indian trading post on the Clear Fork, as heretofore related, reopened the First and Last Chance Saloon, bought from Noel Burton. He had no competition. According to Howard Peak's description in his history of Fort Worth, this saloon was west of the square on Weatherford Street in a one-room shack. In the center of the one room was a box stove. On the east side of the room, a "long bench on which sat customers awaiting the anticipated call of a newcomer or one of the gang to 'set 'em up.' " On the west wall were a few shelves displaying bottles of imported peach brandy, gin and whiskey. A crude counter served for dispensing the drinks, and upon it was placed a wooden pail filled with water to supply the chaser.

Observing everything with his keen blue eyes, Ed Terrell maintained a cheerful countenance. From behind the counter he dispensed not only good and bad liquor, but also advice, yarns and ready humor; and he perpetrated practical jokes upon his fellow townsmen, which kept his customers amused for weeks. Many men, not chronic imbibers, tarried at Terrell's for the news that was exchanged in spirited fashion. He held his monopoly of the liquor trade until Fort Town became known as Cowtown when it acquired the reputation of being a "wide open town" in the 1860s during the cattle drives when the cowboys refreshed themselves.

In May of 1858, talk was of high interest about the trip in early spring that Colonel Johnson, Junius Smith, and others had made through the counties north and west of Fort Worth to Camp Cooper, on the Clear Fork of the Brazos, a military post, then commanded by Robert E. Lee. There were expressions of pleasure when the fact was made known that Junius Smith had decided to remain in Fort Worth, forming a partnership with A. Y. Fowler in the practice of law. At once his practice became lucrative as well as his name better known, so that by late 1860 when Dabney C. Dade resigned as district attorney, Smith was appointed as his successor.

When a stagecoach driver from Weatherford, in August 1858, brought the sad news of General Edward H. Tarrant's death, church services were held in his memory. The general had many friends in Fort Town, visiting here occasionally. He and Mrs. Tarrant had recently spent one day in Fort Worth en route to the west on a business trip, at which time there was a social gathering about which Mrs. Peak wrote an account:

General Tarrant was a medium-sized, dark haired, vigorous looking man with a ruddy complexion, showing he had spent his life in the open. He was not of military bearing but a plain frontiersman, strong, alert, capable, the type of man to meet the difficulties of pioneer life, and was highly respected.

Of course, he and Dr. Peak were attending to business and were with the men of the little community most of the day, joining the ladies at the mid-day dinner table. I shall add that Mrs. Julian Feild was one of the guests.

I had heard that Mrs. Tarrant was the second wife of General Tarrant and of Indian extraction so I was particularly interested in her. I found her quite an intelligent woman of handsome features, pale complexion, dark eyes and hair and altogether she impressed me as quite charming. We had a most enjoyable social visit and then they continued their journey westward.

Trials of travel under summer heat sickened the general. Traveling on the Fort Worth-Fort Belknap road, he was stricken with illness, and was received in the home of W. B. Fondren of Copper Hill, Parker County. Mr. Fondren was county commissioner of Parker County and postmaster at Copper Hill. In the Fondren home, at the age of sixty-two, the Texas hero died on August 2, 1858, and was interred in the Fondren cemetery.

In March of 1859, General Tarrant's body was removed and reinterred near his plantation on Chambers Creek in Ellis County. The governor of Texas, leaders of Texas Masonry, and hundreds of friends attended the services. The funeral procession was a quarter of a mile long, showing homage to a veteran of the War of 1812, the Texas Revolution, a soldier of the Army of the Texas Republic, a Texas Ranger, an Indian fighter, a statesman, and a state leader of Masonry.

Though General Tarrant did not live in the county named for him, he was a visitor. In the late 1830s he had become a large landowner in the southern part of Ellis County, which he had petitioned the legislature to create. He was also instrumental in constructing the first corn mill in that area in 1847. He prospered and acquired slaves.

Time obliterated the grave until L. W. Kemp of Houston began a movement in 1928 to provide General Tarrant a hero's resting place. Seventy years after Tarrant's death, with befitting ceremonies, he was reburied in Pioneer Rest Cemetery in Fort Worth. Three years later, the state of Texas, the Willie Brewer Chapter of the United States Daughters of 1812, and public-spirited citizens of Tarrant County erected a monument over his grave.

The "disinterment of General Tarrant's body [from the Ellis County grave] was attended to personally by Kemp, with the assistance of Frank Hughes of Italy [Texas] and George Hawkins, the only two who had known the location of the grave until recently." Hughes' father was

manager of Tarrant's property at the time of the general's death; while
Hawkins' parents had been slaves owned by Tarrant. Both had attended
the funeral, when Hughes was thirteen years of age, and Hawkins, a
child of five. Both, tied to the past with affectionate reverence, labored
with care in the disinterment. They found that "the earth had acted as
a preservative. Every bone was intact, and there was much of the old
home-made coffin left, which had been made of hand-hewn oak and held
together with square hand-wrought nails."

1859

Birdville's agitation in Austin was growing more clamorous. Captain
Daggett had a plan for silencing the vociferation. Like the Biblical wise
man who built his house upon a rock which stood under the stress of
storm, he thought Fort Worth should construct a county courthouse of
stone and brick with foundation so deep in rock, and walls so thick it
would not collapse under Birdville's attack. Before the month of January
of 1859 closed, a contract was signed by Fort Worthians for a new building to replace the frame one. Forty-one citizens subscribed $2,700 to
erect it, and from the group was selected a building committee composed
of Thomas O. Moody, Lawrence Steele, M. T. Johnson, Julian Feild,
E. M. Daggett, and M. J. Brinson. They agreed that when the work was
completed, if the subscribed amount was not sufficient, this committee
would take care of the balance. The contract was signed January 12.
David Mauck, the contractor, promised to complete the construction
within that year of 1859.

The contract called for a two-story building fifty by sixty feet, to be
constructed of brick and stone work with eight rooms, one room in each
corner, and cross alleys running through the structure. The east-west
alley was to be fifteen feet wide, the north-south alley sixteen feet wide.
The foundation was to be dug down to rock and laid eighteen inches in
thickness. The building was to be heated by four fireplaces, "two in the
east end of the house and two in the west and opposite the outside."

The town fathers seriously assumed their responsibility. According to
their plans, they were building for a century of permanence. In the contract, they included a clause that the building committee would superintend the work, and approve of the material and the construction as the
building progressed. Delay in construction of the courthouse was one
enemy the town builders were determined to avoid in their quiet strategy against Birdville. Therefore, the contract provided that in event of a
dispute between the building committee and the contractors, each party

was to choose a competent judge of such work, to arbitrate; and in case they disagreed, an umpire or third party was to be summoned to resolve the trouble.

David Mauck contractor was to be paid at the rate of ten dollars per thousand for the brick and one hundred dollars extra for the stone work, the payment to be made of the following subscriptions to the extent of the same. To wit: Mauck and man, $250.00; E. L. Terrell $200.00; A. D. Johnson $100.00.

A. C. Coleman	$25.	I. N. Petty	$25.
John Kinder	25.	J. K. Allen	25.
Ples More	25.	W. A. Sanderson	25.
Los Purvis	25.	B. P. Ayers	25.
George Kinder	50.	A. Harris	50.
I. L. Hanley	25.	W. D. Conner	50.
I. W. Chapman	25.	C. G. Davenport	100.
G. P. Farmer	50.	S. Gilmore	50.
S. P. Loving	25.	I. C. Andrews	100.
Francis Knaar	25.	Wm. Moseley	50.
L. I. Edwards	50.	Wm. M. Robinson	50.
I. W. Conner	50.	Dr. Gounah	150.
N. Terry	200.	W. B. Tucker	25.
E. Wilburn	50.	L. Terry	150.
T. O. Moody	200.	Paul Isbell	50.
G. T. Petty	50.	P. E. Coleman	50.
C. M. Peak	100.	Wm. L. Brizendine	50.
L. Steel	100.	Jack Inman	25.

Making in all $2700.00 and if the amount of said subscription is not equal to the amount of said work when completed, the committee is to guarantee and provide for the payment of the balance.

In testimony whereof we the parties have hereunto subscribed our names and seals using scrawls for seals this 12th day of January, A.D. 1859.

Attest.   David Mauck
A. G. Fowler   Thos. D. Moody
                                           Lawrence Steel
                                           M. T. Johnson
                                           Julian Feild
                                           E. M. Daggett
                                           M. J. Brinson

Early each morning David Mauck brought his slaves to the public square. Throughout the winter, businessmen of Fort Town's square were forced to lift their voices to be heard above the clink and the clank of chisels and hammers, and above the grinding of the stone-cutting saw as the slaves prepared the stones. Mauck and Jere Asbury, the other contractor, were men under pressure, working under the storming protests of Birdville. Then it happened. An aggressive city spirit, as old as the world, broke out in Birdville.

Without Fort Towners' knowledge, Colonel A. G. Walker of Birdville, the senator representing Tarrant County, declared in the legislature that the election of 1856 in Tarrant was a fraud. He called for a discussion "concerning Birdville or Fort Worth as the county seat." Joseph C. Terrell said of the colonel, who was his client, that Walker "was a good citizen, though pertinacious even to stubbornness. He never surrendered nor yielded a point."

The legislature agreed to consider the issue. A joint committee was appointed to present Fort Worth's case: Colonel Johnson, representative of Tarrant County, J. W. Throckmorton, representative of Collin County, Colonel Walker and Doctor B. F. Barkley of Birdville.

The committee had legal advice. Two young lawyers from Fort Worth, Joseph C. Terrell and Peter Smith, were in Austin for a masquerade ball which they shunted aside in order to help Colonels Johnson and Throckmorton in their fight. According to Terrell, they delved into a cart of legal papers of Tarrant County in order to equip their friends with winning facts. The joint committee sat through most of the night. Instead of handing down a decision of fraud, they made a compromise. The legislature passed a bill calling for an election on the second Monday in April, 1860, at which time citizens of Tarrant were to vote for the permanent seat which might be "the geographical center of the said county, Fort Worth, Birdville or any other place." The place receiving the majority of votes would be the permanent county seat, and if no place received a majority of the legal votes, a second election was to be held.

The bill took cognizance of the courthouse then in the process of construction, and of the fact that it was being built free of charge to Tarrant taxpayers by generous Fort Towners. Section 4 of the bill stated that if Fort Worth won the election, the contractor would have twelve months after the election in which to complete the building. If Fort Worth was not chosen, the contractor and the parties who had bound themselves to build from their own purses would be released.

The legislature had given Fort Worth an opportunity to battle again— this time to retain the county seat. Another battle would not discourage the leaders. For six years since the evacuation of the fort in 1853, a small group of about ten men had struggled to convert an abandoned military post into a town. And they had been making headway. There was a public square now in place of the former prairie, where a well-beaten wagon road circled it, horsemen's paths criss-crossed; and three stagecoach lines made Andrews Tavern, formerly Steele's, the terminal. Another economic testimony was the many oxteams dozing before their freighters, loaded with hides, wool, or cotton waiting to be lashed into motion toward Jefferson, Shreveport and Houston. Other freighters carried locally milled flour into East Texas to be exchanged for finished lumber, for in 1858, twelve families were camping on the outskirts waiting for houses to be built.

Steele, becoming a stock farmer in the White Settlement late in the 1850s, had sold the tavern to Albert T. Andrews, who had come from Kentucky in 1854. Andrews had refurbished the building, adding a two-story ell of concrete and stone. On the lower floor of this addition was the dining room about thirty feet in length. The dining table was almost of equal length with benches at either side. At mealtime, many Negro waiters stood behind the guests to serve them from the too many dishes of vegetables and the too numerous platters of fish, fowl, game, and fresh meat. In summer, a large fan suspended by a rope hung over the table, spanning its entire length. Propelled by a Negro boy seated at the far end of the room, the fan shooed away the flies and cooled the guests. Andrews' was considered the most elegant dining place in the area, a center for parties and banquets; and it remained so until the 1870s.

There were many distinguished guests who had visited this hotel, and among them were: General Tarrant, Colonel Johnson, Congressman John H. Reagan, Governors James Throckmorton, Sul Ross and Oran M. Roberts.

In the center of the square, the three-room frame courthouse was without a clock, but what need did it have for a mechanical contraption, for the courthouse, itself, was an excellent timepiece. When cow ponies, mules and horses began to appear at its hitching rail, men looked from the windows of their homes across the prairie and knew the day's business had begun. Log cabins, frame shacks for stores and concrete and stone buildings were set down here and there around the square as if the town's builders had tried to make a little look like a lot.

On the southwest side of the square, the present-day southwest corner of Weatherford and Houston, was the imposing two-story concrete store of Brinson and Slaughter. On the south side, the Daggett and Turner store was in the center of the block between Main and Houston. On the north side, towards the west end, near present-day Belknap and Bluff streets, was Andrews Tavern. Also on the north side, toward the east end, was the jail, a frame building. On the east side, corner of Weatherford and Commerce, was Dick King's blacksmith shop and Tom Hagood's carpenter shop. Frank Knaar's saddlery was also on the square, its exact location unknown now.

From the high bluff on the north side of the square, men who enjoyed distant views could look toward the west and see the White Settlement. Toward the north, south and east, they could see cabin homes built in the valley near the sinuous Trinity and its tributaries: Clear Fork, West Fork, Sycamore Creek, Marine Creek, Fossil Creek, and Deer Creek. They could also see a few homes built on the bluffs outlining the Trinity.

Just off the square, looking east one could see the two-story Masonic Lodge and the cabinet shop and home of Abe Harris. Looking south was the post office in what was to be Second and Main streets, and the Maitland-Peak Drug Store and Peak home in the block between Houston and Throckmorton, with Ferguson's Drug Store nearby. Looking west, a stone's throw from the square was the First and Last Chance Saloon; while a short distance down the Belknap Road was the two-room concrete building of the First Christian Church. At the end of the first mile on the Belknap Road was the mill.

Two hundred inhabitants lived on the periphery of the town square in log and frame houses, clustered in groups, or scattered over the prairie in the area today embracing the streets around the square. South of Fourth Street was open prairie which was lighted at night by the campfires of the settlers driving wagons west. This area was interspersed with a few homes. W. H. Wiggins, who had come in 1854, settled upon land three miles west of town, later returned and bought the block now bounded by Throckmorton, Taylor, Fifth and Sixth streets. After a few years residence, he traded the entire block for five Spanish mares. Another home south of the square, famous as the first brick residence in the town, was located on the southeast corner of present-day Seventh and Taylor streets. A log house on the south prairie was that of Tom Cogdell. In 1854 he had erected a log cabin for his family between present-day Eighth and Ninth streets. Charles Louckx, an immigrant from France in 1856, had pursued the American dream to Frenchtown four miles west of Dallas. But when prosperity eluded him, he came to Fort Worth, locating where today is the Fort Worth Public Library. On the block between Main and Houston, Tenth and Eleventh, was the home of Captain Daggett. South of Daggett's and beyond the present Texas and Pacific Railway Station and yards were his fields of cotton and corn.

Now this thriving village was under the storm cloud of the county seat controversy. Perhaps this is what drew one ox-drawn wagon across the square one afternoon, rattling towards Andrews Tavern. Driving was a tall lean man, whose features with the exception of wise eyes, were hidden behind a mass of whiskers and whose skull was concealed with long hair streaming from under his broad-brimmed hat. The winds of a young month in 1859 blew this hair to and fro on his shoulders. A fighting politico since young manhood, Albert Banning Norton always sought a contest weighty with uncertain outcome rather than choosing his way in a serene valley. Fort Worth's struggle for the county seat was a battleground for his nature. No doubt he had heard the full details from Colonel Johnson, Peter Smith, J. C. Terrell and other Fort Towners frequenting Austin on business; and doubtless, too, they had spoken a challenge. It was like a bugle call to Norton that Fort Worth did not have a newspaper, while its rival, Birdville, did. So, though he was editor of the *Intelligencer* in Austin, here he was with his three-legged Washington press, bundles of paper stock, pots of ink and a small trunk. The town's leaders would ride to distant neighbors gathering subscriptions for Fort Worth's first newspaper, the *Fort Worth Whig Chief*.

Norton fitted in to Fort Town, for like many of its citizens, he had cut a figure in events of national concern. At twenty-three years of age, this educated young man had stumped Ohio in behalf of Henry Clay for president of the United States. A Whig, obsessed with his party's cause, Norton dared to debate on the platform with a seasoned statesman of Ohio, Caleb J. McNulty, campaigning to elect James K. Polk president on the Democratic ticket. Youthful Norton's presumptuousness in politics so aroused the ire of the older McNulty that during an oratorical combat, he spoke to the audience in galling derision. "A smooth-faced youth had better tarry at Jericho and grow a beard before he assays to teach men their political rights."

Unabashed, Norton bounded on his long legs to the front of the platform, where he swore that he would neither shave nor have his hair cut until Clay was elected. Henry Clay was never elected president, and Norton went to his grave without either cutting his hair or shaving his beard.

After Clay conceded the presidential election of 1844 to Polk, Norton, following the action of David Crockett in political defeat said, "The country might be going to hell, but I am going to Texas." When he arrived in 1848, he went directly to Austin in order to be in the thick of politics. With a gilt-edged introduction into political circles—an ashwood walking cane with a silver dollar head given him by the famous Henry Clay—Norton strode into Texas politics. In 1850 he bought into the Austin newspaper the *Intelligencer*, splashing its pages with his Whig philosophy. His pen was moved by a legal mind. At the age of nineteen, he had been admitted to the bar in Ohio. Well-born at Mount Vernon,

Ohio, in May 1821, he had attended Kenyon College. Such a political dramatist and scholar, who drew strength from being a centrifugal force in politics, could not remain long in Fort Worth, the outer rim of the political current. Returning to Austin, he left his newspaper the *Fort Worth Whig Chief*, in the hands of Editor George Smith. However, he did not surrender the reins, continuing his editorials until late in 1860 when he drove Fort Towners' opinion into a blasting furor.

Fort Worthians in the fifties were never done with politics. In 1859, Sam Houston was again campaigning for governor as an independent candidate. His platform was loyalty to the constitution and allegiance to the Union. In the summer of that year, the old warrior, engulfed in a linen duster and seated in a two-horse drawn buggy, toured the state at a clipping speed. Fear and dismay of the Union's destruction over the slavery controversy, had confounded men. "Be strong and of good courage; be steadfast," the aging hero pleaded in his speeches. As the days grew warmer, he removed his shirt and continued his crusade. Appearing before the crowds shirtless, he campaigned away the fears of many. His opponent was Governor Hardin Runnels, who had defeated him for governor in 1857.

By the fourth of July, the two adversaries were to meet in debate at Cold Springs near the foot of present-day Samuels Avenue. Colonel Terry was chairman of the committee of arrangements. Handbills had been circulated throughout Tarrant County promising political fireworks and a "Grand Barbecue and Tournament." All county residents were invited. The day before the celebration, Colonel Terry had his slaves take a wagon loaded with watermelons to Cold Springs to be chilled in the bubbling waters.

The day became glaringly hot. The crowd was huge, so large that it was difficult to find a place to hitch one's horses. Colonel Johnson introduced Runnels. The crowd cheered. Colonel Terry introduced Sam Houston. The crowd roared for their hero of San Jacinto.

The political debate over, the crowd gathered around long tables, which had been improvised under a grove of giant pecan and oak trees for the "Grand Barbecue." Terry was a lordly host. He had risen early that morning to superintend the barbecuing, and at noon, his slaves had loaded the tables with platters of steaming chicken, beef, and pork. There were warm pies, hot bread, and cakes. There were slices of cold watermelon. Food for every palate was in greater abundance than the hundreds required.

After the feast, the crowd assembled for the "Grand Tournament." A spectacular game which appealed to everyone, was known as the game of hoops. Hoops were strung on wires that stretched the length of the field. The contestants were six pairs of horsemen, each pair composed of a man and a woman. The man wore a bright-colored sash about his waist to match the colorful dress of his partner. When the signal was given, each pair dashed the full length of the field—about a quarter of a mile—attempting to gather on their baton, which they carried between them, the hoops from the poles that they passed with speed. The couple gathering the largest number of hoops won the prize. It was a contest of graceful and skillful horsemanship.

The great day ended in contentment. By mid-afternoon, wagons began to rumble homeward with talkative occupants. They had seen and heard the hero of San Jacinto once more. His optimism had stilled momentarily their anxiety concerning the national issue: "slave or free soil." Houston remained the night as guest at the Terry plantation, while Governor Runnels spent the night with the Johnsons at Johnson Station.

Houston won the election for governor of Texas in November 1859, defeating his opponent, the incumbent Runnels, by nearly nine thousand votes, on the platform "allegiance to the Union," even though in October, John Brown's raid at Harper's Ferry, had thoroughly frightened Texas slaveholders. Texans in their anxiety over the slavery controversy, wondered if their state could remain within the Union under their popular governor, Sam Houston.

Fort Worthians' hopes were brief and in vain. The new decade of the sixties would be fraught with difficulties. The year 1860 was election year, doubly important to citizens of Tarrant County. In April, they would hold the final election to decide the county seat, and in November, they would vote for president of the United States and congressmen. Slavery was the national problem. There was apprehension. Congress was no longer a legislative body, but two warring factions. The new Republican party, supporting "free soil" was gaining strength in the nation. Orators of the South were debating secession of their states. The Democratic party was splitting into two parties.

The approaching crisis would stay the hands of Fort Town builders through the decade of the 1860s, but it would not be able to obliterate the vigorous handiwork hewed in the decade of the 1850s—the seedtime of Fort Worth. Captain Daggett's plan, born out of a calm survey of history, had completed its first chapter. "Fort Dearborn became Chicago, and in the same fashion, Fort Worth would become a metropolis."

This was a slogan Daggett used to keep the dream glistening before Fort Town builders. In a buoyant faith, he had given the community its first county jail. In the legislature, he had worked to bring about the election of 1856 which made Fort Worth the disputed county seat. In 1857, he had given the first county courthouse, and in 1859, had led the activities for construction of a brick and stone replacement. A man with wide enough sympathies to reach the hearts of good, bad, and indifferent men, Daggett had worked with them all to build a city. Thus he had won a title, as Captain J. C. Terrell was to express it a few decades later: "M. T. Johnson was the father of Tarrant County, as E. M. Daggett was the father of Fort Worth, his image being on our city's seal." (This image of Captain E. M. Daggett was placed on the seal of the city of Fort Worth in 1883).

Thus diligent visionary men in the 1850s snatched an abandoned army post from oblivion, gathered families within its deserted walls, and brought forth a thriving village on its way to fulfilling greater plans with each decade of the century.

Shadows
on the Prairies

CUMULUS CLOUDS floated like ancient galleons across the limitless expanse of sky, casting shadows upon the prairies; it was an unusual characteristic of the new country into which the homeseekers had come —this Great Southwest. Perhaps watching the shadows on the prairies caused the settlers to forget the squeaking of the wagons and the monotonous rhythm of the turning wheels slowly nibbling away the hundreds of miles to the rolling land and the East Cross Timbers.

Silhouettes of the billowing clouds rolled before and around the wagons passing over the wooded groves in the distance, making them appear to be lush green in the steaming heat. Probably to some pioneers who lived by faith, the cooling dusky shapes were the fulfillment of God's loving protection, for "The Lord is thy shade upon thy right hand. The sun shall not smite thee by day, nor the moon by night." It was not so with those who were ruled by superstition, to them the dark shadows engulfing the wagons portended trouble.

Shadows on the prairies literally and figuratively did exist during the 1860s. In North Texas, Indian hostilities spread a prophetic canopy across its rolling expanse, halting the advance of the settlers, while the Civil War, inevitably approaching, forecast trouble for Tarrant County's frontiersmen. In their anxiety they could not be silent because they

knew that the time for a fateful decision was upon them. So under the
shadows of political and economic trouble, the pioneers' faith in their
way of life on the Grand Prairie at the forks of the Trinity was to be
tried and tested during the decade of the 1860s.

CHAPTER 19

Vexations of 1860

INDIANS CAME suddenly, stole horses, and were gone without molesting the settlers if the women gathered their families into the house, closed the shutters and quieted the children. There was trouble only when the savages encountered the settlers in the field or when the white people fired upon them. By 1856, the constant dread of Indian massacres had been stricken from the list of frontier problems for the inhabitants of Fort Worth and Tarrant County. Cattle thieving was the extent of Indian hostilities, and those were desultory affairs, because the swift vengeance of the Volunteer Guard of the White Settlement was an accepted fact in the red men's camps.

After 1856, there were other reasons for the lessening of Indian hostilities. The Second Cavalry of the United States Army was in charge of Texas defense, and never in the annals of our army in the West did the roster of officers include so many famous warriors: Albert Sidney Johnston, Robert E. Lee, George H. Thomas, George Stoneman and John B. Hood. Another reason for the surcease from Indian troubles was the chain of forts west of Fort Worth swinging like an arch from Red River to the Rio Grande.

Then, too, Texas in cooperation with the federal government had removed Texas Indians to two reservations. One was at the junction of the

Brazos and Clear Fork rivers on which lived the remnants of friendly red men: Caddo, Anadarko, Ioni, Waco, Tonkawa, and other small tribes. On the Clear Fork in present Throckmorton County, was the second reservation for the Penateka Comanches, although only half of that tribe lived on the reservation.

However the calm was brief. Indian affairs began to deteriorate in 1858, and again there were reasons. Part of the United States Second Cavalry had gone to Utah the previous year while outlaws had increased in numbers; and those Texas Indians who had refused to live on reservations, joined with the northern Comanches. Hostilities multiplied.

In the spring of 1858, John S. Ford with 100 Texas Rangers and a band of friendly Indians from the Brazos reservation, crossed into Indian Territory and inflicted defeat on the Comanches. Red men under the command of white men frightened their Indian brothers. White men, quick to forget their promises, had attacked them on their hunting grounds. These incidents provoked Indians to greater fury.

Frightened settlers, believing that the reservation Indians were joining their brothers in the raids, demanded that they be removed from Texas, even threatening to massacre them on the reservations. The issue became current politics on Fort Town's public square, as there were divided opinions. Angry tension mounted, until in August of 1859, the Indians were moved from Texas reservations to Indian Territory. In consequence, Texas law made it illegal, with the exception of a few remnant tribes in East Texas, for any Indian to roam in Texas.

But could Indians be expected to understand the law? They continued to hunt on Texas plains, to the confusion of the sedentary ones. Some in their perplexity joined the warriors. Indian terror from the Red River to Corpus Christi marked the year 1859—one of the factors that defeated Runnels and elected Houston governor. The year 1860 did not improve affairs. In December 1859, the Comanches raided Parker County, scalped alive and shot with arrows Mrs. Sherman of Weatherford. Several whites were killed in the counties of Palo Pinto, Young and Jack.

Faithful to his campaign promise of a hard-hitting Indian Policy, Houston authorized the raising of Texas Ranger companies. Each frontier county was empowered to raise a company of not more than twenty-five men each. He called upon his old friend Colonel Johnson, the father of Tarrant County, on March 17, 1860, "to organize a sufficient number of mounted rangers to repel, pursue, and punish the Indians now ravaging the north and northwestern settlements of Texas."

These Rangers were to volunteer for three months' service and were to cooperate with the federal troops stationed at Fort Belknap. Houston's program was applauded in Ft. Worth's paper, Mr. Norton's *Whig Chief*.

The nation's economy in 1860, if not in a slump, was certainly static, and such conditions were felt on the frontier. It was election year, and the choice of a president for the United States would mark a turning point in national affairs. So, young men in Tarrant County, restless and ready for action under the lull, heeded Governor Houston's call.

Colonel Johnson from the neighboring counties, raised five companies of Rangers of eighty-three men, commanded by Captains Smith of Mc-Lennan, Darnell of Dallas, Woods of Fannin, Fitzhugh of Collin and his own son, Tom Johnson of Tarrant. The latter county was well represented. Dr. Carroll Peak joined Captain Tom Johnson's company. John Peter Smith, through with teaching, had been surveying and studying law preparatory to taking the state bar examinations in 1860. He now became a captain in charge of a band of Indian spies friendly towards the whites. Young Captain Johnson's company rode out of Tarrant County in April, while five companies of Rangers met at Fort Belknap.

War, or defense against war, would always consume men's energies it seemed; but then too, men in war or peace would always lift their voices and bow their heads in Divine worship. Fort Towners were no different. They had time in 1860 to turn from war to receive the distinguished Reverend Gregg, Episcopal bishop of Texas. Riding horseback from South Texas, the Reverend Gregg came and conducted the first Episcopal service ever held in Fort Worth. The candle was lighted and would be kept burning by itinerant ministers until 1873 at which time local services would be organized.

Tarrant County's young men went off in April to fight Indians, while the older men remained at home to battle politics. There were political conflicts to be won locally as well as on the national front. The election of 1856 which had made Fort Worth the county seat, and declared fraudulent by Birdville, was to be resolved by the legislature convening the second Monday in April.

These events set Fort Town leaders to waging their campaign the first month of 1860. In a meeting at White Settlement, silver eagles came out of purses to add to the money already contributed the year before to build a courthouse. Even in 1860, Fort Towners knew that it paid to advertise. Having made a new bond for a courthouse, these men prepared and printed in February a political circular for distribution among the Tarrant County voters so they might know the plans for keeping Fort Worth as the county seat.

This handbill included a reprint of the bill passed by the legislature in 1859: "A Bill to Locate permanently the Seat of Justice of Tarrant County." It also contained an editorial which would get the vote of any economy-wise voter. It stated that the agitation of the past four years had existed too long.

Our interest (and we mean every man's interest in the county) individually and collectively has suffered from this strife. It is surely best for us then to put a stop to it at once and forever. How shall we do this? Let each candid man consider the facts and answer the questions:

1. Will true interest of the mass of people of the County be advanced by removing the County Seat from Fort Worth?
2. Should the Tax Payers be taxed to erect public buildings for the County when the erection of a Court House has been guaranteed free to tax payers?

Every one knows that the Bond for the early completion of a $10,000 Courthouse in Fort Worth and creditable to the County is entirely good.

The editorial of the flyer continued to reason and persuade by informing the voters that gentlemen of ample means and integrity were pledged and bonded for the completion of the courthouse; that the work was progressing and would progress; that "the determination is, the courthouse shall be built"; that the committee was at work; and that before January 1, 1861, Tarrant County would have "a courthouse superior to any in Northern Texas and without taxation." Furthermore, the undersigned supporters of this circular pledged to the voters their "entire confidence in the ability and willingness" of the gentlemen who had given their money for the construction of the courthouse to fulfill their bonded word.

The undersigned of this political handbill dated Fort Worth, February 18, 1860, were Charles Turner, W. B. Tucker, L. E. Holt, A. C. Nethery, R. H. King, W. T. Ferguson, T. W. Burr, Jas. P. Alford, Robert Gilaspie, G. Nance, Nat Terry, C. M. Peak, J. B. York, M. T. Johnson, E. M. Daggett, Geo. W. Smith.

Early that March Fort Worthians had dauntlessly laid the cornerstone of the courthouse. They believed that their work and strategy for the coming April election would bring them success.

By the second Monday in April, Fort Worth had more citizens than in the election of 1856. Nevertheless, underneath the outward confidence, anxiety built up tension in the guarantors of the bond as they moved about the town on election day.

Fort Worth won by a majority of 243 votes with thirteen votes not counted. It was alleged that the feud between Birdville and Fort Worth "cost the State of Texas in legislation $30,000."

"Three Cheers for Fort Worth," was the introduction of an editorial in *The Dallas Herald*, April 18, 1860, which published the election returns. From the balloting, it may be concluded that the contest was not between Fort Worth and Birdville, but between Fort Worth and a point at the exact geographical center of Tarrant County.

Polling Places	Fort Worth	Center	Birdville
Fort Worth	316	1	
Birdville	6	116	3
Grapevine	3	111	1
Hutton's	1	10	
Leonard's Mill	19	34	
Walnut Creek	29	14	
Gipson's	16	1	
Deer Creek	32		
Hanley's	32	2	
McCrakin	12		
Young's	36	9	
Johnson's Station	46	3	
Total	548	301	4

The four-year controversy between the rival towns was now over. It was history. Fort Town was made.

David Mauck and Jere Ashbury, contractors hired in 1859, now continued their work but with new zest. Their courthouse had grown from a $2,700 building to a $10,000 edifice, which was to be surmounted by a graceful dome. Among the counties of Texas, it was unusual indeed that any county should possess a courthouse built by popular subscription and without a penny of taxation from county residents. It became the life throb of its community until the late 1870s, since all businesses were located around the handsome structure or nearby as far south as present Fourth Street.

The election brought new businesses before the outbreak of the Civil War. Among them was the mercantile firm of Berliner and Samuels; and a small store in the first block west of the square, William T. Ferguson opened a drug store selling "staple drugs, peewee marbles, candy lozenges, and some notions."

For Tarrant County citizens, April was beset with political "goings-on." Back and forth they turned from state to national politics. The nation was to elect a president in November for which Texans prepared in April. The state Democratic convention assembled at Galveston April 2, 1860, to elect Texas delegates to the national convention in Baltimore and to formulate a policy which Texans would support in the November national election.

To the Galveston convention went men in various mental states, men of trepidation, men of doubting minds, and men eager to act on the rights of the states. Done with wavering between issues, the eager men carried the doubting ones with them to the declaration of a policy which laid the foundation for the future secession movement.

"Embracing the only doctrine which can preserve the integrity of the Union and the equal rights of the states," the Democratic convention of Texas denounced squatter sovereignty (the right of the people in the territories to decide whether their territory upon entering the Union would be a slave or a free state) because, it asserted that under the Constitution of the United States every citizen had the right to take his property, including slaves, anywhere in the United States. It reasserted the adherence of Texas to the Kentucky and Virginia Resolution set forth by Thomas Jefferson and James Madison in 1798 and 1799, which expounded the doctrine of state rights, among them being the right of a state to nullify an act of Congress when that act violated the rights of the state.

Texans were well grounded in asserting the right of Texas as a state, for the convention proclaimed that "Texas as a sovereign and independent nation had joined the confederacy of the United States," and by so doing had not surrendered any part of her sovereignty. Furthermore, "should the Federal government fail to accomplish the object of the confederacy, of which failure Texas alone could judge, she asserted a full right to withdraw from the confederacy." The convention used the word "confederacy" and judiciously avoided the word "Union" although it was the correct word to use.

In order that there would be no doubt concerning Texas' position among the men of the North agitating to abolish slavery and those men working to keep free soil in the West, the convention declared that if these men elected a president, it would become the duty of the people of Texas "to hold themselves in readiness to cooperate with our sister states of the South in a convention to take into consideration such measures as may be necessary for our protection or to secure, out of the confederacy, that protection of their rights which they can no longer hope for in it."

Thus invested with an incisive policy which made quibbling impossible, the Texas delegates answered present when the national Democratic convention convened in Charleston, South Carolina, on April 23, 1860. Fiery oratory in the assembly failed to win a majority for either of the political issues, squatter sovereignty, or the right to carry slaves into the territories under the protection of the United States. This Charleston convention split asunder over these issues and became two conventions assembling later at Baltimore. There, Northern Democrats nominated for the presidency the "Little Giant," Stephen A. Douglas of Illinois, who upheld squatter sovereignty. There was no bickering in the Texas delegation. Straightway they joined the Southern Democrats, nominating John C. Breckenridge of Kentucky as their candidate.

Another Texas delegation composed of A. B. Norton, editor of the *Whig Chief* in Fort Worth, and editor of the *Southern Intelligencer*, in Austin and J. H. Manly went to Baltimore to attend the convention of the Constitutional Union party. "The Union, the Constitution and the enforcement of the laws" was their platform. On the first ballot, Governor Sam Houston was nominated as the presidential candidate by fifty-seven votes while John Bell of Tennessee received sixty-eight and a half votes. On the second ballot Bell won the presidential nomination for the Union party.

The national Republican convention, meeting in Chicago, nominated Abraham Lincoln for the presidency. Their platform asserted that "Congress had no right to interfere with slavery in the states where it already existed, but Congress should exclude slavery from all the territories of the United States."

News of the state Democratic convention in Galveston set Fort Worth agog with talk. News of the Baltimore convention rocked the town with turbulent politics; and the citizens were about evenly divided in their support of the Southern Democrats and the Unionists. Colonel Nathaniel Terry, among the Fort Worth leaders, favored the secession policy of the Southern Democrats. District Attorney D. C. Dade supported the Constitutional Union party. Colonel Johnson, Peter Smith, and J. C. Terrell led the cautious talk and argued against the tack toward secession which the Austin and Baltimore conventions had taken. As the summer heat bore down, the swelling buzz of politics, flies, and mosquitoes did not improve men's moods.

A small fire here, a large fire there, a roaring conflagration elsewhere, and all happened on the same Sunday afternoon of July 8, 1860. When smoke had cleared from eyes, when news from various places had been patched together to get the overall picture; when abolitionists had been caught and made to confess, then Texans concluded that abolitionists had organized a Texas slave insurrection for the summer as the commencement of their "good work."

At Dallas on Sunday that day in July, a conflagration destroyed every building on the western and northern sides of the square and on the eastern side, about one-half of the buildings. The loss was $400,000. At Denton, an hour and a half after the Dallas fire, business houses and twenty-five kegs of gunpowder in a hogshead were destroyed by flames. The loss was $80,000. The same afternoon, fires destroyed property at Pilot Point, Denton County; Ladonia, Fannin County; Milford, Ellis County; Honey Grove, Waxahachie; Austin, and in many other towns. Tarrant County did not escape these incendiary fires. Archibald Leonard's mill, eight miles northeast of Fort Worth, was burned.

For an account of the Dallas fire we have the report of the then District Judge Nat M. Burton one of the old settlers of that town.

I am satisfied the town was fired by Negroes. Mr. Cameron who lived on the Fort Worth road 12 miles from Dallas had a Negro boy about twelve years old, who came to town every Sunday to get the mail. When he returned home that Sunday after being in Dallas his master saw the smoke from the burning town and asked what it was. He replied that Dallas was burning. He was asked how he knew it. He said that as he was going to Dallas that morning Uncle Cato who was then a notorious Negro in these parts told him to look out that Dallas would be burning before he returned home.

This to my mind was most convincing proof. Old Cato was captured and he implicated the other two Negroes who were hanged with him. Their stories were corroborated by other Negroes. They stated that two white preachers from the North put them up to it, and a committee waited on the preachers . . . Whipped them and told them to leave the country.

Judge Burton further reported that in the mass meeting of Dallas citizens held on Monday following Sunday's fire, the moderate wing compromised with the radical faction by agreeing to hang the three Negroes and appoint a committee to whip every Negro in the county. The three Negroes were hanged on Wednesday and most of the people took their slaves to witness the hanging. Judge Burton said that he did not take part either in the hanging or the whippings but that his Negro cook was whipped, although she said that it was a light whipping.

Tantalizing suspicions that abolitionists from the North with their agents were also working in Tarrant County became convictions in the early days of that eventful July. Fort Towners' temper and July heat were hot—a fact made public in an early August issue of the *Houston Telegraph*, quoting the *Fort Worth Whig Chief* dated July 25, 1860: "Fort Town's men hanged an abolitionist in the early morning of July 17 on a pecan tree near the banks of the Clear Fork, three-quarters of a mile west of Fort Worth. They left him hanging there. All through the day people thronged to gaze upon an abolitionist."

Excitement accumulating through the daylight hours spent its tumultuousness in an evening meeting. Fort Worth's newly formed Vigilance Committee, membership unknown, received endorsement of their action, for there was no doubt among Fort Towners that the hanged abolitionist was guilty of distributing the six-shooters among the Negroes. Fifty were found among slaves on farms near Fort Worth.

In August, enough strychnine to fill half a barrel, if gathered together, was discovered in the possession of many slaves in the vicinity of Fort Worth. It was said that poison was another weapon which abolitionists used in doing away with slaveholders and their families. In Washington County near Brenham, slaves caught by the vigilance committee confessed that the Negroes had agreed to a general insurrection in Texas scheduled for Monday, August 6, 1860.

Another day in August, Paul Isbell, the slave trader, rode into Fort Worth from his plantation in the White Settlement with his next door neighbor, George Grant, also a rich farmer. On the public square they met Captain Daggett and Nathaniel Terry. Greeting them, Isbell spoke in muffled tones, "Follow us, the lid of Pandora's Box is about to be lifted." Daggett and Terry heeding the alarm followed Isbell and Grant into the courthouse. They had a statement to make before the county clerk.

Sworn under oath on August 10, 1860, Isbell made known a frightening event. He, with Grant, had found near Grant's residence a letter which was proof that an underground abolitionist's organization was operating in the county. Authenticity of the letter was not to be doubted when a man of Isbell's unimpeachable veracity made known the facts under oath, and it was a plausible occurrence to have found an abolitionist's letter in the vicinity of the homes of Grant and Isbell, because both were slave owners and there were usually about two hundred slaves on Isbell's White Settlement farm, some slaves for field work, others that were for sale.

Deputy County Clerk T. M. Matthews adjusted his chair so the light from the window would be on the paper. It was a lengthy document and not a word was to be misconstrued.

Denton County, July 3, 1860

Dear Sir:

Our glorious cause is progressing as far south as Brenham [Texas]. I traveled up through the frontier counties under a fictitious name. I found many friends who had initiated and understood the Mystic Red. . . .

Upon hearing the words "Mystic Red," the title of the abolitionists' secret order of incendiaries, Captain Daggett, who had been relaxing on the bench, bolted upright exclaiming, "So the order of the 'Mystic Red' is among us in Tarrant County! We have not been dreaming nightmares, I tell you!"

County Clerk Matthews shifted in his chair, then continued in a slow drawl:

. . . If we can break Southern merchants and millers and have their places filled by honest Republicans, Texas will be an easy prey. Lincoln certainly will be elected; so we will then have the Indian Nation . . . When we get to Texas we will have a connecting link from the Lakes to the Gulf, slavery will then be surrounded by land and by water and soon sting itself to death.

In swift motion Colonel Terry lifted from the bench his stovepipe hat bringing it down on his head with a thump. He could see his new world falling apart. His first world had come to an end in Alabama, when he was defeated in the race for lieutenant governor, and his slaves were seized for debt. In Texas, he had built a new domain. Now its survival was threatened. Stunned and angry, he decided that this new evidence of "Black Republicanism" in Tarrant County, would force him to organize this very day a new and cautious routine among his forty-odd slaves.

Matthew's voice, now brittle with excitement, rushed along:

. . . I repeat, Texas we must have. Our only chance is to break up the present inhabitants in whatever way we can. We must have frequent consultations with our colored friends, . . . let your meetings be at night. Impress upon them the blessing of freedom, induce all you can to leave, and tell them that our arrangements for them to go North are improved.

Charles Turner, hearing of the impending excitement in the courthouse, had run from his store across the public square in time to hear the political fireworks. Turner had listened in silence to the reading of the document as if he were objectively calculating his profits and losses for the year. This last barbarous design of the abolitionists and evidence of an underground railroad working to take slaves from Tarrant County to the free North blasted Turner's silence. In deliberate tones he spoke, "Here are the answers to our months of questioning, this letter sets a man's reasoning, we can no longer ask—is it right or wrong. We must act." To Turner's challenge, the group loudly responded in unison.

County Clerk Matthews read on:

We need more agents,—appoint a local agent in every neighborhood in your district. Brother Leake recommends a different match be used about towns. Our friends sent a very inferior article, they emit too much smoke, and do not contain enough camphine—I will send a supply when I get home. I will reprove you and your co-workers for negligence in sending funds for our agents but few have been compensated. You must call on our colored friends for money.

[Signed] W. A. Bailey

Matthews looked up from the letter. Deep indignation gripped the men. Hastily, the county clerk's eyes returned to the document. Then he said in a casual tone. "There is a postscript. Reverend Bailey is sending to the agent in Tarrant County a few copies he has of Hinton R. Helper's book, *The Impending Crisis*. Reverend Bailey bids his agent, "farewell."

To that twist of the reading of the letter, a member of the group replied, "Farewell it will be"; and "be not surprised because we will hang every man who does not live above suspicion."

To make certain that men in Texas would know the intentions of the inhabitants of Tarrant County, this last phrase was published in A. B. Norton's *The Southern Intelligencer* of Austin under the title, "A Letter from Fort Worth, August 12, 1860." No doubt this was a reprint from his other paper the Fort Worth *Chief*.

Isbell's revelation unleashed much talk, correspondence, and visiting among the county's men of action until all citizens were alerted as the newspaper in Austin, *Texas State Gazette*, revealed in a published communication dated at Fort Worth, September 8, 1860:

No more fires or abolitionists hung within the last few weeks. Several are running however just in time probably to save their necks.

These words, moods, and actions explained the huge crowd which attended the public meeting on the square September 11. It was the largest public meeting in the county's history. Colonel Robert Gilaspie was called to the chair. Terrell, the lawyer, was appointed secretary. For many inhabitants, it had cost effort to ride into Fort Town to the meeting, but it was worth it. Terrell in his best form as a spellbinding orator, read the letter from the Texas abolitionist, Reverend Bailey to his Tarrant County agent.

Listeners also heard that the incendiary fires, crimes, and Negro insurrections in Texas were known by the abolitionists in Lowell, Massachusetts, three weeks before the news of these events were heralded in Texas papers; furthermore, the people were informed that the "Black Republicans" had enrolled over a hundred picked men to repair to North Texas in the fall.

Then it was done. Under the stress of emotion, there seemed no need for debate. Straightway the citizens of Tarrant adopted seven resolutions.

In the first resolution, they declared that since there was an organized effort by "Black Republicans" to overthrow the laws of Texas by stirring up the Negroes to insurrection and by incendiarism, murders, and other inhuman crimes; and since society had no security under the law against such depredations, the citizens of Tarrant County considered all persons connected with the crimes "as having placed themselves beyond the pale of the law's protection."

Resolution two provided for the organization throughout Texas of committees of discreet men to operate secretly and compile the names of all "Black Republicans, abolitionists or higher law men of every class," and make two lists in every county. List number one should contain names of suspected persons. List number two, the "Black List" should record the names of those "to be exterminated by immediate hanging."

Resolution three was vehement. "There should be no abatement or exemption from entire extermination of the Black List."

Resolution four declared that "all men worthy of the name of citizen will sustain" the foregoing action as the only remedy.

In the fifth resolution, Tarrant citizens declared that the editor in Austin, A. B. Norton of the *Southern Intelligencer*, editors of other papers, and persons who attributed the late fires to accident, and persons who asserted that the hue and cry about abolition incendiarism had been raised for political effect should be placed at once on "List One of suspected persons," and that they should be carefully watched by the committees. This was because their explanations of these events insulted the intelligence of the people of Texas.

Resolution five was the only one not adopted unanimously but was finally passed by a small majority of seventeen votes. There were too many Union party men in attendance.

Resolution seven made it the responsibility of the Tarrant County committee to correspond with the others in the state in order that a state convention might assemble to take into consideration what further was to be done.

Although the fifth resolution of Fort Town's mass meeting did not pass unanimously, nonetheless it terminated publication of the *Fort*

Worth Whig Chief, for by that resolution, a majority of Fort Towners made known their hostility toward Norton, and certainly citizens would not continue as subscribers.

Doubting nothing, the county's vigilantes moved rapidly. Their attention was directed to two men newly emigrated to town from the North, a Mr. Crawford and a Mr. Anthony Bewley. By trade they were brick masons. Mr. Bewley, a Northern Methodist, was also a minister when he could find a church. Imprudent men, these Yankees worked harder at circulating their "Northern sentiments" than wielding their trowels. They were warned to leave town. Turning deaf ears to warnings, they continued to crusade in the small churches scattered through the county, where slaves were allowed to gather for worship.

In such a church located on the Clear Fork at the extreme end of present-day West Belknap, evidence of the "evil acts" of Bewley and Crawford were obtained by a loyal slave, Ned Purvis, of the Purvis family. Ned denounced abolitionists as "De tools of de debbil." Vigilantes hid Ned under the floor of the church several hours before a meeting of the Negroes. What he heard convinced him "Dat de debbil wa'r unchained. Dees Yankee men tol' de colored folks to rise up agin'st dar marsters."

Men do not run away until they lose hope, and that was what happened to Bewley. He was caught on the border of Indian Territory and returned to Fort Worth bound in rope. Another account states that Bewley had gone to Missouri to visit friends, was arrested in Springfield, Missouri, and returned to Fort Worth charged "with implication in a nefarious plot to poison wells, fire towns and residences and in midst of the conflagrations and death to run off with the slaves."

Too much evidence and too much anger were stacked against Bewley and Crawford. West of town on the Clear Fork in the dark woods, on September 13, 1860, hundreds of saddled horses milled around, leaves and twigs crackling under their restless hoofs. Animal instinct told them it was a sullen occasion. Not far off stood their masters, good men at heart, who hated murder and bloodshed, but to whom this was not murder: it was an act to save their individual and civil rights. Their countenances revealed their moral conflict, as they stood in a circle hearing Mr. Bewley, the abolitionist brick mason and preacher, give his last confession. Sworn under oath and knowing that these were his last words on earth, Mr. Bewley stated that Mr. Bailey's letter of instruction was a genuine document; that Bailey had sent him the letter for guidance in his activities in Tarrant County; and that he had lost Bailey's letter at the place testified to by Isbell and Grant.

On the same limb of a giant pecan tree about three hundred yards west of the intersection of present-day Jacksboro Highway and White Settlement Road, the two abolitionists Bewley and Crawford were hanged until dead. They were left to hang there as a startling object lesson for any Negro inclined to waver from his path of loyalty or for any man ruled by "Northern sentiments."

Vigilantes, searching their consciences for justification believed that a man must be loyal to the ideals inside of him, one being state's rights, the taproot of freedom and independence, which they were compelled to preserve. These hangings should be sufficient warning to rid Tarrant County of "Black Republicans." Such were the thoughts of the horsemen as they rode home, but their minds were not at peace. They knew that the world went on in spite of hangings, and the problems which split their universe wide open still rode with them.

The Dallas Herald, dated October 10, 1860, published the news of the hangings. According to the December 26, 1860, issue of this paper, the Fort Worth vigilantes missed one of their men. They reported that a Mr. Willet, supposed to have been hanged on the same tree with his father-in-law, Bewley, had arrived safely in southern Kansas, but not without a struggle. For eight days, he had lived in Texas woods with nuts and herbs as his only food until the angry search of the Tarrant County vigilantes subsided.

Willet may have escaped Fort Worth's vigilantes, but their alertness in ferreting out an abolitionist or a Northern sympathizer never waned. According to Harry B. Catlett, a newcomer who did not meet the unrestrained hospitality as those arriving in Fort Worth a year earlier:

Excitement was very high in Fort Worth preceeding outbreak of war. Every newcomer was closely scrutinized. His sentiments probed and if his proclivities were toward the North, woe unto him. He was a branded man and his best bet was to get away while getting was good.

Citizens are never of one mind concerning political issues or a crisis. In Tarrant County many citizens criticized the September mass meeting, the lynching, and the mob. They were of the same opinion as Norton's *The Southern Intelligencer* which stated that any fires occurring were accidental and not the work of abolitionists, scoffing at the "evidence" found by Isbell and Grant, asserting the whole affair had been perpetrated by secessionists for political reasons.

The young men who had gone to the Indian country in the spring of 1860 were no happier over events than Tarrant County's vigilantes.

Colonel Johnson's five companies of Texas Rangers had been joined at Fort Belknap by two companies under the commands of Captains Ed Burleson and W. C. Dalrymple, and had started for Indian country in May. But Governor Houston failed to follow up his plan with material support and the campaign, which had begun in enthusiasm, vanished into disappointing futility. Houston's indifference still remains an enigma. It has been said that Houston wished to keep the Rangers organized in order to have them in readiness for an ambitious plan, a new republic with Texas as the core.

On July 30, 1860, Colonel Johnson ordered a portion of his Rangers to return. Without achievement, they came home an unhappy lot. The others, remaining on the frontier, advanced into Indian country beyond the line of Kansas. They had action, but penuriously equipped, they experienced torturous privations when summer came with scorching heat. In the fall they returned to Fort Belknap and were disbanded by the governor's order.

Wearing tattered clothes and in boots without soles, thirty half-starved men of Colonel Johnson's Rangers walked into Fort Town in October of 1860. Ninety miles from Fort Belknap in the wilderness, Indians had set upon them, stampeded the horses, stealing fifty-nine of their sixty-five mounts, pilfered their blankets, and left them without supplies. Subsisting upon what they could find in the countryside, they had almost starved on their homeward trek. They were a deplorable sight. Nonetheless, their tragic appearance did not arouse to action the habitual crowd who frequented the public square. In October, men already were too vexed. Indian hostilities and frontier defense were now minor problems buried beneath the complexities of irascible politics. Too much had been said by the presidential candidates and their supporters in the campaign during the summer of 1860. Angry words as well as desperate and fearful acts had piled up. There could be no equilibrium among frightened men.

November came and with it election day. Fort Worth men went to the polls. None voted for Lincoln. Some cast their ballots for Bell, candidate of the Union party, standing for the preservation of the Union and the Constitution. The majority voted for Breckinridge, candidate of the Southern Democratic party, opposing squatter sovereignty. Their votes cast, Fort Worthians fretfully waited. One afternoon in mid-November the stagecoach from Dallas came in. Its arrival in Fort Worth was in the tempo of a crisis.

"Hurry with the unloading of those papers," the crowd nagged the driver. Subscribers to the *Dallas Herald* and the Austin papers, *The Southern Intelligencer* and the *State Gazette*, hurried after the driver into the post office.

"Lincoln elected president–" was on every tongue. Yes!—but what of the news? How was the country reacting to the election? What did the statesmen in Austin say? The crisis had come! Upon a swell of emotion these questions arose. In nervous haste, readers unfolded newspapers and tried to grasp the whole news in a glance. Some men read silently, others aloud. They learned that from the moment the account of the election of Lincoln reached Austin on Sunday, November 11, the question spread through the capital city: what should Texas do? A group of statesmen were demanding the immediate secession of Texas from the Union and were preparing formal requests, asking Governor Houston to call a special session of the legislature to consider Texas secession from the Union. Leaders of this group were Associate Justice O. M. Roberts of the Texas Supreme Court, Attorney General George M. Flournoy, State Comptroller C. R. Johns, and William Bird, editor of the *Texas State Gazette*.

"I am with Justice Roberts and his group," said Captain Daggett without lifting his eyes from his paper.

"Wait! Captain Eph," young lawyer Terrell retorted from behind his paper, "Read what Governor Houston has to say."

As if that would make any difference to Captain Daggett, the individualist! Daggett loved Houston but did not approve of what he read. When the governor was asked for a statement in regard to Lincoln's election, he replied that the election of Lincoln was a misfortune but in his opinion not disastrous. And to the tense politicians in Austin clamoring for immediate action, Houston advised them to wait for "an overt act of aggression." Since Lincoln would not be inaugurated until March, he said, the wiser course was to wait for a statement from Lincoln. Houston insisted that Lincoln would uphold the Constitution; in fact, he might make an able president. Lincoln's election, Houston declared, was no cause to destroy the Union. "Wait," he pleaded, "until after Lincoln's inauguration."

"Yes, the crisis has come," said Doctor Peak.

"Only the first stage of the crisis," replied Peter Smith. "There will be others."

From their newspapers, men turned to predicting what would happen. Unionists, supporting Houston, and secessionists, following Justice Roberts, each in turn produced their arguments. They would await more news and directives from Austin. And without delay, both news and directions came for them. The news would end an era of magnificent freedom for early Fort Worthians, and never again would they live on the prairies and East Cross Timbers of Tarrant with such grandiloquent individualism.

Rabid secessionists in Austin and from Red River to the Gulf would not heed Houston's advice. They would not wait for Lincoln's inauguration and statement of policy. On Monday or Tuesday following the announcement on Sunday of Lincoln's election, the secessionists held a consultation in Justice Roberts' office, and decided to request the governor to call a special session of the legislature in order to arrange a state convention of the people's representatives to determine whether or not Texas should leave the Union. They did not await Houston's reply. They organized to wage their campaign. They wrote letters to leaders throughout the state. They published articles in newspapers, made public addresses, and went on speaking tours. Their campaign was aided by a secret society at work in Texas—Knights of the Golden Circle.

This organization was known in the deep South as the Sons of Liberty. It had existed for many years with a colossal plan to build a southern empire established on the institution of slavery. True to fantastic plans, the limits of their dream empire sprawled across two continents and embraced the islands of the Caribbean. It would extend from Philadelphia to Bogota, Columbia, and from the West Indies to Chihuahua, Mexico, including most of Texas. Havana, Cuba, was to be the center of this empire.

Some Fort Worthians undoubtedly were members of this secret order and were workers for its success. Into Texas, General George Bickley, leader of the Knights of the Golden Circle, had come in the late 1850s organizing many local secret units called "castles." Through these castles, political leaders worked to stir up the mass of Texans in order to obtain their votes at the proper time for the withdrawal of Texas from the Union.

While Houston delayed, secessionists toured the state. Few counties escaped their haranguing speeches.

When George Baylor of Weatherford, whiplash of the secessionists, on tour in northwest Texas, arrived in Fort Worth in late November, he was greeted by Colonel Nathaniel Terry, now the outspoken secessionist; by W. H. Griffin, a newcomer from Georgia; and by the three largest slaveholders: Paul Isbell, Captain Daggett, and Charles Turner. Other slaveholders listed in the Fort Worth area were Stephen Terry, Baldwin Samuels, Sam Evans, and H. C. (Tobe) Johnson. The general public had no way of knowing whether this reception committee received Baylor with the secret handgrip of the Knights of the Golden Circle, since few men knew of the organization. The crowd gathered at the courthouse to get the latest news from this bigwig who knew.

Secessionists were succeeding in agitating the people. In many counties, citizens were holding mass meetings. Tarrant County citizens, always in full swing when it came to politics, were now in furious motion. Baylor's speech had scored. Citizens of Tarrant County held a mass meeting in Fort Worth on November 26, 1860. Their purpose was to consider what action should be pursued as a result of the election of Lincoln. Colonel Johnson opened the meeting by urging calmness and prudence and closed his speech with the cryptic advice, "First know the right; then maintain it."

A committee between Union men and those favoring secession was appointed. The members were J. P. Smith, Captain Daggett, Captain Griffin, A. T. Fowler, and Colonel Johnson. Two resolutions were adopted unanimously. The first stated that citizens of Tarrant call upon Governor Houston to assemble the legislature at an early date. The second declared that as a pledge of their fidelity to Texas and her institutions, also as a pledge of their prior allegiance to the sovereignty of the state, the citizens of Tarrant, by public acclaim, would hoist in the public square in Fort Worth on November 26, 1860, the Lone Star flag of Texas as the banner of their liberties.

Before this second resolution was adopted, there was debate. The question arose as to whether the hoisting of the Texas flag in Fort Worth as a pledge of their allegiance to the state would be an assertion by Tarrant County citizens that they supported immediate secession. By majority vote, the assembly agreed that such action would not commit them to support secession, and ordered that the secretary so state it in the report. The meeting adjourned with a provision that the next assembly of citizens would be held on December 8, 1860.

And on November 26, 1860, with public acclaim and accompanied by robust cheers, the Lone Star flag ascended the old flagpole on Fort Worth's public square. Tarrant County citizens had pledged their faith to Texas and the institutions of their state, slavery being one of those institutions.

On December 1, Justice Roberts acridly denounced Governor Houston's policy in a public address in Austin. Given much publicity in the papers, news of the speech reached Fort Worth just in time for a bit of discussion before the Tarrant County mass meeting, to be held on December 8.

To the December meeting in Fort Worth, went Tarrant County men whose questions had been answered by the forces at work. These citizens, acting upon the votes of the majority, sent a second petition asking Governor Houston to convene the legislature in special session in order that it might provide for the election of delegates to a state convention. Tarrant County's petition added one more to the growing stack on the governor's desk.

Houston's stubbornness and the secessionists' willfulness hurled events into an irreconcilable course. At Austin on December 3, 1860, Justice O. M. Roberts and Attorney General George M. Flournoy with other leaders, acting on their own initiative and finding legal right for their action in Article 1, Section 2 of the Texas Constitution, which gave men the right "to alter, reform or abolish their form of government in such manner as they think expedient," had issued a call for a state convention of the people's representatives.

January 8, 1861, was set for the election of delegates to the state convention which would assemble in Austin on the twenty-eighth of the month. The call was published in every newspaper in the state.

Houston had lost the first round in his campaign of watchful waiting but was determined to continue the fight. He therefore issued a call on December 19, 1860, for a special session of the legislature, hoping that it would prevent the secession of Texas from the Union. Colonel Johnson, Peter Smith, Terrell and Dade, as leaders of the Tarrant County Unionists, would fight on with Houston.

In Fort Worth, men no longer moved to and fro about their affairs. One place, which did not feel the sharp contraction of business, was Andrews Tavern. Transcontinental tourists continued arriving by the Dallas and Weatherford Stageline and spending the night or a few days before making connection with the Butterfield Overland. Only the arrivals and departures of these stagecoaches gave the public square a temporary air of bustling business. When the stagecoach was out of sight, the town sank into inertia.

Wool did not sell at Jefferson. It was not worth the price to drive cattle to the Shreveport market. Hard money was seldom seen. The cost of living was high because goods imported were scarce as well as costly. The business drive, all of it, seemed to have gone out of Fort Worth men. On the square they sat on bales of cotton, leaned against the hitching rails, whittled some, talked much and smoked or chewed tobacco. Then they stood awhile or took a turn around the square or went over to watch Mr. Mauck direct his slaves busy at building the courthouse. They sauntered into Ed Terrell's First and Last Chance Saloon for a nip. Then returned to sit, to talk, to stand, to walk; and all the while they brooded. Some men became intoxicated, would jump on their horses, ride around the square and fire their revolvers into the air. At least, their action tore away the paralyzing calm. Sober men hurried to safety, while mothers hid their children.

Then a diverting thing happened one day in late December. A veil of dust arose from the Weatherford Road which led into the square. Winter wind blew the dust about a two-seated buggy rolling at a fast clip behind two handsome horses driven by Isaac Parker of Birdville. Beside him sat a woman apparently an Indian, with a baby in her arms. The horses harnessed to the buggy were keeping pace with several men galloping on horseback who had joined Parker when he forded the Trinity in front of David Mauck's mill.

These horsemen always gathered at the mill to hear the news. Today, they followed Parker, knowing that he would have a tremendous story to relate. Men in walking distance of the square ran to get the news. Men at the edge of the village, seeing the excitement, mounted their horses and galloped to join the gathering group. Parker did have a great story to tell.

In order to prevent a renewal of Indian raids in North Texas, Governor Houston had ordered Captain Lawrence Sullivan Ross and seventy Texas Rangers to establish their station beyond Fort Belknap, where they arrived in mid-October of 1860. In December as they scouted the North Texas plains with a detachment of the Second Cavalry, United States Army, they met on Pease River about seven miles west of present-day Vernon, a large band of Comanches led by Chief Nocona, and virtually annihilated them. Chief Nocona, with the remnant of his tribe and his two small sons, fled to the northern part of Indian country.

After battle confusion had cleared away, Parker related, the Rangers discovered the squaw they had captured with a child in her arms was of white blood, because Indians do not have blue eyes. The Rangers began to talk to her. She did not understand them. Then one of the Rangers suggested that perhaps she was Cynthia Ann Parker. This Ranger had grown to manhood on his father's story of the bloody raid of 1836 on Parker's Fort near the Navasota River in Limestone County.

Attacking Parker's Fort, three hundred marauding Comanches and Kiowas killed eight of the settlers and carried away five prisoners, including Cynthia Ann Parker, nine, her brother John, six, Mrs. Elizabeth Kellog and Mrs. Rachel Plummer with her son, James, eighteen months old. James later was ransomed. After several years of slavery among the Comanches, Mrs. Plummer was purchased by a Mexican trader operating between Missouri and Santa Fé, and soon afterwards freed. Mrs. Plummer returned to her relatives in Texas, where she wrote and published an account of her trials among the Indians; but the whereabouts of Cynthia Ann and the others remained a frontier mystery.

Isaac Parker, being a good storyteller, increased the crowd's suspense by describing the Rangers' struggle with the problem: who was the white squaw? Captain Ross concluded, Parker said, that the Ranger's supposition was a likely answer. Perhaps the squaw was Cynthia Ann Parker, although it had been twenty-odd years since her disappearance, and during that time, the Comanches had stolen many white children. So hoping that the Ranger was correct and since some of the Rangers stated that her Uncle Isaac Parker lived near Birdville, Captain Ross had sent a rider to Tarrant County to summon Parker to Camp Cooper forty miles west of Fort Belknap in order to identify the captive.

"I didn't tarry," Parker said. "Hitching my team of horses to the two-seated buggy, I traveled several days to Camp Cooper."

His listeners traveled vicariously with Parker even experiencing his perplexities during the journey. Parker was dramatic, telling them:

"It was not a happy journey. Twenty-five years had passed since the tragedy at Fort Parker. My mind was troubled by the task before me of deciding whether the captive at Camp Cooper was Cynthia Ann. Doubts led me to distrust myself, for now I am sixty-seven years old, and years of separation change loved ones into strangers."

Waving his hand toward the squaw in the buggy he continued, "And how strange to me was the sight at Camp Cooper of my thirty-four-year-old niece, browned by sun and disheveled from the lack of a white woman's grooming."

"Did you recognize her?" queried one in the crowd.

"No!" retorted Parker. He told of how he and the interpreter had struggled to talk with her, but she had lost every word of her native tongue, and he despaired of identifying her, when he turned to the interpreter and said very distinctly that the woman he was seeking was named Cynthia Ann. The name distinctly spoken seemed to reach the long forgotten recesses of her memory. Isaac continued:

The moment I mentioned the name, she straightened herself in her seat and patting herself on the breast, said 'Cynthia Ann, Cynthia Ann!' A ray of recollection sprung up in her mind, that had been obliterated for twenty-five years. Her very countenance changed, and a pleasant smile took the place of a sullen gloom.

But twenty-five years of living as an Indian princess had blotted out for this young woman the bond of kinship for her uncle, which Parker understood. He expressed the hope that she could be restored to the family fold, because she always responded to him in a grateful manner.

Parker returned to the buggy and took Cynthia Ann and her baby into the Daggett-Turner store. Under the gaze of the men and the air of excitement, she clutched the child, Prairie Flower, close to her breast and wept. She was told there was nothing to fear, and efforts were made to give her comfort. But the food, the straight-back chair, and civilized ways deepened her sorrow and fear. Too late and too weary to complete the journey to Birdville, Parker with his niece remained in Fort Town for the night.

News spread around that the long-lost Cynthia Ann Parker was in Fort Worth. Next morning, people left their work to see her. In the words of Medora Robinson, daughter of Milt Robinson, school was closed, and Fort Worth children were taken to the store to see the heroine of their folklore stories, now in their midst.

Excitable joy seized Medora, for it was no ordinary occasion to go to the Daggett-Turner store in the first place. Her mother did not take her there often because of the usual crowd of hunters, cowboys and farmers. Going to the store with her teacher, Professor Hudson, Medora considered it to be a double adventure, for she would not only be seeing Cynthia Ann, but also the alluring shelves and counters filled with goods from faraway places so fascinating to a frontier lass. She had never been allowed to remain long enough, anyway, to satisfy her curiosity.

That day, the crowd was so large that Medora could not see the counters or the shelves, only the high walls of the store which were hung with buffalo meat, wild turkeys and partridges. Hanging on one wall was a huge sign which informed customers that all meat and poultry sold for ten cents a pound.

The schoolchildren slowly worked their way through the crowd to the back of the store, where they found their folklore heroine. Soft little gasps of sympathy arose from the awestricken schoolgirls when they beheld her. High above the gazing crowd, Cynthia Ann "stood on a large wooden box, bound with rope." Instead of being dressed in Indian attire, she wore a torn calico dress. Her blond hair bronzed by the sun, was cut shoulder length and hung straight in squaw-fashion. Tears glistened on her tanned face as she mumbled her Indian language. This was Medora's description.

The young girls sorrowfully left the store, saddened by what they saw, and repeatedly asked, "Why does Cynthia Ann weep? She has returned home!" Someday they would understand how justifiable those tears were. Cynthia Ann had been treated with every consideration by Captain Ross, and now Uncle Isaac Parker told her that she had nothing to fear, and no cause for weeping.

Could a mother, heavy with sorrow, restrain her tears, being subjected to the stares of curiosity seekers crowding around her in noisy excitement, none of which she understood? Cynthia Ann, an Indian princess, was grieving for her Indian Chief Peta Nocona and her two sons, ages fifteen and nine, whom she believed to have been killed in the battle on Pease River. Never would she know that although her chief was killed, her two sons were somewhere in Indian country lifting up their chants to the Great Spirit, for omens which would tell them of the return of their mother.

Meanwhile, in an oak grove on her Uncle Parker's farm near Birdville, Cynthia Ann each day offered her supplications to the Great Spirit and did penance, Indian fashion. According to her belief, she must atone for her sins and assuage the anger of the Great Spirit by self-inflicted punishment. So, to her shrine in the oak grove, she performed a final act of penitence by slashing her breasts and dropping her blood upon a small fire she had kindled. Her supplication went unanswered. Then to her grief, another bewildering experience had to be endured. Isaac Parker took her from Birdville to Austin.

There, accompanied by a group of ladies and gentlemen, she was presented to the state convention meeting to consider the secession of Texas from the Union. Gaping faces sent ravaging fear through her grief-wracked being. These men, she thought, were chiefs in a war council considering her execution. Lawmakers' hearts succumbed at the vision of this fear-tortured victim of Indian raids. Straightway the legislators approved an act April 8, 1861, granting Cynthia Ann Parker a pension of $100 a year for five years, dating from January 1, 1861. The act also required the county court of Tarrant County to appoint a guardian for her. The guardian of the bond was "conditioned for the faithful application of the pension, and for the support and education of her child."

Back in Birdville, Cynthia Ann each day retreated into the woods with her child where she could live in her Indian way. In the seclusion of the oak grove, she fashioned from cloth of brilliant colors, which her uncle had given her, clothes for herself and child. Confounded by his thwarted efforts to restore Cynthia Ann quickly to her rightful place within the family, and unable to give her the attention required to redeem her to civilized ways, Parker took her to Van Zandt County to live with her Uncle Silas Parker and his family.

Again, she became the subject of legal proceedings. On January 8, 1862, the legislature passed an act.

Silas M. Parker of Van Zandt County is hereby constituted as agent of Cynthia Ann Parker formerly of Tarrant and now of Van Zandt County, and on his given bond in the sum of $400 to the Chief Justice of Van Zandt County for the faithful application of said pension to the support and education of her child Tohassannah, the State Treasurer shall pay said pension to the said agent, on his order.

On December 16, 1863, the legislature made the last appropriation to pay Cynthia Ann's pension for the years 1864 and 1865.

Uncle Silas Parker's family, like Uncle Isaac, met failure in trying to comfort her. Their solicitations, she did not understand. For the Indian princess would not forsake her ways but retreated to dwell in the secret places of her Indian mind. In 1864, the loss of her daughter, Prairie Flower, left her arms empty. Then death, so kind to sorrow-ravaged hearts, freed Cynthia Ann four years after her return to civilization.

Her relatives buried her near their home in the Fosterville burying ground on the line between Henderson and Anderson counties. Cynthia Ann's mortal prayers to be reunited with her chief and her two sons were answered in part after death. Today, at the foot of the Wichita Mountains near Cache, Oklahoma, on the Indian reservation over which her son, Chief Quannah Parker presided, Cynthia Ann lies buried beside him. When Lawrence Sullivan Ross was governor of Texas, 1887–1891, Chief Quannah, a friend of many Texans, was given the right by the United States government to remove his mother's remains from her Texas grave to the Indian reservation.

CHAPTER 20

Decisions
of 1861 and 1862

FOR FORT WORTHIANS there would be several decisions to be made in the year 1861. Should Texas secede from the Union? Should the state return to the status of a republic or join the Confederate States of America? Should Fort Worthians haul down the United States flag, born of their grandfathers' blood, saved by their fathers' blood in the War of 1812, and for which they themselves fought during the Mexican War? Should Fort Worthians go to war, consign all their worldly goods and give their sons to battlefields as the price of their allegiance to a new nation?

Incisive decisions were to be met in 1861, and straightway. Eight days after the New Year's celebration, Tarrant County voters made a choice. Heeding the call of Justice Roberts and his group, because Houston had refused to act, Tarrant men went to the polling places to elect delegates to a state convention which was to consider secession.

There were four candidates: Colonel Johnson of Johnson's Station, and D. C. Dade, district attorney of the Sixteenth District, opposing secession; Colonel Nathaniel Terry of Fort Worth and Josiah Cook of Birdville urging secession. The latter two were elected to represent this county in the state convention when it assembled in Austin, January 28, 1861. From the official roster of delegates to the convention published in the *Texas Almanac*, 1862, the following information is given concerning the two delegates:

Terry, Nat C., Born Virginia, Age 62, immigrated to Texas 1854, planter, Postoffice Fort Worth. Cook, J. E., Born South Carolina. Age 39, immigrated to Texas 1858, blacksmith, Postoffice Birdville.

Governor Houston, hoping to forestall secession, had convened the legislature in extraordinary session. It met on January 21, one week before the state convention assembled. Dr. R. M. Gano, of Grapevine, represented Tarrant County in the House of Representatives. Tarrant County in the Twentieth Senatorial District was grouped with the counties of Johnson, Erath, Parker and Palo Pinto. The senator from this district in the Ninth Legislature, 1861–1862, was a citizen of Weatherford.

Houston's message to the legislature was packed with caution as well as fantasy. He counseled against secession, urged concerted action with the Southern states, and if secession became inevitable, he wished Texas to remain independent; because, he said, "Texas has views of expansion not common to many of her sister states, although an empire within herself, she feels that there is an empire beyond [her limits] essential to her security."

What rampant imperialism and what a plan! But the old hero of San Jacinto seemed dispossessed of his magnetism. His dazzling design fell upon deaf ears. In one thing only was Houston victorious—he urged that "whatever was done it should be referred to the people."

According to schedule, the state convention assembled in Austin on January 28. It immediately drafted an ordinance of secession; directed that this ordinance be submitted to the qualified voters of Texas on February 23; and if the majority of votes called for the secession of Texas from the Union, it would take effect on March 2, 1861. It would require every moment until March 2 to call the election and tabulate the results, because the state must secede before Lincoln's inauguration on March 4. Some secessionists said it was a point of honor, as Texas must avoid the necessity of submitting a single day to "Black Republican rule." Only eight of the 170-odd delegates in the convention voted against the ordinance for secession, and Colonel Terry was not one of them.

While the convention was meeting in Austin, six states: South Carolina, Mississippi, Florida, Alabama, Georgia, and Louisiana, were writing a constitution for the Confederate States of America. Although Texans had not voted for secession, the Austin convention believed that Texas would, and that Texas would join the Southern confederation.

Therefore seven delegates were sent by the convention to Montgomery, Alabama, in the hope that the legislators would be home to vote on the epoch-making day, February 23, 1861. The legislature had walked in harmony with the convention by passing an act to submit the ordinance of secession to a vote of the qualified electors on the same day as that set by the convention, and that returns be made to the secretary of state. Thus two sets of returns and two separate counts of the voters were to be made from each county.

Between February 5 and March 2, the battle in Fort Worth between the secessionists and antisecessionists, or Unionists, fervidly rushed toward the climax. C. B. Mitchell said, "It got so that up to four and five nights a week we'd hear debates and speeches in the Masonic Hall." Fort Worthians were the recipients of their share of the propaganda which filled Texas. The conservative *Dallas Herald*, the chief source of news for Fort Worthians, came out decisively for the cause of secession, Another source of printed persuasion for secession was the "Declaration of Causes," prepared by the convention. Some of the 20,000 printed were distributed in Fort Worth. The antisecessionists or Unionists of the town found their chief support in the Austin newspaper, *The Southern Intelligencer*. Soiled and frayed from much reading, these Austin and Dallas newspapers many days old were to be found by the shoppers in the mercantile stores on Fort Worth's public square: Daggett and Turner, Brinson and Slaughter, Berliner and Samuels, and Alexander Neatherly. In those days, trading was mixed with talk and leisure.

Colonel Terry returned from the convention to Fort Worth in a triumphant spirit, but it was not unanimous acclaim that greeted him. When he climbed from the stagecoach at Andrews Tavern, the bell was ringing for the supper hour. Before joining his friends in the hotel, he hired a rider to go to his plantation and instruct his body servant Uncle Daniel, to come for him in the buggy. Over well-filled platters of fowl and meat in the Andrews hostelry the town's political leaders dined with him. In all eagerness they wanted details of both events and subtle happenings which occurred at the Austin convention, as well as an account of the innermost thoughts of the men in high places—little things but vital ones which do not become printed lines in the newspapers.

Johnson, Peter Smith, Dade, and Terrell were pleased with Terry's telling of James Throckmorton's dramatic speech. Colonel Terry said that when Throckmorton was called upon to vote yes or no on the question of the secession, he arose and said: "Mr. President, in view of the responsibility in the presence of God and my country—and unawed by the wild spirit of revolution around me—I vote 'no.' "

Colonel Terry, in order to emphasize how unanimous was the secession, said, "Remember only eight delegates voted 'no.' " Continuing with enthusiasm, he described how hisses arose from all parts of the hall in response to Throckmorton's statement; whereupon, Throckmorton again arose and replied, "Mr. President, when the rabble hiss, well may patriots tremble."

The legal minds of Terrell and Smith reacted with gusto. "Where could we find more men with such courageous individualism?" asked Terrell. Then he posed another question: "If the majority vote for secession, cannot Texas take a separate action?" His challenge evoked emotional opinions.

Colonel Johnson, as an intimate friend of Governor Houston, no doubt understood the workings of Houston's mind which opposed secession, but if it came, Houston had a plan that Texas should return to her sovereign status of republic and set in motion a movement to bring Mexico under the control of Texas and other territory to the West, possibly New Mexico and Arizona.

Johnson, Terrell, Smith and Dade could not lessen Terry's ardor for secession and a southern confederacy, although in the past he had followed their advice. He dismissed their counsel with a confident shrug. Too long had he heard the arguments of the Sons of Liberty in Alabama, and now those of the Knights of the Golden Circle held him fast.

In the late dusk of February, Colonel Terry seated himself beside his faithful slave, Uncle Daniel, and for the moment, relaxed as his buggy rolled along the Cold Springs Road behind his excellent horses. He mentally praised the freedom of life on the prairies of Tarrant County. His pride in his plantation in the Trinity lowlands cheered him to the extent that he temporarily forgot the bitter defeat and humiliating losses in Alabama. "All this new way of life must be saved," he thought, "and it will be, if the people of Tarrant County will only vote right on February twenty-third." Meanwhile he would exert every effort to lead them in the path of "right" balloting.

On February 23, 1861, ballots were almost evenly divided for and against secession. The vote for secession carried by a majority of only twenty-eight out of about 800 votes polled.

Colonel Terry, having cast his vote, left the following morning in order to reach Austin in time for the reconvening of the convention. Captain Daggett and Isbell gathered a group to give him a good send-off.

On March 2, 1861, the twenty-fifth birthday of the Declaration of

Texas Independence from Mexico, the conventions reassembled and declared Texas once again a free sovereign state. That was the mandate the people of Texas had given at the polls on February 23. Two days later, the convention adopted an ordinance, providing immediate union with the Confederate States of America. This last act Houston declared illegal. The people, he said, had voted for secession; therefore he accepted it, but the people had not given the convention authority to join the Confederacy.

Defying Houston's objection, the convention requested all state officials to appear before the body and take an oath of allegiance to the government of the Confederate States of America in Montgomery. Houston refused. Colonel Terry was vexed with his old friend, and voted with the majority to remove him from the governorship by declaring the office of the governor vacant, and to make Lieutenant Governor Edward Clark, governor. On March 24, the convention, having ratified the Constitution of the Confederacy, adjourned. On March 14, the convention had passed an ordinance qualifying the following officers for Tarrant County: chief justice, William Quayle; district clerk, W. B. (Bony) Tucker; county clerk, Gideon Nance; assessor and collector, J. A. Hust; sheriff, W. O. Yantes; surveyor, F. Wilcox.

Knights of the Golden Circle and the Sons of Liberty were well on their way toward their realization of a great sovereign power built upon the institution of slavery. Colonel Terry returned to Fort Worth to join others in their work to make the Confederacy a "going concern" in northwest Texas. He was not completely happy, for he realized that only the first hurdle was cleared, that now Texas faced war and that in war, the game of chance and fortune burdens a man with anxiety.

Many others could not hold fast to the Biblical admonition, "Be not overanxious." A luminous heavenly body lighted the northwest skies in the spring of 1861. It was a natural phenomenon, a comet putting on an astonishing show. Wondering faces looked into the heavens at its ominous glow. "An omen of bad luck for our people," asserted those who were perturbed over the contentious issue of slavery, and foreseeing the approach of war.

Before dawn, April 12, 1861, Confederate guns opened fire from three sides on Fort Sumter, South Carolina. A small Federal force, hungry and with little ammunition under Major Anderson, had refused to surrender the fort to the new Confederate government. Three weeks after the fall of Fort Sumter, the news reached Tarrant County.

Men did not think—they acted. Horsemen rode the backwoods of the county telling the isolated farmers the news. In consternation each indi-

vidual heard that drilling grounds had been designated in various parts
of the county for volunteers going to war. Men too old to fight, were expected to join the frontier guards organizing to defend women and
children against the Indians. The horsemen rode on. Each farmer looked
at his fields. His plans for clearing timber and other chores, were
swallowed up in the sorrowful vision of seeing sons go off to fight for a
new government, the Confederate States of America. This government,
he had not yet learned to love. "Why didn't Sam Houston save the
Union?" he mused. "I voted for him because he promised to preserve
the Union, if elected governor in '59; then he repeated the promise when
inaugurated on December 21, 1859."

Little did this toiler of the earth, believing so profoundly in the power
of democracy and the common man's vote, understand that his will and
the will of some men like himself, could not have prevailed in a dexterous
campaign waged by adroit statesmen determined that their will was
best. Of that which had taken place in far-off Austin and in high circles
of politics, he had no knowledge.

Like an avalanche, the war broke and swept men from their routine
paths. Men too old to fight remained at home with troubled hearts.
Their sons gone, their shoulders were bent with heavier burdens to keep
the economic and political wheels turning. Young men rushed to arms
marching away with their comrades in selfless action, while their women
carded wool, spun, wove, and knitted. For four years such was the pattern of every Tarrant County inhabitant.

From the state tax record of 1861, Tarrant County was able to contribute her just share to the war. The total value of taxable property
was $1,342,614. There were 199,730 acres of taxable land valued at
$541,825; 756 Negroes valued at $337,552; 5,293 horses valued at
$206,429; 32,999 head of cattle valued at $161,536; and 13,800 sheep
valued at $24,948. The value of miscellaneous property was $19,625.
Poll tax collection amounted to $385; and the ad valorem tax was
$2,818.17.

Men with the most acreage and slaves, and farmers with the greatest
"know-how" in the environs of Fort Worth such as Colonel Terry and
Henry Daggett, northeast of town; Captain Daggett and Jeremiah Ashbury, south of town; Paul Isbell, George Grant, James K. Allen, Doctor
Woods, and Elijah Farmer of the White Settlement; Jeff Earl, James
Ventioner the grain farmer, and Abraham Anderson the stock farmer,
north of town; Lemuel Edwards, cattleman, and Wright Conner, farmer,

west of town; and Samuel Loving, R. J. Tandy and Benjamin P. Ayers east of town, all took inventory of their wheat, corn, stock, and wool and made plans to step-up production in order to have larger harvests in the fall.

Some of these men rode the county talking with the small farmers in order to know how deep the Confederate government could dip into the barrel of Tarrant County supplies. On May 15, 1861, J. N. Dodson wrote from Fort Worth to Justice Roberts, leader of the secessionists in Tyler, reporting that "Colonel Terry and the leading spirits of Tarrant County were alive to the times," that grain crops in Tarrant were good for the Confederate Army, and that the great difficulty Tarrant County men faced was the question of where to get arms. Nevertheless they were, he said,

... trying to arm themselves so far as their means will go—recently a thousand dollars was raised in a few minutes, some persons putting in their last little morsel of pocket change. Where will we get the arms—shall we turn out and get workmen and make arms? Please advise.

Dodson knew that Fort Worth men were a determined lot in spite of difficulties, a fact of which he wished Justice Roberts to be aware. In his report he wrote, "They are much more cool and deliberate in this section." In truth, Tarrant men were calm and decisive; therein lay their strength.

Julian Feild, in Mansfield, offered himself for military service, but his offer was declined, and instead, he was given a commission in the Quartermaster Department. He was instructed to stay at his mill, grind wheat, load his freighters with flour, and keep them moving to Shreveport and Jefferson.

Charles Turner, although in Houston's camp opposing secession, buckled under when Texas joined the Confederacy. Prominent ranchmen were designated as "government stock raisers." They were to furnish the Commissary Department of the army with beef for which the Confederate government paid $40 a head. Thus Charles Turner was placed in charge of the Beef Commissary of this area. Food Commissary would have been nearer the correct title for he had as his task to gather beef, wheat, flour, and other food supplies for the soldiers, and to freight them to the Red River stations. All day long and part of the late evenings he worked at the job with about eight men to assist him. Sam Chapman was his chief aid.

Paul Isbell, also given a commission in the Quartermaster's Department with headquarters in Dallas, traveled northwest Texas and as far south as Waco, gathering horses and mules for the Confederate Army.

Lawyer J. C. Terrell was commissioned by Judge Devine of San Antonio as "Confederate states receiver of tax in kind for fifteen counties in northwest Texas." Tax in kind meant that the Confederate government tithed the products of the earth from the inhabitants which had to be received by officers bonded for the purpose.

Colonel Johnson laid aside his correspondence with President Jefferson Davis of the Confederacy concerning organization of volunteers long enough to take stacks of leather, and piling them high on the bench of Uncle Dave, one of his slaves, told him to make boots and saddlebags because he, his sons, and the neighbors' boys would be needing them soon.

Junius W. Smith left Fort Worth to accept his appointment as Confederate States Receiver.

Little men and men of affluence whose military knowledge was confined to Indian warfare joined the frontier guard, an imperative need. Tarrant County had lost her northwest wall of defense. No longer were there United States troops stationed in the chain of federal forts which had formed an arching bulwark against Indians.

Early in February 1861, before the secession of Texas took effect, Major General D. E. Twiggs, in command of United States forces in Texas with headquarters in San Antonio, had surrendered under force his garrison and supplies to General Henry E. McCullough. On February 18, he had agreed to evacuate all forts in Texas, surrender their garrison equipage and their arms, only allowing the soldiers to retain their side arms, and such facilities of transportation as were required to carry them out of the state. Thus, by the last of February, General McCullough, acting upon orders of the Committee on Public Safety, had "without the firing of a shot put out of action more than ten percent of the regular army of the United States, and has acquired military supplies and other property valued at $3 million."

These troops, however, did not leave Texas. After the fall of Fort Sumter, the Federal troops were held as prisoners of war. Therefore, during 1861, volunteer minutemen—and there were many from Fort Worth—replaced United States soldiers on the frontier to keep the Indians in check. In 1862, Texas organized the Frontier Regiment which many joined. In 1863, it was reorganized, becoming the Mounted Regiment of Texas State Troops. By December of 1863, conditions were serious; therefore, men liable for military duty were required to serve part of their time in frontier defense.

With children bouncing about on top of the coverlet stretched over the wagon loaded with the freshly clipped wool, Mrs. Noel Burton, the wife of Fort Worth's first saloon owner (who had abandoned that business for farming), drove the wagon to the creek to wash the wool. On the seat beside her was a neighbor, and under the wagon seat was a large hamper of lunch. All hands, even those of the little boys and girls, were needed to get ready those extra yards of jean for uniforms, and those extra socks before the boys marched from Tarrant County to war. Mrs. Burton wanted to help fill Tom and Ben Johnson's saddlebags with socks and gloves, a small thank-you for Mrs. Johnson and the colonel, whose mercy and bounty were always a benediction to all the farm families who knew them.

Lucy Burton, age five, was given knitting needles made of turkey quills and taught to knit. She was told that when she had learned the stitch she would be given steel needles, since she, too, must help win the war. There were many mothers like Mrs. Burton, as well as countless little girls like Lucy, learning to knit on turkey quills at the age of five.

Mrs. Archibald Franklin Leonard and her aged mother, who had moved to Birdville after Mr. Leonard's mill (located nine miles from Fort Worth) burned, organized the women of Birdville community to spin, weave, make uniforms and bandages. With such industry, the women met the crisis. Most Tarrant men marched away with plenty of socks and well covered in jean uniforms.

While older men gathered supplies, and the women made clothes, the young men and boys rushed to the designated drilling grounds in Tarrant County to drill through the summer and fall of 1861. Volunteers, enthusiastically backing up their beliefs with their lives, drilled back and forth and around Fort Worth's public square, until some of them fell from exhaustion. Sprawling for awhile on the prairie grass, they continued their military training in gay boisterousness. The giant Captain Eph Daggett, his robust vigor undiminished by fifty birthdays, became master of ceremonies; and with other veterans of the Mexican War, they demonstrated how they had drilled; and how they had fought hand-to-hand skirmishes with Mexicans adept with the dagger. No better instructors could have been found, for warfare was no novelty to these feuding Sabine River men. They had spent years in East Texas feuds, and it was said that they were the core of the fighting in the Mexican War, helping General Worth win at Monterrey.

To Howard Peak, six years old, and his little playmates, the public square was a panorama of military glamor which surpassed a boy's dream of something great. They no longer needed to plan their amusements. There was so much excitement on the square, it was almost a strain on their attentive powers to grasp all the sights. There was Colonel Griffin, newcomer from Georgia, who had presided over Tarrant County's mass meeting in November, and of whom it was said "he knows more about the latest military tactics than any man in town." He shouted orders like heavy firing artillery to the volunteers of Tom Johnson's company, as these raw recruits blundered. Men on the sidelines laughed.

There was Doctor Peak astride his horse, Grey Eagle, leading his cavalry through maneuvers. There was "old Withem's Fife and Drum Corps" which brought everyone out of the stores and houses, as they entered Fort Worth from Birdville playing "The Girl I Left Behind Me."

And there was William Quayle's company of Mounted Riflemen. Quayle, sea captain for many years, had settled at Grapevine. Endowed with two talents: one for discipline, the other for giving orders, he was quick in training a company, and the first to leave Tarrant County.

On August 20, 1861, there was no space left at the hitching posts around the public square, lined with buggies, wagons and horses. Crowds had come to wave good-bye to Quayle's company of Mounted Riflemen, who had volunteered for twelve months' service. There were ninety-eight privates and thirteen officers: Captain Quayle, three lieutenants, five sergeants and four corporals. What a parade of manhood—mere boys, young men, and older men molded strong by frontier hardships. There was sixteen-year-old Mark Elliston of Birdville, whose venturesome spirit had always disquieted his relatives, and this same spirit had now sent him headlong into war in spite of his widowed mother's pleadings. There was thirty-six-year-old A. M. Hightower from Smithfield, a six-foot-three Scotch-Irishman, weighing 200 pounds and wearing size thirteen shoes. He had the distinction of bringing to Tarrant County the first breech-loading shotgun, and was later remembered as being strong in thought and direct in action.

It was no miracle that Captain Quayle had succeeded well in assembling a company on this frontier. His horsemen were clad in jean uniforms of varying blue hues, some of which were well made and others with multitudinous defects of tailoring. In evidence were guns and rifles of different kinds and ages, some inherited from the American Revolution. There were six-foot squirrel rifles, shotguns, caps and balls, and what not. Each man had one or two six-shooters and a homemade saber. Some of these sabers had been fashioned in Fort Worth to meet the arms crisis. There were Choctaw ponies, domesticated mustangs, fine horses and a few mules. Homemade saddles and bridles were to be seen as well as some made by expert saddlers, such as Frank Knaar. At the head of the cavalry troop floated a hand-sewn Confederate flag made by several women at Grapevine, among whom were Mrs. Martha C. Quayle, sister-in-law of the captain.

In leaving Fort Worth, this assemblage of frontiersmen-turned-soldiers circled the public square to demonstrate to the crowd for the last time, their newly acquired military training; then descended the high bluff and disappeared from sight. The crowd hastened to the edge of the bluff from where they watched the Mounted Riflemen cross the Trinity, ride away over the prairie until they became a blur on the north horizon. Grayson County was their destination. Here they were mustered in as Company A, 9th Texas Cavalry Regiment, which was organized October 2, 1861. At that time, William Quayle became lieutenant colonel and Thomas G. Berry, who left Tarrant County as a sergeant of Quayle's company, became the captain of Company A.

There was no end to farewells. Fort Worthians in September, 1861, said good-by to the second company of volunteers to leave Tarrant County. It was led by a man who struck out to do things without delay —Captain M. J. Brinson. He had been merchant and co-owner with Mr. Slaughter of Fort Worth's first concrete store building. He was also one of the charter members of the first Masonic order; a plantation owner near Johnson's Station, and a son-in-law of the colonel. His company had an uproarious send-off. Tarrant citizens were as demonstrative in September as they had been in August when they had cheered the departure of Quayle's company. Almost the entire populace of eastern Tarrant County rode to Fort Worth to see the patriots off. They waved good-by to James and John Watson, sons of Patrick Watson, founder of Watsonville community four miles northeast of Arlington. There were others from the families of the first settlers in eastern Tarrant County which included Louis Finger, Charley and Will Goodwin, and Dart and Burt Anderson. There were only a few volunteers from Birdville and Grapevine, because most of them had left with Quayle's company. People of the White Settlement went en masse to cheer their boys as they galloped off to fight "Black Republicanism." Among these young men were T. S. Coleman, Tom and Ben Hagood, and Sam Petty.

Citizens whistled, cheered, and waved as Brinson's cavalry paraded. Captain Daggett roared in his lion-like voice when Bunk Adams, his kinsman and Fort Worth's famous fiddler and square dance caller, passed in parade. Antone, a lonely Mexican in typical Latin fashion, did his pompous best to give the crowd a show and, although without relatives, he received his share of cheers. Young boys, whose parents prevented them from volunteering, yelled approval when their fifteen-year-old comrade, Merida Ellis, rode by. He had withdrawn from Dr. Peake's company which did not get off soon enough to gratify his youthful enthusiasm. Women wept in the din of cheers.

In order to end quickly the bitterness of parting and to demonstrate their fine horsemanship, Captain Brinson ordered the company to gallop around the public square. Then without further ado, he led the cavalry across the Trinity and rode northward over the dusty, dry September prairies toward Grayson County. Seventy volunteers had joined him for twelve months' service. In Grayson County, they met their comrades who had gone away with Quayle's company. Under the command of Captain M. J. Brinson, they were mustered in as Company D, 9th Texas Cavalry Regiment.

Peter Smith had opposed Texas secession and union with the Confederacy, but he knew that a few men of his opinion could not preserve liberty in their way. The will of the majority had decreed differently; so he decided to fight for frontier liberty in his neighbor's way. At first, he joined Dr. Peake's cavalry company, but having made up his mind to fight, he was in a hurry. He assisted Captain Thomas A. Moody, a man of property—whose contribution made him one of the important guarantors of the Tarrant County Courthouse—to raise a company of 150 men. In the fall of 1861, Captain Moody's company left Fort Worth soon after that of Captain Brinson's.

As Smith, astride a fine horse, rode out of town and headed south toward San Antonio, he no doubt was contemplating the happy years spent in his adopted home. In the fall of 1853, he had walked into Fort Worth a penniless youth just out of college. Perhaps he hoped that destiny would bring him back from the war to help build Fort Worth from village to city, and that such would be Fort Worth's manifest destiny.

Beside him jogged Louis Wetmore, the former dragoon of the old fort. Wetmore had fled from Germany to escape compulsory military service, arrived in New York in time to fight in the Mexican War, and to help build the military post at Fort Worth. Then upon mustering out of service, he became a prosperous stock farmer south of town. He had but recently returned from New Orleans, where he had gone to take passage to Germany in order to claim his father's estate. Refused a passport because of the approaching war, Wetmore had spent his money for luxuries in New Orleans for his wife and two little daughters. Among his gifts were crystal goblets and a set of French china dishes which would adorn the wedding feasts of many brides of Fort Worth during the late sixties and seventies. Now Wetmore was thirty-three years old and riding to war again. "Would it always be war?" he queried.

Upon reaching San Antonio, Smith and Wetmore, with their Tarrant County comrades, were mustered into Confederate service as Company K, 7th Texas Cavalry under Colonel William Steel, General H. H. Sibley's brigade, and ordered to the campaign in New Mexico. John R. Baylor, commander of Texas troops, had by proclamation in August, 1861, established the Territory of Arizona, which included New Mexico, so that Confederate troops were sent to conquer the area as a part of the plan for a "greater Confederacy."

Drilling, volunteers leaving, and the war news coming to Fort Worth convinced Dabney Dade that Americans were really faced with a long struggle. Like his law partner, Terrell, he had opposed secession; but now Terrell was considering joining the Confederate Army and in doing so, he would support his state of Texas. Dade, a Unionist, could not accept his partner's reasoning. Fort Worth's law firm of Terrell and Dade closed. On April 22, 1861, townsmen gathered at Andrews Tavern to see Dade off on the stagecoach. He was returning to his native state, Missouri, which had remained faithful to the Union. In both masculine and feminine camps despite their divergent creeds, sorrowful good-bys were said. With Dade gone and the Confederacy needing men, Terrell resigned his commission as "Confederate states receiver of tax in kind." An older man could fill his place. Early in 1862, he opened a recruiting station. Being an orator and possessing magnetism, he was able to organize a company of volunteers.

From all parts of Tarrant County men answered Terrell's call: thirty-eight privates and nine officers. Among the privates were James Grant and William T. Allen, sons of the first home-builders of the White Settlement. There was also Horatio Brown, whose father had farmed with slaves near Marine Creek since 1858, and whose mother was sister-in-law of Jerome Bonaparte, brother of Napoleon. Another private was Jacob Samuels, son of Lemuel Samuels, who had opened a mercantile store on the square in 1860. Little Jacob, thirteen years old, was on Dr. Peak's muster roll until he heard Terrell's speeches. Jacob loved oratory, and Terrell became his idol. Love of oratory carried Jacob away to war, and the music of oratory lived in his future son Sydney Samuels, who in the twentieth century would contribute much in legal knowledge to the city. Among the officers in Terrell's company was Tobe Johnson, whose parents settled northwest of the fort before the troops left in 1853; and John Frank Elliston of Birdville, whose father had died there in 1857.

In blustery March of 1862, with their hats pulled well down on their ears, Captain Terrell's company rode away to service through the waving prairie grass of Fort Worth's future Main Street. Two wagons of provisions rumbled behind them. They were bound for Lafayette, Louisiana, to join Lieutenant Colonel Ed Waller's five other companies. They were mustered in as "Company F, Captain J. C. Terrell, Waller's Battalion, Cavalry, Tom Green's First Brigade, then Hardeman's Brigade, Walker's Division, Texas troops, Trans-Mississippi Department."

> Johnson Station, Texas
> February 9, 1862

Captain C. M. Peak
. . . Have your company at Dallas by tomorrow. I will extend time to Thursday night. You should by all means swell your number of privates to 60 by that day if possible.

These were the instructions of Colonel Johnson, a tense man, who for many months had been pushing and pulling a giant project to fulfillment. He had become a centrifugal force in the military organization of Tarrant County in the summer of 1861. Now, Johnson planned to raise not a company of cavalry, but a cavalry brigade. President Jefferson Davis, in correspondence, had assured Colonel Johnson that if he succeeded in organizing a brigade of Texans, he would be commissioned brigadier general in the Confederate Army.

Men and youths converged upon Johnson's Station from Tarrant and adjoining counties. At night, Johnson's Station blazed with campfires. By day it bustled with the recruiting and drilling of men past fifty, who had received their baptism of gunfire in the Mexican War; and of youths, clutching awkwardly their heirloom guns and homemade sabers, who had come to learn the dreadful business of war.

"I paid $40 for a double-barreled shotgun and entered as a high private in Captain A. R. Reagan's company F, in Colonel Johnson's First Cavalry Regiment at Johnson's Station," recalled Abe Harris in 1920, then a historic personage in the record of the founding of Fort Worth. He had been offered a commission as colonel of Tarrant County's Militia, but would not accept, since he felt that he had urged too many youths to join the service. Then, too, desire to go with them was deep.

Harris, Fort Worth's cabinetmaker, closed his shop near the public square; and took his three motherless children to the farm of their grandparents, Mr. and Mrs. Wright Conner. During the fretful days after the outbreak of the Civil War, his wife had died. A veteran of the Mexican War, he had remained, as stated earlier, a soldier in the fort, and was instrumental in selecting the best timber for the building of that fort. After his honorable discharge, he had tried farming for a time, but he was a cabinetmaker by talent, and had prospered in Fort Town at his trade. Ten years ago, he thought that he was done with war, but in 1862, he rushed to embrace it. Perhaps it would renew his spirit.

Colonel Johnson had commissioned Dr. Peak to raise a company for his brigade which he was assembling at his place. Peak was to draw upon the men of Fort Worth and the western section of Tarrant County.

During the first weeks of 1862, Dr. Peak organized the company of Tarrant County Rifles. He worked diligently at turning out a well-drilled company, daily stirring the dust into clouds on Fort Worth's square; and the volunteers, living up to the best of their abilities, had become proficient troops. Dr. W. P. Burts, who voted for secession and approved of the war, was company surgeon but later paid a substitute to take his place as did other officers: P. C. David, John R. Garaghty, W. O. Yantes, George Boone, and Thomas M. Matthews.

Among the privates were J. B. Andrews of Andrews Tavern, Nathaniel Terry, Junior, son of Colonel Terry, the leading secessionist, and Ephraim Albert Dickson, promising young businessman engaged since 1856 in the mercantile business with his father in Fort Worth. There came David Snow from Birdville; W. J. Terry and Gideon Nance from the White Settlement; Jeff Earl, northeast of Fort Worth; and W. R. Loving from the first family to settle in Sycamore Creek east of town. There were those who had arrived in Fort Worth in 1860 and 1861— James P. Alford and Harry B. Catlett.

The latter young man had come to Fort Worth to look after 28,000 acres of land, his share of a large real estate partnership, which his father, H. G. Catlett, had formed in 1845 with Senator Toombs and Governor Crawford of Georgia. The older Catlett surveyed 84,000 acres; but death ended his extensive plans for land sale. Young Henry Catlett forgot about the 28,000 acres, joined Peak's company, went to war, experienced the postwar depression and sold the land for very little, because he could not keep paying taxes on his profitless holdings.

This story, however, explains to thousands of Tarrant County property owners today, holding land northwest of Fort Worth in the Lake Worth area and extending into Wise County, the reason for the names Toombs, Crawford, and Catlett appearing on their deeds.

In the last session of drilling before the troop's departure, Grey Eagle, Dr. Peak's horse, fell with the physician. The men had to ride away without Captain Peak, who was so seriously injured that he was incapacitated for military service until later in the war, when he served as an army surgeon in Louisiana. Perhaps Dr. Peak's accident made it necessary for Dr. Burts to send a substitute in order that he might remain at home to care for the health of the community. Soon afterwards, Burts was appointed conscript surgeon for Tarrant County. At the head of Peak's company now rode Captain Ben Johnson, Colonel Johnson's second son. In the words of Harry B. Catlett, "Doctor Peak's captaincy went to Ben Johnson, first lieutenant, and I was promoted from second to first lieutenant."

Preparation, worry, toil, then Colonel Johnson's work was established. Seated in his saddle, he patted his horse, breathed deeply and shouted orders. Johnson's Brigade rode eastward in February of 1862. Dallas would be their first stop, where formalities of organization would be completed before their long ride to Little Rock, Arkansas, headquarters for the final induction into the Army of the Confederacy. Perhaps the colonel was happy. He was off to the war to fight as of old for his beliefs, and with him were his two eldest sons, Tom and Ben, each an officer and worthy of his rank. Likely his fifty-one years of successful living had given him a grateful spirit. Jobian losses and defeats were to be his measure in the remaining four years of his life.

On April 17, 1862, Johnson was appointed colonel, "Provisional Army, Confederate States from the state of Texas to rank from February 15, 1862" and was assigned to the 14th Regiment, Texas Cavalry. Following instructions, he led his Texas brigade to Little Rock, Arkansas. There on May 8, 1862, they were mustered into the regular Confederate Army as a part of the 14th and 15th Cavalry regiments. At this time Abe Harris, who had left Johnson's Station a private, was made a lieutenant colonel in the 14th. This regiment was to serve in Louisiana and Arkansas, but its principal service was to be in Tennessee and Georgia.

Colonel Johnson, having mustered his troops into Confederate service, left Little Rock and hastened to Richmond, doubtless happy in the thought of the pleasurable pride with which President Davis would receive his report of the Texas brigade, but politics take devious courses.

Perhaps from an unfriendly source, President Davis had heard not only of Johnson's opposition to Texas secession but also of his opposition to Texas joining the Confederacy, even after Texas seceded. Then, too, it was remembered that Johnson was an ardent Houston supporter. The reason for President Davis' action is not important, but the result of his action is significant to the history of Tarrant County. No reason had been given, but President Davis, contrary to his assurance to reward Johnson with the rank of brigadier general if he raised a Texas brigade, conferred no such rank. Johnson's military renown, integrity, and popularity brought the brigade together; but now military rank as commanding officer went to another. Astounded and mortified, Colonel Johnson left Richmond and returned home.

However, later, he was commissioned by the Richmond government to supervise the blockade running, so necessary to the life of both soldiers and citizens of the Confederacy. He maintained communication with Liverpool, England, through Mexico and Cuba. Texas cotton, together with cotton of the other Confederate states, was sent across Texas to Tampico, Mexico, from where it was shipped to Britain, or it was loaded on ships in Texas ports, which ran through the Union blockade to British Jamaica and Spanish Cuba. Texas, by way of Mexico, or through her own ports, was the Confederacy's only gateway to Europe from whence came needed supplies of medicine, arms, and manufactured goods.

Johnson did serve and served well. One of his soldiers in this economic war for survival of the Confederacy related his story to a reporter which was published in the Fort Worth *Star-Telegram*, May 4, 1916.

I drove an ox-team from Bonham to Laredo working for M. T. Johnson, hauling cotton to Mexico. Cotton was worth its weight in gold. The shipments from this section of Texas was [sic] destined for Brownsville but Texans were not confident that Brownsville would remain in Confederate hands. Therefore, much of the cotton was hauled to Laredo or towns higher up the Rio Grande, sold there and then hauled down the Mexican side to Brownsville. A trip by ox-team from this section to Brownsville took the better part of a year.

At least ten companies of volunteers, it has been said, left Tarrant County during the years 1861 and 1862. According to official war records, the first company in one regiment was from Tarrant County. This account follows:

Thirty-fourth (Alexander's) Texas Cavalry Regiment organized in Indian Territory February, 1862 was composed of ten companies. Company A was from Tarrant County and its captains from first to last were M. W. Davenport, —— Crowley, and —— Baldwin.

By way of summary, the other volunteer companies from Tarrant were those of Captains William Quayle, M. J. Brinson, J. C. Terrell, Thomas A. Moody, Alexander C. Neatherly, C. R. Reagan, Carroll M. Peak, Ben Johnson, Charles Turner, M.T. Johnson, and Richard R. Gano.

The latter was one of the few Texans rising to the rank of general in the Confederate Army. Richard M. Gano had settled near Grapevine in 1856. Versatile and successful, he was a doctor, stockman, farmer, and representative from Tarrant County in the state legislature, 1860–1861. Favoring secession, he resigned from the House of Representatives. Then from his friend General Albert Sidney Johnston, he received authority to raise troops and report to him at Bowling Green, Kentucky. It was done. The official war record states:

Gano's Cavalry Battalion. Merged into 7th Kentucky Cavalry, September 1862—Lieutenant Colonel, Richard R. Gano.

Assigned as captain of a squadron of cavalry in the army on the Tennessee, Gano displayed such military expertness that it raised him to the rank of brigadier general, and prompted his promotion to major general when the war was ended. After the war, Gano sold his property in Birdville and became a citizen of Dallas, where he entered the ministry. As a Church of Christ minister, Gano achieved much success in the field of evangelism.

Among the Tarrant County volunteers joining Gano's company was H. C. Holloway, who returned from the war a colonel, became a prominent Fort Worthian, and a future leader of the movement which established the Fort Worth stockyards.

Apparently there was no need for a conscription law in Tarrant County after such an exodus of her manpower. Nevertheless, there was a Conscription Act passed by the Confederate Congress April 16, 1862. Men from eighteen to thirty-five years of age were required to answer to the call. By September, need of manpower was greater; hence the age limit was raised to forty-five, then changed again to include men from seventeen to fifty; and if a man could afford it, the law permitted the hiring of a substitute. Texans engaged in frontier defense, the professions, agriculture, and industry were exempt.

Troops departing, an emotional outpouring, then an emptiness of spirit—endlessly it had gone on through 1861 and 1862—so it seemed to those who remained at home. In 1863, the saddest sight of all to Fort Worth oldsters was that of Captain Charles Turner departing with a company of sixteen- and seventeen-year-old youths. Boys were needed in 1863 to sustain Confederate troops dwindling by death, disease and desertion. Fort Worthians did not fear for the well-being of Captain Turner's company of youths. A very rich man, Turner had not spared his gold in outfitting the company and drilling them. Fort Worthians grieved because war would destroy their youth, place in their eager eyes a new expression born of the cruel horrors of battle; then, too, death would take its toll of future Tarrant County builders.

Charles Turner led his company to the mouth of the Red River. There they joined Sweet's regiment, Walker's Division, to prevent the Union Army under General Banks from invading Texas. Hardships of campaigning to which forty-year-old Turner, the merchant, was unaccustomed, made him ill with fever. To take his place, he paid a substitute five hundred dollars in gold and returned to Fort Worth to fight the war on the economic front.

CHAPTER 21

Harvest Time
of Decisions

VOLUNTEERS were gone to the Confederate Army. Other men were riding in the Frontier Guard to keep the Indians beyond the new frontier line of defense extending from Lampasas County through Brown, Comanche, Erath, Young, and Jack counties to the Red River.

Few men were left in Fort Worth. The town was almost depopulated, and would remain a village of a few hundred until the late sixties. In 1861, the population numbered some 350 persons. Now was the harvest time of those decisions made by Tarrant County citizens in 1861 and 1862, to secede from the Union and join the Confederacy. Four years they would wait to learn the outcome of their resolve to fight for slavery and the theory that the rights of each state were supreme. And each day of those years would unravel slowly a portion of the harvest in mounting hardships and losses.

Fort Worthians left at home waited and worked—labored to keep women and children in food. Men formed a "beef club." Each member contributed from time to time a beef for the needy families. Boys hunted wild turkeys and prairie chickens; they gathered wild honey also to provide sweets for the table or for cooking. Supplies dwindled until Fort Worthians were thrown back upon an entirely local and primitive economy. Supply trains arriving from Jefferson and Houston were luxuries of the past. Medicine, coffee, and sugar now came by way of Mexico but were purchased before the few freighters advanced beyond San Antonio. Small quantities which escaped from eager purchasers and found their way into Tarrant County were bought by the few who had the enormous price to pay.

War's inflation in Fort Worth was described by Constant Dodson in a letter written on October 9, 1862, to his son, Jasper Dodson, serving the Confederate Army. Dr. Dodson lived on a farm in the vicinity of the present location of the United States Public Health Service Hospital. He listed the prices of goods on the Fort Worth market:

A bushel of wheat	$ 4.00
100 pounds of flour	15.00
A yard of cloth	4–5.00
A bushel of corn	2.00
100 pounds of pork	20.00

Of his own problem, he wrote: "I have breadstuffs enough to do me if I could keep it, but there are so many passing soldiers it seems like they will eat everything I have."

Food prices soared. A fact the *Dallas Herald* spread on its pages for the readers of North Texas:

June 19, 1861		September 23, 1863	
Ham	16 to 18 cents a pound	Ham	35 cents a pound
Beef cattle	$12 to 15 per head	Beef cattle	$30 per head
Corn	50 cents a bushel	Corn	$1.37 a bushel
Wheat	60 cents a bushel	Wheat	$2.50 a bushel
Oats	50 to 40 cents a bushel	Oats	$1.50 a bushel
Sugar	15 cents a pound	Sugar	35 cents a pound

Statistics could explain high prices. In 1858, it was estimated that 16,000 acres of land were under cultivation in Tarrant County. After 1861, acreage in crops on farms without slaves shrank to meet only necessities—enough cotton for clothes, and enough corn and wheat for bread.

Oats advancing from fifty cents to one dollar and a half a bushel meant starvation for teenage George H. Mulkey. In 1862, at the age of fourteen, he had become a pony express rider. On a daily salary of one dollar, he maintained himself and fed his horse on his route from Waxahachie to Johnson's Station, which he rode in one day; spent the night there, and rode to Birdville and Fort Worth the second day. In 1864, prices were still high, too high for a pony express rider; and George was eighteen, old enough to drive a freighter—a job with more financial re-muneration. He hauled goods from the Houston and Texas Central area near present-day Bryan to Fort Worth, Dallas, and Waxahachie, a dis-tance of about 200 miles. Soon afterwards, George Mulkey joined the Confederate Army, serving one year until the war ended.

Our job was to confiscate meat for the army. We would go through a man's herd and cull out the beeves that were over four years old, and drive off the steers for the army. No, we were not popular and oftentimes the cattlemen took a shot at us, and we had a pretty tough time in general. It was hard too, because we did not want to do it.

Regardless of high prices, good managers in Fort Worth provided suffi-cient food for their families. Olive Peak related how her "Mama," with their slave, Louisa, and other mothers, worked to keep a vegetable gar-den, a home patch of corn, as well as some cane for sorghum molasses. They maintained a few cows, so that there would be plenty of milk, buttermilk, butter, and clabber. They parched wheat and barley as a substitute for coffee. They soaked sycamore balls in oil to light their homes. Candles, or the materials with which to make them, were scarce. Bolts of cloth which formerly could have been purchased at Fort Town stores were nonexistent. Cotton, even that raised in Tarrant County, was difficult to obtain and then at a price too strenuous to meet, because cot-ton and wool were purchased by the Military Board of the Confederacy or taken from the farmers to pay their tenth, or "tax in kind."

Women labored to keep their families in clothes. White hands and black hands carded, spun, and wove. They clothed the man on the home front in coats and trousers made of jean. They dressed their boys in cotton shirts, jean pantaloons, and bedticking suspenders. They made linsey-woolsey dresses for their daughters. For the soldiers, they sewed garments which the Confederacy could not supply in abundance, cut bandages for hospitals, and knitted socks for marching feet and mittens to bear better the weight of the guns.

Before the war the few looms in Fort Worth were usually lent from housewife to housewife. But now every household, or every other one, needed a loom, and there were no freighters hauling lumber from East Texas with which to make the required number. Men provided for them. Members of Masonic Lodge, Chapter 148, went to their lodge building, ripped joints from the first floor and made looms. It had to be that way for survival. So the clatter of the looms along with the tick of the clock marked the slow passing of time.

Though the women could keep their families scantily clothed by constant toil, they could not keep the children in shoes. Most of the children in Fort Worth were barefooted by the winter of 1864. Notwithstanding, Howard Peak, then a child, related that he and his playmates managed to ice skate on the Trinity. A pair of shoes could be shared, and boys at play have always had a genius for devising. The Santa Claus myth, he said, was the greatest war casualty among Fort Worth children. There were no toys, and they watched their mothers bake the animal cookies which they found in their stockings.

Man is born to act. To wait as a spectator of events which would determine answers to their questions was almost intolerable for Fort Worth men. Their tribulation of waiting was made bearable by talk sessions on the public square.

Talk concerned the Confederate government's "tax-in-kind," which each man was paying to the collector at Marshall. His administration extended over fifteen counties of the fifth district, of which Tarrant County was a part. Texas was divided into six districts for the collection of this tax. A few men muttered complaints, as they watched the stacks of cotton collecting on the courthouse grounds, growing in width and height before being hauled away to Marshall.

Men talked about John Chisum, who in 1862 had moved his herds from the range of Denton and Tarrant counties to the Concho country. One thing certain, they said, John would not be shackled by Confederate agents collecting this and that.

Chatter was brisk when it was learned that the mercantile firm of Daggett and Turner had paid to the Richmond government the $30,000 which they owed New York merchants, this being the Confederacy's policy of confiscation of property held by Northern enemies. (After the war, the firm paid their Northern creditors.)

Gossipers surmised about how much gold the various citizens had; and whether the rich men of Fort Worth wholly complied when the Confederate government required all citizens to exchange their gold for Confederate currency. Some men did not obey, but that remained a secret.

Mr. Dickson, one of the merchants on the square, had seen his two sons march away to die for the Confederacy. To him, that was sufficient sacrifice, so he concealed much of his gold in a field on his farm six miles southeast of Fort Worth.

Charles Turner, with his trusted slave Uncle Ben, went in the night and buried a sizable amount of gold under his favorite oak tree which still shades the circle at the entrance to Greenwood Cemetery. Turner reasoned that he had been liberal with his gold. In addition to the $30,000 paid the government, he also had outfitted one company, as related earlier. There was a chance, he reasoned, that the Confederacy might lose. Wars were uncertain, and gold would be needed to start the wheels of trade on Fort Town's square at the close of the war.

Newly elected county officials of Tarrant were conversational topics on the square. There was Chief Justice Stephen Terry, a scholarly lawyer always on the line of duty. It is to be remembered he had come with the Kentucky caravan in 1854, buying land in the White Settlement, and later moving into Fort Town. He replaced William Quayle, who had led a company of Mounted Riflemen to war in August, 1861.

District Clerk W. B. (Bony) Tucker had been inducted into office. No man could chide him for careless work, for he had served well as an official since the late 1850s.

There was County Clerk Gideon Nance, of whom it was said that he was as inflexibly willful in pursuing a cause as his determined scowl indicated. He won distinction for serving sixteen years as county clerk of Tarrant.

There was Assessor-Collector J. A. Hust. Since the creation of the county, he had plodded on horseback from farm to farm. An artful purveyor of public news, he made pleasant the procedure of assessing and collecting taxes in one visit.

The sheriff was J. W. Gillespie, while W. W. McGinnis was surveyor. All of the foregoing men would carry the load of office through the war years.

Townsmen discussed, too, their regret at having to remove the flagpole of the old fort installed by Major Arnold. Its waving in the winter winds of 1862 was a hazard to passersby. Patriots of intense spirit found another flagpole in the woods at the foot of the bluff and erected it on the right side of the main entrance to the courthouse. Thus the Lone Star flag and the Confederate, symbols of the people's patriotism, could again flap to and fro in the winds blowing across the bluff. Seeing the flags, soldiers of former wars saluted when they passed and pondered the need of the Confederacy's law fixing punishment for any person discouraging enlistment in Confederate service. Then they joined other oldsters to discuss the lack of wisdom of the younger generation who did not know that to possess liberties, one must safeguard them even to going to war.

Compassionate women were vexed when they heard in December, 1862, that an Arkansas trader had left in the woods north of Fort Worth a string of one hundred slaves scantily clad in torn cotton clothes to shiver in the winter's cold rain, and to suffer hunger. Begging at farmhouses and at Fort Worth doors to work for shelter and food, the Negroes spread the news that "Marster Carrol, de ole debbil, couldn't sell us and up and went off in de night, leavin' us in de woods!" Fort Worth men rationalized with their wives that panic must have sent Carrol rushing to Texas, where he probably expected to sell his slaves to Tarrant County men whom he thought would not have his acute business discernment so far from the battlefront.

Events of 1862 were enough to frighten a large slave owner and forewarn him of financial ruin if the present trend in affairs continued. General Benjamin F. Butler, also known as "Beast Butler," and Commodore David G. Farragut had captured New Orleans in April, 1862. By that summer, the rumor was that Louisiana and eastern Arkansas would fall into "Beast Butler's" hands. In September, Lincoln announced his Emancipation Proclamation, which was to take effect on the first of January of 1863. In October 1862, Galveston had been captured by Union forces. The cause of the Confederacy appeared dismal.

Master Carrol from Arkansas was wrong in his thinking. Fort Worth men did have business astuteness, also knowledge of events even though they lived on the northern frontier of Texas.

Slaves were not selling. Furthermore, East and South Texas were crowded with Negroes sent to Texas for safekeeping by southern planters east of the Mississippi. The Negro population of Tarrant County also had increased since 1861 by 194 slaves. The state tax record for 1862 listed 950 Negroes valued at $417,180.

In spite of war, the economic picture was not dark in the second year of the conflict. There were 264,887 acres of taxable land valued at $293,925; 37,813 head of cattle valued at $208,047; 14,245 sheep valued at $29,890; the total value of property was $1,701,785, an increase of $359,171 over the year 1861. The state ad valorem tax collected was $5,431.81. The poll tax collected was $882, an increase of $497, which leads one to question the great increase in voters. Perhaps there was more political interest in 1862 than 1861; and another explanation may be the fact that there were still many men in the county who paid their poll tax in 1862 before going to war. Only two companies of volunteers left Tarrant in 1861.

The news of war deaths came all too soon to Fort Worth's square. In late July 1862, the mail hack arrived. John B. Dickson learned that his son and partner, Ephraim Albert Dickson, was dead. The young soldier had gone away in what had been Captain Peak's company, and was mustered in at Little Rock, Arkansas. In the first skirmish, which was with a Kansas regiment of abolitionists, he was shot through the head in the Battle of Black River near Paroquet Bluff, Arkansas, on July 8, 1862. He was buried there with other Texans.

In a few months, the Dickson store closed. Mr. Dickson retired to his farm southeast of Fort Worth. Grief engulfed him. His second son, Dempsey Powell Dickson, having enlisted upon leaving college in 1861, was killed at the Battle of Elk Horn in March of 1862. From a comrade, the father learned that the Texans slain at Elk Horn were rolled in their blankets and buried apart from the others. With this information, Mr. Dickson sent a relative to remove his son from the battlefield to the Dickson burying ground in Arkansas.

Another blow felled Fort Worthians that same late July day that had brought Ephraim Dickson's death notice: Captain Tom Johnson was also dead. Every inhabitant of Johnson's Station mourned. Mrs. Lucy Calvert recalled that as little Lucy Burton, she had wept for this much loved man of Tarrant County, remembering the day he came to say good-by. He gave her an apple from his patent leather saddlebag and kissed her doll farewell.

He was killed in the same cavalry skirmish at the Battle of Black River, Arkansas, that took young Dickson's life. Tom Teague, a private, saw his captain fall. In quick anger, he raised his gun, killing the Union soldier who had taken the life of his leader. For this story we also have the words of William Jesse Boaz and Taylor Thompson, who were witnesses.

Many months later, in the winter of 1862, Fort Worthians, taking camping equipment in their wagons for a two-day journey, went to Johnson's Station to attend the funeral of Captain Tom Johnson. Colonel Johnson had had his son's body brought by rail to Houston and from there by oxteam to his plantation for interment in the family plot. The many friends of the Johnson family would not withhold their last tribute to the youth. In the final rites at the cemetery, according to the custom of that day, each friend in turn placed a shovel of dirt on the grave with a prayer that earth would gently rest upon their departed comrade.

In 1949, one could find his grave near that of his famous father in Mill Branch Cemetery, the burial ground of the Johnson family three miles south of Arlington.

Sorrow continued to strike swiftly in Fort Worth. The news, it seemed, was all bad during the summer and fall of 1862; a fact substantiated by the decline in numbers on the muster roll of Captain Brinson's Company D, 9th Texas Cavalry, Sul Ross Brigade, ordered to Indian Territory to work with the five civilized tribes with whom the Confederacy had a treaty for protection from Union soldiers crossing into Texas.

In crossing Red River and pursuing hostile Indians, Joe Boggs Crow was killed. The Texans pursued to the Kansas line, then turned south into northern Arkansas. There at Clarksville, the company lost a cavalryman and another at Jonesboro, Arkansas. They battled their way into Tennessee, losing Lieutenant Watson in the campaign. Then they rode into Mississippi to meet defeat.

In the battle at Corinth, Mississippi, which lasted two days, October 4 and 5, 1862, Lieutenant Jim Kelly fell with nine comrades from Tarrant County: two men of the Kemble family, two Mannings, Charlie Goodwin, and two Daltons, who had buried their other kinsman, Jasper Dalton, in the Arkansas campaign.

The battle at Corinth stabbed Captain Brinson with bitter pain, for his son Fred fell before him, and he had to witness the terrible deaths of the other Tarrant boys, sons of his respected friends. Suddenly he felt old and sad. The fire gone out of him, he returned home to his farm. His twelve months' service was completed, and he was too old to reenlist. Twelve others, sad and tired, did not return to the army when their terms of service ended. Among them was the rancher, Dart Anderson, overage, and the Reverend T. A. Ish. But remnants of Brinson's company fought on; they went to the defense of Vicksburg, and lost again. Avery Crouch and Hugh Taylor died in the battle of Vicksburg July 4, 1863.

Elasticity of youth had enabled Merida Ellis to bear the arduous campaign until, wounded and sick, he was discharged at Tupelo, Mississippi. Having become a veteran at eighteen, he could not remain out of the fight. Soon after his discharge, he reenlisted at Fort Worth in Captain Archie Hart's company, Martin's regiment, serving west of the Mississippi until the war ended.

Hiding their grief in work and banal talk, Fort Towners engaged in good-natured gossip about Colonel Nathaniel Terry's patriotism. It was known that he had sold, on July 29, 1863, his extensive plantation near Cold Springs to David Snow, a shoemaker and a rabid antisecessionist, for $20,000. He refused the sum in gold, accepting only Confederate money. Some of this money Colonel Terry converted into Confederate bonds in order to comply with the law of 1863 passed by the Confederate Congress, compelling the funding of citizens' money into these bonds. However, it was alleged that David Snow was not championing a losing cause. He buried $10,000 in gold under a dirt floor in a back room of Number 109 Weatherford Street, which he resurrected in 1866. The

Terry family moved into town, occupying a house in the 300 block of West Belknap, west of the present site of the Criminal Court building.

Men talked, then went out to see Fort Worth's new industry in the process of construction, for Colonel Terry was building a brewery three-quarters of a mile down the Trinity from Julian Feild's former mill, and Fort Towners liked to watch the slaves at work on it, a diversion in their lives. It was said Terry had big plans—one of which was to change the course of the Trinity. His brewery facing that stream, was located west of present-day Bennett Street which parallels Samuels Avenue and north of Morrison Street, where it intersects Bennett.

The colonel built well, for in 1930 the foundation, cellar, other parts of the brewery, and marks of the dam and watercourse were still in evidence. Admirers said he had business sagacity, because he did not put all his economic eggs in one basket. His wife, Elizabeth, had purchased in her name 412 acres from Colonel Johnson, where the Terry slaves were already busy in the fields.

Across the map of the Confederacy, soldiers of Tarrant County visually marched and fought. The map hung in the Daggett-Turner store. Around it men gathered waiting for the mail. War had interrupted scheduled service. George Terrell, son of Ed S. Terrell, carried the mail once a week between Fort Worth and Dallas. He rode to Dallas one day and returned the next. After the mail was opened, one man read aloud the war bulletins from the papers, while another located the areas on the map. Dr. Peak read to the others his letter from John Peter Smith. Another day, Turner passed around his missive from Captain Terrell. Sometimes Lemuel Samuels brought a boyishly scrawled message from his son, Jacob. Thus with the newspaper accounts, bolstered by letters relating personal experiences, battles were re-fought. Spirits of Fort Worthians soared and fell according to what they heard and reacted to on the map. Like a stock market ticker, the map sessions in the Daggett-Turner store affected daily activities of Fort Worth men.

Standing before the map of the Confederacy, they vicariously lived the military campaign of Company K, 7th Texas Cavalry under Colonel William Steel, General H. H. Sibley's brigade. It was a walloping campaign from start to finish. How could it be otherwise with such responsible hometowners in the fight as Captain T. O. Moody, Peter Smith, Louis Wetmore, and James Woods, of the White Settlement. The newspapers from 1862 until 1865, did not neglect their story which was supplemented by Smith, an able letter writer. After mustering in at San

Antonio, Company K went with Sibley attempting to make their grand dream of that "Greater Confederacy" come true, by occupying the Confederacy's recently created Territory of Arizona, which included at that time, New Mexico.

Victory at Valverde February 2, 1862, gave them control of Albuquerque and Santa Fé. A series of engagements in March reduced the brigade's strength; and the Battle of Glorietta Pass forced Sibley to retreat from New Mexico, blasting their dream kingdom.

With a remnant of toughened veterans, Sibley returned to San Antonio that summer. On the retreat from Glorietta to San Antonio, Smith was assigned to escort several wagons of 111 wounded men. Weak from improper nourishment, they bore their discomfort well as the wagons trundled through sand and cacti. Upon entering El Paso, Smith met a Mexican with a herd of goats. He made a bargain: the Mexican, with his herd, was to accompany the wagons. Under Smith's orders, the sick men drank goats' milk. Unpopular though the drink proved, the majority of the ill were recovered by the time they rode into San Antonio.

But Smith, Woods, and Wetmore, with their Tarrant County comrades, were not through. Their New Mexico experience had prepared them for a battle on January 1, 1863. Union forces had captured Galveston in October of 1862. Confederate General John Magruder, in command of the District of Texas, New Mexico and Arizona, was determined to free every inch of Texas soil from the invaders.

He sent from Houston's Buffalo Bayou, two river steamboats, the "Bayou City" and the "Neptune," buttressed with cotton bales behind whose soft walls 380 veterans of Sibley's New Mexico campaign, serving as marines, besieged Galveston with the aid of a land force stationed at Virginia Point opposite the city.

Smith and Wetmore, with other hometown soldiers, were aboard the faster boat, the "Neptune." Wetmore's firing skill of Mexican War days, was evident again, while the everyday experience in marksmanship of the other Tarrant men proved of value. Nor could the enemy put an end to their firing by "picking them off." Union bullets sank into the deep soft cotton bales, while the marksmen continued firing. Texans recaptured Galveston, seized four Union vessels and took 300 prisoners. Fort Worthians at home cheered.

Meanwhile the vicarious warriors viewing the map in the Daggett-Turner store were aware that the Confederacy faced decisive battles in 1863.

Since the spring of 1862, the Federals had been trying to secure control of the Mississippi, and David Farragut had captured New Orleans on May 1 of that year. In May 1863, General Grant was moving down the Mississippi into Louisiana while other Federals were driving up the river from New Orleans. Fort Towners knew the Confederates must keep Louisiana, so a special anxiety held them, especially since Tarrant County men were there holding the line: Captain Terrell's Company F, and Company K with the veterans Wetmore, Moody, Woods, Smith and others.

Under General Tom Green's command, Tarrant men in fierce fighting, took Donaldsville, Louisiana in June, and attacked Fort Butler at the mouth of La Fourche River. Here, Confederates paid a bloody price, and many troopers of companies F and K departed from the area without their comrades. One greatly mourned was the beloved Mexican War veteran and soldier of Major Arnold's command, Wetmore, who had taken honors in founding the fort. Near the place of his death, in the Confederate Cemetery at Donaldsville, one can find the grave of this soldier-citizen, as well as those of other Tarrant County heroes.

In August of 1863, there was a deluge of news. Slow mail service brought information which plunged into men's spirits like a double-edged sword: Sam Houston had died at his home in Huntsville on July 26, aged seventy; and worst of all, General Robert E. Lee had been defeated at Gettysburg in a three-day battle July 1-3, 1863.

Fort Town's news analysts—and there were several—said that Lee's defeat was a tragic blow, because the war now would be fought on Southern soil, not in the North as Lee had hoped. Added to the news of Lee's first decisive defeat, was that of General Grant's capture of the Confederacy's strategic terminal of Vicksburg, Mississippi, on July fourth.

The analysts explained to their fellow Fort Worthians, that the fall of Vicksburg split the Confederacy in half; that the Confederate Army was cut off from Texas and Arkansas, their chief sources of food and supplies; and that the only open port for the South to Europe by way of Texas and Mexico, was now closed. For Tarrant County stockmen and cotton farmers with many slaves, their small market was completely gone. Fort Worth's wealthier men such as Turner, Terry, Eph Daggett, Isbell. and Grant, were certain to be detrimentally affected.

The collapse of the Texas cattle market proved a windfall for some Fort Worth wives. The price of a Texas beef plunged from $50 to $5 a head, producing despairing talk among men, while women commented about the price of beef at B. F. Bamberg's Butcher Shop, the only one in Fort Worth. It had opened in 1862 in a ramshackle building on the corner of present-day Belknap and Commerce streets. In 1864, Bamberg beef sold for one, two or three cents a pound, depending on which cut was wanted. Do not think Bamberg was a careless butcher—to the contrary. Each morning, he killed a beef at his place in the country, brought it to his shop in town and hung it to drip. Regardless of the customer's affluence or the extra price offered, Bamberg would not sell a pound until the next morning. By that time, the beef had thoroughly dripped.

On the heels of the reports of Confederate defeats at Gettysburg and Vicksburg, reports of serious Indian raids aggravated their anxieties. In Clay, Montague, Cooke, Jack, Wise, Palo Pinto and Parker counties, Indians were driving off many thousands of cattle and selling them to the Union Army. Raids and atrocities occurred with monotonous repetition. Mail from Dallas and Fort Worth to Fort Belknap had been irregular since 1862, and the mail route west of Weatherford had been discontinued. Fort Worth, in early August, was filled with militiamen. Brigadier General Nathaniel Terry, State Militia, 20th Brigade, called the militia to assemble at John Robinson's mill for the protection of the outlying counties. Terry was acting under the law passed by the legislature December 21, 1861, providing for the organization of a frontier regiment subject to the rules and regulation of the Army of the Confederate States of America.

The regiment was to be officered by one colonel, a lieutenant colonel, and a major appointed by the governor of Texas. Each company was to elect its own officers which included a first lieutenant and a second lieutenant. The staff officers were a surgeon, a quartermaster and a regiment commissary. Men enlisted for twelve months and occupied a chain of eighteen stations which extended from Red River to the Rio Grande.

Fear for their families among the militiamen from Parker and Johnson counties, made it almost impossible for Terry to retain the men in camp long enough to complete the organization. Every hour their people were in danger. Just before receiving Terry's call to report to Tarrant County, Indians in Parker County had killed two women, carrying away the four children of one and murdering the two children of the other. Indian depredations in the neighboring counties west and north of Tarrant were to make trouble for militiamen until 1866. At the close of the war, Indians would become once again the problem of the United States government.

There was one victory in the fall of 1863 to lift the depressed spirits in Fort Worth. Admiral Farragut and General Banks had a major plan to invade Texas, taking Beaumont and Houston. The campaign began in September in an attempt to take Sabine Pass. Lieutenant Dick Dowling with forty-seven men of the First Texas Heavy Artillery, defeated four Federal gunboats bearing more than 5,000 troops. But Fort Towners' joy was lessened when word that General Banks in November 1863, had succeeded in occupying the Texas Gulf from Brownsville to Indianola, leaving Galveston and Sabine Pass as the only free ports in Texas.

Fort Towners scowled with worry in the spring of 1864, when it was learned that General Banks was making a fourth attempt to invade eastern Louisiana and Texas in order to replenish the Federal commissary with Texas beeves, to seize Confederate cotton stored at Jefferson and Shreveport, to capture the foundries at Marshall and Henderson, and to occupy the productive farming area of East Texas. It was to be the Union's knockout blow in the West.

Leaving Alexandria, Louisiana, General Banks moved up the Red River with 25,000 troops which were to be reinforced by General Steele's army, advancing southward from Little Rock. Together they were to overrun southern Arkansas, northern Louisiana, and East Texas.

Desperate for men to meet such an onslaught. General Kirby Smith in command of Confederate forces west of the Mississippi, called for more men to be rushed to him. Boys were enlisted to march eastward from Texas along with every company that General Magruder could spare from Texas defense. Walker's division of Texas infantry and Green's brigade of cavalry, sped to join troops from Louisiana, Arkansas, and Missouri, assembling under Richard Taylor in command of the army which was to face Banks.

Survivors of Tarrant County's companies of volunteers, who marched from home in 1861 and 1862, serving west of the Mississippi in different brigades, converged upon Louisiana to answer General Smith's urgent call. And they were victorious in this last decisive battle at Mansfield, Louisiana, fifty miles below Shreveport, near the Texas border.

On April 8, 1864, 11,000 Confederates met General Bank's army of 25,000 Federals. Banks was badly beaten. W. H. Harrell, a Texas Confederate who was there, said that the Union troops fell back slowly fighting every inch of the way, but the next day, they made another stand at Pleasant Hill about eighteen miles from Mansfield. Here, Federals succeeded in defeating the Confederates. It was an empty triumph. The defeat at Mansfield had so weakened Banks that he could not hold his position in the area any longer and retreated to the Mississippi. Confederate Harrell elaborated:

Our Western boys were too much for them, the Federalists fled in disorder, Steel's army retreated to the northeast, and Banks' army retraced its route to the Mississippi closely pursued by the Confederates who would have captured Banks' army if the Union gunboats had not shelled us unmercifully. Confederates captured wagons of supplies, teams of mules brought by Banks from the boats, and more than 2,000 prisoners, many of whom as well as the dead on the battlefield wore on their caps the words: 'To Texas or Hell.'

Banks' last and fourth attempt at invasion had failed. A grand march of the Union Army through Texas was denied him; and Texas was spared another "Sherman's march to the sea." Peter Smith, now colonel of his regiment, Captain Terrell, and other Tarrant Countians were there. Their proficient marksmanship was a part of the victory. Every battle won, though, wears a price tag of sacrifice. Victory at Mansfield spared Texans desolate fields and charred homes, but not desolate hearts. A walk among the tombstones of Confederate cemeteries tells the story of the sacrifice Tarrant County citizens made to keep Texas soil free from invasion.

After Mansfield and its subsequent engagements, young Jacob Samuels had time to write his father, Lemuel Samuels. Jacob, the thirteen-year-old boy in 1862, was now a mature fifteen. His letter told of Wetmore's death; of Peter Smith's valor which had brought him severe wounds in the campaign to take Donaldsonville in 1863, then of his (Smith's) promotion to colonel of his regiment and of further slight wounds Smith had received at the Battle of Mansfield. Jacob went on to tell of his own experience in the engagement at Blair's Landing on the Red River on April 12, 1864, when he had stood beside General Green, pleased at being near this man whom he considered to be great. Then he stated that a moment of horror followed. In an instant, a cannon ball from a gunboat on the river exploded, sending his hero to death on the ground before him.

In the same letter, Jacob confided to his father that Captain Terrell was not only an able orator, but was also a warrior as well as a model for his soldiers who were devoted to him; that added to Terrell's well-known military ability were offers of promotion, which the captain refused, because he did not wish to leave the company he had raised in Tarrant County and had led to war.

Young Jacob did not tell his father about his own record as a soldier. But Captain Terrell did so later. Never, said Terrell, did he want for food. Better than ten Spartan soldiers—history's famous foragers—were Jacob Samuels and his (Terrell's) Negro servant. Both variety and abundance of food they brought to camp.

There were not many events east of the Mississippi about which to be grateful, for there the powerful Union, with superior manpower and equipment, pressed down with great strength upon the Confederates. With vanishing resources and declining numbers, the troops of the South struck back in bleeding exhaustion.

Abe Harris, now a lieutenant colonel, David Boaz of Sul Ross's brigade, and other Tarrant men, along with William Mill's regiment of Granbury's brigade, served east of the Mississippi in Jackson's division of Forrest's Cavalry Corps of the Army of Tennessee.

No wonder that Fort Town's Mexican War veterans, too old to fight in 1861, continued to serve as self-appointed military strategists in the Daggett-Turner Store. They critically followed the progress, especially, of Harris. He was their comrade, and they expected a sheaf of victories, because Mexican War veterans were fighters. When news reached Fort Worth that General William S. Rosecrans, with his Federalists, had attacked General Braxton Bragg and his Confederates in December 1862, at Murfreesboro, Tennessee; and after three days of ineffectual fighting, Bragg had been forced to retreat to Chattanooga—they grumbled. One of them allegedly questioned "What's happened to our Texas know-how on the battlefield?"

In the fall of 1863, these same veterans gave thanks for the return of "Texas know-how," because General George H. Thomas was defeated at Chickamauga, Tennessee, and their Abe with other Tarrant County troopers, no doubt played a part in the victory. But Chickamauga was to be the last Confederate victory east of the Mississippi.

Generals Grant and Sherman had, in the latter part of November 1863, battled for two days at Missionary Ridge and Lookout Mountain. They won, taking Chattanooga, the railroad terminal. This gave the Union control of Tennessee and the passes through the mountains to Georgia.

To Fort Worthians, letters from the battlefront and death notices came. Christmas of 1863 was not celebrated. People's hearts were troubled by the letters they received. The men in the Daggett-Turner store no longer glibly explained how they would have fought the battle and won. Heavy in spirit they gathered to hear reports, not to argue among themselves.

In late September 1864, they heard that Sherman, after marching from Chattanooga into Georgia, had taken Atlanta and burned it. Abe Harris and his Tarrant comrades, were in Georgia serving under General John B. Hood. After their defeat in Atlanta, Hood and his men turned back into Tennessee. Hood expected that by threatening to cut off Sherman's base of supplies, Sherman would withdraw from Georgia.

But that wily Northerner ignored Hood's strategy, and marched to the sea, destroying all before him in a swath sixty miles wide, extending from Atlanta to the coast, and taking Savannah, December 21.

January 1865 came—a new year toward which people did not reach with zestful resolutions, for it appeared to begin another season of burdens in a hopeless war; and teen-age boys were leaving home to re-inforce the Confederates. Among them was the former pony express rider and freighter, George Mulkey.

With February came a heavy weariness, which reached even to the high command, and laid hold of the people. General E. Kirby-Smith, commander of the Trans-Mississippi Department, offered secretly his services to Emperor Maximilian of Mexico in case the Confederacy fell. Then when March blustered in, many spirits broke. Men deserted the army. Nevertheless, there were many defiant Texans; some were to be found in Fort Town.

Late April brought the news of Lee's surrender, producing consterna-tion. Rebellious ones, like Colonel Terry, declared that the news was but a "Yankee rumor." Throughout Texas that was the reply of radical secessionists to the news; so the final confirmation of Lee's surrender, seared their souls.

When the word reached Waco, Paul Isbell and his fourteen-year-old son Mel, were watching over a corral of mules and horses which next day they were driving to the Confederate Army. A horseman brought the news to Isbell. It was alleged that in silence he walked to the corral, opened the gates and said, "It is all over, Mel. Help me drive the animals out upon the road; perhaps they will wander back to their owners." Next morning, Isbell started his son Mel with his faithful Negro, on the road to Fort Worth. In a few days he followed.

Jogging home from Waco, Isbell was enmeshed in dejection. He was a man shorn of riches. Land he possessed, but no Negroes to cultivate it, for he had lost a fortune in slaves now that Lincoln's Proclamation would become law. What were the thoughts of his comrades: Terry, Turner, Eph Daggett, he wondered. When he reached Fort Worth, he sought his friends in order to find solace in common troubles.

But men on Fort Town's square were not discussing their own prob-lems. Lincoln had been assassinated on April 14, 1865. That was the baffling news just come by stagecoach. Some men were rejoicing and celebrating; others were perplexed. "To troubles now would be added confusion," one was quoted as saying.

"Who was this Vice President Andrew Johnson?" queried another. Formerly a tailor, a self-made man from Tennessee, was the answer, and being a Southerner, perhaps he would be more likely to understand the South's problems. One very courageous man in the crowd said, "It would be more difficult without Abe Lincoln because he had a sound program." Only a wise and fearless man could have uttered such a prophesy in the midst of men celebrating the assassination of Lincoln with gunfire and other means.

Howard Peak, eleven years old at the time, described the rejoicing:

Brick Pomeroy's *Democrat* was a newspaper that my father subscribed to during the war. It was a rabid Democratic journal published in La Crosse, Wisconsin, and was filled with cartoons of Abraham Lincoln and other leaders of the North. It served to fan the prejudice of us Southerners and made me, as a boy, look upon Lincoln as a devil incarnate. I recall the day when the news came (though it was weeks afterwards) that the President was assassinated and the joy given vent to by the populace yours truly included. But time has changed all that and I, like all other Southerners have grown to regard Lincoln as a martyr and one of our greatest Americans.

Lee had surrendered, and Lincoln had been assassinated. From these two events Texas "die-hards" would try to salvage some gain. Through the papers, they made known their hope that some of Lee's army had escaped and were with General J. E. Johnston, who would retreat with his army across the Mississippi and join General Kirby-Smith.

Then word came of General Johnston's surrender to Sherman, April 26. That meant that the war was over for Tarrant County men serving east of the Mississippi. Those west of the Mississippi were still in service and at war. Lieutenant Colonel Abe Harris in late April surrendered his men at Meridian, Mississippi—237 of them laying down their arms out of the 887 who had gone from Texas with him. Abe traveled to Rome, Georgia, to marry Sallie Logan, whom he had met while stationed there. Several years later, he brought his wife to live once more in Fort Worth.

Still some Texans would not acknowledge defeat. Among them were a few Fort Towners. The atmosphere on the public square became strained with more vociferous arguments. Gone for a time was the jovial comradeship. Newspapers in May reported that Governor Pendleton Murrah of Texas and Generals Kirby Smith and John Magruder were making speeches to rally the soldiers to fight on. In editorials and in town meetings held elsewhere in the state, people were told that if Texas resisted, better terms of surrender could be obtained than those granted Lee and Johnston; furthermore, Texas could fight on, the editors said, because Texas would not be invaded. They thought that it would require one year of preparation before the Union Army could campaign in the wide spaces of the Texas empire; and by that time, perhaps Texas might receive foreign aid.

Editions of mid-May newspapers reported that army meetings were poorly attended; soldiers scorned speeches, and town meetings failed to revive a spirit to resist to the "last ditch." Words, words of acrid hatred, the veterans heaped upon the "exempts" who had remained at home; and upon the cotton speculators whom they blamed for the failure of the war. One Fort Towner, who had both wisdom and understanding, exhorted his comrades to stop wrangling. He said that the inexorable law which God had for mankind was that, "slavery must be wiped from the face of the earth."

Thus Fort Towners, in strain and arguments, watched events spin the Confederacy to an agonizing end. But they forgot their troubles momentarily by attending the May wedding of Medora Robinson, fifteen-year-old daughter of the Milt Robinsons, to William Turner, son of Captain and Mrs. Charles Turner. To accommodate the hundreds invited, the wedding took place at Andrews Tavern. A day of feasting was followed by a night of dancing; and there were plenty of partners for the girls, because many Confederate soldiers had returned ill or on furlough. Captain Turner had delicacies freighted into Fort Town for the celebration. One account states that the festivities lasted two days.

In early June 1865, the war was formally over when the Confederate Army west of the Mississippi surrendered May 26. The returning hometown soldiers were welcomed through the summer and fall of 1865. The male frequenters of the square, gathered in the shade of the oak trees in front of Andrews Tavern, greeting conquered heroes. Men, bodily whole returned in undefeated spirits, eager to ride the range, plow new fields or hang out their law shingles. But some, like Sam Dorsey, came home with an empty sleeve. Endless was the drama of welcoming returning soldiers, once perfect of body, now bearing injuries of the conflict. Some of the town's patriarchs were seen turning away clumsily concealing the tears. Others wept openly upon greeting their dead sons' comrades.

Julian Feild's son, Lieutenant Julian Theodore Feild of Company C, 15th Texas Cavalry returned with the zeal of youth. He had left for the war at the age of seventeen, had seen men suffering from lack of medical care, and had decided to study medicine. He began his famous medical career in 1865 by preparatory study with Doctor Peak before entering medical college in Kentucky and New York.

Captain Terrell with his company came buoyantly into town. But Colonel Peter Smith turned toward Mexico. In May, he (Smith) had mustered out of service 600 men on the Trinity River in Navarro County. Contrary to his blueprint for a career in Fort Worth after the war, Smith went to Austin to join his comrades whose foreboding of "an era of Yankee oppression" had produced an ambitious design. Fifteen Confederate officers had agreed to meet in Austin in early June and ride together to the court of Emperor Maximilian in Mexico City. Their departure was delayed until June 18, at the request of state officials who wished them to remain in order to restrain disbanded soldiers in case they should become lawless.

These Confederate officers, fertile in brain and firm in belief that each man lives by his own design, did not lack plans. One scheme of taking a slice from Mexico on the Rio Grande border and organizing a republic, ended with the disastrous defeat of the Confederacy and the lack of support from any army of volunteers for such a project. There were no barriers for these men. When one design failed, they pursued another. Mid-June, they left Austin with plans for new kingdoms in the valley of Mexico where, free from Yankee tyranny—their greatest compensation for exile in a foreign land—they would enjoy ownership of lush plantations along with offices at the court of Maximilian in which to expand and to satisfy their political and military aptitudes.

One of the astute designers of this Mexican project was Judge Alexander Terrell, who understood the importance of diplomatic protocol. Knowing that the master key which opens doors in foreign countries is a state paper elaborate with gilt, ribbon, and an official seal, he spent his last evening in Austin—June 17—in the executive office with his friend Governor Murrah of Texas. Judge Terrell wrote a letter of introduction to Emperor Maximilian extolling the eminence and superior qualities of the party of Confederate officers seeking new homes in Mexico. Among them, in Terrell's words, were "General W. P. Hardeman, Colonel George Flournoy, Colonels Peter Smith and M. T. Johnson of Fort Worth, General King of Walker's Division, Major Hill, my Brigade Commissar, Captain Roberts and myself." Junius ("June") W. Smith, a lawyer also of Fort Worth, was in the party. Governor Murrah signed the letter of introduction written on stationery with the caption, "Governor of Texas."

Because of their delayed departure of several weeks, these Confederates had to hasten from Austin if they were to escape apprehension by Federal soldiers. It was known that General Grant had sent General Philip Sheridan to the Rio Grande with a force of 52,000 for the purpose of strongly indicating the displeasure of the United States government to the presence of the French in Mexico.

Mounted on fine horses, the party rode continuously but judiciously toward the Rio Grande. A good horse ridden with care can carry his master a tremendous distance within twenty-four hours. So every thirty minutes they stopped, removed saddles and blankets and permitted the horses to graze or rest for five minutes before remounting. Colonels Johnson, Flournoy, and John Peter Smith, had no extra lead-horse, but each had an exceptionally fine animal.

On approaching the Rio Grande the crossing of whose waters would bring them a new life in exile, disquieting emotions took hold of these refugees. There was the pain of sorrow that comes to a man as he breaks with a part of his life, all that he has known. There was the excitement of anticipation that pounds through a man as he enters into a new phase of his life. Nor did events make easy the crossing of the Rio Grande into Mexico. They met a group of Mexican horsemen. Feigning interest in the welfare of the Americans, they told the Confederates of the location of United States troops guarding the Rio Grande border, and advised them of the most desirable place to cross the river. The Mexicans rode on and reported to Union soldiers the approach of men of high station.

Riding toward the river crossing, the refugees met a Mexican whose information revealed the treachery of the other Mexicans. Turning their horses around, they rode ninety miles down the river to find another crossing, for they were determined to outwit the United States troops waiting to capture them. Such a contingent of Southern men entering Mexico would stimulate Unionist fear of Confederate activity in Mexico, for already there was some suspicion that certain recent Confederates desired to channel the energies of Mexicans and the resources of Mexico into another war in order to create their nefarious empire of slavery.

Reaching the crossing of their own choice, Judge Terrell swam the river and found a safe landing on the Mexican side. His comrades followed, crossing their Rubicon into Mexico. Entering the town of Mier on the Rio Grande, they were detained, disarmed and held as political prisoners during the night. Both the gleam of pistols and the handsome steeds lighted with avarice the eyes of the Mexican commander, as he praised the equipment of his captives, whom he was charged with keeping. Terrell noted the Mexican's covetous admiration for their rich accessories, and straightway began negotiations. A horse and a pistol bought release and restoration of arms and horses to the ex-Confederates.

Next morning, before officialdom of Mier had arisen, the Confederates were on their way. Twelve of them rode toward Mexico City. Three of them—Johnson, Junius Smith, and Peter Smith—rode along the Mexican side of the Rio Grande to Matamoros. These three Tarrant County individualists decided to say farewell to their companions. The decision was their own, made during the night of imprisonment at Mier. Johnson and Peter Smith had mentally and verbally thrashed out their problem. Why not go home again—it was yet so near. Perhaps on the road to Mexico City, dangers would be a constant threat. The incident at Mier had indicated that likelihood. Even though conditions at home now would be different, life would have more elemental certainty. Mexico City was far away, and their future life at the court of Maximilian was chimerical.

Good fortune brought the three Tarrant men through the valley of the Rio Grande on the Mexican side in spite of it being inhabited by roving bandits and Mexican peasants who, for a small price would surrender them to Union troops stationed across the river, and whose business it was to hunt Confederates fleeing to a Mexican exile. Near the mouth of the river at Matamoros, the crucial point in their escape, they again eluded enemies, sold their horses, and took a boat carrying a cargo to Galveston. Disembarking at that port, they moved northward to Fort Worth in September 1865.

On the prairies of Tarrant County, putting behind their defeat in war, Confederate veterans would consider their tomorrows. Their strength, like that of other Fort Towners, lay in overcoming the bitter aftermath. On the hard road of Reconstruction, they would find courage to keep their dreams for the future of their county.

BOOK V

Re-sowing
on the Prairies

FORT TOWNERS were moved by two great drives—politics and town building. Along with earning their bread, politics for these men was serious business as well as their chief sport and amusement. But at the end of the Civil War, radical Northerners in control of Congress stripped them of their political rights and interfered with their unrestrained economic freedom. For nine years, from July 1865 to January 1874, the Era of Reconstruction in Texas, Fort Worth men would learn the meaning of imposed authority and would know the bitterness which rankles Americans forced to submit to a government not of their own making. Fort Towners did not permit their pent-up feelings to break out in open defiance. Their political sagacity saved them, and their ingenious methods of solving problems spared the town and county many distressing incidents experienced in East and South Texas during this same period. They would fret because of the works of the reconstructionists—the carpetbaggers, scalawags, Union men, and Republicans. Inwardly fuming, but committing their ways to the new laws from Washington, D.C., they set their minds to conform in order to hasten the day for their restoration to the nation's fold.

CHAPTER 22

Chastisement, 1865-1869

WHEN JUNE days of 1865 were wearing to an end, a Fort Town news analyst was heard to say on the public square, "Well, it's not over, if you mean the war." For the big news quickening the spirits of the inhabitants was startling, and they were adjusting their minds to it.

General Sheridan, commander of the military division of the Southwest, with headquarters at New Orleans, had sent General Gordon Granger to Texas to preserve order until civil government could be established. Fort Towners learned that General Granger landed on June 19 at Galveston with 1,800 men and had proclaimed, in the name of President Andrew Johnson, the authority of the United States over Texas. He also declared null and void all laws enacted since 1861; required all Confederate soldiers to register; ordered all persons "having in their possession public property of any description formerly belonging to the late so-called Confederate States or the state of Texas, to turn it over to the proper United States officer" at the nearest designated stations: Houston, Galveston, Bonham, San Antonio, Marshall and Brownsville; and announced the freedom of all slaves. This is the reason that Texas Negroes observe June 19 as their emancipation day.

Such headline news, arriving by stagecoach in Fort Worth, was disconcerting, but to the printed words were added grotesque rumors of things to come—treason trials for prominent rebels before Yankee military commissions, dreadful punishment for rebels, and wholesale confiscation of rebels' property. Stagecoach drivers had sharp ears and glib tongues. The more they heard of disorders in East and South Texas, the more their tongues wagged of impending punishment. They reported with truth that many other Texans were emigrating to Mexico to escape retribution by the Union. It was already known in Fort Worth that Generals Kirby Smith and Magruder, with Governor Murrah had fled to Mexico. There was no Texas government.

Facts and rumors were spiced with stories related by groups of soldiers coming home, some of whom had new blankets tied to their saddles, others had saddlebags bulging with bolts of domestic or bolts of flannel, or shoes or a new mule whip, or a hammer, or a string of buttons—the latter a luxury gift for mother. They told their fellow townsmen of disorders in the state. Some brows knit in perplexity, as the soldiers described how the troops at Galveston, when hearing the order on May 21 for the evacuation of that port and believing that the end had come, and that they need not wait for formal discharge, had broken rank, moved upon Houston and raided the ordinance building, taking everything portable.

Moving homeward, they were raiding other commissaries, taking what they believed rightfully belonged to them, because it had been collected for their use, but had not reached them in their dismal need in the last months of the war. Private property was respected; however public opinion did not usually condemn the soldiers, because they were the heirs of Confederate property rather than the Northerners, having fought to protect it.

Fort Towners learned that confusion was everywhere. Panic had seized many people in Texas, but it did not grip the leaders of this town. They looked from the bluff across at the prairie with its limitless power found in space, fertility and beauty. They saw that the land, in the fullness of its strength, was still there in spite of a lost war and new masters. Gaining new vigor from the sight, they were unafraid. These men thought that they would proceed in their own way to work out their problems—they always had.

Captain Eph Daggett and Charles Turner read their late June papers and memorized General Hamilton's instructions to Texans. Then they walked across the square to the courthouse grounds and took a survey of the cotton, wool, hides and grain stored, awaiting the freighters which were a month overdue. These supplies belonged to the Confederate government; some had been purchased by the military board; others had not been paid for, and much of it was Tarrant County farmers' payment of their "tax-in-kind."

Captain Eph contemptuously grumbled, "Surrender Confederate property to the Yankee military officers at Bonham and Marshall when our frontiersmen are in need? How much is demanded of men?"

Turner thoughtfully retorted, "We have contributed a fortune to the Richmond government—now it is Washington."

Then Daggett in his role as "Pappy Daggett," an affectionate title bestowed upon him by Fort Towners, spoke, "We must provide for our own; that is our first duty."

The two men came to an understanding and returned to join the talk session in the Daggett-Turner store, which was deliberating, pro and con, General Granger's orders to Texans. While making his giant body comfortable on top of a barrel, Captain Eph heard one of the group say:

"So General Granger will rule us with 1800 soldiers until civil government is restored? How small does he think Texas is? With most of the Union troops on the Rio Grande, to frighten the French out of Mexico, that leaves only a handful of soldiers for the various military posts—from where he plans to control us."

Like a patriarch, Captain Eph allegedly spoke from the flour barrel throne using his favorite admonition, "Fret not thy gizzard; frizzle not thy whirligig."

This was a preface for good advice. Men became attentively quiet. Pappy Daggett trying logically to explain away their anxiety said: "There are no disorders in Tarrant County. We have always governed ourselves and maintained order. Fort Worth, located on the frontier and not a commissary headquarters, will escape raids and Yankee soldiers."

A man in threadbare clothes looking at Daggett, perhaps questioned in a nasal drawl, "Are the Yankees rightfully entitled to the property of our defunct Confederate government?" With a wave of his hand in the direction of the courthouse grounds, he testily continued, "Some of that Confederate cotton is my 'tax-in-kind.' Now it will be taken by Yankees!"

"Mighty temptin', that Confederate corn. I ain't got none—shore do need some fer plantin'," snapped an ex-soldier clad in remnants of a grey uniform faded and soiled.

A man in want, and especially one of his own hometowners, moved Turner to reply with an artful hint. "Bonham and Marshall, the stations to which Confederate property is to be taken, according to orders, are too many miles from here, and the haul is too costly for us. Let us wait. It will be several weeks before the Yankee agents or soldiers reach here."

Ideas were building up, just as Captain Eph, the molder of events, anticipated. Turner's intimations were placing a new light in listeners' eyes. He saw that it was time to heighten the power of suggestion. In his deep voice, magnetic with the proper inflections, he intoned:

"Too many families—too many Negroes in Tarrant County are without clothes—without shoes—without corn. Men can't let their own suffer."

Moving off the barrel, he stood an instant looking at his fellow townsmen. His expressive face added impact to the question he hurled at them.

"It will be a hard winter. Or will it?"

Walking away his words boomed over his shoulders, "Somehow frontiersmen always find a way out of their troubles."

Fort Towners and farmers around about did find a solution. When the United States Treasury agents, who were swarming over Texas taking everything they could claim as property of the former Confederate government, arrived in Fort Worth, they found Confederate property small in quantity.

On the other hand in Dallas, men, women, and children—many of them hungry and ragged, also solved their problem. Moving upon the government supplies stacked on an open lot, they fought and scrambled for cotton with which to clothe themselves, as well as hides and grains. They hauled them away, while officials watched the riots undecided whether to enforce law as officials, or as humanitarians to extend merciful charity.

On the eve of its collapse, the Confederacy had offered freedom to slaves if they rendered military service; but its defeat prevented fulfillment of the promise. Tarrant County citizens, being avid readers and well-informed, had known since 1864 that slavery had collapsed in the areas east of the Mississippi occupied by Federal armies; and in early spring of 1865, four months before General Granger's emancipation announcement of June 19, 1865, they anticipated freedom of the slaves.

Turner and Isbell, the largest slave owners in the county, freed their slaves before word of Granger's proclamation reached them. Turner granted freedom to 150; but being a man who handled his affairs wisely, kept his slaves at home in order to protect and to care for them until legal action was taken by the government. He had gold buried, as well as means with which to feed and clothe his slaves until the dark period of adjustment had passed.

With Isbell, it was not the same. The greatest portion of his operating capital was always invested in slaves, for he was a slave trader; and the remainder of his capital was now lost in Confederate bonds. Without cash or means to provide his slaves with food or clothes for many months, the problem overwhelmed him. So when he heard of Lee's surrender, he rushed home from Waco to free his slaves.

Under the branches of the great pecan trees in the assembly yard of his White Settlement home, Isbell stood on a worktable, looking down into 200 or more black faces. It was an early May morning, time for their field work, but they had not been sent to their chores. Instead their "master" who had returned the previous evening, had called them to him.

"The war is over. You are now free to come or to go. The roads and fields are open to you to travel where you will." The Negroes were stunned.

Lean, tall, yet bent by age, Ott, Isbell's loyal field slave, groping in bewilderment, quaveringly asked, "Master, whar will we-uns go, and what will we-uns do?"

These few cogent words articulated for them the blacks' terrible dilemma. If their white masters were disconcerted in trying to reconstruct their world, how much more were they overwhelmed with this new situation. Their bonds were cut asunder, but what were they to do with their freedom? Two kinds of freedmen evolved: those who stayed with their masters, to be helpful as well as to be a care; the others who left their owners to wander up and down the roads and through the towns, becoming economic and political problems of the nation.

Those freed slaves who trusted in the mercy of their masters, now beseeched "their folks" not to remove them. Unless these masters were brutes or devoid of economic resources entirely, they did not refuse homes to their former faithful workers. Among such understanding men were Eph Daggett, M. T. Johnson, Turner, Nathaniel Terry, Isbell, and others.

Many Negroes, the record states—about fifty percent of them—left Tarrant County. It was not a hasty exodus. Slowly becoming aware of the meaning of freedom, the emancipated, through the summer and winter of 1865, left in groups to journey back to East Texas and the southern states from whence they had come. They were the blacks who had resisted the reins of their masters, or those who longed for their kinsmen from whom they had been separated in bondage, or those with ambition to reach beyond the horizon, or those who had never been reconciled to the Texas prairies swept with penetrating cold in winter and seared with smiting heat in summer. The prairies had deepened their yearning for the mountains, hills, and timbered valleys of Tennessee and Kentucky. Late into the eighteen-seventies, there would be the sight of freedmen going home.

After the first news of General Granger's proclamation of emancipation and the rush of some slave owners to comply, there followed hesitation in carrying out the order. Diverse statements in the press confronted the well-informed citizens. Statements issued by wishful optimists attempting to convince people there would be a lenient North offering the South compromises and compensation, were stumbling blocks in the road to recovery.

The weekly paper of East Texas, *Texas Republican*, printed such wishful opinions. This periodical gave several reasons for not freeing the slaves. First, it would demoralize the country. Second, slavery was not terminated, because it would be necessary for the Southern states to ratify the Thirteenth Amendment, abolishing slavery before it became constitutional, which the Southern states would not do. Third, perhaps emancipation, if accepted, would be gradual, covering a period of ten years; and there would be financial compensation. Fourth, if slavery were abolished in name, it would remain in the form of compulsory labor for the safety of the nation and the welfare of the Negro. In this latter stand, the *Houston Telegraph* agreed, stating that the emancipation of slaves was certain, and their unpaid service would be replaced by paid compulsory labor.

The general opinion of Tarrant County slaveholders (as previously discussed) was to keep at home those who were willing, and consign them to work temporarily at wages, in the form of shelter, food and clothing for themselves and their families, since money was nonexistent. So General Granger's order to do just this, was unnecessary in this area.

When the military posts were established at various points, the commanders issued orders containing the same advice. They also announced that Negroes would be assured of their freedom and protection from injustice, but if found idle, the freedman would be punished by hard labor without pay; also they should not travel on public roads without passes from their employers. These orders, however, could not be enforced since army posts were too far apart to keep the Negro under surveillance.

East and South Texas had their problems with Negroes to whom emancipation meant freedom from labor and freedom to roam the countryside. But in Tarrant County and North Texas where Federal troops had not yet penetrated in late summer of 1865, Negroes did not roam the country or break their contracts. This was explainable. It was generally understood among men of this county not to employ a freedman without the consent of his former master. Recalcitrant Negroes, leaving their former masters, were brought back by force or made to leave the county if they had been freed, or had declared their intention to return to their kin elsewhere and had a pass to do so from their former owners.

But apparently the most effective deterrent to wandering illegally, was the "Patta-roll" (Patrol). This was a patrol organization of whites maintained by Tarrant County slave owners, who were horsemen with bullwhips or black-snake whips, riding the countryside at night, whipping Negroes found roaming from their homes. Until the Ku Klux Klan appeared a few years later, this "Patta-roll" kept order in this county. So great was its fame for terrifying punishment that a jingle often repeated by the slaves themselves was, "Run, Nigger, run, the Patta-roll'll get yuh!" Even white parents disciplined their young with this threat.

When September of 1865 came, there was still talk among ultraconservatives and former secessionists that emancipation would be gradual, and accompanied by financial compensation. These ideas, published in newspapers, hindered work of reconstruction and increased confusion in South and East Texas. Experience during that summer proved that free labor was a failure; that the labor famine brought crop failures. In the presence of the military, the whites in East and South Texas could not apply coercion, and the Negro did not work or, if he made a contract to labor, he broke it. Negroes spent the summer and winter of 1865 in idleness, thieving, begging, and vice. They were waiting under false ideas, that at Christmas the land of their former owners would be divided, and that each would receive as a gift, forty acres and a mule. Texans declared this "Forty-acres-and-a-mule" propaganda was traceable to Northern radicals and federal soldiers.

Since in Tarrant County, most of the Negroes stayed with their former masters, the fields were cultivated without incident that summer and fall. As proof of the faithfulness of the ex-slave one can read the statement by a citizen who lived through this period of transition.

There were some mighty faithful Negroes about Fort Worth during war times and Reconstruction, and they were reliable in every particular. Old Dan Hall, Dan Daggett, John Pratt, and Old News, who assisted Uncle Ed Terrell and Uncle Jesse Burton and many others are deserving of mention. They did their duty as prescribed by their white employers and never sought to transcend their humble position in life. There were occasional exceptions. . . .

General E. M. Gregory in charge of the Freedmen's Bureau in Texas, arrived in September 1865; but not until December was his organization perfected when he appointed a dozen local agents of whom five were civilians, to operate at strategic centers in the interior of the state. General Services Administration, Washington, D.C., reveals that:

For purposes of administration the Freedmen's Bureau, divided the State of Texas into districts: the District of Dallas, with headquarters at Dallas, Texas included Dallas and Tarrant counties. In October 1867 Ellis County, and in February 1868 Johnson County were added to the district. The records do not show exactly when this district was established or how long it remained in existence. However, in accordance with the Act of Congress of July 25, 1868, the operations of the Freedmen's Bureau, except the activities of the Education Department and the payment of servicemen, was discontinued on December 31, 1869. The following individuals served as Sub-Assistant Commissioners in charge of the District of Dallas: 2nd Lieutenant Alfred H. Manning, from February 1867; William H. Horton, from February 1867; William A. Bledsoe, from June, 1868; 1st Lieutenant Henry Horton, from August 1868; and Dewitt C. Brown, from November 1868.

The bureau had authority over all affairs concerning former slaves. Freedmen were required to make contracts to labor. These contracts were to be drawn up, approved and registered by the bureau, which would also give ex-slaves protection of person and property. On November 17, 1865, General Gregory issued a message to freedmen which the chief justice in each county was to read. They were instructed to work under contract; that idleness would be considered a criminal act subject to severe punishment, and were informed that they would not receive gifts at Christmas, or at any other time. To comply with the law, Chief Justice Stephen Terry of Tarrant County read General Gregory's message to freedmen. For several weeks, he rode the county circuit dutifully fulfilling the law. But the slaveholding men of this area did not need Gregory's message. And when Christmas came and passed and the Negroes did not get their forty acres and a mule each, they settled down to working for wages.

General Sheridan announced on June 30 that no home guards or bands for self-protection would be allowed anywhere in the state since the regular soldiers were sufficient. But Fort Towners were certain that Sheridan was mistaken. So they spared neither stress nor accent in their denouncement of what they called "Sheridan's Yankee ignorance," while townsmen of milder tempers were often heard to ask as the Indians' thievery increased, "What does Sheridan know about Indian defense?"

August politics in Fort Worth was concerned with President Johnson's plan for reconstructing the states of the former Confederacy. In May of 1865, he had issued a proclamation of amnesty, extending pardon and restoring property, except slaves, to all men in the former Confederacy, who would take the oath of loyalty to the United States. All high military and civil leaders of the Confederacy were excluded, and Johnson added a few others including those holding property worth $20,000 or more. These groups might, however, petition the president for pardon. He also made known his plan for reconstructing the governments of the seceded states. He would appoint a provisional governor in each of the Southern states until qualified voters through state conventions could form state governments, elect legislators who would ratify the Thirteenth Amendment, nullify the ordinances of secession, and cancel all Confederate war debts. Etc. . . .

In July, 1865, President Johnson appointed A. J. Hamilton provisional governor of Texas. Hamilton was a Texan, an ex-congressman, and a Unionist.

President Johnson's plan obliterated the fortunes of Nathaniel Terry, Isbell, Johnson, and other Tarrant County citizens; and it would have despoiled the fortune of Turner if some of his wealth had not been invested in the Daggett-Turner store. Economic loss was accompanied by political loss as well. The president's program of Reconstruction also disfranchised some Fort Towners. Provisional Governor Hamilton filled the state offices with only those Texans who had always been loyal to the Union. He further announced that he refused to recognize local officers in counties and towns who had served under the Confederacy; and that throughout the state he would replace them by men recommended by his Union advisers at Austin.

Certain officials of Tarrant County—Chief Justice Stephen Terry, County Clerk Gideon Nance, Sheriff J. P. Davis, District Clerk W. B. Tucker, Assessor-Collector H. C. Daggett, and Surveyor M. Booth, would be the victims of the new law along with most of the men who had been the political wheels in the machinery of the county and towns of Tarrant.

Legal leadership had returned from the war to Fort Worth in the person of Captain Terrell. Men sought his aid. He had been paroled from the service in Austin on August 25. Under the president's Reconstruction program, public office was closed to him. But civil practice in Fort Town would be his bread and meat, though temporary civil chaos threatened his immediate livelihood.

Aggressive citizens refused to wait until Governor Hamilton got around to the appointment of Union men to civil offices in their county.

They sent Terrell and Edward Hovenkamp of Birdville, who had been
district attorney in war time, to Austin to obtain the appointment of
county officers. They called upon Governor Hamilton, the former law
partner of Terrell's brother, Judge Alexander Terrell. Friendship sometimes cuts through iron-clad politics. Hamilton gave Terrell a note in
pencil to his secretary of state, Judge James Bell, whom Terrell knew.
Affluent prestige of Terrell would soften the governor's order for Tarrant County.

Directly Bell asked for a list of names for appointment. Terrell and
Hovenkamp held a two-man Tarrant County election, bypassing Ham-
ilton's order. They handed a list of their duly elected officers to Bell.
Next morning they received the commissions signed and sealed. Thus
Tarrant County was among the first northern frontier counties of the
state to have a legal government in the early fall of 1865.

Among the key appointments were County Judge Stephen Terry,
County Clerk Gideon Nance, and District Clerk Louis H. Brown, who
was, according to Terrell, "an aged man but an elegant hospitable gentleman of the old school" whose son, Horatio, had served in the Civil
War in Terrell's company. He had presented the elderly gentleman's
name because of Mr. Brown's worry over the loss of his slaves, but most
of all from a personal sorrow, for in the winter of 1864, he had buried
his wife, Susan.

Cool, brisk fall winds of 1865 blew in like a tonic upon Fort Town.
Tarrant County men, on their way to the original three-room frame
courthouse built in 1857 by Captain Daggett, looked in the opposite direction or closed their eyes to the sight of the incompleted stone courthouse begun in 1860 but abandoned during the war. Only the outer rock
walls of the first story with their weather-beaten joists stood as markers
of arrested progress, and as unpleasant a sight as that of a human skele-
ton. Citizens were trying to forget the bitterness of the past and to meet
the present by complying with Governor Hamilton's instructions. That
they had willed to do so was evident by the sound of their boots and
spurs clumping down the wide hall of the little courthouse to take the
amnesty oath from the new Tarrant County officers.

On August 19, 1865, Governor Hamilton had issued a proclamation
providing for the registration of voters in order to provide for the election
of delegates to a constitutional convention. This would restore Texas to
full status of a state in the Union. President Johnson's plan was: "In
each county the chief justice, the district clerk and the county clerk were

to act as a registration board and sit at least one day in each week at the county seat." They were to do two things: one, extend the oath of amnesty to those eligible under the Amnesty Act and register them as legal voters; two, administer the oath of amnesty to those excluded under the act as a preliminary step toward their special pardon. Separate rolls were to be kept of these two classes.

Although the governor's proclamation was made in mid-August, it was not until November that a majority of the voters of Texas had qualified. The delay was explainable: there were no mails; and there were men living far from the county seat whose chief source of information was newspapers several weeks old. The newspapers, however, were united in urging the people to register in order to hurry the return of normal government.

Another stimulant to hasten registration was General Hamilton's address to the people on September 11, 1865. He urged Texans to put an end to ante-bellum delusions which caused some to delay taking the amnesty oath, and he warned them against the press and politicians who were misleading them. He declared that slavery was ended; that it could not be resurrected in any form; that compulsory labor laws would be considered by the North as an evasion of emancipation; that the Negro must be equal with white men in civil rights; and in all cases in courts, be admitted to testify. He entreated the people to hasten to take the amnesty pledge, thereby qualifying them as voters; after which the convention, enacting the necessary measures for taking Texas back into the Union, would be held.

The Stars and Stripes on Fort Town's square did not create violence, nor was there any attempt to take the flag down. By November, however, there were reports throughout the state of hostile action. One crowd allegedly tore to pieces a United States flag on the courthouse at Weatherford. At Bonham, according to another report, a flag was destroyed and some Negroes shot. There were also disorders in Grayson and Bell counties. In November, Governor Hamilton called for the organization of a police force in some counties. But Tarrant County men had affairs in hand and were spared violence. That did not mean that some of them were not guilty of subjecting Union men, especially Dr. B. F. Barkley of Birdville, to insults and threats. Barkley had opposed secession, and had remained loyal to the Union during the war, although as a humanitarian, he kept an open house at Birdville, feeding and clothing widows and orphans of Confederates, even to lodging those returning soldiers in need of a helping hand. Now he was in Governor Hamilton's favor, and gossip claimed he had been an informer of conditions in Parker and Tarrant counties. It was alleged that he had told the governor of the flag incident in Weatherford. Reward would come for his loyalty to the Union party in the election of 1866. At that time, he would become county judge and later United States commissioner during radical Reconstruction.

The need of hard money with which to buy goods sent Captain Daggett to Shreveport. He could not view the prairies west and south of Fort Town literally "black with cattle" without seeing there an opportunity to be grasped. Since the fall of Vicksburg in 1863 and the loss of the Confederate market, it is said that unclaimed cattle covered the prairies from Tarrant County to the extreme western boundary of Palo Pinto County.

"The local market belongs to Tarrant inhabitants," Daggett allegedly confided to his comrades, "and I do not like the recent appearance in this county of Yankee ex-soldiers who are seeking to earn for themselves some specie dollars in our prairies by gathering up a herd and driving them north."

Many of these outsiders did not purchase cattle; they stole them and drove them off or slaughtered them for their hides. Formerly camp followers whose occupation was stealing, they continued their operations after the war on the Texas cattle ranges. Their extensive thievery, it was said, was one reason John Chisum moved his ranching industry to New Mexico.

Daggett did not scan a newspaper—he read every line in it, even discerning the significance of the unprinted news hidden between the lines. From his Austin and Dallas papers, he learned that there was a demand for beef in the North, also that if the owner accompanied his cotton or goods to the point of shipment and produced evidence to the United States agents that it was not "surrendered property" of the former Confederacy, he could ship to New Orleans or New York.

Late October found him on the trail to Shreveport with a large herd of cattle aged four to eight years. From Shreveport, he would ship the cattle to the New Orleans market. What he had seen in the land between Marshall and Shreveport affected his course in the period of Reconstruction which ominously stretched ahead. With a detailed plan for action, Captain Daggett returned to Fort Worth in time to help organize the campaign of Colonel Johnson, candidate for delegate from Tarrant County to the constitutional convention at Austin.

On November 15, 1865, Provisional Governor Hamilton had issued a proclamation fixing the date of election of delegates for January 8, 1866. The purpose of the convention was to write a constitution for Texas which, when acceptable to President Andrew Johnson, would terminate provisional government and restore Texas to normal relationship with the Union. It was to meet on February 7 in Austin.

Daggett felt resentment toward the more rabid Unionists, for there were rumors from the North that this group, not satisfied with abolishing slavery, were now talking of granting suffrage to Negroes. Texas Unionists, he feared, might become pawns of radical Northerners, especially Dr. Barkley of Birdville who might be one of them. Daggett had engineered other elections. In December 1865, he expended his wrathful spirit to prevent Barkley's candidacy and to bring about the election of M. T. Johnson in the coming election of January 1866.

Daggett thought his fear was justified by John Reagan's letter to Texans which had been published in all papers. Reagan, former Texas congressman, first postmaster general of the Confederacy and later its secretary of the treasury, had been captured in May of 1865 and was a prisoner of war at Fort Warren, Boston. From there on August 11, 1865, he wrote the letter which determined Daggett's stand.

Reagan urged his fellow Texans to hasten their return to civil rule by complying with the terms imposed upon them and by accepting their status as a conquered country. He further advised that there was no such right as secession of a state from the Union; that Texans must recognize this principle and accede to the supreme authority of the United States; accepting the abolition of slavery and the right of the freedmen to the privileges and protection of the law; furthermore, it was probable that the Northerners would demand suffrage for the Negro.

He went on to outline steps for putting an end to both the hostility between the races and the agitation between states of the North and South. First, Texans should "admit the testimony of Negroes in the courts subject only to the same rules as applied to whites." Second, Texans should fix an intellectual and moral test, also the possession of property as a qualification for voting regardless of race or color, providing no person previously entitled to vote was deprived of the voting franchise.

Fort Towners knew and admired Reagan. He had been their district judge of the state district court. His advice to accept limited suffrage of white men, the supreme authority of the Federal government, and the abolition of slavery was thought reasonable by most. But his advice concerning the freed Negro was considered rampant radicalism astounding and angering them.

The viewpoint of the moderate conservatives was stated by Middleton Tate Johnson. In sharp-cut words and plain sentences, he "opposed granting the Negroes any political right whatever," but on the other hand insisted that the freedmen now in "their helpless state be treated with justice and kindness," which Texas should guarantee; and asserted that the "Negro should be made to work under uniform laws" which the Texas legislature should pass regulating "pauperism, labor, and apprenticeship."

With his manuscript, Johnson rode to Fort Worth to seek his friends' approval and their rhetorical corrections. There were County Judge Terry, Colonel Smith and Captain Terrell whose opinions he valued, and he could expect good advice with wisdom from Doctor Peak, Captains Daggett and Turner. There were also Nathaniel Terry and Isbell with the mood and mind of dispossessed slaveholders, and there was Gideon Nance, a rugged frontiersman. Here was a cross section of minds representative of Texas thinkers. In Fort Town, these men read Johnson's manuscript, and studied its content to observe if there were any sentences which might be misconstrued. In their enthusiastic approval, they sent his editorial off for publication. It was published in several Texas newspapers, appearing in the San Antonio *Daily Herald* January 3, 1866.

Governor Hamilton had declared no person eligible who was excluded from general amnesty unless pardoned by the president. Colonel Johnson no doubt, like all good citizens of Tarrant, took an oath of amnesty at Fort Worth in September of 1865. Whether he was eligible for general pardon or took the oath as a step in obtaining special pardon from the president is uncertain without documentary proof. Johnson could have been excluded because of his war record—the raising of a regiment for the Confederate Army and for blockade running. He might be able to obtain special pardon from President Johnson. There were, however, several other delegates to the convention, who were definitely excluded by the general amnesty, and had not been pardoned by the president. Among these was O. M. Roberts, president of the secession convention which had taken Texas out of the Union.

1866

Tarrant County citizens elected Colonel Johnson on January 8. On February 7, he was in Austin joining the conservative group of the constitutional convention which held the balance of power. There was a strong minority of Unionists but only one among them, E. Degener of San Antonio, openly advocated suffrage for freedmen. There was an equal number of aggressive secessionists, some of whom were excluded from the general amnesty and had not been pardoned by the president.

The delegates were to rewrite the constitution of Texas, which, when approved by Congress, would meet the requirements for the restoration of the state to the Union.

In military or political battles, Fort Towners had always vocally fought with vigor. From February through mid-April, they concentrated their interests upon the convention. And to please subscribers, the *Dallas Herald* devoted more than half of the front-page space of each issue to an account of the proceedings in Austin.

Beginning its work in guarded restraint, the convention soon moved into wrangling momentum. Disputation reigned until adjournment April 2. When it first met, there was general unanimity on the various questions; but there was wide divergence as to the manner in which these things should be done.

A. B. Norton, formerly editor of the *Fort Worth Whig Chief*, also the *Southern Intelligencer* of Austin, who had gone to Ohio during the war, had returned to Texas and was publishing the *Union Intelligencer* at Jefferson. His paper of strong Republican aroma was an offense to many, and as the mouthpiece of the radicals, it accused the convention of failure, because it had not declared the act of secession from its beginning null and void, and had not given the Negro his full share of civil rights and liberties.

Fort Towners did not agree with Norton. Mostly conservatives, they railed at him and approved in general the work of the convention. Political betting being one of their chief amusements, they began to arrange wagers as to whether J. W. Throckmorton or E. M. Pease would be elected governor.

In the midst of this betting and campaigning for the June election of 1866 (which was also to elect county and district officials), the *Dallas Herald*, May 26, published the account of the death of Colonel Johnson on the previous 18th of that month in Austin. Fort Town's leader and the father of Tarrant County had died of apoplexy. His last work for Texans had been completed. Eight weeks of battling political issues, followed by work with the nominating caucus in preparation for their spring campaign—in order to elect in June all conservatives to state offices—was too much tension for a grief-burdened soul. The giant body, worn by sixty-odd years of zealous living, by campaigns of the Mexican War, by Ranger service, by service in the Civil War, and by frontier building, had fallen.

Johnson was buried in Austin. But in the winter of 1866, his life-long friends, Captains Daggett and Turner, went to Austin to arrange for the removal of his body to the family cemetery at Johnson's Station. No headstone marks his grave. The state of Texas, in 1936, erected a granite monument, with a bronze plaque, inscribed in memory of Colonel Middleton Tate Johnson, Father of Tarrant County.

Good men, thrifty men, hardworking men, freedom-loving men, and men with faith in the future lived in Fort Town. They were not sanctimonious men. Many of them persistently and intensely hated tyrants—Yankees, like William Lloyd Garrison, the Boston abolitionist, and Harriet Beecher Stowe, author of *Uncle Tom's Cabin*. They were harsh in their treatment of liars and dishonest men, and swore softly or uproariously according to the event. They drank in the saloons for comradeship and placed bets on both horses and political candidates. They drove good bargains but were always ready to lend money to a trusted man, and without contract or note.

The rank of the town's men was strengthened in late December of 1865, with the coming of Major Khleber Miller Van Zandt, who placed his name above a mercantile store on the square in January of 1866. From that day, every undertaking which would make the history of Fort Worth would have as one of its chief underwriters Major Van Zandt, who lived by the grace of God, his own prudence, and his labor.

Van Zandt was born in Tennessee in 1836. Two years later, his family came to Texas. In 1842, President Houston appointed his father, Isaac Van Zandt, minister from the Republic of Texas to the United States. Accompanying his parents to Washington, D.C., six-year-old Khleber, lived in the boarding house where Senator John Quincy Adams, former president of the United States, made his residence. In the same house lived Senator John C. Calhoun, and Daniel Webster.

Young Khleber became a friend of Calhoun, and each morning walked a part of the way to the Capitol with the aging senator. In Washington, he attended his first formal school, while his father sought the annexation of Texas to the Union. When the Van Zandt family returned to Texas, making their home in Harrison County, his father Isaac became a candidate for governor of Texas in 1847. Tragedy struck before the election. Isaac Van Zandt died of yellow fever at the Capitol Hotel in Houston on October 11, 1847.

Without a father, and his mother a widow with five children, Khleber, a lad of eleven years, realized that he must make his own way in life. He took a job in a mercantile store. Soon after each daybreak, he swept the store and built fires in the stoves. When the doors opened at seven, he waited on customers. A printing shop soon lured him, and until he was almost fifteen, Van Zandt worked as a printer's assistant. Then he left the employment of the printer, returning to his Grandmother Lipscomb in Tennessee. From there, he went to Franklin College in Nashville, and at the end of three years, graduated valedictorian of his class, delivering the valedictory speech in Latin. He presented his diploma to his grandmother, for she had sustained him through the college years. Her graduation gift to him was an unbroken mare. Khleber made of the animal a saddle horse and named her Dido in honor of Virgil's heroine in the Latin classic, the *Aeneid*.

In the fall, after graduation, eighteen-year-old Khleber rode Dido from Tennessee to Marshall, Texas. Soon after his arrival there, he sold Dido for $100 and gave the money to organize a Christian church. He was not a lukewarm Christian, as his action proved. Reared in the Baptist faith, he joined the Christian church at Franklin College.

He took a job buying land for the Vicksburg and Shreveport Railroad. When he had earned sufficient money to meet the minimum essentials for living, he began to study law in the office of his brother-in-law, J. M. Clough, with whom he soon formed a law firm. In 1861, Texans were marching away to defend the Confederacy. Khleber was twenty-five and already a leader in Marshall. He recruited a company, was elected captain, and led his men to Hopkinsville, Kentucky. They were mustered in as Company D of the 7th Texas Infantry. After desperate fighting to save Fort Henry on the Tennessee and Fort Donelson on the Cumberland—the chief gateways to western Tennessee—they surrendered at Fort Donelson to General Grant on February 16, 1862.

Captain Khleber Van Zandt was a conquered Confederate, but not a beaten one. Direct and aggressive in manner, he wrote to the victorious Grant asking permission to remove the body of his brother-in-law, Clough, and a comrade, killed at Fort Donelson. He wished to take them to Kentucky, from which state they would eventually be removed to Marshall, Texas. Grant complied; and Van Zandt, a war prisoner, was sent to Camp Chase near Columbus, Ohio, then transferred to Johnson's Island, remaining there six months. During an exchange of war prisoners between the Confederacy and the Union, he was exchanged for a Union major and sent home on furlough.

In January 1863, he returned to the battlefield as a major. At the battle of Chickamauga, he led his brigade, since the officer in command was ill. Chickamauga was his last battle. Having received a chest wound which grew worse, he was sent to the hospital in Dalton, Georgia, where, for a time, death threatened to be the victor. In 1864, having recovered sufficiently, he returned to Marshall, and managed the Confederate warehouse which stored cotton and other goods collected for the "tax-in-kind."

When the South surrendered and the Federal agents came to seize the property of the Confederacy, Major Van Zandt demonstrated his skillful leadership and fighting spirit. He told his assistant to lock the warehouse and to tell the Federals that he had lost the key. That night, the destitute inhabitants in and around Marshall found supplies in the warehouse to meet their direst needs.

Disorders broke the routine life in Harrison County, which had one of the largest slave populations in Texas. Confounded by the chaos, Federal officers asked Major Van Zandt to work for them, and requested that he take the oath of loyalty.

"I will work, but a loyalty oath I will not take," was his answer. Confronted with the choice of confusion or order, the Federals employed this defiant but capable Confederate without requiring the usual oath; for they were certain he could bring about peaceful rule.

Here was a man who was living by his own conviction, motivated only by his own prudence, and capable of maintaining his own rights. Here was the manifestation of the spirit of the man who later in adversity brought by drouths, crop failures, and financial panics (which would sweep the nation in the years to come) could yet be able to help Fort Worth prosper and grow.

After smoothing the troubles in East Texas, he decided to seek the higher altitude of North Texas in order to improve his broken health; and to find a home in a frontier county populated by few ex-slaves and fewer Union soldiers, for there he would be able to purge his heart of pent-up resentment.

In August 1865, Van Zandt traveled from East Texas astride the horse on which he had ridden home from the war. He was accompanied by three other mounted men, who left him at Dallas. He rode on through the East Cross Timbers in search of his Franklin College friend with whom he had graduated—Leigh Oldham, a merchant of Fort Worth. Dismounting on Fort Town's square, the first man he met was Dr. Woods, formerly of Harrison County, but then a prosperous farmer of the White Settlement area. Together they found Oldham, and a jovial reunion followed.

Van Zandt liked the prairie country. Choosing to stay, he rented a house located near the present-day northeast corner of Commerce and Fifth streets, then returned to Marshall for his family. On the way home, he rented two teams of oxen with which to move his family and household goods. Although penniless, he prepared for the journey. Mrs. Van Zandt had saved seventy-two dollars which would finance the trip to Fort Worth. Before leaving Marshall, one of the four children had been exposed to the measles, a fact that Van Zandt withheld from his wife. For three weeks they traveled amid the worst November weather. There were windy blasts, snow, sleet, and rain. On the journey, traveling seven miles a day, all four of the children became ill with the measles. Without medicine, Mrs. Van Zandt toiled to keep the children bundled in blankets with hot rocks around them. Arriving in Grapevine, they found comfort in the home of the Lipscomb family, Van Zandt's kin from Tennessee.

By January of the year 1866, the Van Zandts were citizens of Fort Worth. The major then went East, bought merchandise on credit, and opened a store on the "south side of the square across from the court house" on today's Weatherford Street in a "ramshackle concrete store erected by Leigh Oldham before the war." Affable and kind, Van Zandt would soon be called a friend by all Tarrant County people, who would address him as "the Major," and by his intimates as "Major K. M." He was now thirty years old.

Another newcomer to Fort Worth that year, who became a friend and co-worker with Van Zandt, and would cast heavy ballast in Fort Worth's favor, was Harrison G. Hendricks. Kentucky-born and self-educated, he had read law in Bonham under Judge A. A. Evarts, a member of the convention of 1845. Hendricks had been admitted to the Texas bar. In the following year he married Judge Evarts' only daughter Anne, and established a law firm in Sherman. His legal fees were paid in land which he converted into commercial value by purchasing slaves to cultivate his land holdings.

In 1861, he moved with his slaves to a large plantation in the Brazos River Valley in Hill County. There he devoted his ability in legal persuasion to the cause of Texas secession from the Union. Freeing his slaves after the war, and believing that Fort Worth was the town of promise, he moved his family there and established a law office.

His legal success made it possible for him to acquire large blocks of land, circling the village. In the north area he located his farm on land which later was to be covered by two meat-packing plants. From his property in the south area, Hendricks would make a land grant in 1872 to the Texas and Pacific Railway in order to bring the railroad to Fort Worth.

Unpleasant events occurred in the spring of 1866. Heavy rains sent the Trinity swirling into the highest flood stage on record. No living pioneer of the upper Trinity Valley could recall that the country had ever been submerged beneath such depths of water. During the planting season, farmers had treasured each expensive grain of the scarce seed corn and seed wheat. Tomorrow's bread was washed away. With homes and cattle moved off down stream, the farmers about Fort Town stayed on the high ground until the water ran off their land. Then they returned to toil all the more in their fields caked with mud and debris of the woods, while some of the merchants began to scheme to obtain seed corn for them.

Misfortunes of the area were not announced to strangers. Instead, the goodness of the town and its environs were described to the outside world in an article written before the June election of 1866—"Description of Tarrant County" by W. S. Tucker, county judge—published in the *Texas Almanac*, 1866–1867. It follows:

At Fort Worth we have one male and female academy. Also the Mansfield Academy on the edge of the Cross Timbers fourteen miles east from Fort Worth. Our churches are the Methodist, Presbyterian, Christian and Baptist. Our agricultural products are:

Wheat	20–30 bushels per acre
Corn	40 bushels per acre
Rye	35 bushels per acre
Oats	30 bushels per acre
Hungarian grass	2 tons per acre
Cotton	1 bale to the acre
Barley	40–60 bushels per acre

We also raise potatoes and tobacco.

The Cross Timbers abound with iron ore also petroleum oil. Quick silver mines have been discovered but not worked. We have several springs in the county of medicinal qualities. Our climate is mild. Winter 50–80 (degrees). Summer 50–100 with pleasant breezes. Summer nights are cool. Prospective railroads have been surveyed. We have timber in abundance, limestone, rock, brick, and concrete for building.

Milk, butter, cheese, eggs, poultry and winter and spring vegetables can be had. Bacon is excellent. Cost of living is comparatively nothing. Hogs can be raised at but little cost and without trouble beyond saving the bacon. Cattle fatten on winter pasturage.

Population is increasing 5 percent. The vote before the war was 700 and is now 1000. Our markets are Houston, Galveston, Millican which is about 200 miles, freight from $1 to $1.50. Also San Antonio, Paris and Jefferson in Texas and Shreveport in Louisiana. No attention as yet has been given to horticulture, though the grapes grow luxuriantly and spontaneously from which much wine is made. The price of land: $3–$15 improved land, 50¢ to $1.50 on unimproved. The negroes have decreased in number 50 percent since the War. Our farmers do not expect to make contract with them but to work their usual crops themselves. We have peaches in abundance, some apples.

Corn is worth	50¢ per bushel	
Beef " "	1–3¢ per pound	

Pork	"	"	4¢	"	"
Butter	"		5–12½¢	"	
Bacon	"		10–12¢	"	
Horses	"		$30–150		
Oxen	"		$30–50		
Cows	"		$8–10		
Stock cattle			$4 per head		
Sheep			$2 " "		

Any devoted son of the soil would conclude that Tarrant County was a pastoral paradise after reading Judge Tucker's description of the county. If one had no ties binding to a home elsewhere, no doubt he would hasten to hitch his oxteam and begin moving to this region.

Regardless of prospective prosperity depicted by Tucker, Captain Terrell was not as optimistic. In a letter to his mother on August 1, 1866, he wrote: "This country is not prospering in improvements as I thought it would. I do a good business but cannot make collections . . . hence if in the course of a few months prospects do not brighten, I will leave for a more populous and enterprising country." However, he revealed that farmers were favored with one dollar a bushel for wheat. Throughout the year, his letters speak of the scarcity of money.

Other events of that same spring of 1866 which attracted attention but shattered precedent and ruffled masculine pride, even to the uttering of oaths against President Johnson's strange ways—were the appointments on May 10, of a woman postmistress at Fort Worth, Mrs. Dorcas Williams, and a fifteen-year-old postmistress at Birdville, Miss Alice Barkley, daughter of Dr. Barkley, the staunch Unionist. Women postmistresses were unprecedented. However, few able-bodied men were eligible. There were few who could take the "iron-clad" oath of office that they "had not in any way aided the Confederacy"; while these two women, when questioned by Federal authorities, as to the extent of their aid to the Confederacy, replied that they "had spun and woven cloth and knitted dozens of pairs of socks for the soldiers." Alice Barkley even confessed to having woven cloth to make Captain Terrell a pair of trousers to take with him to war. These were minor misdemeanors, which cleared them from rebel status. So Fort Worth had a woman postmistress for eleven months until April 23, 1867, when Charles J. Louckx became postmaster.

Confronted with this new idea of women in public office, amazed men were spurred to drive for the election of conservative officials in the June election of 1866, which Provisional Governor Hamilton had called after the constitutional convention had completed its work in Austin that April 2, preceding. By overwhelming majority, Tarrant County men elected Throckmorton for governor, because he opposed Negro suffrage. In general, the citizens were pleased with the outcome.

In the newly elected legislature was Sam Evans, age thirty-three, born in Kentucky, post office address Fort Worth, occupation, farmer, representative for Tarrant County. The senator from the Twentieth District (which included Tarrant, Erath, Johnson, Parker, and Palo Pinto counties), was not an inhabitant of Tarrant. To serve in the state court of the Fifth District, were Judge J. J. Good; and E. E. Hovenkamp of Birdville in the office of district attorney. The slate of elected officers for Tarrant County listed: W. B. Walker, county judge; G. Nance, county clerk; J. T. Turner, district clerk; H. C. Daggett, sheriff; A. G. Gardner, surveyor. Tarrant County voters did not elect senators or representatives to the Congress of the United States, for it was provided that the Eleventh Legislature would.

On August 9, 1866, the Eleventh Legislature of Texas convened, soon followed by the inauguration of Governor Throckmorton, Lieutenant Governor G. W. Jones, and other state officials.

August 20, President Johnson proclaimed that insurrection was ended —Texas was restored to the Union. The fact that Texas was the last state to be readmitted to the Union under President Johnson's plan of reconstruction, did not detract many Texans from their sublime sense of security derived from the belief that Texas had been rewarded for her compliance with the complete restoration to the Union.

Keen politicos of Fort Worth watched with foreboding the affairs at Washington and Austin. Congress early in 1866 extended the term of the Freedmen's Bureau, passed a civil rights' bill giving blacks equal civil rights with whites, and in June of 1866, Congress guaranteed these rights by presenting the Fourteenth Amendment to the states for ratification.

The Eleventh Legislature of Texas did not act upon the Thirteenth Amendment, and by overwhelming majority, rejected ratification of the Fourteenth Amendment, which provided civil rights and citizenship to male Negroes, punishing any Southern state denying these rights by reducing their representation in Congress.

The third and fourth sections were the hardest on Tarrant County males by disqualifying them from both federal and state offices if they had participated in rebellion, and canceled all public debts and voided all claims of loss caused by emancipation of their slaves.

Even President Johnson advised the Southern states against the ratification of the Fourteenth Amendment. Texans were strong in their opposition to it. They could not accept first, civil rights and citizenship for Negroes; second, reduction of representation in Congress for any state denying the right of suffrage to male Negroes—such reduction to be in proportion to the number of blacks disfranchised; third, disqualification for both federal and state offices of all Southerners who, having taken an official oath to support the Constitution, later participated in rebellion; and fourth, canceled the public debts and voided all slaveholders' claims of loss caused by emancipation of their slaves.

Colonel Smith and Captain Terrell had legal perspective of events both state and national. Captain Terrell had written his mother in a later letter, that he did not and would not take active part in political matters since he had sworn loyalty to the United States and intended to keep his oath. Nevertheless, he dispensed political advice. He, with Smith, tried to spare their friends a jolt from their enjoyment of false security. These friends erroneously believed that Texas was safely in the Union, thus all was well. Smith and Terrell began to point out danger signals. They said, for one thing, that Reagan had been right in his advice the year before, that Texas should submit as a conquered area in order to hasten the day of restoration; that now Congress was prepared to defy the president and tyrannize over the South. Furthermore, the Texas legislature had erred in refusing to act upon the Thirteenth Amendment and ratifying the Fourteenth; also it had passed a compulsory labor law and black codes, and had elected to the United States Senate two men who could not take the iron-clad oath: David G. Burnet and O. M. Roberts. Thus Texas had made herself vulnerable for deep whiplashes by Congress.

Fort Towners listened to these two trusted logicians; nevertheless, they approved of the work of the legislature, for they were not yet prepared in thought to submit as conquered men. And in order to push back despondent omens, they tried to remain even-tempered when Congress refused to seat the Southern states. They tried to watch the quarrel between President Johnson, fighting to keep his program of reconstruction, and Congress steaming up to ride roughshod over both the president and the South.

They sympathized with the people of Europe because a fellow named Otto von Bismarck of Prussia was fighting Austria and the lesser German states. They dismissed affairs in Mexico with the hope that conditions would improve. Emperor Napoleon III of France had promised the United States, endeavoring to enforce the Monroe Doctrine, that he would withdraw French troops from Mexico. (However, some were still there.) Whether Mexico would be ruled by Maximilian as emperor or by Benito Juarez as president, was an issue beyond the people of Fort Worth. They did not neglect, however, to read the column reporting foreign news in their newspapers which came twice weekly.

Only a semi-weekly mail operated from Dallas to Fort Belknap in 1866, so states the *Texas Almanac*, 1866–1867; and in its chart of "Newspapers Published in Texas," there was none listed for Fort Worth. Therefore the *Dallas Herald* and Austin and Galveston papers were the chief informants. But Fort Worthians record that in the eighteen-sixties, their town did have a newspaper, *The Chieftain* which, in 1867 was sold to men in Cleburne, Texas.

Good medicine for forgetting national problems and international woes was to concentrate upon earning bread and meat and attending to affairs in Fort Town—that was the decision of the village doers. Construction on the courthouse, for one thing, needed to be resumed, and they saw that it was done in 1866.

Sometimes Fort Towners had the opportunity to welcome heartily the masters of covered wagons, who in their rumbling voyage westward paused to enter the stores on the square inquiring about obstacles to avoid on their road, and to purchase a few necessities. The town people considered that hospitable interest extended to homeseekers or visitors to be an investment in future customers. Such a visitor was a cowman who entered the Tarrant County Courthouse in April, 1866, to inquire about the best crossing on the Trinity for a herd of more than one thousand cattle which within an hour would be upon the town.

Quick to grasp that this cowman's question for a good driver crossing was opportunity knocking at Fort Worth's door, Charles Biggers Daggett, with a few other townsmen, replied with cordial gusto, "Bring 'em on!" Rushing from the courthouse, they leaped upon their horses and rode with the cattleman to his herd which was then advancing to the south prairie now lying between present-day Jennings Avenue and South Main Street.

Daggett and his companions escorted the leadman of the herd to ford the Trinity just east of the present-day Samuels Avenue railway bridge, known as Daggett's Crossing. This was the vanguard of other drovers who would trail millions of cattle from the Gulf Plain of Texas through Fort Worth between 1866 and 1886. So it was that Fort Worth became a cattle town.

From the published chronicles of the trail drivers themselves, the facts are established that this first herd belonged to Colonel J. J. Myers of Lockhart, Texas, that epochal spring of 1866, on his way to the Missouri-Pacific railway which offered transportation from Sedalia and Saint Joseph, Missouri, to Saint Louis and Chicago. Monroe Choate and B. A. Borroun also drove a herd from Karnes County, crossed the Red River and went to Iowa. There was a Mr. A. F. Carvajal of Spanish descent, who related, in an account of his journey in 1866 from Fort Worth, that his party drove to Montague and thence to Red River Station. These men were the Magellans of the cattle trails. The period between 1866 through 1868 was one of trail explorations in which the McCoy-Chisholm Trail from the Gulf Plain to the North was to be charted and fixed.

Drovers were adventuring with no security and all risks. In the North after the war, there was a beef shortage, and on Christmas Day of 1865, the Union Stockyards had opened to handle the cattle of the western plains; so Chicago packing houses began to bid for Texas cattle. Average market price then in Texas, was three to four dollars a head. At that price, speculators were few. Market quotas in the North ranged from thirty to forty dollars and even fifty for mature beeves. The pioneer trail drivers were experimenting in the game of cost and profit. The problem was how much would it cost to deliver their five-dollar beeves to a fifty-dollar market.

The drives were more than a financial gamble, they were a contest in patience and hardships. In southeastern Kansas, southern Arkansas, and southern Missouri, cowmen endured all kinds of troubles. Armed mobs tried to prevent the movement north of cattle which they claimed to be infested with Texas Fever, but the true motive of many an armed band, was robbery. Bad news travels with speed, and the drovers following the first trailblazers, avoided the eastern route to Sedalia, Missouri. They drove west about 150 miles along the southern boundary of Kansas beyond farm settlements. When far enough north, they backtracked east and reached the railroad at Saint Joseph, Missouri, from where cattle were shipped to Chicago.

In that first year, it is estimated that 260,000 head of Texas cattle crossed the Red River for northern markets. Many of those thousands no doubt, plodded through Fort Worth. During the spring and summer of 1866 Fort Towners, seeing hides and horns treading past them, predicted there would be more herds next year. Prominent among these percipient men was M. B. Loyd, who would earn cattle gold that would change the financial life of the village.

Captain Loyd, under Colonel McCord during the war, had a company of Rangers protecting the frontier. He had ridden the western prairies and had seen, after the fall of Vicksburg, the cattle become numerous. During the next five years he had spent his days gathering and marketing herds. With profits from trail driving, he was to open an exchange or loan office on the square in the first years of the eighteen-seventies. In 1873, he was to invest in one of the first commercial banks, the Texas and California Bank of Loyd, Markles and Company; and by 1877, to establish the first national bank to operate in Fort Worth.

In the meantime, undisciplined boys, without schooling since about 1862, became a problem. In August, measures were taken to repair the Masonic lodge building for school purposes. Since the floor had been torn out to make looms during the war, Dr. Peak, Judge A. M. Milwee and Milt Robinson purchased a load of flour at Mauck's Mill on the Cedar Fork, and drove to East Texas where they traded it for lumber.

At eight o'clock upon one morning in September, the bell in front of Andrews Tavern rang to summon youths to the "Hanna High School." Captain John Hanna, with all the military bearing which his title indicated, stood at the double doors of the Masonic building to greet his students who had reveled in the three-year holiday from school.

Blustering hectors tried the mettle of the new professor, age thirty-five, and a newcomer from the rival town of Dallas. Their bullying insolence could not intimidate a captain with a record of distinguished service in the Confederate Army, nor a scholar who had graduated with honors from Miami University in Ohio, a lawyer who had practiced in Missouri before the Civil War, and since the end of the war had taught school in Dallas.

Professor Hanna closed his school each year in a mood of gaiety. Visitors from Dallas, Jack, Johnson, Denton, Wise, Parker and Tarrant counties came in hacks, buggies, wagons and on horseback to be present at such ceremonies, and to see the students display their achievements. Hotels, boarding houses, wagonyards were filled, and private families opened their doors to the visitors. The evening of the school exhibition, the enormous audience seated upon every available bench, chair and box in town, pressed the walls of the Masonic hall. Hanna, assisted by Carl Vincent, had rehearsed the program for months.

At the base of the stage erected across the auditorium sat an orchestra consisting of Theodore Feild, and Tom Moody, violinists; Miss Jane Ferguson, pianist; Jim Bradner, second fiddle; and Tucker Boaz, accordionist. When the last strains of "The Downfall of Poland" had ceased to reverberate, the curtain raised in the quiet hall. Dressed in their best were the girls and boys who filled the stage. Recitations, orations, essays, and debates—all were heard in the course of the evening. The best declamations in the opinion of the boys were those about Indians, the most popular ones being: "Red Jacket," "Lo the Poor Indian," and "The Death of Logan, the Indian Chief." The climax of the evening was a drama. Indians, cowboys, robbers, barroom scenes, and a shooting were enacted. The drama was alleged to have "been creditably acted and highly received by the enthusiastic audience."

It was to be in 1868 that Hanna formed a law partnership with J. V. Hogsett, which was to be recognized throughout the Southwest for its exemplary jurisprudence. And when he died in March 1884, he was buried in Pioneer Rest Cemetery.

While boys, unaccustomed to school routine wrestled with their studies at Hanna's school in 1866, men worried about the means of acquiring money. The lack of specie since the war had prodded men to seek new ways to carve out a livelihood. In October, 1866, George Holland was an item of conversation. For weeks he had been gathering flocks of wild turkeys fattened on grass, wild grain, and insects of the prairies around the town and in the vicinity of Turkey Knob Hill, the favorite turkey roost. Today, this place is located directly south of the present highway passing through the main business block of old Handley. With a chuck wagon and several men and boys to drive the flock of many thousand birds, Holland left Fort Worth with the wish of his friends that he would return bowlegged under the weight of gold and silver eagles. If fortune was with him, Holland expected to arrive in New Orleans in time to sell his turkeys for the Christmas market.

Another road to riches was freighting. Every man who could get a wagon and team began hauling to Jefferson, Houston, or Millican. Word had come to Fort Worth in 1866 that eastern buyers were at Millican, the terminal of the railroad two hundred miles south. They were offering specie for hides, tallow, and beeswax. Four yokes of oxen pulling freighters each loaded with cow, deer, bobcat, and sheep hides, tallow, and wool left Tarrant County for Millican. Gold and silver dollars were not all the freighters brought back. Like the ships returning in the fifteenth century from the Orient bringing wondrous goods to Europe, these freighters too, brought luxuries to Fort Town: hickory shirting, spool cotton, brown and bleached domestic, knives and forks, cups and saucers, plates, a few clocks, and a novelty—tin milk pans.

"Bony" Tucker, an officeholder in Tarrant County since 1856, was now one of the displaced political leaders under Governor Hamilton's decree which barred from office all men who had held a position in either town or county government under the Confederacy. He turned to farming as the certain way to acquire the scarce hard money. By 1867 he had built a house on a prominent hill south of the town near the intersection of what is known as Tucker and South Main streets, and was said to be the first house erected south of the present Texas and Pacific Railway station on West Vickery. His farm covered what is known today as Tucker Hill and extended from present-day Bryan Avenue in the area of the Fort Worth Fire Station Number Five, west across South Main, Galveston, Saint Louis and May streets to Jennings Avenue, incorporating approximately the four hundred and five hundred blocks of those streets. On today's Jennings Avenue, Bony Tucker built a treadmill operated by a treadwheel powered by oxen treading round and round, grinding corn and wheat.

1867

President Johnson had lost the struggle as to whether the president or Congress had the right to reconstruct the South. Northern radicals had won complete control in the autumn election of 1866.

When the new Congress convened in 1867, it was dominated by two radical Republicans. Charles Sumner of Massachusetts, impaired in health because of a severe head beating from a cane wielded by Representative Brooks of South Carolina in the Senate in 1856, for his speech against slavery and Southern leaders, now drove the Senate to vengeful acts. The other, was Thaddeus Stevens, age seventy-five, on the verge of the grave and embittered by the loss of his ironworks near Gettysburg, which General Lee's army burned during its invasion of Pennsylvania, lashed the House of Representatives to inflict harsh retribution upon the refractory South.

So hammer blows of Congress were to fall upon Fort Town's supreme individualists with stunning impact. They were to be scourged into political exile by a series of three acts passed during the period from March through July 1867, fomented by the two splenetic Republicans.

First, Congress declared that the governments in the Southern states reconstructed under President Johnson's plan, were illegal. This was done to punish Texas and other states for accepting the work of their constitutional conventions, leaving their governments in the hands of the white race; and they had also rejected the Fourteenth Amendment granting freedmen civil rights.

The South was placed under military rule dividing it into five military districts, each to be ruled by a military commander and federal troops. The commanders were to call elections based on Negro suffrage; and at these elections, delegates were to be chosen to attend a convention which would write a new state constitution, granting Negro suffrage and ratifying the Fourteenth Amendment. Later, Texas, Virginia, and Mississippi as the last three states to reenter the Union, were also required to ratify the Fifteenth Amendment as a requisite for readmission.

Texas and Louisiana made up the Fifth Military District ruled by General Phillip H. Sheridan, in New Orleans; while General Charles Griffin, commander of the Texas division governed from Galveston. Governor Throckmorton, the people's choice in the 1866 election, pledged his cooperation. But Sheridan and Griffin, "prejudiced against Texans" as obstinate rebels, began a most tyrannical rule.

General Griffin brought civil government under his control. He threw the courts into chaos, practically voiding them by transferring from the civil courts to military tribunals all cases involving Negroes, Union men, or soldiers, by requiring jurors to take the iron-clad oath; and by establishing the competency of Negroes to serve as jurors.

On July 30, 1867, General Sheridan removed Governor Throckmorton as "an impediment to reconstruction." Throckmorton was a friend of Fort Towners ever since he had, as a legislator, helped them in their quarrel with Birdville over the county seat. E. M. Pease, a loyal Unionist, supporting Negro suffrage, and against whom Fort Worthians had voted in 1866, was made governor. Pease, a Texan since 1835 having served twice as governor, was a man of unquestioned honesty, as well as the most lenient of the radicals. These latter virtues, however, did not make him acceptable to Daggett, Turner, Isbell, Stephen Terry, Major Van Zandt, and others of Colonel Johnson's following.

Meanwhile, the military government proceeded to carry out the act of Congress passed in March of 1867, requiring the military commander of each district to appoint a registration board in each county and register the legal voters, who would then be permitted to vote for delegates to a constitutional convention. These delegates would write a new constitution for Texas establishing Negro suffrage. The registration of voters was to be completed by September 1, 1867. There were thirty-three such military district posts in Texas. Those posts which were nearest Fort Worth were located at Brenham, Waco, Palestine, Marshall, and Jefferson.

Squire B. F. Barkley of Birdville, was appointed by the military commander to be head of Tarrant County's registration board. Those who could be registered as legal voters included all male citizens twenty-one years of age, resident of the state one year, of whatever race or color or previous condition, and able to take the iron-clad oath.

Generals Grant and Sheridan interpreted the franchise clause of the Fourteenth Amendment to exclude from registration and voting not only persons who had held a state or federal office, but even those persons who had served in such minor capacities as mayors of cities, sextons of cemeteries, and school trustees. On July 19, 1867, Congress wrote into law the Grant-Sheridan interpretation and gave discretionary powers to local registration boards to register or reject an applicant. The board at Dallas, consisting of one white and one Negro, made full use of its power. It is said it refused to register as voters all white men who admitted that they were opposed to Negro suffrage.

Throughout the summer the registration in Texas moved slowly in an atmosphere ominous with rebellion. When registration was completed, it was estimated between 7,500 and 10,000 white men had been disfranchised. There were 59,633 white voters registered, fourteen percent of the white population. There were 49,479 black voters registered, twenty-seven percent of the Negro population. There were between 112,000 and 189,000 qualified voters in Texas.

In Tarrant County, registered voters were not numerous according to the statistics that A. B. Norton in his newspaper, the *Fort Worth Whig Chief* of September 12, 1871, reported:

Tarrant County—had in 1860, a population of 5,170 whites and 850 blacks, making a total of 6,020. In 1867, there were 833 registered voters of whom 636 were white and 197 colored.

Indeed, the radicals in Congress had cut deep in restricting the right of males to self-government in Tarrant County.

By September, the great body of incumbent officers, judicial and administrative, had been removed and replaced by the appointees of the military commanders of Texas. Those new appointees in Tarrant County listed November 7, 1867 were: County Judge B. F. Barkeley, County Clerk L. H. Brown, Sheriff M. T. Morgan, County Treasurer H. T. Brown, and dashes in places of names followed the offices of district clerk, surveyor, and tax assessor-collector. Charles J. Louckx favorable to Unionists, having succeeded Postmistress Mrs. Dorcas Williams in April, remained as postmaster. To the Fifth District state court which included Tarrant County, the military government awarded the judgeship to a nationally known leader of the Union party—A. B. Norton, and Green J. Clark was to serve under Norton as district attorney.

After the anger arising from the thought of being governed by military authorities had spent itself, reason once more took hold of the former Confederates of Tarrant County. Before Andrews Tavern some of these men gathered to visit with Stephen Terry, former chief justice of the county, who had recently returned from Washington, D.C., where he had to report concerning Confederate taxes collected in Tarrant. He was moved by his vision of Thaddeus Stevens in Congress snarling denouncements of the South.

"I don't want to intrude my opinion," he said, "but have you men considered what Tarrant County has escaped? Spared a carpetbagger or a radical Northerner bent upon spiteful vengeance as the county judge, the key man responsible for enforcing the new order? We should give thanks that Dr. Barkeley, our new county judge, is a Tarrant citizen—one of us. We admit that he has an iron will; has in the face of insults and threats, stood steadfastly loyal to the Union party throughout the war. But you cannot deny that he is a man of a good heart and is fair-minded." Both Major Van Zandt and Captain Terrell were among the group who agreed.

On September 15, yellow fever removed General Griffin in death. General J. J. Reynolds succeeded to the office, beginning immediately to scourge Texas rebels. Good days had come for carpetbaggers, radical Republicans, and Negroes in Texas. The Union League, formed in the North for the purpose of teaching freedmen of the South loyalty to the Republican party, sent agents moving over the state. They were to organize local Union Leagues in each county. Tarrant County quickly experienced their disruptive influence. Mrs. Stephen Terry, on several occasions, upon going to the kitchen when dinner had not been announced finding the meal burning on the stove, her cook, Maria, gone, and Joe the houseboy responding with insolence to her instructions, then realized, along with other residents in the town, that there were Union Leaguers among their former slaves.

In November of 1867, General W. S. Hancock, a Democrat disliking the program of the radicals, replaced General Sheridan as commander of the Fifth Military District. In December, Hancock ordered an election to be held in each county of Texas early the next year, from February 10 through 14, 1868, to determine whether or not a convention should be held to write a new state constitution and at the same time to elect delegates to the proposed constitutional convention.

"By hector! Let the radical Republicans rule to their own ruin. We will comply in order to regain our inalienable right to govern ourselves," was the angry resolution of disfranchised males. And with that attitude, men of Fort Worth in September of 1867, turned from politics as an avocation and a sport. The merchants—Lemuel Samuels, Major Van Zandt, Daggett, Turner, and others—took inventory in their stores and supplied their shelves with goods for the caravans wheeling westward and goods for the expected increase of trail drivers bound for Kansas with their cattle.

Since the first herd from South Texas had come through the town the year before, the program of these businessmen had solidified. Fort Worth was the last place of any size on the lonely trail of two or three months across Texas and Indian Territory to Northern markets. They were determined to place their town as the most important on the route, and not permit Dallas to capture the trade of supplying the grub wagon of the trail drivers, and entertainment for the cowboys. It was true that the adventurers of 1866 had fought their way through Arkansas, Missouri, and Kansas, and for some of the drovers it had been disastrous. But others had returned to South Texas with more specie than had been seen in those parts in years. So the canny Fort Worth businessmen reasoned that as soon as the range grass turned green in the spring of 1867, the cowmen would adventure again, and this time in greater numbers.

From spring of 1867 through the summer and fall the herds from South Texas plodded east of Fort Town's public square, filling the village with dust—a signal for the idlers on the square to jump on their horses and ride a safe distance to see the sight of a sea of brown hides bobbing up and down. Among the trail drivers, drovers of the year before were recognized. They would become familiar figures on the square, patrons of Fort Worth's hotels, friends of the town's leaders, and would anchor the cattle trail through Fort Town. Among these were "big-time" names —hallmarks for Fort Worth—Monroe Choate, Colonel J. J. Myers, and J. L. Driskill.

Choate, a rancher of Karnes County since 1855, a reputable trail driver to the Louisiana market, and one of the first ranchers to drive north in 1866, became known the whole length of the trails to Abilene and Dodge City as a man among cowmen—"generous, whole-souled, thoughtful of his men, full of wit and humor, and the life of his outfit on the trail and in camp." So difficult had been the drive to Kansas that first time, that he turned his herds to New Orleans in 1867, 1868; but would return in 1869 to the Kansas market and become a perennial trader in Fort Worth.

Colonel Myers was the figure of destiny in the spawning of the northern cattle trails which transformed "Fort Town" into "Cowtown." He was a small man of strong build. At that time his hair was gray, but it was said that the years had not robbed him of a body structure which seemed incapable of fatigue regardless of hardships. As a youth he had joined John C. Fremont on Fremont's exploring expedition to the Pacific coast in the 1840s. A successful Texas rancher, a Confederate colonel, a horseman of ability, yet a quiet man, he was known for honesty and sincerity.

After experiencing on that first drive in 1866, the battles on the trail, he decided to drive to western Kansas, bypassing the settlements, and to take the chance of finding a purchaser on the far western frontier. His gamble succeeded. In Junction City, Kansas, an incident significant both to Texas and to Fort Worth occurred. There Colonel Myers met Joseph G. McCoy who was on his first visit from Illinois to western Kansas, surveying for a location in which to establish a cattle shipping depot for the cattlemen of the West.

According to McCoy, he met Myers at the Hale House in Junction City. He was soon convinced that Myers was an astute man in whose word credit and confidence could be placed. McCoy unfolded his plan for providing a cattle shipping depot for Texas drovers. He asked Myers for his opinion, and that pioneer of the cattle trail had a ready answer for McCoy.

"A cattle depot operating upon legitimate business principles," he said, "is the greatest need of Texas stockmen," and he sagaciously concluded that such a business would be both a benefit to Texas and a boost out of the post-war depression generally.

The two men talked, made a plan, shook hands as if to seal their faith in the design and departed, each to his own business. Such was the birth of the McCoy Trail to Abilene, Kansas, the cattle boom in Texas, and the pattern of Fort Worth as cowtown on the trail.

In 1867, the Kansas-Pacific Railroad had built past the farmers' frontier and had reached Abilene, Kansas. The cowmen, for a time, would not have interference from farmers or their fences, so McCoy built the cattle depot with speed and confidence, while Myers returned in haste to Lockhart, Texas; and was soon on the trail with his cattle bound for Abilene, Kansas.

Upon reaching Fort Worth, he related the good news of an assured cattle-shipping depot at Abilene, grazed his cattle north of Fort Worth, resupplied the chuck wagon from the shelves in the town's stores, and then drove north to Abilene, becoming a figure in history. For the next seven years, he was to drive from one to 16,000 head of cattle annually to Abilene. Since the limit of a herd was 3,000 head, there was always a Myers herd somewhere along the trail during the season.

That could also be said of J. L. Driskill, a citizen of Texas since 1848, later a cattle drover for the Confederate Army, and after the war a drover to the New Orleans market. In 1867, he turned his herds toward western Kansas, and thereafter, according to Joseph McCoy writing in 1873, from 1,000 to 6,000 head of Driskill cattle arrived in the Kansas market each year.

Trails through free grass country from the Texas Gulf Plain to Kansas would triple the drives in 1868. Abilene would remain the chief cattle market for Texas drovers until the railroad reached Dodge City, Kansas, in 1876. But whether Abilene or Dodge City was the destination, most of the herds would pass through Fort Worth. Trail drivers in later years, relating tales to their grandchildren, used the names McCoy Trail, Dodge City Trail, and Chisholm Trail, applying all to the trail through Fort Worth.

The McCoy Trail, the chief one of the north during 1867–1876, extended from South Texas through Fort Worth to Red River Crossing where it joined the Chisholm Trail which crossed Indian Territory. Like fingers on a hand, cattle trails led from the grasslands of the Texas Gulf Coast to San Antonio; from there several trails converged at Austin, where the many trails became one as it moved northward through Waco and Cleburne to Fort Worth.

The season of trail driving, though burdensome to housewives of Fort Worth who were kept busy raising and lowering windows in order to shut out the dust, was a procession of entertainment for the children of the town. Safe behind a picket fence Elizabeth Frances Terry, four years old in 1867, and the only daughter of Judge Terry, stood in the yard of her father's home located on Pecan Street, between Fourth and Fifth, and watched the herds coming across the prairies from the south and moving up what is today Commerce, Jones, Grove, and Pecan streets.

An obedient child, she stopped playing about the yard, remained quiet and restrained her desire to wave at the Mexican cowboys, who sang softly the phrase, "Oh-ooh-ooh" which they trilled up the scale, trailed down the scale, then allowed to fade away like the sound of an echo. Sounds and sights causing stampedes, usually were wafted away from the herds on the notes of the cowboys' song. For an hour or more, the herd plodded past the Terry home, and Elizabeth's interest would lag. Moving cautiously into the house so as not to frighten the herds, she remained indoors until it was time to see the last part disappear over the bluff—a scene she delighted in. And there was another reason. Following some distance behind the herd was the chuck wagon with the cook and driver, creaking and swaying to the slow rhythmic tread of oxen; and in the rear, a teenage cowboy in command of the remuda. All the trail travelers in this rearguard of the herd waved to her.

Somedays, large herds passing through provided more amusement for Elizabeth. There were so many cowhands to watch the herds, that some were able to observe the scenery of the town. Mexican cowboys, seeing a rosebush heavy with blooms climbing over the double doors of the handsome brick residence of the Terry's, would sometimes ride to the fence, dismount and in their Latin charm ask Mrs. Terry if they might pick a rose or two. With many a smiling thank-you, each man then rode away with a rose in his hatband.

After the cattle disappeared over the bluff, they moved along a trail east of the Pioneer Rest Cemetery and of present-day Samuels Avenue— which at that time had not taken form, followed the Cold Springs Road to Daggett's Crossing, forded the Trinity, swung around the hill where today is located Old Trail Drivers Park, turned north onto Decatur Road, and pointed toward the Red River and the Chisholm Trail. If the herds forded Daggett's Crossing near sundown, the cowhands "bedded them down" for the night in the prairies where the packing houses were to be some years later. Leaving a few men to guard the sleeping herd from the lobo, coyote, and panther which were numerous, they returned to Fort Worth, their last chance for an evening of pleasure before the desolate drive ahead. They crowded Ed Terrell's small saloon and Andrews Tavern. They indulged in the best spree the small town could afford in the eighteen-sixties.

Cowboys and cattle erased from men's countenances much worry. Apple peddlers, something new, were the wonder to Fort Worth children. From Missouri and Arkansas in the coolness of the fall of 1867, came the first apple peddlers in bright green wagons with red wheels drawn by well-groomed horses or mules decked with silver-mounted harness and bridles and with red tassles nodding about their heads. "On the end of a long stick, stuck in the side of the wagon, an apple swayed enticingly to and fro, beckoning children, housewives, and men to come buy the fruit which filled the wagons. Fort Towners took the fruit as fast as the peddlers could hand it out and make the change. The wagon, emptied of apples, was a subject of sale. Men asked the cost of the team, harness, and wagon. The sale price ranged from $500 to $700 the outfit. Of course it would not pay to haul apples from Missouri to Texas. The actual reason for the appearance of the apple peddlers was that horse and mule breeders, and wagon and harness manufacturers back in Missouri were seeking markets in Texas and sent the apples along to attract buyers. Apple peddlers also had another purpose—that of encouraging Texans to drive cattle North. Penetrating the state as far south as Austin and San Antonio, they spread the news. The effect of the peddlers' visits would be realized in 1868 when herds, from early spring to late fall, would kick up the dust along the trail through Fort Worth.

It was an alive town in 1867, moving forward in spite of military government. The courthouse was roofed and completed. Its small tower-like dome served as a central focus from which encouragement, in ever widening arcs, drew newcomers within its circle. That was the reason Captain Daggett led the movement in 1860 to build a spectacular court-house that would halt the newcomers' trains. As a result, Fort Towners had an impressive structure, flashing the message that times were looking up.

Migrants observing the imposing building, felt inspired to remain. Among them was George H. Mulkey, former pony express rider. After the close of the war, he had gone to McKenzie College in Clarksville, Texas. He stayed there a year until chills and fever sent him home to Waco; but Fort Worth beckoned him as the place for opportunities. He moved to Fort Town and found a job making brick with a Mr. Frazier, a builder. He earned one dollar a day and board. Years later, Mr. Mulkey explained: "I could get meat to eat by working for board too, and we didn't always have it at home." Supplies were scarce, and people frugal.

Mulkey's frugality made him ingenious. He wove his own hats of wheat straw to shield his head from sleet and sun. Hardships and sickness were companions. He suffered chills like most of the pioneers. A sizable amount of his dollar-a-day wages was spent on quinine, retailing at ten dollars an ounce—its weight in gold. These toughening ordeals forged Mulkey into a man of strength and wisdom. When an octogenarian, Fort Worth citizens would salute him as a City Father, capitalist and philanthropist.

Quinine was almost as necessary as bread according to one pioneer describing conditions prior to secession of the states.

In early days we had drenching dews and heavy fogs. The country reeked with malaria. It was quite the thing for every normal person to undergo the agony of a chill every other day. It was not unusual for the family of eight or ten to make it unanimous and all fall to shaking at the same time. There was a tariff on quinine to protect the home manufacturers of the precious drug who demanded from $5 to $7 an ounce. It was before the day of capsules. Therefore quinine was taken in coffee and in whiskey often with the result of turning us against coffee and in a few instances against whiskey. The death toll from malaria directly and indirectly was very heavy in Texas.

Northerners were responsible for the excessive price after 1862 according to Captain Terrell. The South, where malaria and fever were prevalent, used twenty times more quinine than the North. After 1862, the South no longer represented in Congress, could not defend itself when Congress ruled by Northerners, placed a tariff on quinine,

raising the tariff from 15 cents under the law of 1857 to 45 cents, and raising the tariff on Peruvian bark from 15 cents in 1846 to 20 cents in 1862 and 1866. The law prevented importation (of quinine) from Europe and enabled the only manufacturers of the drug in the United States to enjoy a monopoly. . . . The law was repealed in 1868, but the high price obtained practically during the reconstruction, for it was only placed upon the free list in 1868, when its price fell to $1.35 an ounce.

Northerners had put quinine into the pack of polygonal difficulties of Reconstruction. Many thousands died because they lacked the price to buy the drug. The substitute for quinine—corn shucks, dogwood and willow bark, did not suffice. During the Civil War, quinine from France was brought into the Confederacy by blockade runners, and its price remained high. When the Federals seized the Confederate commissaries— or the Confederates raided one, quinine was the prize of the loot. Captain Terrell received from a client in Johnson County, his legal fee in French quinine which his client had confiscated when a guard of the Confederate Army at the commissary in Tyler, Texas, at the close of the war. Captain Terrell returned to Fort Worth and disposed of his fee at $16 an ounce at the drug store of Samuel J. Darcy, a wounded veteran.

News of 1867 in Tarrant County, no different from that elsewhere in the West, reported death of its citizens and Indian hostilities.

Mr. Andrews of the famous Andrews Tavern, died May 2, 1867, and was buried among the other graves clustering about that of Major Arnold and his children.

That summer in the northeastern part of the county at cotton-picking time, the Hamilton home was attacked by Indians. Mr. Hamilton was away at a distant mill. Mrs. Hamilton, at home with eight of their children, was weaving at her loom. Three older children were in the field picking cotton. The Comanche chief, Satank (who would be captured with Satanta and Big Tree in 1871) led a band of Indians upon this farm. They killed Mrs. Hamilton, kidnapped three of the children—one of whom they killed the next day, and carried away all portable household goods. Tarrant men railed bitterly at the Reconstruction government which forbade them to maintain their own home guard as formerly.

However, conversation in Fort Town also dealt with subjects other than denunciations. The Baptists were inviting townsmen to come to church in the Masonic Temple. In August of 1867, Reverends A. Fitzgerald and W. W. Mitchell organized the first Baptist church in Fort Worth. Fitzgerald, a controversial man constantly embroiled in disputes and a subject of gossip, did not last but two years.

In mid-October, Fort Town lost one of its leading bachelors. The townsmen chatted about the marriage of Colonel Smith to Mrs. Mary E. Fox, daughter of Colonel James Young of Tarrant County. It was a social event of interest not only to Fort Worth, but to the state as well.

In spite of much narrating of hardships experienced by citizens, a glance at the tax report of "assessments made in Tarrant County in 1867," would indicate that the year had been a prosperous one. The tax assessments published in the *Texas Almanac, 1868–1869* listed 198,256 acres of land lying in the county valued at $592,694. There were 10,117 horses valued at $356,143; cattle, 28,862, their value $160,607; sheep, 9,909, valued at $19,906. There was merchandise worth $36,703; and money on hand or at interest was $21,754. Miscellaneous property was worth $88,328. The total value of assessed property was $1,378,860. The state collected $1,630 in poll tax, and the total amount of taxes collected, including poll tax and ad valorem, was $3,195.25.

1868

Fort Town males had furiously sworn in 1867 to be done with politics, and let the radicals rule. Therefore, those who had not been rejected as qualified voters in the summer of 1867, went to the polls between February 10 and 14, 1868, heeding the call of General W. S. Hancock of the Fifth Military District. They voted yes or no on the question whether a state convention should be held to write a new constitution guaranteeing Negro suffrage; and at the same time, they cast a vote for delegates to the proposed convention. Little more than half of the registered voters of Texas exercised their franchise. Many whites, especially in South and East Texas, refused to vote, saying they preferred "Yankee rule to Negro rule." By this refusal they planned to defeat the radical Reconstruction program of Congress. Total votes cast in February were 56,156 of which

44,689 voted for the constitutional convention: 11,440 against it, 37 blank.

Negroes organized and directed by branches of both the Freedmen's Bureau and the Union League, carried the issue in South and East Texas. Major J. M. Bonner said that the voters in Dallas passed between two lines of Federal soldiers, some of whom were Negroes; and that Negro voters in Dallas carried the vote for the convention.

From the public square, the political leaders of Fort Town, now disfranchised, watched the proceedings of the February election and directed their influence, so that the qualified white voters cast conservative votes. The disfranchised leaders—Major Van Zandt, Colonel Smith, Captains Daggett, Terrell and Turner; Dr. Peak, Judge Terry, Gideon Nance, Bony Tucker, and others, warded off unpleasant incidents in Tarrant voting. They were without temerity even though a company of Federal soldiers was now encamped near the courthouse, at the foot of the bluff in the area of present-day Franklin Street, according to the record of Mel Isbell, who as a boy, accompanied his father, Paul Isbell, to the public square. He noticed that there were about twenty Negro soldiers among the Federals.

Charley Louckx was one of the Fort Town citizens maintaining order. In 1868 he had been appointed by Judge Norton, the Unionist, to serve as sheriff, though he was also the postmaster. The latter office, he said, did not keep him busy but the office of sheriff did as "there was plenty of law in Tarrant County at that time, but there was need of a strong-hearted man to enforce it."

Negroes may have rushed the voting polls in many parts of the state, but they did not crowd the polls at Fort Worth. However, they came. Faithful ex-slaves were kept at home, while recalcitrant Negroes of Fort Worth were led by the Northern members of the Union League. Seeing soldiers, some of whom were their own race, guarding the polls, the Negroes went forward, after a backward glance at the Union Leaguer standing nearby, who, by an encouraging nod or wink, sent him between the line of soldiers to cast his first vote.

The aforementioned disfranchised leaders disappeared into their own business houses. Their anger, contained only by will, was spent in a spurt of labor, tidying up shelves and moving barrels for a better arrangement in their stores. Out on the square, many other disfranchised men as well as the aged qualified white voters were huddled together. In bewilderment, according to Bud Daggett, they witnessed the almost incredible sight of Negroes voting, and white voters being compelled to pass between files of Negro soldiers in order to reach the polling place in the courthouse. A stillness pressed down on the disconsolate group gathered at the former little frame courthouse. For a long while in silence they gazed at the activities until the stillness was allegedly broken by an elderly farmer with these words: "As the Holy Book says—'Thou has shewed Thy people hard things, Thou hast made us to drink the wine of astonishment.' "

On June 1, 1868, ninety delegates assembled in convention in Austin to write a new Texas constitution. The results of Negro suffrage were much in evidence. Among the delegates were nine Negroes, twelve conservatives, and "six or eight were of the true carpetbag variety." W. F. Carter and Arvin Wright were the delegates from the Seventeenth District, representing Tarrant, Ellis, Palo Pinto, Parker, and Shackelford counties. The Republicans, in the convention were divided into two sharp factions—the radicals led by Edmund J. Davis, and the moderates by A. J. Hamilton, former governor.

In session fifty-five days, the convention spent $70,000 and without funds, adjourned August 31, 1868. A special tax was to be levied in order that the convention could reconvene on the first Monday in December and finish its work. Instead of completing a constitution, the convention had wasted time chartering railroads, debating the proposal to divide Texas into two or three states in order to assure the supremacy of the Republican party, and hearing complaints from the committee on lawlessness. This latter committee reported on July 2 that since 1865, there had been killed in civil strife 509 whites, 486 Negroes, and that ninety per cent of the crime was committed by whites.

The Fort Town men, in the summer of 1868, followed reports in the *Dallas Herald* of the proceedings of the convention as well as General Grant's campaign for president. They both derided the radical Republicans and resented bitterly the special tax to provide funds for the continuation of the convention which was ruled, so they said, by venal, inept, powerseekers. As for lawlessness, which they feared might spread if Grant were elected—they knew that somehow they could meet it.

By an act of Congress July 25, 1868, the Freedmen's Bureau was removed from Texas except for certain educational activities, and was discontinued by December 1869. (Since 1866, the local bureaus composed of either civilians—Republicans, carpetbaggers and scalawags; or a captain, lieutenant, or sergeant supported by a company or squad of soldiers, had been located throughout Texas towns.) They had been the sole judge of complaints made verbally to them by freedmen. They had succeeded in making labor contracts between ex-slaves and the former slaveholders in most of Texas.

According to the record of County Judge Tucker in 1866, few contracts were signed in Tarrant County. Men, refusing to do so, were working their own fields. Other records show that the large slaveholders were clothing and feeding their ex-slaves and permitting them, without cash payment, to labor in their fields for their own support as well as that of their former masters.

With the Freedmen's Bureau removed, agents of the societies—the Union League and Order of the Grand Republic, increased in number and multiplied their activities in order to preserve progress which had been achieved for the freedmen, and to organize them for active assertion and participation of their rights as citizens under the Fourteenth Amendment.

Negroes asserted their equality with whites by occupying the whole road or sidewalk, by refusing to give way to whites in public places, by attempting to force their way into public assemblies, by knocking at front doors, by roaming the highways when they willed, and by insolently refusing to do their work. The Union League, directed by leaders from the North, did work among the Negroes of Tarrant County, and some freedmen were enticed by promises of a new world for them, to be created by Republicans.

Maria, one of Judge Terry's four ex-slaves, was told by the Union League agents that she could enter the front door and be seated in the parlor; and young Joe was told to act as a free man. There were times of disobedience. To Joe's impudence, Mrs. Terry one day reacted intrepidly, although the judge was away from home. She was weary from many hours at the loom, for she clothed her ex-slaves well, and wove every thread of their clothing, while Judge Terry kept them in good shoes. In return for her personal bounty—instead of appreciation—there had been disobedience. On this particular occasion of Joe's insolence, she ordered him to go to the creek, gather willow switches, and return directly. Then she sent one of her sons to Captain Terrell to come to her aid. Terrell ran most of the way from his law office, arriving at the Terry home, breathing heavily.

Terrell found Joe thanking Mrs. Terry for showing him "de right," and promising that "I won't listen to dem men no mo', I'll tend to de Cullud folks who give yuh trouble." Mrs. Terry had changed Joe's attitude by standing on a tub, in order to reach his shoulders, and whipping him with the willow switches which he had gathered. From that day, he remained a loyal member of the Terry family.

But Maria followed after the false prophets. After months of repeated runnings away, each time forgiven and rewarded with another chance to do right, Judge Terry carried out his threatened punishment. He ordered the furniture in her room and her clothes to be placed outside the Terry's fence. He told her he would give her these things in order that she would not go destitute into the world, and bade her farewell. Two strangers came and hauled away Maria's possessions that day. Many months later, Mrs. Terry, hearing that Maria was in distress, went to her aid. She found the woman sick and dying in a tent on the bank of the Clear Fork where other errant freedmen were living under the directions of the Union Leaguers, who provided the tents in present-day Trinity Park, according to Mel Isbell.

Colonel Smith's wife was another white woman to have trouble with the new breed of ex-slaves. When her cook did not arrive until ten o'clock one morning to cook breakfast, and was impertinent in explaining her tardiness, Mrs. Smith struck the woman with a rolling pin and told her to go home.

The cook left, and under the guidance of a carpetbagger, reported to the county court. A complaint was sworn out against Mrs. Smith for assault and battery. Colonel Smith paid the fine and thought it a good joke which he often related to the grandchildren. Never recovering from her indignation, the affair held little humor for his wife.

On the otherhand, Paul Isbell's aged ex-slave, Ott, had refused to leave his master; also had stubbornly refused to make a labor contract. Instead, he had condemned "de niggers lisenin' to de debbils." Reprisal took place. He was found murdered, lying beside Isbell's wagon and team. He had hitched the horses to a tree near Silver Creek where he had gone to gather willows and bark for Isbell.

Such incidents as these, the fear that more would occur, and the forebodings of the future when Grant should become president and enforce the Fourteenth Amendment—which he would surely do, led to the organization of the Ku Klux Klan in Tarrant County sometime in the spring of 1868. By August, the ghosts were riding through Tarrant County.

They made their first appearance, though, in Dallas in April of that year. Citizens there found notices posted in conspicuous places all over town.

K. K. K.

Demon's Den, Dark Day.
Cloudy Moon, Time Out,
Dumb Ferret

Shrouded Brothers, Dallas Division
The Great Past Grand Giant commands you. The hour to act has come. The

knife and the pistol to use are given. The Foreman's chain must now be riven. On the eleventh of this mortal's month go forth to the harvest of Death. Come from the shadow of the grave and dye your hands red with the blood of your victims.

(Name of Victim)   Beware: The Pit yawns to
                                                  receive you.
              By Order of the Great Grand Cyclops

The order of hooded night riders in Tarrant County directed their activities chiefly against the Union League and confined their nocturnal sessions to frightening Negroes. Horsemen in white flowing robes, paper-covered faces, tall paper hats whose heads sometimes came off and were carried on long poles, rode horses covered with white sheets. They spoke to one another in low tones. Negroes were intimidated, and soldiers quartered in the town to enforce Reconstruction laws, made no attempt to arrest the masqueraders; they did not even show their heads outside their quarters. Dudley G. Wooten, in his *A Complete History of Texas*, stated that these spectacular demonstrations were more effective than guns and cannons in preventing the impending calamity of aggressions by Negroes falsely led by radical Republicans and imported politicians.

Tarrant County Ku Klux Klan, provoked by incidents, several times threatened Judge Barkley. His son related that one day a menacing notice appeared at their home. The hooded men were courteous enough to notify the judge that they were coming that night. The son rode to alert his father's friends, then sat at the gate all night in order to signal his father of their approach and to defend his home. The blackness of that night passed unpierced by white robes. That these threats were not illusions, may find verification on one pioneer's reminiscenses. Charles Ellis Mitchell recalled seeing Judge Barkley coming every day from his home in Birdville to his office in the courthouse at Fort Worth, and returning each evening, always escorted by Negro soldiers.

White men were not thinking—they were feeling, and were distraught. Negroes also, were despoiled in spirit during the days of Reconstruction by Congress. Thus the rod of Congress smote the people, and its yoke rested on white men and black alike. Tarrant County Negroes recounted their past woes long after the events had occurred.

By Sam Bush, Ex-Slave:

Uncle Dave tells me often about the time after surrender. A crowd of niggers from Colonel Johnson's place went to Village Creek to a dance. Now de Cullud folks am free and have de right to be thar. All de Johnson Station niggers am good folk. Marster Johnson learnt dem dat way, so evahthing am all right, cuz dere waz good order. All a-sudden some one looked down de road and saw a string of guised men on hawses a-comin'. De niggers sez to Uncle Dave, youse do de talkin' and we-uns stand behind youse.

Uncle Dave met de Klux at de doah. He tells dem, de niggers had de right to be thar. Then Uncle Dave looks behind him and no nigger wuz in sight, deys went up de chimney, out winders—anywhar deys could hide. The Klux warn't aftah to interfere wid de dance, des wuz aftah one partikler nigger. But dey whupped Uncle Dave cuz he talked like de niggers tol' him. De Klux tol' Uncle Dave if he want to be left lone by de Klux, to stay at home.

By Andy Nelson, Ex-Slave:

Fo ten or twelve yeahs aftah de war, some of de fool niggers had lots of troubles. De wust trouble round dis place wuz, cuz de Cullud folks would run round wid out de pass befo' deys could leave de place. Klux would whup dem. De niggers sho quave'd when deys think de Klux wuz aftah 'em. One time de Klux came to John Parker's house. He crawled up de chimney dere wuz a little fire and de nigger began to git powerful hot and drapped out ob de chimney. De Klux sho whupped him.

In the ranks of crusading organizations, sometimes are found fanatical men whose zeal carries them into unreasonable action. This was true in Tarrant County. White men were forced to take measures against the Ku Klux Klan in order to protect their property, their crops, and the black laborers on their land whose toil made possible a living for both. The organization was to grow in power, however, until 1871. After that time, it would wane and disappear as suddenly as it had come, for Congress would pass the Ku Klux Klan Act which permitted the president of the United States to suspend the writ of habeas corpus in cases of secret conspiracy.

The story of the ex-slave Sam Kilgore, is testimony of the evil excesses of the Klan.

Dey burned my mother's house. She lost evahthing—$100 in greenbacks— 300 pound hawg in de pen died from de heat. When de Klux came weuns all runs to Marster Rodgers place.

De riders gits so bad dat deys come most anytime an' run de Cullud folks off fo no cause but jist to be o'nery an' to plunder de homes. Marster Harris had several families on deir place and other white folks. It gits so bad de Cullud folks am fraid to wurk de land. Twas between Fort Worth and Cleburne. Weuns were told to dig a trench long and wide cross field. Marster Rodgers brought home several guns. Riders came in de night. Dere was a volley of fire—twelve riders crossing de ditch weuns dug, fell off dey hawses. Klux didn't bother de niggers on our place anymo'.

Hooded men at first had made freedmen afraid, devouring their strength, but constant persecution aroused a new anger which gave some Negroes boldness to strike back. Uncle Joe, an ex-slave described these tormented Negroes who lived between Fort Worth and Johnson Station.

In de Village Creek section on de Ditto's, Cannon's and Johnson's plantations and most of de Cullud folks stay on dere Marster's place. Dey joy demselves wid parties and dances. Dey had good times until Klux organized. Klux came to places whar de niggers dance and go on picnics and whup 'em. Dey do it just to keep de niggers skeert.

Sometimes Klux came to our houses when twarnt no dance or party. Twas always aftah dark when deys comes and ketch de men an' whup 'em fo nuthin.' It gits so bad dat men folks always eat der supper befo' dark and take a blanket an' go to de woods fo to sleep.

One time de Klux come to our house. Jean wuz 300 pounds an' as wide as de doah. I couldn't git out of de house. I hid under de bed. Jean filled a bucket wid embers from de fire place an' throws dem in de face of Klux when dey knocks on our doah.

Fort Worth Klansmen were demons by night but charitable men by day, helping the upright black men. They patronized the blacksmith shop on the corner of Weatherford and Rusk (now Commerce). It was owned by a former slave, John Pratt, Fort Worth's first Negro businessman. When his master went to war, he cared for his "white folks" and disregarded the emancipation order. His master was killed in the war, but years later, John repaid that master's kindness with the profits earned from the good patronage of Fort Towners. He financed the college education of his master's youngest son.

In 1868, while hooded men of Fort Town galloped under the stars of August skies, cattle herds thundered through the town during the heat in their haste to get up the trail before winter, and while prices were high. Cowboys told Fort Towners of cattlemen, returning to South Texas loaded with money from their spring drives which had passed through there. In Kansas, they were getting $30 a head for four-year-old steers, $25 for dry cows, and $30 for a cow and calf. Optimism resurged among men, while schoolboys scowled, for September was approaching and that meant confinement in school.

Colonel Smith, like General Robert E. Lee, disfranchised and excluded from office by the Fourteenth Amendment and by other acts of Congress, and following the example of General Lee who believed that the hope of the South lay in the education of the youth, opened the town's school in the Masonic Temple assisted by his bride of almost a year.

The town's school population included a few grown ruffians who thought of school as a campaign to outwit and outfight the teacher. Colonel Smith prepared to meet the leader of the toughs. The first day before opening the doors, he unscrewed and loosened the leg of the front bench. The school day began. Straightway the brawler began to fulfill his boast made to the other boys he could break up any school. The colonel, meeting the challenge, reached down and with one wrench, ripped the leg from the bench, waved it in the air and in a quiet tone, announced that he would silence any trouble with the new paddle. The ruffian had tested the new teacher and found him to have muscle. There was no more trouble. Smith, a war hero, a classical scholar, and a lover of youth, coaxed his pupils with anecdotes; entertained them with stories of the war when they grew restless, inspired them with lessons from Caesar and other classics, and awakened their interest in geography by relating his travels through the South and Mexico. After such inspiring instruction pupils soon went home each day with a will to study. They marked their assigned lessons in their books with bookmarkers of Confederate money, ranging from ten cents to one hundred dollars.

Well taught, Fort Town's children were also well cared for when sick. In 1868, two doctors arrived in town making four—Drs. Peak, Burts, and the newcomers, Drs. J. F. Shelton and Isaac L. Van Zandt. Major Van Zandt had so convinced his brother in East Texas of the merits of the town that Dr. Van Zandt had come to Fort Worth in 1866. Thinking that the place was too small to support another physician, he moved his family to Dallas, but by 1868, he decided to make Fort Town his home. He was twenty-eight and a doctor of experience. When war began in 1861, he had completed half of his medical studies at Tulane University in New Orleans, so he immediately entered the medical service of the Confederate Army, and after the war, finished his training at Tulane. His skill, administered with genuine regard for his patients, made him the chosen physician of hundreds of citizens of Tarrant County.

Dr. J. F. Shelton, a Tennessean, became a practicing physician in Kentucky in 1855, and the next year moved to Texas, practicing medicine in Tarrant County until he joined the Confederate Army as a surgeon. After the war, he returned to Tarrant County devoting his attention to farming until 1868. That year he was attracted by the growing cattle town. Itinerant cowboys and citizens of Fort Worth would need drugs and sundries, and following this reasoning, he opened Fort Worth's third drug store in a two-story frame building at No. 6 Weatherford Street. At this place, he dispensed excellent medical advice, and became characterized as a man of honesty and integrity. His youngest daughter, Anna Shelton, would become the organizer and founder of the Woman's Club of Fort Worth in the 1920s. Another new inhabitant who heartened the town promoters and housewives in 1868, was Mr. William E. (Buck) Trippett who opened the first store dealing solely in hardware.

John Robinson's circus, a rival with whom Colonel Smith had to compete for the attention of his pupils, came in the early fall of 1868, held sway two days, and was gone. But the magic of the circus lingered, changing the play habits and ambitions of Fort Town youths. John Robinson's circus had come overland from Jefferson, Texas. It was Fort Worth's first such show. People drove in from all parts of Tarrant County and camped in the open fields south of Fourth Street. The marvel of it dazzled the unsophisticated frontiersmen, whose eyes had only beheld a few school charades, Indian dances and antics of cowboys and cow ponies. The lady bareback riders enthralled the boys, ages eight to eighty. The trapeze performers and clowns were irresistible. The elephants, lions, tigers, and giraffes made them aware of a faraway continent called Africa.

For a time, Fort Worth boys abandoned their ambition to become "cowpokes" or Texas Rangers. Howard Peak and his little companions went into the circus business and trained for the day when they could join the circus. They erected a trapeze, and also practiced riding their ponies bareback turning somersaults. Then they held public performances for their parents and playmates. And on one such an occasion, Howard turned a somersault on his pony. Instead of landing on his feet, he fell on his back and the Fort Worth Circus went out of business.

In late November, issues of the *Dallas Herald* confirmed the election of General U. S. Grant to the presidency of the United States. Grant's victory further demoralized the Texas Democratic party, while the Republicans, flexing their power, cheered their delegates on their way to the constitutional convention reconvening in Austin December 1. The purpose, one Fort Towner remarked, was to "spend wastefully Texans' scarce money." Its true purpose, of course, was to finish the work which the last session had failed to do, i.e., to complete the constitution and to provide for unrestricted Negro suffrage so that Texas might be readmitted to the Union.

Another bit of news disturbing Fort Towners with emotion and envy, was the launching December 18, 1868, of a boat by Dallas, their rival city. This boat, the "Sallie Haynes," was eighty-seven by twenty feet.

Dallasites were prophesying that it would open a great river trade, making their town the prosperous river port of Texas, abolishing the expensive hauling of goods to and from Jefferson and Bryan, and attracting the many riverboats then operating between Galveston and Trinidad in Henderson County.

In May of 1868, Dallas merchants paid a $500 bonus to Captain J. M. Garvey of Job Boat No. 1, to navigate his boat from Trinidad to Dallas. One envious Fort Town male allegedly growled, "Don't them Dallasites know that there is too much brush and too little water in the upper Trinity for a steamboat?" A careful reader of the *Dallas Herald* retorted, "Dallasites think that they can do all things. Headed by Colonel G. W. Record, they are planning to clear the Trinity of brush and get an appropriation from the legislature for the project." "Not with my tax money," blasted another townsman.

To vaunt their pride, to inflate their ego, and to heal the envy pangs, one Fort Towner prophesying that since Charles Biggers Daggett had established that year the first ferry on the Trinity, and it was a good one, that his town would draw away from Dallas the immigrants using the Dallas ferry, making Fort Worth the immigrants' fording and shopping center of North Texas. He was right in part, for hundreds of immigrants bypassed Dallas in the late eighteen-sixties and seventies, using the Daggett ferry. There was also a raft maintained near the confluence of the Clear Fork and West Fork which was pressed into service only when the Trinity was at flood stage.

When men in Fort Town had time on their hands and boys were free from school on Saturdays, they went to the foot of present-day Samuels Avenue to watch the operation of the ferry. Heavy teams of mules were stationed opposite each other on either side of the riverbanks. When passengers were ready to be ferried across, they were loaded on a large raft and ropes were thrown across to the mule skinner on the opposite side. It was entertainment to hear the chant of the men as they swung the ropes, and hurled them across the river to be caught by the man on the opposite bank; to listen to the mule skinner bellow to the mules and crack his bullwhip so loudly that his voice and whiz of the whip, echoed in the nearby groves of oaks; to see the mules lunge forward, with muscles taut in legs and back, as they climbed the steep banks, pulling the raft across the river.

Mules and mule skinners were only a part of the entertainment. There were many wagons all alike but different in their signs scrawled across the covered tops. Conveyances of newcomers approached the north bank where they had crossed the Red River and were bound for homes in the present vicinities of Burleson, Alvarado, Mansfield, Cleburne, Waco, and even as far south as Austin, or points in Tarrant, Parker, Palo Pinto and Hood counties. On the north bank were also the fancy wagons of the apple peddlers. There were vehicles of settlers on the south bank coming from Central and South Texas who, discouraged, were moving back to Missouri or Kentucky. The ferry operated near the cattle ford; thus the boys of Fort Worth had two points of interest: the ferryboat with the wagons, and the herds crossing the Trinity.

Trail drivers, preparing the cattle to ford the river, proved to be an unusual sight. A mile from the river, the cowboys milled the cattle. The leadman led the animals round and round into a tight circle which, when finished, was a circle of hide and horns with a circumference of several blocks—a magnificent spectacle. Milling placed the herd in complete obedience to the drivers. Then slowly unwinding the circle, they were led to Daggett's Crossing. All the while, the cowboys were singing, and there would often be one cowpuncher riding down and roping an uncooperative steer. As many as 40,000 cattle, Charles Biggers Daggett reported, annually forded the Trinity there during the eighteen-seventies. Of this crossing, Howard Peak recalled:

Many times, I have followed the herds to the Trinity River, and watched the milling animals as they plunged into the swollen stream with heads above the surging waters, tails afloat, bawl and horn their way across, then see them scramble to the steep bank beyond, shake off their watery covering and proceed on their way northward.

Among the many herds crossing the Trinity in 1868, was one driven by M. A. Withers, twenty-three years old, who had been a trail driver since a boy of thirteen driving cattle from Texas ranches to Shreveport for the Confederate Army in 1862. He had left Lockhart, Texas, on April first with a herd of "600 big wild steers" valued in Texas from eight to ten dollars, and with eight cowhands had passed through Fort Worth reaching Abilene, Kansas, on July first.

Then there was the herd of Dave Puckett, "1000 longhorn steers, full grown and good walkers," bossed by Steve Rogers. When strung out on the trail, the herd covered one-half mile. A chuck wagon drawn by oxen and a large remuda brought up the rear.

Other well-equipped outfits belonging to Myers, Choate, and W. G. Butler of Karnes County, passed through Fort Worth that same year. Many herds, though, treading through the town were driven on credit, or rather the pledged word of a man to his neighbor that he would drive his cattle and pay on the return trip. George Steen was one of these. He said that in 1868 he had no money, and banks were not gambling in cattle credit, but people permitted him to drive for them on credit; and he purchased with his pledged word a few more steers at ten dollars a head, hired six cowhands, and drove his herd from San Marcos, Texas, through the then "small village of Fort Worth to Abilene, Kansas."

Another herd of 600 steers stirring up dust in Fort Worth, was driven by the owners Forehand and C. Cockrell. Leaving Bastrop County with eight cowhands and a cook, they trailed to Dallas where they were told by some of the citizens there—so the cowhand W. F. Cude related—that "they would reach the Chisholm Trail a few miles north of Dallas." Driving on, they camped in the evening northwest of Dallas; and during the night an electric storm struck their camp, killing one cowboy, and badly burning another. The herd moved on with six cowboys, and reached a small town called Fort Worth where they learned that the Chisholm Trail was not a few miles north of Dallas, but about a week's drive north of Fort Worth.

Herds and herds—75,000 head in 1868—hoofed up fogs of dust over Fort Worth and trailed on to the Kansas market, although the drovers were aware that 1867 had been a "lallapolooza" of bad luck due to rains, flooded rivers that "worked the starch out of the cowboys," and the flesh off the bones of cattle forced to graze on grass made sappy and coarse by the rains. Drovers that year (1867) sold bony steers with swollen stomachs for immediate slaughter, and other herds were forced to "winter graze" around Abilene, Kansas. Hard luck, the drovers thought, but it turned into good luck for it added a new twist to the cattle business. The winter grazing of those cattle of 1867, showed them that Texas cattle could not only stand northern winters, but would grow fat for an early market. This realization accelerated the cattle drives, thus helping Fort Worth, as a strategic gateway, to prosper for two generations.

For a while the drive of 1868, in the vernacular of a cowboy, "ran as smooth as molasses." Cowhands had it easy on the trail, but then a temporary reverse occurred in the market. Spanish fever developing among the cattle, caused the Illinois legislature to place an embargo on Texas stock, by passing the Anti-Texas Cattle Act. Lobbyists for Texas drovers obtained an amendment to this law permitting the entrance into Illinois of Texas cattle "if wintered in Kansas." Enforcement of laws and their effects sometimes move slowly. Meanwhile half the cattle of the drive of 1868 remained on the range surrounding Abilene, Kansas. This condition, unless corrected would destroy Abilene as a cattle-shipping market.

Citizens of Abilene decided to save their cattle town. They tried advertising. Loading wild buffaloes into a freight car, they sent them to the North and East, showed them to curious crowds, distributed handbills which praised Texas cattle, and announced that Abilene, Kansas, was the place to buy them. It paid to advertise. By the fall of 1868, cattle buyers came in numbers from the North and East, and before the year's end all the cattle of the 1868 drive valued in Texas from eight to ten dollars, sold from twenty-five to thirty dollars a head. Citizens of Abilene, had saved their town as a cattle market, and by so doing had saved Fort Worth as the grub wagon supply station on the trail—an economic fact attracting a new type of businessman who would make Fort Worth the cowboy's "town with the gates wide open."

New riches came to Withers the fall of that year, as he had been one of the lucky drovers to profit by the market change in Abilene. His riches were not acquired wholly by luck, but rather by a bit of Withers sagacity. Since July his cattle had grazed on the plain near Abilene after the long walk of four months from Lockhart. Now it was fall and he had sold out at top price, had taken $1,000 in cash, and the remainder in drafts on Donald Lawson and Company of New York. With his new wealth he bought wagons and harness, made workhorses out of his cow ponies, and sent his cowhands home, instructing them to load the wagons with apples in Arkansas and to sell them in Texas. This apple trade also made a profit. While his cowhands took the slow journey, Withers took the easy way by railroad to St. Louis, down the Mississippi by fast steamer to New Orleans, then by boat to Galveston, from where by railroad and stagecoach, he traveled to Lockhart, arriving home Christmas Day. News of good money in Kansas swept like wind through the grass of the Texas range. The drive of 1869, cowmen predicted, would be a bell ringer.

1869

Outwardly, Fort Town was tranquil, but underneath there was discontent. Exclusion from politics was a smarting indignity they could not eradicate from their being. So they gave their usual attention to the political news in February's newspapers. On February 8, the constitutional convention, completed the Texas Constitution of 1869 at a cost of $200,000 to taxpayers. It provided for unrestricted Negro suffrage, a centralized government, a governor to be elected for four years with the power to appoint the secretary of state, attorney general, and the judges of the courts. County courts were abolished. The best feature of the

document was its provision for public education. The Texas Constitution
had been sent to Congress for its approval.

Meanwhile military rule continued, and a few troops were still
camped off Fort Town's public square at the foot of the bluff. Male citizens
tolerated the Federals when they met them in Ed Terrell's saloon
or in the stores on the square. The soldiers bought goods with specie.
Civilians and soldiers did not clash; only minor incidents occurred, and
those indicated little bitterness, such as was the incident in the winter of
1869. A crippled veteran enveloped in the overcoat of his Confederate
uniform was walking on the square when a soldier approached him, demanding
that he remove from the coat the Confederate buttons. The
veteran refused. The Federal then rushed at him attempting to tear off
the buttons. The veteran struck the soldier in the face with his cane.
Men gathered as if to help the veteran. Tense was the atmosphere.
Trembling in fear after his anger had passed, the veteran said, "I'll take
off the buttons, but you won't." The commander of the soldiers had the
arrogant Federal removed and loudly announced to the gathering of
citizens: "I saw the incident. Neither the Confederate veteran nor the
citizens shall be punished for any disrespect to a Federal."

Judicious conduct was not constant among the former Confederates;
and in Ed Terrell's saloon, too much liquor unloosened their buried bitterness.
Howard Peak told of a recent Confederate soldier farming near
Village Creek. Having never surrendered, he was still fighting the war.
One cold day he came to town, imbibed too much, and began to upbraid
the Federal soldiers with all the oaths in his vocabulary. Another drink,
and he was boasting that he could "whup a whole company of them." Ed
Terrell, using every opportunity for a prank sent an habitué of his
saloon to don both the overcoat and hat of a Union soldier. Returning
dressed in the uniform and with a rifle, he entered the back door of the
saloon as the Confederate was shouting his bravest boasts. Seeing what
he thought was a Federal, the inebriated Confederate ran from the saloon,
mounted his horse, and sped from town. No doubt the intoxicated
man galloped most of the way home. At any rate, he was so exhausted
that upon reaching the creek near his home, he fell from his horse and
unable to remount, lay in the cold water. Next morning, he was found
frozen to death.

General Grant was inaugurated president of the United States on
March 4, 1869, and Fort Towners decided to bet on horses instead of
politicians. Across the Trinity, just north of where today is the present
American Cyanamid Company plant, a few men interested in sports,
built Fort Worth's racetrack. Floods washed it away, and the town's

second track, built in the eighteen-seventies was on the west side of the Cold Springs Road, about one-half mile north of the Pioneer Rest Cemetery.

There was little money in the Southern states since the North often refused credit to the South. When a loan was extended, the terms were too harsh. Without gold and credit, the former states of the Confederacy carried on farming by devising the share-crop system and continued to trade by barter. In the words of Major Van Zandt:

There wasn't too much money in Fort Worth. Most exchange was made by trade and barter. We traded wool, hides and flour for lumbers and other things that we needed. A beef steer brought $12.50. I have accepted many of them in payment for dry goods.

Fort Towners schemed to get gold, and merchants accumulated more specie than others, selling to the newcomers, Federals, and cowboys going up the trail to Kansas. A man who could get together enough cattle or wool to send to market, had gold. An individual with a wagon and team could earn a few gold eagles in the business of freighting. Major Van Zandt said:

We did everything we could to bring more money into Fort Worth. I remember once I heard that they needed beef over in Mississippi. It was just hearsay as communication was slow and uncertain. Upon the strength of it, I bought up some steers and sent them there for sale. I got word back that they did need meat badly but that they had no money to pay. It was money that we needed down here, so I sent the steers to Chicago. I sold them at a profit. The money was then started in circulation in Fort Worth.

To the average citizen of Fort Town in 1869 the saying "gold was as rare as a raindrop in a Kansas drought"—was no jest. Press Farmer, living on a farm south of town was the center of an allegedly true story concerning gold. One day he came into town, tied his horse to the hitching rail, and told his friends he had something rare to show them. Press dug in his pocket and brought out a $20 gold piece. It was the first money he had seen in four years. His sudden wealth had come through a horse trader, driving a herd of Texas ponies back East. He had rented Mr. Farmer's "stalk pasture." The horses feasted upon the numerous stray nubbins which the horse trader considered to be good forage worth twenty dollars.

A friend of Press suggested, "Let us brand it," and they did. Farmer had many creditors, and he had to decide which one should get the gold. Gratitude directed him to pay it to Dr. W. P. Burts, who had attended his family during the Civil War without a cent.

After giving the physician the gold piece, Press, free of one less debt was jubilant and stayed in town all day. Toward late afternoon, while mounting his horse to return home, a man called out, "Wait, Press, I want to pay you some money I owe you." He handed Press the very $20 gold piece which he had branded that morning. All the male citizens of the town, it is said, were on the square. They laughed and began to count the number of debts the same gold piece had paid. It had changed hands ten times during that day, and had paid $200 worth of debts.

The gold drouth did not last forever. Three million dollars—even more than $3 million dollars in specie, an astonishing sum to circulate in Texas in 1869, was brought from Kansas by Texas drovers. The cattle from the drive of 1869, the largest since 1866—350,000 head—were sold in Abilene at $25 to $30 a head. Fort Worth, the cowman's town, glittered with gold money, when the drovers came up the trail in the spring and summer of 1870.

Herds through Fort Worth were not all pointed up the north trail to Kansas. By 1869, many longhorns nosed westward toward New Mexico, among them the herd of Frank Winbarn. In Fort Worth, looking for a man who knew the New Mexico country, Winbarn found him—James Preston Wood, son of Dr. Wood of the White Settlement. Wood, twenty-five years of age, was many years older in experience. A Confederate veteran, he had fought through the New Mexico and Arizona campaign, had helped recapture Galveston, had survived the Battle of Mansfield; and after the war, had turned to freighting from Millican and Bryan to Fort Worth and Northwest Texas. In 1869 as a cowhand for Winbarn, he eagerly adventured into New Mexico to revisit the country where as a lad of seventeen, he had been baptised in the fire of war.

The western trail to New Mexico was opening up in 1869. More Indians were giving up the fight and retiring to reservations to be fed upon Texas beeves, which the federal government was buying at top prices. Midwest and California ranches were "giving paying prices" for stock cattle. In 1866, Charles Goodnight and Oliver Loving had blazed the Pecos Trail by the Concho, Horsehead Crossing on the Pecos, and up the Pecos to New Mexico.

Whether drovers took the northern trail or the western trail, Fort Worth was a pleasant place for trail-weary cowboys and cattle in need of good grazing. George C. Briggs as a child at the age of ten, began to drive the western trail from Orange, Texas, to New Mexico. He related that Fort Worth was his outfits' trail stop. After crossing the Trinity in the area of present Trinity Park, they found good grass "so high," he said, "that it reached the bodies of the cattle. It was a pretty country with giant trees along the river from which swelled the sea of high grass." After a day or two of good grazing, the herd was headed west.

Twenty years had passed since historic 1849. The fort was no more. A few residences had been made of the officers' barracks. An impressive brick and stone courthouse now stood in a field, and beside it, the original little frame courthouse remained to serve as the clerk's office. This array of administrative authority was encircled by a wide road around which Andrews Tavern and merchants' stores formed the public square. In 1869, there were more stores than in 1859 in spite of the war and Reconstruction; and among them were specialty stores. The Bateman Brothers, (K. D. and Q. Q. Bateman) in 1865, had opened a grocery store which would operate many decades. Other specialty stores were the Bamberg Butcher Shop, and the Buck Trippett Hardware Store. There were three drug stores: one owned by Ferguson, the second by Doctors Shelton and Dorsey; and the third by Maitland and Dr. Peak.

There were several industries in operation: Stephen Terry's brickyard, Charles Biggers Daggett's ferry transportation, Mauck's mill, Bony Tucker's treadmill, Frank Knaar's saddlery, Tom Hapgood's cabinet shop, Dick King's blacksmith shop and a second one operated by John Pratt, the ex-slave. There were two hotels, the Hurt House opened in 1860 by Mrs. Anna S. Hurt, and Andrews Tavern. There was the Concho Wagon Yard, named for the Concho River. Located in the 400 block of present-day East Belknap, it was a popular place for visitors in town to shop and for immigrants, because of its nearness to the square, the hub of affairs in Fort Town. The leading general mercantile stores around the square were owned by Berliner-Samuels, Van Zandt, Daggett and Turner, Henry Davis, and Jesse Jones.

The two latter men were newcomers to Fort Worth. Henry Davis had come from Missouri in 1866 and had located his store on the square at the corner of present-day Weatherford and Main streets, operating it as one of the popular mercantile stores until he moved to Oak Grove in Tarrant County in 1875.

A mercantile neighbor of Mr. Davis within the same block, was Jesse Jones, who opened his store in 1869. A North Carolinian, he settled at the age of twenty-three in Ashland, Tarrant County, opening a mercantile store in 1860 only to close it within a year to fight for the Confederacy, serving as lieutenant of infantry through the war. Returning from the conflict, he located in Fort Worth where each business day until 1893, his store opened for trade.

With all the gains, Fort Worth lost in 1869, the mercantile business located on the northeast corner of present Houston and Weatherford, operated since about 1865 by Mr. P. A. Huffman, a Kentuckian, who had lived elsewhere in Texas since 1857. A businessman, envisioning large-scale enterprises, he had opened another store at Fort Griffin in 1868 while at the same time engaging in buying and selling cattle on both northern and southern markets. Through the cattle trade he envisioned another field. Selling his Fort Worth and Fort Griffin stocks, also his home in Fort Worth, located on Fourth Street, he moved to Galveston and invested in a meat-packing business. His son would return in 1870 to become one of the town's leading businessmen.

Besides the cluster of business houses fringing the courthouse square there were other buildings adding their structures to fill in the wilderness space: the jail, post office, Masonic building, and the Christian Church near today's Belknap and Lamar streets. Just off the square, was the town's oldest law firm, that of Captain Terrell, housed in a two-room office building since 1857.

The residence of a prominent citizen near the square was that of Dr. Burt on the northeast corner of present Second and Commerce streets, and across the road on the northwest corner was Ferguson's drug store.

Into the public square entered three important roads. The Dallas Road, now known as Throckmorton Street, was the south road. Dr. Peak's home was located on it. The Birdville Road, after crossing the Trinity at Daggett's Crossing near the Cold Springs, entered the square from the east. The old Weatherford and Fort Belknap Road after crossing the Trinity near Mauck's Mill, entered the square on the west. Where this road crossed the ford, a raft was tied to a pecan tree for use as a ferry during the spring and autumn freshets.

"Sunflowers as tall as a mule's back," so Bettie Wetmore McKee said, tossed their yellow heads in fields along present Main and Houston streets, south of Fourth. In the south prairie a few houses were scattered. Among them were those of Dr. Van Zandt in the vicinity of the six-hundredth block of present Throckmorton Street, John Hershfield's brick residence on the present southeast corner of Seventh and Taylor, and Postmaster Louckx's near the site of the public library. In the outskirts of the village was Captain Daggett's home in the block bounded today by Main, Houston, Tenth, and Eleventh streets. West of the square there were a few homes and among them was that of Colonel Smith which had been located in the vicinity of what is now the six-hundredth block of West Third.

Houses were interspersed along the Belknap and Weatherford roads. Just off the square on what is today West Belknap in the first block where the Ripley Arnold Housing Center is located, was the home of the Frenchman who dug the second well in Fort Town. The water of this well he shared with the townsmen.

Most of the houses were located east of the square along present East Bluff, East Belknap, and East Weatherford. Among them was the residence of Mr. Ferguson, the druggist. Southeast of the square were the homes of Major Van Zandt, located on the northeast corner of today's Commerce and Fifth, and in the area of present Pecan Street. On Fourth and Fifth streets was the brick residence of Judge Terry whose farm lands extended to the Trinity.

Each house in Fort Worth had its log smokehouse filled with every kind of processed beef and pork, a garden, a chicken yard, a cow lot and a pigpen. Any citizen without these accessories, Captain Terrell said, was considered by the townsmen as a shiftless person worthy of little respect. Hunger was a strange word to Fort Worthians.

Boys had a part in producing the harvest of plenty. Their problem was to keep the fences mended in order to keep the razorback hogs, which ran wild about the town, out of the gardens and from under the houses where their wallows bred flies. Razorbacks were the boys' greatest trials. In the dog and hog fights, many a dog was ripped to death by the sharp tusks of a boar.

Fort Worth's first new citizens of the year 1869 were Mr. and Mrs. Addison Clark, a bridal couple. They arrived in January, rousing much laudatory talk among the townsmen, who commented that the handsome, scholarly, twenty-seven-year-old Addison Clark was an enriching adjunct to Colonel Smith's school.

He had come to assist the colonel in the school session January to June of 1869, for now the school's enrollment was large, drawing students from the surrounding counties. When the school year closed in the spring of that year, Peter Smith announced that he was returning to the practice of law. Clark was to continue the school in the Masonic Temple, which would begin its session in September. He published his plans for the coming term in which his brother Randolph would assist. The fact that the Fort Worth school was to continue and in the hands of scholars, encouraged the town boosters, because a school would attract settlers and be another stone in town building. So they published the fact in conversation with the stagecoach drivers, powerful salesmen for the town;

also they made known the fact to farmers and cowmen who came to Fort Worth to trade.

Addison and Randolph Clark were the sons of Joseph Addison Clark and Hattie D'Spain. The D'Spain family lived in Nacogdoches County where Hattie married Joseph Addison Clark, printer, surveyor, lawyer, later preacher and editor of a newspaper first at Rusk, then at Palestine, and finally at Galveston where in 1850, he assisted W. Richardson in planning for the publication of the *Texas Almanac*.

The first teacher of the two Clark sons, was their mother, a woman of beauty with an academic education, and talented in art and music. She taught them the fundamentals; also the Bible and nature study along with art. An important part of their education was each evening's concert in their home. Their father and mother sang hymns, which their mother played upon a square piano, whose polished wood added beauty to the uncarpeted rough floors. Songs supplemented with reading of ballads of Scott and Burns completed each evening's concert. When the boys mastered the fundamentals of education, they turned to the family library which was rare in most pioneer homes. The Clark library contained volumes of history, biography, literature, and natural history.

Addison, believing that education was a personal matter, used the family library educating himself beyond the average teacher available on the frontier. At the age of twelve, he attended an academy at Palestine for one year, studying in the advanced classes of the school. In 1857, at the age of fifteen, he went to Tennessee Colony school in Anderson County, Texas, where a Mr. Averett, a Baptist preacher and teacher, former president of a college in the East, measured up to Addison's ideal of a teacher. For two years he studied with Mr. Averett, using his library which was said to have been a university in itself. When Addison was nineteen the Civil War opened, and he and Randolph, a year and a half younger, went to war. Although soldiers, they continued to educate themselves. In Addison's knapsack was a small Bible, a pocket edition of Byron, and a translation of a French work in higher mathematics.

After Addison and Randolph returned from the war in May 1865, they took off their tattered Confederate uniforms and resumed their education. Addison, with a neighbor, built a log schoolhouse and taught rural school one year; then he moved to town, instructing there one more year. In 1867, he and Randolph went to Kentuckytown, Texas, to study with Charles Carlton, a graduate of Bethany College, who combined pedagogy and religion in training young men for their careers. When Carlton founded Carlton College in Bonham, Texas, Addison and Randolph went with him to complete their education; and Addison served as an assistant teacher. At Carlton College, Addison further educated himself in higher mathematics, Hebrew, and Greek, since there were no instructors for these subjects. In January 1869, in the assembly room at Carlton College, Addison married Miss Sallie McQuiggs, niece of Mrs. Carlton, and moved to Fort Worth to assist Colonel Smith.

To Fort Worth had come a scholar and a teacher who would be assisted by another educator, his brother Randolph.

Christian tenets became the fundamentals of their educational system. Addison's philosophy, formulated in his youth and based upon the teachings of his mother, are stated by his brother Randolph in his book, *Reminiscences*:

From them [his parents], he learned that God is an everloving Father, that the world and all things, even the commonplace things, belong to Him, and that the people must be about the Father's work—idleness is sin, and that there are no high and low callings, but that honor lies in doing some needed work well, and that to engage in any work or calling that did not benefit others is a waste of the time and the talent with which God had endowed him.

For five years the majority of Fort Worth's children and young people were to attend a school with a curriculum for scholars, advanced far beyond most frontier schools; and were to be under the guidance of these Clark brothers, who in time were to become the founders of Texas Christian University, and rank among the great in Texas education.

During the summer of 1869, Addison made preparations to open the Fort Worth school in the Masonic Temple in September, assisted by his brother. Meanwhile the spirit of sectarianism was revived in the town. Randolph in his *Reminiscences*, related that some few Fort Worthians said a preacher and most especially a preacher of Addison's particular faith, should not have the school. To meet this criticism, a few townsmen suggested that Addison give up preaching while teaching. This he refused to do, nor would he abandon the teaching of the Bible, an important part of his school's curriculum.

A Masonic meeting was held, and a resolution was passed that the lower story of the house belonged to the Masons, and that a Masonic school would be taught there beginning the first week in September.

In spite of the Masons' decision, there were people determined to maintain the Clark brothers' school. Major Van Zandt, Dr. Peak, Colonel Smith, other members of the Christian church as well as other citizens, repaired the two-room concrete building at Lamar and Belknap which had not been used for school since the opening of the Civil War in 1861.

Here, in September 1869, in accordance with his published schedule, Clark opened school. It prospered and offered promise of a permanent academy.

But there arose another obstruction to hurdle in the troublesome time of Reconstruction. Under the Reconstruction government, a free public school system was provided for all children from six to eighteen years of age irrespective of race and color. (The Texas Constitution of 1866 had been nullified by Congress, but its provision for education was retained and amended to include Negroes.) Proceeds of a poll tax, one-fourth of the revenue from state taxes, and revenue from the sale of public lands were assigned to the support of public education.

There were state, district, and county superintendents and teachers, all appointed by the state government and required to take the "iron-clad oath." Officials and teachers were paid high salaries. Teachers were required to obtain a certificate and authority to teach from the state school board. Patrons could send their children to private school and be exempt from the fine for non-attendance at the public school if the teacher of the private school was certified to teach by the State Board of Education.

Addison Clark refused to take the so-called "iron-clad oath" which would ally him with the political machine, he thought. However, he obtained a certificate from the state examiner, took it to the county board, and was given permission to continue his school in Tarrant County. From that day until it closed in the spring of 1874, the Clarks' school prospered, and its enrollment grew.

Addison taught the mature students, and Randolph had charge of the younger pupils. Little Elizabeth Frances, daughter of Judge Terry, enrolled in the Clarks' school. According to her account, Randolph was her first teacher whom she, like all the children, loved, because he was so kind and patient when a pupil stood beside his chair, haltingly reading the primer lesson.

On July 20, 1869, President Grant had made Joseph Addison Clark, the father of the two Fort Worth teachers, a postmaster, which office he held until February 1873. Postmaster Clark, bought a sizable lot between Ninth and Fourteenth streets near Calhoun and Jones, where it was planned an academy should be constructed, since Addison had selected Fort Worth for the location of his life's work, and had built a home on a block near this property.

Meanwhile the Clark brothers taught school in the Christian church's little building. However, their benefactors looked to the future. Major Van Zandt and Judge Terry, accumulating a little wealth for the first time since the war, shared their profits with the church. The major sold a lot for two hundred dollars, and the judge sold two lots to equal the major's contribution. Together they bought the block between Houston and Main and Fourth and Fifth streets, and gave it to the First Christian Church which had outgrown its two-room concrete structure.

Ladies of the congregation, denying themselves new ribbons for their bonnets contributed the money for the new church. Men gave brick, lumber, stone and their teams for hauling and labor. In 1870, the church, a one-story brick building, was completed on the southwest corner of Main and Fourth. On the same block, the church members constructed a box house twenty-four by thirty-six feet. These two buildings served the purpose of the school. Although a denominational school, it is said most of Fort Town's youths attended the school as well as did the children of well-to-do farmers of Tarrant and surrounding counties. Work was play and play was work became the spirit of the scholarly school.

Other incidents in the chronicle of 1869, were the publication in the *Texas Almanac* of an account of the low-cost food prices in Tarrant County, and a list of the county officers, moderate men, giving good government. They were "County Judge, B. F. Barkley; County Clerk, A. G. Walker; Sheriff, Ganders Elliott; Assessor-Collector, Henry C. Daggett; County Commissioners, William Evans and H. C. Jefferson; and Justices of the Peace, twelve in number."

Congress had approved the Texas Constitution of 1869, therefore an election was fixed for November 30, at which time, qualified voters of Texas were to vote upon the adoption of the constitution and were to elect congressmen, members to the legislature, and the governor.

The year had opened with an election, and now it was closing with another. Politics, always politics, to provoke Tarrant County's disfranchised males. Radical Republicans had nominated E. J. Davis for governor. Tarrant County males were again emotionally aroused. They reviled those whom they considered to be the political buccaneers. A target of their bitter contempt was General Reynolds, military commander of Texas who allegedly packed the registration boards with radical Republicans favoring Davis, and the Union Leaguers, who aligned the Negroes with the Davis supporters.

On election day, a few aggressive Fort Towners, although disfranchised, tried to register as voters. The registration board presided over by Judge Barkley, and supervised by Federal troops, some of whom were Negroes, turned these citizens away. Humiliated, they stood aside in bitterness to watch Fort Worth Negroes vote.

Throughout Texas, timid members of the Democratic party, qualified to vote, refused to cast their ballot, believing that even if the conservative Republican candidate Hamilton were elected governor—for there was no Democratic candidate—Congress would not recognize the new Texas government. Nearly half of the voters of Texas stayed away from the polls rather than to vote for E. J. Davis.

In December of 1869, Fort Towners sighed with impatience and wondered how long they would be afflicted by their enemies in high places, who still scourged most of them with disfranchisement. There was no news as yet concerning the results of the November election. Texas remaining an outcast from the Union, had crawled only a few steps nearer to her redemption.

However, changes for the good of all would come in the eighteen-seventies with a new decade. Already shadows on the prairies that had hung so heavily over Fort Towners during the decade of the eighteen-sixties were being lifted by the songs of the cowboys, the rumbles of emigrant wagons, and the faint echo of the distant whistle of the railroad bringing a new era.

A distant echo it was. Nevertheless, the saving grace of Fort Worth builders, was their enthusiastic imagination bolstered with power to keep their minds staid on future projects. Their elation for the future had mounted in May, when newspapers headlined the most tremendous event of the year for the United States. Leland Stanford of California had driven a golden spike near Ogden, Utah, to connect the Union Pacific and Central Pacific railroads forming the nation's first transcontinental rail line. The Atlantic and Pacific coasts now were tied in economic bonds unloosening the torrential vigor of American business.

The restless South, seeking fresh opportunities, immediately increased their clamorous demands in Congress and their state capitols for subsidies to build a southern transcontinental railroad. The United States must have a snow-free route to the Pacific.

Fort Worthians, never holding thoughts of limitation, began plans to place their town on that southern transcontinental line.

This photograph depicts the courthouse built between 1876 and 1878, following the March 1876 fire that destroyed the county's first stone courthouse. Miss Garrett made a common error in her original caption for this photograph, incorrectly identifying the building as the first stone courthouse which was begun in 1861 and completed at the beginning of the 1870s.

Major Khleber M. Van Zandt became a merchant in Fort Worth in 1866. He was a mighty force in transforming the village into a "little metropolis."

The public square of Fort Worth in the late 1860's.

ANDERSON'S
Gun Store

STORE

TIVOLI HALL

The business section of Fort Worth was located next to the courthouse square. This picture was taken in the 1870's.

Thomas J. Jennings. A civic founder who contributed extensively in land donations to the Texas and Pacific Railway.

Joseph Moody Peers. Owner of the fashionable Peers House Hotel (Virginia House).

A view of Houston Street in the 1870's.

B. B. Paddock. Editor, historian, and frontiersman. He became the editor of the *Fort Worth Democrat* in 1873.

CHAPTER 23

Redemption, 1870-1872

1870

I T WAS EARLY January of 1870. General Reynolds, military commander of Texas, proclaimed without making public the election returns, that Davis was elected governor and that the Texas Constitution of 1869 had been adopted. He also announced the names of the four congressmen elected. Three of these were radical Republicans and the fourth congressman, J. C. Conner, was a carpetbagger but a member of the Democratic party. And to further intensify displeasure of conservatives was the fact that radicals had won control of both houses of the legislature.

Hamilton, candidate for governor of the conservative Republicans, believed with all of his followers that he had been counted out. Conservatives did not contest the election, although it was known that fraudulent acts were committed by the registration boards stacked with Davis men and by Federal soldiers in attendance at all the polls.

On January 8, General Reynolds appointed to office the successful candidates of the election. They were to hold their offices as provisional officers until the Constitution of 1869 became law. The legislature convened on February 8, ratified the Fourteenth and Fifteenth amendments, and elected two senators to the United States Senate.

For Fort Towners, that April was more invigorating than usual. Early issues of the April newspapers informed readers that Texas was readmitted to the Union. President Grant had signed, on March 30, the act of Congress admitting senators and representatives from Texas to Congress, thereupon the "provisional government of Texas" with its "provisional officers" moved into the status of full-fledged sovereignty. On the sixteenth of the month, General Reynolds formally terminated military rule in Texas.

It was not a time for unrestrained exaltation, for Reconstruction had not ended, the sharp thinkers of Fort Worth told their fellow townsmen. They were right, for in future years the historians would give January 1874 as the date for the end of Reconstruction in Texas. Fort Town's legal analysts gave as their reason that in a republic the majority rules, and many of their townsmen remained outside the political pale.

The Twelfth Legislature was convened by Governor Davis on April 26, 1870. It wrote into law the radical Republican program, violating the new constitution by postponing until November 1872, both the regular election for congressmen—which would have been held in the fall of 1870, and the election of state officers, which should have occurred in 1871.

By this latter act they prolonged the rule of the radicals elected in 1869. This legislature, whipped by radicals into a mood of unwarranted overbearance, arrested and excluded temporarily a part of the minority of eleven Democrats and three conservative Republican members who blocked their acts. The legislature, by an enabling act, gave the governor power to appoint district, county and city officers; gave him a state police force, provided for the organization of a militia, and empowered him to use it by invoking martial law in any county. (Governor Davis would abuse his police power until 1874, by using Negro policemen to supervise political rallies and elections.) The legislature further wantonly gave land and money to railroads, and spent Texas into bankruptcy.

Wisdom, however, guided some of its acts, making provisions for good roads and education.

Fort Towners that winter, kept an eye on these affairs in Austin, remarking that politically, there was much to perplex a man. On the other hand there were material blessings for which to be grateful.

The population of Tarrant County was 5,788, and assessed value of taxable property was $1,392,877. Greater attention was being given to farming 16,000 acres in cultivation in the county. Wheat was becoming an important crop. More cotton was being raised, and the market price was rising—a condition promising a new opportunity for making a little money, which the enterprising Major Van Zandt grasped. He bought a cotton gin and established it on Judge Terry's property. Sterling P. Clark said he brought in the first bale of cotton his father raised, to Van Zandt's gin, located on present East Fifth Street in the vicinity of the Acme Fast Freight Depot which would be built in years to come, near the spur of Highway 287.

In 1870 a new decade was breaking with new opportunities. This was the thought which powered the six feet of energy that was William Jesse Boaz, Confederate veteran and clerk from the mercantile store of John B. Shipley of Birdville.

In Fort Worth, on a visit, he saw fortunes in the cattle trail dust blowing about the unpainted wooden and rock buildings of the village which all men said was a cattle town on its way up—at times, they called it "Cowtown." Boaz, twenty-nine years old, decided to risk investing in Fort Worth the few surplus dollars he had made in trading horses and cattle while clerking in Birdville. With Mary, his wife of two years, and all his worldly goods, he moved to "cattle town" to make a fortune.

When Boaz left Birdville in 1862 to fight for the Confederacy, he had experienced the fearful realities of many battles; had suffered cold, hunger and difficulties of two prison camps; and had struggled to survive economically during the hard times of 1865—all of which had forged him into a man of will.

Now in 1870, he formed a partnership with James Franklin Ellis, who too, had been through the crucible of war. They erected a plank lumber building, opening a general mercantile store where old-timers went to trade with thirty-two-year-old Ellis whom they had known since he was a boy of nine; and had watched the serious-minded boy mature. Boaz and Ellis were both men of good repute and attracted business. Within twenty years, Boaz would become one of Fort Worth's first millionaires.

Notices published about Fort Worth also had power of attraction. The editor of the *Cleburne Chronicle* printed a notice which was copied by the *Daily State Journal* of Austin, June 12, 1870:

Fort Worth shows signs of improvement. It is located on the banks of the Trinity River in a high and healthy locality surrounded by rich and fertile land. An immense trade is carried on. Fort Worth has the finest courthouse and jail in northern Texas, and built too, by voluntary contributions which shows a public spirit and enterprise seldom found elsewhere.

Another new citizen was Dr. Elias James Beall, Georgia-born and with a medical degree from Tulane University in New Orleans. He had first located in Corsicana in 1860 where he married Miss T. C. Van Zandt, a daughter of Isaac Van Zandt. In 1861 he had gone to war as a surgeon of the 17th Texas Regiment, later being promoted to chief surgeon of Walker's division. In 1870 Dr. Beall, thirty-six years old, tempered by training and experience, chose Fort Worth as his career town. His surgical and medical skill practiced on the Grand Prairie was to bring him both local and national renown.

Other blessings flowed upon Fort Worthians about which there were no doubts. During this year, Captain Daggett was snaring homeseekers of undetermined destination by offering them as gifts, town lots south of Tenth Street between Main and Houston, if they would settle in Fort Worth and build a home on the lot. New citizens and new businesses were the apparent result.

One new family was that of Mr. and Mrs. C. J. Gambrell and their two daughters. The Gambrells, a young couple, had come alone from Mississippi to Fort Worth in 1867, spent two weeks in town, then moved to a farm near Dido on the West Fork of the Trinity. Indian raids had compelled them to move closer to Fort Worth on a farm located on Marine Creek five miles from the public square. In 1870 they moved into town where they bought a lot fronting on West Belknap, adjoining the old fort grounds, for which they paid $500 in gold. The price included the lot and a two-room framework dwelling constructed from one of the officers' houses of the old fort. Mr. Gambrell opened a grocery store "on the west side of the square just across the street, west from the public well."

Randolph Clark, the young teacher, brought his bride, the former Ella Blanche Lee from Bonham. They returned to Fort Worth for the school year opening in September.

At this time the new Christian Church, and the block schoolhouse beside it, which had been started in 1869, were now being made ready for occupancy. For the Clark family their future in Fort Worth promised a life of amenities. The elder Clark continued to be the postmaster, and his elder son, Addison, had built his home a block away.

Fort Worth was indeed pulling out of the wilderness status. This same fall, another school opened its doors to the town's youth, thus boosting the town's assets. In the Masonic building, Professor Oscar J. Lawrence and his sister, Miss Mary Victoria Lawrence, welcomed children taking their first steps in learning; also young adults seeking advanced courses in Latin, Greek, and literature.

The Lawrences were Tennesseans by birth, children of a successful large landowner who had been told that land in Texas was better, so had brought his family by ox wagons in 1856, to Covington, Hill County,

Texas, where his son and daughter received the rudiments of learning.

Fort Worth boys surveyed the field that first day of school in September 1870. What they saw foretold them that a year of serious business lay ahead, not a season of pranks, for Professor Lawrence was no neophyte in the schoolroom. He had taught previously in Hill and Milam counties, at Belton, Marshall, and Galveston. His manner was that of a commander of situations. Thirty-two years of age, he was said to have been of medium height, erect carriage, serious face, and luminous eyes. He wore black sideburns, kept his clothes well brushed, and shoes polished regardless of weather. He had the demeanor of a scholar. His education had been gained under the guidance of the Reverend J. W. P. McKenzie, called the old master of Texas educators. To booklearning, Lawrence added humanizing experiences and hobbies. A musician, he played the flute, horn, and violin to good purpose in school programs.

When he was twenty-three, he had gone to war as a field photographer in the Intelligence Service in J. B. Hood's Brigade. Later, the Federal government bought his films and pictures for the archives of the United States War Department. An entertaining speaker, he spent summer vacations lecturing in rural communities, and these experiences flavored his classroom lectures. A fluid writer and a persevering teacher, he taught many a Fort Worth youth how to express thought in writing.

In fact, Lawrence was to move to Mansfield later, directing his literary talent to an editorial crusade against intemperance. He won the battle, forcing saloons to move out of Mansfield across the creek. By 1876, he was to move to Arlington, open a school, and become the editor of the *Arlington Messenger*.

In the meanwhile, his sister, Mary Victoria, was his assistant in Fort Worth's Masonic school. She was a tall, gracious lady with a ready smile, and "regarded as one of the best educated women in Texas." Since childhood, books had been her associates through which she trained herself. At the age of eighteen, she had begun to teach in her hometown of Covington, and for five years alternately taught and attended school. She became proficient in Latin and higher mathematics, and had knowledge of French, Spanish, and Greek. After leaving Covington, she taught at Port Sullivan, and then at Waco Female College before coming to Fort Worth. Fort Worth children were to have but one year of the guidance of this inspired lady, for she attracted to her, Fort Worth's "most eligible bachelor," Captain Terrell. The two were married after the school doors closed in May, 1871.

A sign of progress in 1870 was the sight just off the public square of William Alexander Darter, peering into his surveyor's level, and signal-

ing to his brother, J. H. Darter, and T. C. Gambrell. They were surveying the streets of Fort Worth from the square southward, with the inter-
secting streets. That same year, Darter made another survey which
placed his name on records of Fort Worth history: the "Old Burial
Ground," as it was called then, but today is Pioneer Rest Cemetery.

During the tragic sixties many of Fort Town's citizens were buried
in this three-acre plot, that already held many of the founders of the
town, and which had been donated by Dr. Gounah. By 1870 more space
was needed. Baldwin Samuels, owning the land north of Dr. Gounah,
designated that an additional three acres could be taken from his property. So, Darter, with his helpers, surveyed and drove down stakes hoping
that someday, prosperous men would fence it.

In 1871, Samuels and his heirs would give to three trustees—Dr. Burts,
Captain Loyd, and Major Van Zandt, a stipulation along with the gift of
land, that it was "to be speedily fenced and laid off in lots. A failure by
the trustees to comply with these conditions would forfeit the land."
Then the name was changed from Old Burial Ground to City Cemetery.

From 1870 until 1880, Darter's services as Tarrant County surveyor,
would be in demand. By 1876, he would make the first complete map of
Tarrant County on file in the Land Office of Texas, and would prepare
surveys for the citizens' committee which were to be brought before the
legislature to obtain its support in bringing the railroad to Fort Worth.

Fort Worth had a town newspaper established in 1870—*The Fort
Worth Whig Chief.* Whether to count it among the assets of the town
was a moot question. A. B. Norton was its owner. This was his second
attempt to publish in Fort Worth, for in 1861, due to his abolitionist
stand, he had been run out of town. Now in 1870, he was still unpopular.
He had served as judge on the bench of the state court, Fifth District, and
in 1868, he had promoted navigation for Dallas on the Trinity. He had
praised too exuberantly the rival town as the future city of North Texas.
The *Whig Chief* further antagonized citizens by this announcement:

Fort Worth Whig Chief
Politically
is
devoted
To the dissemination of Republican principles
and the
Maintenance of Constitutional Liberty
It Advocates
The restoration of good feeling between the North and South
Prompt Acquiescence in the General Government
and restoration of all men

Such publicized Republicanism no doubt aroused their suspicion of Norton's behavior. When Fort Worth's political experts saw an exaggerated editorial published in the *Daily State Journal*, Austin, August 16, 1870, they accused the *Whig Chief* as being its likely source, since newspapers exchanged news items. They concluded that the editorial was a design to extend the power of Governor Davis in Fort Worth and Tarrant County through government by a Davis militia. The editorial read:

We have reports of anything but a cheerful state of things from Fort Worth, Tarrant County. William Gillum deliberately murdered Jack Stateham and made his escape to Smith County. The next victim was a half breed from the Indian nation named Joe Cox whom certain parties accused of horse stealing and shot to death. No arrests were made. The next day a colored woman was shot. On the second of August a dentist at Fort Worth was chased through the streets and fired upon by rowdies in the presence of the deputy sheriff, for the crime of being a newcomer. The deputy did nothing. An attempt was made to kill a freedman named Rucker which failed as Rucker had fled to Waco to save his life from assassins. Altogether it looks as though a strong dose of the militia law would be a wholesome thing for Tarrant County.

Reaction to the article caused thoughtful citizens to exclaim, "an exaggeration with mal-intent" because citizens of Fort Worth, with a few exceptions, were law-abiding—which was true.

Governor Davis declared martial law three times in his administration, but the Fort Worth area was never affected.

Old hands and new hands at trail driving set out in 1870 with the first new grass, praying for cowboy's luck—"a smooth drive" and profits at Abilene. Drovers began the year with encouraging information. Profits for the drives of 1869 had been $3 million. Fort Worthians were among the new hands. Dr. Burts gathered a herd on the Grand Prairie and hit the trail for Kansas. He, Van Zandt, and others had accepted political restrictions placed upon them, but in the realm of economics, they foresaw that the coming decade of the 1870s should be their opportunity to capitalize on Texas beef.

Captain Terrell also raked in gold in that year, for a Mr. George Lang, proprietor of a butcher shop in Leavenworth, had set out with his outfit from Kansas in March to scout the trail in Texas for good beeves, and he had to search no farther than Fort Worth. He contracted with Terrell for 700 beeves with the promise that they were to be gathered as soon as possible. Honesty being the trademark of Fort Worth, the herd started for Kansas in April.

With the coming of the trail driving season, Fort Worth pulsed to the tread of the herds. Cows were the hub of life. Cowtown welcomed as friends the drovers of previous years, Myers and Choate. There was Colonel J. F. Ellison who had lived on the San Marcos River since 1850. He had returned from the war bankrupt, and had turned to driving cattle from his ranch in order to support "a faithful wife and five children."

There was Colonel John O. Dewees. He had come to Texas with his father in 1849, had gone to war in 1861, won his military rank, and returned to ranching in Wilson County. Success on the trail would spread his ranches over many Texas counties. By 1871, he would form a partnership with Col. Ellison; and as the cattle drives boomed, Fort Worthians recorded that Dewees and Ellison cattle were thick on the trail for many years. Between 20,000 and 40,000 of their beeves annually passed through Fort Worth.

There was a Captain E. B. Millet who had served in the 32nd Texas Cavalry throughout the war. From 1869 until 1882 he was to be a close friend of many Fort Worthians and a familiar figure in the stores and hotels of Cowtown. Forming a partnership with a Mr. Mabery, the Millet–Mabery outfits annually herded 100,000 cattle from Texas.

Other drovers in the year of 1870 were W. H. Mayfield with 700 big steers, R. J. Jennings as boss for Crunk Jennings and Company with 1,600 head, C. H. Rust with 1,500, W. G. Butler with "an enormous herd," and "Uncle" R. B. (Bob) Johnson with a young Negro man as personal servant and a good herd. W. T. Waggoner in Fort Worth, made his first large cattle deal in that year.

Fort Worthians were pleased when Col. Ellison returned to town in April and it was related by a witness:

'That herd of 750 mixed cattle I drove through here last spring on credit paid off. I sold cattle and outfit at Abilene, came back by boat, paid my creditors, and pocketed $9,000.'
'What's the drive this year?' a man asked.
'About 1,500 head are through Fort Worth today. I'm counting on sending several herds up trail this season,' Ellison optimistically answered, 'and that means plenty of bacon to buy.'
'I can supply it,' retorted a merchant.

According to the statistics of Pleasant Burnell Butler, expert trail driver, whose brother W. L. Butler, was one of the biggest drivers and prominent patrons of Fort Worth merchants, it required three quarters of a pound of bacon and the same of flour for a cowhand each day. "At

Fort Worth, it was necessary to take on supplies for one month," he said, "there being no big stores between Fort Worth and Abilene, Kansas." Butler's chuck wagons, always drawn by four oxen, groaned with the weight of "flour, coffee, bacon, beans, and dried fruit," as it left Fort Worth with a supply for thirty days to feed from ten to eighteen hungry cowhands.

Men without an acquaintanceship with honesty also came to Cowtown to make dollars. T. M. Turner, riding with W. L. Butler, met such men in the environs of Fort Worth.

We met two shorthorn cowboys who were yelling and shooting and we came near having troubles with them because they turned our cattle back. Mr. Butler and I told them in a very emphatic manner to strike a high ball to town, and they struck it, and the last we saw of them was a streak of Fort Worth dust.

Winter came. The drive of 1870 had been a banner year. About 300,000 Texas cattle arrived in Abilene. The season had been dry, the grass fine, and when cattlemen reached Abilene, they profited by the freight war between the railroads. Trainloads of cattle were transported for $1.60 per car from Kansas to Chicago. Buying was brisk. Cattle worth $20 in Texas sold for $50. Of these financial facts and figures, the merchants of Fort Worth were aware; and travelers in town from South Texas said the entire Gulf Coast range was in action—every man with a cow or two, was talking about hitting the trail in the spring of 1871.

So saloonkeepers of Cowtown stacked their money received from the cowboys, and mailed their orders for additional barrels of whiskey. Merchants counted their money taken from the drive, made pencil figures in the largest digits ever, as they estimated their orders for supplies to meet demands of the drovers expected in 1871, and wrote hopefully on their ledger pads projected possible profits.

1871

Prosperous Texas drovers, homeward bound from Kansas descended the Mississippi on luxury boats. They discussed with male passengers national politics and the cattle industry. They spoke of booming cowtowns on the McCoy-Chisholm Trail. Fort Worth became a geographical fact "back East" among men contemplating a change in fortune. Cowtown, longhorns, and Texas prairies were magnetizing words attracting men from north of the Mason-Dixon Line. Conrad Bretz Morgan of Sycamore, Ohio, was one of these.

Back from the war, he saw his freighting business dwindle as the Ohio country was spanned with more railroads. At freighting points, he heard of the cattle town of Fort Worth. Freighting would be a good business in a cowman's market on the "railless prairie."

In the summer of 1871 Mr. Morgan's caravan, bearing his family and freight hands who had taken their chance in life to reach the West by entering Mr. Morgan's hire, was something to see as it rolled into Fort Worth. There were four freight wagons drawn by two, four, and six yoke of oxen, several sturdy buggies, a fashionable carriage, and a string of race horses which his English wife, Hannah J. Shields, cherished as the part of her English life transplanted to America.

Mrs. Morgan's father had been sent by Queen Victoria on a special inspection tour to Canada. North America won him. He removed his family to Canada although his wife, a lady at court, reluctantly consented. Later the Shields moved to the United States. Now, Mrs. Morgan's delight in horse racing, was responsible for placing a string of racers on the track in Fort Worth, which, as previously related, was located during the seventies in the present vicinity of Paddock Viaduct. In good weather, men on horseback and couples in their buggies drew up around the unpretentious track to watch the racers. Morgan's fine string of horses were an adjunct to the amusement-hungry Fort Worthians, while Morgan's freighters, plying between East Texas, Dallas, and Fort Worth, conveyed trade to the town.

He established his home on a farm on the east side of Baldwin Samuels' road. Possessing an inventive mind, Morgan created many gadgets to simplify frontier toil, establishing him in a lucrative business. His fame as well driller would bring him a contract in 1881, to drill all the water for the Fort Worth and Denver Railroad as that line was being constructed.

Mr. Morgan's caravan, though, was only one in the procession of covered wagons whose masters in 1871, were seeking the combined trade of a cattle town and a farmers' market on the Grand Prairie of Texas. Even early settlers of Fort Worth were venturing onto new paths. Dr. Burts, having laid aside his medical profession for trail driving, entered the mercantile business that year. On Main Street, just off the square over a building appeared a new sign announcing the firm of Newman, Young, and Burts, General Merchandise. This enterprise of the doctor's prospered. The story of his trail driving venture was different. Though he made a great deal of money in the drives of 1871–72, the one to be in 1873, would prove disastrous, and he would return to the practice of medicine.

Never in the memory of Texas ranchers had their branding irons seared so many hides as in the spring of 1871. The legislature in 1866 passed an act recognizing brands as proof of ownership, and now a new law made it illegal to drive an animal to northern markets without a road brand. The drive of 1870 had brought wealth to many Texans, and surely, they argued in American fashion, that there was enough wealth in Abilene awaiting any man who would risk the hardships of the trail. It was predicted that 700,000 Texas cattle would reach the Abilene market in 1871. The *Whig Chief* issue of September 12 that year, quoting from the *Cherokee Kansas Sentinel*, said:

360,000 head of cattle by a careful register have passed Fort Worth! Where is there another route that can count as many cattle?

Herds, like ocean swells, constantly rolled in upon Fort Worth. The citizens gaped at the sights that gave them a feeling of living successfully. In May, 1871, the rains came and remained, making it a soggy spring. The Trinity reached flood stage, and herds crowded around the town.

To Amanda Burks, "the first lady trail driver" according to records, it meant a delay of days on the route. In April, her husband and Jasper Clark, each with a herd of a thousand head, left Nueces County. Each outfit had ten cowboys, mostly Mexicans, a cook, and wagons. After a day out on the trail, Mr. Burks had sent word by a rider for his wife to join him, bringing their black boy, Nick, to care for her comforts. In a day's time, Amanda Burks, in a little buggy drawn by two good brown ponies, overtook the herd and followed it day after day. Nick prepared her meals, and each night put up her tent. In Johnson County they were beaten upon by a great hailstorm. Then they trailed on into Tarrant County. She wrote:

We camped a long time at Fort Worth, waiting for the Trinity River to fall low enough to cross our cattle. I counted fifteen herds waiting to cross.

If Amanda Burks behaved as a normal woman—and no doubt she did —her buggy was seen tied to a hitching rail at Fort Worth as she looked about in the stores at the fashionable goods from "back East." It was an amusing pastime while awaiting a Trinity crossing. Amanda, her buggy, and her black boy would become a familiar sight on Fort Worth's square. It was perspicacious of Mr. Burks—taking his wife with him on his first trip up the trail, for soon afterwards he was killed by bandits in the streets of Cotulla, the town near his ranch; and Amanda, having been initiated as a drover, would continue following the herds from the

Burks ranch to the Kansas market, receiving from the drovers the accolade, the "Queen of the Trail Drivers."

The raging Trinity and the mud in the spring caused cowmen to fuss and fume but heightened the excitement of Fort Worth boys who gathered to watch the daring cowboys drive frightened herds into the fast flowing, muddy Trinity. One trail boss really gave them a show.

"Neither a forty-dollar horse nor a high river will throw me," was the iron-willed decision of Colonel G. W. Neil, boss of a herd, as he watched the cattle pile up around Fort Worth waiting for a crossing. Impatient to be on the move before the trail became too crowded, he talked to Fort Worthians on the square, then ordered his cowhands to go up the river west of town, cut timber and brush, haul it back to the cattle crossing and construct a cattle chute to the river in order to force the animals down the eight-foot bank.

W. B. Foster, one of the lead cowboys in the herd, related that he always led the cattle across river, and on this occasion he went down the brush chute into the swirling water in front of a bawling herd. After crossing to the north bank, his horse, ascending the bank, bogged down in the mud. He dismounted into an audience of several Indians sitting on a log, entranced by the sight of man and beast struggling with nature. Foster shouted to the men on the opposite bank that there were Indians. Before the men could cross on the ferry and join the herd, the Indians had disappeared.

It was at that time that a seventeen-year-old youth on his first trip up the trail enjoyed new experiences and sights in Fort Worth. The lad was George W. Saunders. In later years he would organize the Old Trail Drivers Association, and would give the name to Trail Drivers Park in Fort Worth. In 1871, Saunders had hired to Choate of the firm of Choate and Bennett. They were sending fourteen herds in the spring drive. When Mr. Choate asked young Saunders which outfit he wished to work in, he replied, "The first one out." Jim Byler was boss of the first outfit which left Stockdale with one thousand steers in April. George said:

We went by Waco, Cleburne, and Fort Worth. Between the last two places, the country was level and untimbered and full of prairie chickens and deer. We held our herd in Fort Worth two days.

Saunders, backtrailing from Kansas through Fort Worth, punctured the dullness of a day with trail news for habitués on the square who had begun to be bored with the coming of fall days that were so uneventful after those crowded months of the trail season.

According to Saunders' story, Choate and Bennett, also Butler of South

Texas, had sold several herds in Kansas. Thus they had a surplus of men and horses in Abilene because ranchers in the Northwest had not yet learned that Texas cow ponies were better for range work than their native horses. When they did discover the fact, cow ponies were readily sold in Kansas, and cowboys came home by rail and boat. But in 1871, the three big cattlemen were compelled, before the season drives were over, to send back to Texas men, chuck wagons, and 150 cow ponies. Saunders said they had a lively time enroute home since they had nothing to do but drive the horses, make camp, eat, and sometimes sleep. They stopped in all towns on the trail, visiting stores and saloons. At Denton, they planned a stop. Officers demanded that they surrender their guns because a recent Texas law prohibited the carrying of pistols. Cowboys replied by drawing their pistols, mounting their horses and riding out of town shooting into the air. "The officers did not follow," Saunders said. The cowboys headed for Fort Worth where they stopped for the usual fun of visiting stores.

The law forbidding the carrying of firearms in Texas, except in the area beginning in Parker County and counties west, was a statute stabbing the comfort of older Fort Worth men. As one pioneer said, "men would not be caught in public without their six-guns any more than they would be caught without their pants." But laws have an amazing elasticity when interpreted to apply to the peculiarities of frontier communities. Fort Worth was a cowman's town. There were permits issued for "gun totin' " to certain citizens, and liberties were silently allowed for transient visitors from the trail. Human law being more powerful, one did not separate a cowboy from his "Black-eyed Susan."

Businessmen in Fort Worth watched news from June through October concerning the success of the cattle drives and the Kansas market. For as the cattle market soared and fell, so did the prosperity of Fort Worth merchants, as well as their orders for stock from New York and St. Louis. The year's drive had been disappointing. Swollen rivers, rain-soaked grass, stampedes, and a crowded trail made it a tortuous drive. Cowboys were so physically spent when they reached Abilene, they said that their "ears flopped"; but their troubles were over, while their employers'—the drovers—troubles began.

Beef prices slumped. The rate war of the railroads was over, causing the freight rate costs to rise. One-half of the drive of 1871 remained unsold in September, and Texas cowboys and cattle were forced to spend the winter in western Kansas and eastern Colorado. A piercing blizzard swept across the Great Plains that winter, striking down many cattle and as a result, some of the ranchers went bankrupt.

For a brief time in June, 1871, the people of Fort Worth forgot the cattle business entirely, when an Indian battle raged along Marine Creek. It was almost at the threshold of the public square since a man could see Marine Creek from the bluff. A band of Indians had raided horse corrals of residents located on the north and west rim of the town. They then galloped away with a fortune in these animals to the little forest along the creek located east of present-day North Main near Exchange Avenue. Here they planned to hide until nightfall. A group of Fort Worth volunteers gathered at once, and sought the Indians through the woods of the West Fork. Their search ended in a battle in an oak thicket. In the words of Bud Daggett, a member of the party, "A memorable fight took place . . . on Marine Creek and a large number of horses and a few men were killed." The Indians fled, and the citizens' guard followed the trail out of the area. It was alleged that some of the people blamed the Indian outbreak on the carpetbag government of Governor Davis for lack of adequate frontier protection.

Fort Worthians were overly sensitive to Indian hostilities, for in May, they had been infuriated over the bludgeoning at the hand of the Kiowas, of their good friend and former townsman, Captain Feild. Owning one of the finest flour mills in North Texas at Mansfield, and also operating a freighting line known as "Feild's Freighters" he had a contract with the government of the United States to freight supplies to the federal forts in the West. His freighters loaded with flour and other provisions consigned to Fort Richardson and Fort Griffin had passed through Fort Worth, exchanged greeting with friends, crossed the Trinity at the ford below the bluff, and proceeded to Jacksboro. On the road from Jacksboro to Fort Griffin, the wagon train was attacked at Salt Creek. Most of the party of teamsters were killed or wounded. The slain men were tied to the wagon wheels, then the wagon train was burned, and for all their bloody work, the Indians were only richer by the dray animals of the train.

Fort Worthians considered Indian raids as late as 1871, in the midst of settlements, to be inexcusable. However, General Sherman, who had been in the vicinity of the area at the time, gained a new stature with them. He had been hated for his destructive "March to the Sea" through Georgia during the Civil War. But now, escorted by Randolph B. Marcy on an inspection tour, Sherman came over the road to Jacksboro shortly after the massacre and ordered the Indians chased. The leading culprit, Satanta and two other Kiowa chiefs, Satank and Big Tree, were captured on the reservation at Fort Sill.

Sherman was convinced that the Indian menace was real, and ordered the Kiowa chiefs to Jacksboro for trial. The court sentenced Satanta and Big Tree to be hanged, but they were never executed.

The distant vista of a railroad was shortened for Fort Worth promoters as they concentrated on development of railroad news. The Twelfth Legislature had convened on April 26, 1870, and ended the first session on August 15. The majority of legislators lacked acumen concerning taxes and debts, so were extravagant with state funds in granting aid to railroads, because the Constitution of 1869 prohibited land grants. Legislators believed that the need of Texas for a transcontinental railroad was greater than a substantial treasury.

In July, the legislature granted a charter to the Southern Transcontinental Railroad Company. Under this charter the company was organized in New York City in October.

On August 5, the legislature incorporated the International Railway Company providing for a railroad from Red River opposite Fulton, Arkansas, to Laredo. They promised the company state bonds to run for thirty years bearing eight percent interest to the extent of $10,000 for each mile of track constructed. These events of 1870 meant railroad progress even though it angered many taxpayers and threatened the financial integrity of the state.

Then on March 3, 1871, occurred the event that would bring the vista of a railroad almost into eye view of Fort Worthians. Congress granted its first charter to a Texas railroad. A new company, the Texas and Pacific Railroad by a special act of Congress was to build along the thirty-second parallel route from Marshall, Texas, to San Diego, California. This railroad was to serve as a national post road for mail and a military route to carry troops and supplies. No state would have power of interference in the performance of these duties.

This event brought shouts of hurrah from Fort Worth promoters and aroused their concern as to railroad measures the Texas legislature would enact during its second session which had convened in January 1871. No doubt the act of Congress in March stimulated the Texas lawmakers to take every measure to promote the construction of transcontinental railroads through Texas. They authorized cities and counties the power to grant "bonuses" to railroads.

On May 24, over the veto of Governor Davis, the legislature generously granted state bonds in aid to two railroads then trying to build through Texas. The first was the Southern Pacific Railroad Company "not in any way connected with the present Southern Pacific Company," whose line was from Longview, westward along the thirty-second degree of latitude. Since 1867 they had been building snail-paced from Marshall. The second company was the Southern Transcontinental, whose route was westward from Texarkana along the Red River. These two roads were to merge at some point east of the eastern boundary of Shackelford County and form one railroad line.

To these two companies which were to share equally in the grant, the legislature voted the transaction already stated. The total aggregate of state bonds was not to exceed $6 million.

Such liberality brought protests from taxpayers, even insinuations that "unblushing bribery" had occurred. Arguments and complaints were heard in Fort Worth. Townsmen with legal minds politicized the dilemma they faced. It was either state bonds or an amendment to the Constitution of 1869. The legislature had implied a future amendment in a provision of the bill granting the state bonds. It stated that if the constitution should be changed so as to permit land grants, future legislatures might appropriate to these "two railroads or their successor twenty-four sections of land" for each mile of track constructed.

Most pleasing to railroad boosters in Fort Worth was the stipulation in the bill that the recently chartered "Texas and Pacific should succeed to all rights and privileges granted to the Southern Pacific and the Southern Transcontinental." This provision was the gem Fort Worthians treasured during the summer and winter of 1871 as they applied their minds in continuous thoughts about measures to be taken to place Fort Worth on that line of the congressional chartered transcontinental through Texas.

September was the month when Fort Worth mothers prepared their children for school and sent them off to the faint ringing of the school bell. This September of 1871, the peals resounded at a greater distance since the resonant bell formerly in front of Andrews Tavern had been moved to the Masonic building.

It was a banner year for education with three schools opening. The third school was a school for girls established for gentlewomen by Mrs. E. S. Scribner, a graduate of St. Mary's Hall in Burlington, New Jersey. It signified that some citizens of the town could indulge in a bit of extravagance in acquiring culture. Tuition in each of the higher branches of her curriculum as English, French, music and voice was five dollars a month, and one dollar extra was charged for use of a piano for practice.

Fort Worthians realized that their community was not only a cow-town to the drovers and cowhands, but also was a town in the West with culture. The seventies would be the beginning of Fort Worth's complex life: entertainment houses for playful cowboys, schools with curriculum ranging from the rudiments of education to higher branches of learning, and a finishing school for "gentle ladies in subjects which were accoutrements of cultured womanhood."

Another center of interest in September was the return of the franchise for many Southern veterans. The "iron-clad oath" which had disfranchised Confederates was repealed by Congress. That was ecstatic news for disqualified Fort Worth leaders. Now they could vote. Good was moving forward. Democrats and conservative Republicans were incited to action. In September, 1871, Texas taxpayers called a convention composed of representatives from ninety-four counties. Meeting in Austin, it protested the extravagance of the Governor Davis regime which was bankrupting the state. It drew up twenty-one counts of violation by the governor and the legislature, of the Texas Constitution of 1869.

S. P. Hollingsworth, representative from Tarrant County, was a member of the committee which drew up the charges against Davis. This display of boldness by Texas voters, expedited another step in their political liberation. Setting aside the unconstitutional ruling of the legislature that postponed the election of congressmen until 1872, this convention provided a special election to be held in October to vote for four Texas congressmen. The heyday of Republicans in Texas was drawing to a close. Four Democrats were elected to Congress in spite of the militia's supervision of the polls.

Political news was improving, therefore Fort Worthians should have a Democratic newspaper. Scant circulation stopped the press of Norton's *Whig Chief* before the expiration of 1871, giving Major Van Zandt further incentive to establish a news journal. He felt that Fort Worth, in order to have status as a town of consequence, should count among its assets a Democratic newspaper.

In October 1871, he sent a load of flour to Quitman, Texas, where he bartered it for an old Washington press and equipment, the property of Major J. J. Jarvis, the former editor of the *Quitman Herald*. Backers of the Major's project were Captain John Hanna and Sam Evans, W. H. Overton, and Junius W. Smith.

After freighting the press from Quitman to Fort Worth, it was set up by a joint stock company with J. W. Cleveland as editor and B. R. Bibb as publisher. They began publishing a weekly, *The Democrat*, in November 1871. Earlier in that year, Cleveland had started a paper he called *The Enterprise*, but the existence of it is not mentioned in F. B. Baillio's *History of Early Newspapers in Texas.*

1872

Momentously constructive would be the year 1872. Fort Worth, commanding several good river crossings had been rescued from oblivion by the cattle drives to Kansas. Leaders, crusading since 1853 to build a town, would see their visions of a railroad become a promise. Men of achievement coming from other states would fuel the economy. And Fort Worth men would have their economic and political shackles broken asunder by congressional and state laws. At last, gray days would be fading in the faith of a new freedom.

However, the year 1872 would begin for the village much as former years had begun since the close of the war. January and February were disagreeable months of piercing winds, occasional rains with their accompaniment of mud, and monotonous days, sometimes spiked with interest brought by tardy immigrants in a hurry to reach a designated place on the prairies in time for March plowing. The big rush of newcomers—those who had planned well—had already come in the fall of 1871. As usual, when spring came, the cattle herds trailing their way toward Kansas, would pass through the town in continuous procession all the day long.

Then in late May, the year of 1872 ceased to be similar. The usual talk of cattle changed to that of the Amnesty Act passed in May by Congress restoring to all except about 750 former Confederates the right to hold office. Fort Worth males talked and solemnly vowed what they would do when November came, as it would be the first time since the war that the disfranchised could vote. Some would run for office, or for a seat in Congress.

Many conversed too, on the subject of the new railroad acts. The phrases of state bonds for railroads and the incorporation of the companies, brightened the vision of Fort Worthians, now planning to get the railroads to come through their town. The town leaders were conversant with recent national developments. Colonel Thomas A. Scott of Pennsylvania, a railroad baron, and owner of mines in California and New Mexico, had been elected president of the Texas and Pacific Railroad Company in February, 1872.

In March, the new company, exercising its power granted by the legislature, acquired the rights and franchise of the Southern Pacific and the Southern Transcontinental railroads. After consolidation of these rail lines along with the Memphis, El Paso and Pacific companies, the Texas and Pacific began to operate the former service of the Southern Pacific between Longview and Shreveport. And Colonel Scott prepared to visit New Orleans, Galveston and many points in Texas.

On May 2, Congress further strengthened the Texas and Pacific by an amendatory act which modified the original charter of 1871 and changed the name of the Texas and Pacific Railroad to the Texas and Pacific Railway Company.

In that same month, Congress became more benign toward the South in its need for a transcontinental railroad by increasing the construction bonds granted the previous year, from $30 thousand for each mile of track laid to $40 thousand for each mile of rail.

Fort Worth boosters watching the railroad news remarked that this act would be a financial bolster for the Texas and Pacific, accelerating its construction across the state.

Meanwhile, the Twelfth Legislature had withdrawn the state bond subsidies of $10,000 a mile. The International Railway Company, after building fifty-two miles of track had applied for the bonds. The comptroller and treasurer of Texas refused payment declaring that the bond subsidy act was unconstitutional. Negotiations for settlement with the company began. Fortunately for the honor of Texas credit and the taxpayers, the bonds were never paid.

Later, in 1875, the legislature would clear the state's debt to the International Railway by granting twenty sections of land for each mile of track constructed, and certain tax exemptions.

Then came June, 1872, bringing another propitious episode. A stagecoach had traveled in the spring from Jefferson, Marshall, Longview, across North Central Texas carrying capitalists who had come to view the much publicized "Land of Promise" where their dollars, and the dollars of little people, as well as of the United States government, were being invested in rails, ties, bridges, and locomotives.

These men, familiar with the ways of eastern industrialism and fortune-making in booming California, no doubt were given a feeling of history-making, as they pictured in their minds the changes to be wrought in this spaceless country as their stagecoach rolled through the pine woods of East Texas, out onto prairies broken by oak timber, across white rock-bedded creeks and rivers, up and down the rise and fall of inland hills, past plowed fields with promise of corn and cotton crops, clusters of farmers' log houses, and finally emerging out of the wilderness upon villages and towns. They searchingly observed the landscape for the pertinent facts of their mission: the selection of a route for a railroad across Texas; also to solicit money and land grants from counties and towns.

Colonel Scott headed this party. With him were James W. Throck-morton, former governor of Texas and a director of the Texas and Pacific Railway; D. W. Washburn, a civil engineer; and the most eminent American journalist, John W. Forney, editor and proprietor of the Philadelphia *Chronicle*, whose mission with Scott was to rally "Yankees" to a realistic support of a southern transcontinental railroad.

Texas captivated Colonel Forney. His pen sent streams of letters to his Philadelphia paper to be read by Eastern city dwellers.

Colonel Scott and party were to visit Dallas, and no doubt their arrival in Fort Worth was expected since town leaders had been following ac-counts of the party through papers from Austin and Galveston; and had been chatting with ready-witted stagecoach drivers, the best carriers of current happenings. This news perhaps caused civic leaders to indulge in the dangerous game of comparing assets with their rival Dallas, a town with a population in January of 1872, of 3,000. Some Fort Worthians, however, believed it was closer to 2,000, as it was exceedingly hard to estimate population in a boomtown. Furthermore, their neighbors were infected with a disease known as exaggeration. To Fort Worthians, Dal-las had an enviable asset—a railroad. The Houston and the Texas Cen-tral was building into the town, and their newspapers spoke of the town as the future rail and mercantile center of the state.

The Fort Worthians who had wanted Fort Worth to be the county seat, were now wanting the railroad to stop here, too. These warriors of the county seat fight, along with the newcomers of the 1860s, planned a campaign to win a party of railroad builders over to their way of think-ing. Some of the group felt that they had reasons for optimism.

For although Dallas had more people, newspapers, and stores, Fort Worth had something to offer railroad investors. It was the very impor-tant, and lucrative supply station for cowmen on the McCoy-Chisholm Trail, as well as the emporium for farmers and immigrants, and was reputed to possess the finest county courthouse in Texas, though its population was only 500. Added to these assets, there was one newspaper, three schools, two stone church buildings, four church organizations, a Masonic hall, a flour mill, a cotton gin, and about thirty businesses, be-sides three doctors and as many incomparable lawyers.

With confidence, it may be surmised, the strategists prepared for the coming of the railroad party at an undetermined date. Negro boys were busy everywhere. Andrews Tavern gleamed hospitably in its crude frontier equipage. Proprietors of stores on the public square did chores of tidying. The courthouse, the pride of the town, was given an extra sweeping and dusting. Town leaders had their broadcloth suits and buggies made ready for a good impression.

Sometimes anticipations do not happen as the mind imagined. So it was with the directors of the village. They were surprised by an unexpected arrival of Colonel Scott, according to the account of Major Van Zandt. He was napping on a counter in his store because "the day was hot and business was dull," when a young man hastened in to inform the major that the railroad men "were in [their] midst," and had taken lodging in Andrews Tavern.

Van Zandt summoned Judge Hendricks to accompany him to welcome the visitors. After exchanging cordialities, he invited the group to his store which was more commodious than the hotel room for a meeting "with other citizens."

Men assembling that afternoon in late June had risen above mediocrity in living American history. These citizens were majors, colonels and captains of the Mexican and Civil wars. There were legislators, who had authored bills which had channeled the course of the state's history. And there was an ex-governor of the state.

After these men had assembled, engaged in introductions and welcoming pleasantries, they were seated for a conference. Former governor Throckmorton, their close friend, had told several men that Colonel Scott was "a very frank man and would tell them what he wanted." When asked in the meeting the purpose of his visit, Scott told the group that he wanted "320 acres of land south of town" in consideration of which he would "proceed as rapidly as possible to build the Texas and Pacific railroad to [their] town."

"Before seven o'clock that night an obligation promising this land bonus was executed by four men—Colonel T. J. Jennings, Captain E. M. Daggett, Judge H. G. Hendricks and me," according to Van Zandt.

When Colonel Scott with his party left the village for California to continue their promotion of the Texas and Pacific Railway, the townsmen were confident that Fort Worth would live. Life and death of a town depended on a contract guaranteeing a railroad; and Fort Worth was protected by many contracts, through both Congress and their own state legislature. Colonel Scott, upon his departure, had given his promise of a railroad and carried in his pocket a "promissory obligation" of four Fort Worth leaders.

In August the Texas and Pacific entered into a contract with the

California and Texas Construction Company to build tracks from the
eastern boundary of Texas to San Diego, California. Immediately after
the contract was executed the Texas and Pacific gained control of the
construction company.

General Grenville Dodge had been lured from the Union Pacific by a
salary offer of $20,000 a year, to become chief engineer of the Texas and
Pacific Railway. He had divided the projection line into five divisions
and organized surveying parties, placing Captain R. S. Hayes in charge
of the division east of Fort Worth, and Hodges, Wilson and O'Neill in
charge of the Brazos division.

Promise of a railroad, though still on paper, began to make its physical
appearance in Fort Worth in the fall and winter of 1872. Surveyors
working west from Longview, had revised the preliminary survey of
1871. William Patrick Doty, one of the surveyors, apparently was not
heartened by the sight of Dallas or Fort Worth. In his narrative he recorded: "Dallas is a struggling village of a few hundred people, and Fort
Worth consisted of a fringe of buildings around the public square."

By Christmas the surveyors reached Weatherford. There was much
to encourage Fort Worth. Besides the actual presence of the railroad surveyors, was the general talk that the legislature when it met in January,
1873, would legalize land grants to railroads, thereby removing all legal
obstructions to progress.

As a matter of fact, projecting into 1873, the "T & P" would begin
building track at three different points. By November there would be the
"Panic of '73," showing 251 miles of completed rails, reaching Dallas
and as far west as Eagle Ford. And the amendment needed, would be
passed in March, limiting land grants to twenty sections for each mile of
track, which Colonel Scott would accept.

Meanwhile, news items about the president of the railroad were ex-
hilarating. Like an evangelist, Colonel Scott traveled the nation, appearing before citizens' committees and town meetings. Five million dollars
was the astronomical sum he had to raise in order to meet the cost of
constructing the southern transcontinental railroad. His zealous speeches,
given wide news coverage, charmed listeners and readers as he described
the undeveloped wealth of Texas, offering opportunities in the fields of
manufacturing, agriculture, ranching, and in exploration for mineral
wealth which he proved by quoting Professor A. R. Rossier's mineral
surveys of the region:

Petroleum springs occur over a space of about fifty square miles in Hardin
County, and it is probable that larger supplies may be obtained by boring.
. . . The iron deposits of northeastern Texas are of the most remarkable char-

acter, equaling in extent and richness those of Sweden, Missouri, New Jersey, and New York. Gold, silver, and copper exist in inexhaustible quantities in West Texas, and on to the Pacific.

Such verbal pictures tantalized the speculators to invest. For the practical man who invested his money on the basis of actual, rather than promissory values, Colonel Scott pictured the need of the United States for a railroad to the Pacific that would never be snowbound. It would shorten the distance between New Orleans and the Pacific Coast to 1,800 miles, and from Texas ports to the Pacific the distance would be less than 1,500 miles.

Fort Worthians with money invested in the Texas and Pacific Railway, and those without money, saved for future investment in the patriotic, as well as, road to riches project.

Railroad tracks came slowly across the prairies, but the word sped swiftly concerning the prospective route of the rails. Fort Worth, the cowtown, was to be on the Texas and Pacific Railway, the shortest transcontinental route to the Pacific Coast. Newcomers, speculating to their last penny, hurried into the village sending prices of real estate upward until values trebled, population doubled, and business houses filled the blocks solid on the square, and then occupied many of the vacant lots just off the square along Main Street. New plank board buildings appeared over night.

Many were the newcomers to arrive. Some were perspicacious men destined to be leaders. Among these were B. C. Evans, the merchant; Sam Furman and J. Y. Hogsett, attorneys; Major Jarvis, lawyer and businessman; Jeremiah Marklee, banker; Captain B. B. Paddock, journalist, newspaper editor and lawyer; General J. M. Peers, future owner of the largest hotel until the building of the El Paso; Z. E. B. Nash, founder of a tin and hardware shop; and former resident Abe Harris, who had returned and opened a photographic studio.

Since these men would toil with the old-timers to transform the village into a little metropolis, their contributions should be noticed.

B. C. Evans, an unassuming young man of twenty-eight, opened in October, 1872, the first store in Fort Worth engaging exclusively in dry goods. It was on Houston Street just off the public square. Older men laughed at this presumptuous young man thinking that his dry goods mart could compete with the general mercantile stores. They were in error. Evans would astonish the natives. Through his practice of integrity, business acumen, and executive ability, he operated business with

luxury items of such excellence as to surprise eastern visitors expecting
only frontier crudities. Success was not phenomenal, but it was substantial. Born in Chesterfield County, South Carolina, in 1844, the son
of a large planter and slaveholder, he was educated at Columbia Military Academy and the Citadel in Charleston. He went to the war in 1861,
only a boy of sixteen serving as aide to one of his brothers, an artillery
officer. The Negro his father had given him when a child to serve and
attend him, accompanied Evans to school and to war. After the conflict,
together they planted a cotton crop on the family plantation. Soon after,
he engaged in merchandising with his brother for about five years in
Cheraw, South Carolina. During this time he was elected to the Assembly
of South Carolina for the session of 1870-71, but did not complete his
term because of the distressing proceedings of the body. Texas offered
a new beginning. In Fort Worth he would be one on whom the citizens'
committee could rely to give substantially to bring the railroad to Fort
Worth, for he was soon earning a fortune from merchandising and the
livestock industry.

A cattletown and a railroad boomtown would be a lawyer's oasis in
frontier Texas, especially for one who stated that the rules for a successful lawyer were "to work hard, to understand his business, to deal frank-
ly and never to take a bad case." Those were the rules of J. Y. Hogsett,
returning to Texas in the fall of 1872. A youth of sixteen in 1859, he
left his birthplace of Anderson, Tennessee, for Texas where he remained
until the Civil War began. From Texas, he marched away to the conflict
as a private but was promoted to sergeant. He fought through until the
end. After experiencing war, he returned home to Tennessee, studied
law, and was admitted to the bar in 1869; but Texas and news of the
Texas and Pacific Railway were the magnets pulling him to the West.
Arriving in Fort Worth in the fall, he formed a partnership with Captain Hanna, acquired a costly law library and a reputation as an able
jurist. Affable and companionable, he was an asset to the boomtown, and
in 1873 Hogsett would write the first charter for the city of Fort Worth.

A party of South Carolina planters, refusing to accept Lee's defeat,
went to Central America to continue their way of life. In the party was
the Furman family with their son, Sam, who at sixteen, had volunteered
as a private in the light artillery, fighting until Lee's surrender. In Central America, tropical sickness decimated the party, and ill health sent
survivors back to the United States. Sam studied law in his native state,
and was admitted to the bar. But his financial status remained adverse.
Texas, the panacea for many difficulties, brought Sam to Fort Worth.
Land, cattle, and money speedily exchanging hands was all for the good

of Sam Furman's profession. Although a newcomer in 1872, four years later, he would be elected county judge of Tarrant.

In 1856, with $100 in his pocket, James Jones Jarvis, aged twenty-five, left for Texas. He walked from Shreveport to the East Fork of the Trinity in Collin County, retraced his steps as far as Quitman in Wood County, where in 1857 he began to practice law. He had but sixty dollars left when reaching Quitman. Loaning fifty-five dollars to a friend, he began his career with only five dollars in his pocket. Born in North Carolina in 1831, he had moved with his family to Tennessee, then Illinois where he read law at Urbana, and was admitted to the bar by the supreme court of Illinois in 1855. His knowledge of literature had been cultivated since a farm boy; his intellectual prowess sharpened by the study of law, and a well-dipped pen made him an able editor. In 1857, he purchased the *Quitman Herald* which he published for two years being his own editor, printer, and devil. At the first call to arms of the Confederacy, he volunteered as a private. Promotions were rapid. He rose to the rank of major. Soon after the war he was elected judge of Wood County, and later was appointed by Governor Hamilton, attorney of the Sixth Judicial District composed of five counties over which he traveled on horseback. Another beneficial change in his life was his marriage to Ida Van Zandt, youngest daughter of Isaac Van Zandt and sister of Major Van Zandt of Fort Worth. During the five years since 1866, Jarvis and his wife saved several thousand dollars which changed the chart of their lives. He had accompanied the chief engineer for the Texas and Pacific early in 1871 on an inspection trip to the North Sabine. One evening about the campfire, the engineer said that the Texas and Pacific would go through Fort Worth some day. Jarvis decided to move there. This decision, no doubt, had influenced the sale of his Washington printing press to Fort Worth men in the autumn of 1871. Arriving in Fort Worth, before the boom began, he invested every penny of his savings in real estate, consisting of several blocks of Main and Houston streets. He joined the law firm of Colonel Smith and Hendricks, the second oldest law firm in the town, Captain Terrell's being the oldest.

New days of expansion came in neat succession by mid-year of 1872. With each new day there were new citizens, new businesses, new buildings, new thoughts about railroads, and a new increase in cattle sales. Managers steering the course of Fort Worth's progress looked into the town's mirror of new prosperity and saw reflected there a need for a new financial system.

Since March, 1869, cattle buyers from the North had arrived in Fort Worth calling for herds to buy, and their numbers had been increasing with each spring. A man with energy could gather a herd in a week or two, by riding the periphery of Tarrant and adjoining counties, but it required money to buy cattle now. When selling to buyers, it was necessary to give formal titles of ownership, because cattle gathered on promise of future payment were no longer accepted as ownership, and no buyers invited legal suits. Frontier bartering and friendly credit without interest were gone forever with Texas filling up with newcomers. Business was becoming scientific and with it the problem—where could a man with push and vision get money? It was true that one could borrow money from the exchange office of M. B. Loyd and pay in gold three to five percent interest a month. But the difficulty was that with no security, few could manage the loan. Nevertheless, some cattlemen's need for scientific business had been met during these early years of the cattle drives. For them, proceedings were easy. In Terrell's two-room office, it was a short walk across the hall from Loyd's money market, to the barrister's office to get legal papers.

Wishes for more accessible money for the growing economy became a reality as several newcomers with wealth arrived, ending the town's financial crisis.

With the upsurge of spring, Jeremiah Marklee had come from San Francisco to visit Fort Worth. Born in Canada in 1827, he had been a lead miner in Illinois in 1844; then joined the gold rush in California where he made $15,000 merchandising in a mining camp. He promptly invested his earnings in cattle and a hotel in Sacramento; but both investments had been washed away in the great flood of 1852. Calamity felled him again. While examining a mine for his employer in 1858, it had exploded, injuring his eyesight. By expending his will and all his dollars as an invalid in San Francisco, Marklee had recovered after one year of inaction. Returning to mining, he had discovered the Marklee mine in Amador County in 1864; had mined it profitably until 1868 when he sold it to a London company for $55,000 in gold, and had retired briefly to San Francisco, only to set out in the spring of 1872 on a journey to Texas. Visiting Fort Worth, he had found it to be pulsing with potentialities. Returning to San Francisco he organized his affairs for the Texas venture. His arrival in Fort Worth in the fall offered a subject for public square gossip. There was talk that Marklee, a bachelor of forty-five, was rich—even had brought with him sacks of California gold dust. His capital interested Loyd with his financial foresight. Deciding to challenge the new competition from a branch bank established in Fort Worth in 1872 by a McKinney, Texas, firm of G. Van Winkle and Company, Loyd and Marklee formed the California and Texas Bank of Loyd-Marklee and Company. And Marklee had numerous ways to earn money. Horticulture was one of these. It was said that he imported the first Bermuda grass from Alabama to Fort Worth, selling the seed at $3.50 a bushel and was praised for his action, since it was rated as a hay crop for farmers.

With autumn, came the founders of another institution using the formal title "bank." Thomas A. Tidball from Lexington, Missouri, and J. B. Wilson of Virginia, had come out of a settled country whose frontier years had long since passed. Business astuteness made Tidball and Wilson hasten their plans as they observed the aggressive growth of the town. Wilson provided the money—a few thousand dollars for capital, and Tidball supplied the banking experience. Their bank opened sometime in the winter of 1872. The partnership would continue in operation for about a year when family responsibilities would call Wilson home to Virginia. Tidball remained to plant deep roots in Fort Worth. For by 1874, Major Van Zandt, Colonel Smith, Major Jarvis, and T. Van Zandt purchased Wilson's interest, and in cooperation with Smith, Jarvis and Tidball, each investing $7,500, the bank reorganized under the title Tidball, Van Zandt and Company. Tidball's early life had been one of constant change. Missouri-born, a "storeboy" at fourteen, a bookkeeper in a mercantile house at nineteen, he had gone to war at twenty-three, fighting under General Lee at Gettysburg, Chancellorsville, and at Appomattox. Back in Lexington, Missouri, he sold merchandise for a short time, then became a bookkeeper in a bank in Lexington in 1868. Four years of application had prepared him for operating a bank of his own with keen perception that would benefit Fort Worth, helping it rise to city status.

Cattle barons making Fort Worth headquarters for several months in the spring while their herds passed through Kansas, and visiting speculators with gold in their pockets, had accustomed themselves to the comforts of fine hostelries of large cities and the luxuries of Mississippi steamboats. For such men, whose money had brought fondness for refined living, a new hostelry in Fort Worth would be a wreath of joy. The proprietor, General Joseph Moody Peers from Virginia, would add the ingredient of fashion and discriminating dining to the little city on the make.

General Peers' life had been interwoven with the sumptuous living

of the Tidewater South. His family held original land grants from King
James I. Like most notable newcomers, he was a Confederate veteran.
President Davis had conscripted Peers from his wholesale tobacco house
in Richmond to serve the Confederate government in an administrative
capacity. Before the war his wholesale business had given extensive
credit to foreign and national buyers. After the war the federal government canceled all debts owed to the Confederacy. Facing bankruptcy,
Peers had turned to Kansas City where fire destroyed his investment.
He moved to Fort Smith, Arkansas, living there for a while until the
publicized news of future prospects in the railroad towns of Dallas and
Fort Worth sent him in search of the prophesy.

With the wisdom of a man of forty-eight, Peers founded a sound establishment. He bought the corner of Fifth and Commerce streets, also
half the block from Mr. Dunn whose log house was located nearby. He
erected a two-story frame hotel facing Commerce and along Fifth Street.
On the inside of his lot, Peers constructed four separate houses, the
kitchen, the storehouse, the icehouse insulated with sawdust, and a laundry where each week many Negro women spent an entire day washing
the hotel's linen and the next day, ironing. Impeccably white fresh linen
tablecloths and napkins were among the features which distinguished
the Peers House. The former general directed most of his attention to the
administration of the hotel's kitchen and dining room. He assembled a
group of Negro cooks who, under his supervision, prepared food for gour-
mets. Meals were served in courses, always with wine and without extra
charge, but each guest was limited to one glass. Men were required to
wear their coats at table; but to prevent embarrassment to farmers and
cowmen who came to town without coats, Peers provided a long rack in
the washroom where were hung about twenty coats in sizes for large
or small, fat or thin men. Proceeding to the dining room, gentlemen were
seated around beautifully set tables adorned with large glass bowls, filled
with dates which Peers requested would always come with his order of
Mexican coffee. These dates served as appetizers for his guests waiting
for service. Many ate them for curiosity's sake, as they were a delicacy
in frontier Fort Worth. In quail season, men breakfasted there to eat
that savory bird on toast. Peers' one difficulty in managing his hostelry
was keeping a sufficient number of waitresses. He "advertised in Saint
Louis and eastern newspapers for waitresses" and although they came,
these women did not tarry long. They served with such ingratiating de-
portment that Mr. Peers soon lost them as brides to his customers.

In winter another distinctive feature provided for guests, was having
a warm room to wake up in, as Negro boys earlier had lighted a fire in

the iron stove. For such deluxe service prices at the Peers House quoted in 1877 were:

Transient board, $2.00 per day; board and lodging, $7.00 per week; board without lodging, $5.00 per week.

One man's talent creates life's embellishments; another, its utilitarian needs. Z. E. B. Nash making Fort Worth his home in 1872 would, like Peers, make a marked difference on life in the community. But unlike other remarkable newcomers, he was a Union veteran. Born in New York of a family of craftsmen, Nash had moved with his parents to Minnesota from where he enlisted in the Union Army. When hostilities ended, he was assigned to the army of occupation stationed at New Orleans. Beauty of the landscape, mildness of the climate, and the apparent ease of acquiring the good things of life, determined him to become a Southerner. As soon as he was mustered out of service, he moved his family to New Orleans and began the practice of his trade as a tinsmith. Customers in his shop early in 1872, talked continuously of wealth that could be made in Texas upon completion of the Texas and Pacific Railway, especially in certain towns—one of which often mentioned was Fort Worth. Nash left New Orleans with his family to become one of the fortune seekers. On the corner of present-day Monroe and Tenth streets across from the present city hall, Nash bought a lot which was then a cotton field, and built a home.

On the public square, he opened his tinshop to which housewives brought their worn-out but cherished utensils inherited from grandmother or mother. Four days later, Nash would hand them copper or tin skillets, teakettles and saucepans fashioned according to their favored designs. Farmers, cattlemen, and businessmen liked Nash for his ingenuity in designing to their special needs, water tanks for cattle, cisterns and water tanks for homes, and for his skill in tin-roofing the new plank buildings rising in the boomtown. His roofs, tightly nailed, stayed where they belonged in Texas winds. It is said that eighty-five percent of the roofs of the business houses in Fort Worth in the seventies and eighties were tin, and most of them were the work of Nash. His fame was further enhanced when his skill made obsolete wooden washtubs that shrank and buckled under the Texas sun. Designing numerous tin washtubs, he placed them on display in his shop—the first such tubs to make their appearance in Tarrant County. A few years later, he created another novelty—a tin bathtub, which immediately had extensive sales.

Diversities of natural gifts but the same spirit, motivated the men choosing Fort Worth for their world. Captain B. B. Paddock came to spend his ability. His business would be printing words and ideas. On a horseback journey from Fayette, Mississippi, across Texas, Paddock met in Dallas former governor Throckmorton who had suggested Fort Worth as the town of promise for a young man of twenty-eight, and directed him to call on Major Van Zandt. Arriving in the first week of November, he went directly to the store of the major, introduced himself, and declared his intention of making his home in Fort Worth. Van Zandt, given to wishful hoping that each newcomer would bring a special profession or craft, straightway asked, "What is your occupation?"

"Sir, I should like to run a newspaper," Paddock replied. Van Zandt's genius for fathoming the value of a man in the turn of a phrase then said, "Well, we have one here if you will operate it."

Captain Paddock became editor and W. H. Graves publisher of the *Fort Worth Democrat* with the masthead motto, "Let the chips fall where they may." Paddock would make the paper at home and in many states in the nation, a broadcaster dramatically describing the productive wealth of Tarrant farms, the fast moving progress of the town, and the magnetic activities of business leaders. His editorials would excel the alluring accounts in the best real estate brochures about the "New West" published in the United States for immigrants. Paddock's paper would be a hammer striking heavy blows in the construction of the town by pounding into readers' minds the promising future it held for men. His unbounded admiration for the little village and surrounding countryside did not arise from limited horizons and few experiences. Editorials of praise from this Confederate veteran, Yankee-born, came from depths of knowledge, drudgery, and war-toughening experiences.

Paddock had moved with his family from Ohio, his birthplace, to Wisconsin Territory where his mother had died when he was only seven. Left entirely to his own devices, he began his voyages through the wilderness, had spent one year with Indians without seeing a white man, and had worked in lumber camps and fur trading posts. Before his fourteenth birthday, he had traveled through all the western territories as far west as Washington Territory and as far north as Hudson Bay. From books he had come to admire the idyllic life of Southern planters.

When the war came, believing that the culture and economy of such a society should be preserved, he had traveled to the South and joined the Confederate Army as a private. In 1862, at the age of eighteen, he was promoted to the rank of captain. Throughout the war he had fought in Wirt Adams' cavalry. The battles of Shiloh, Corinth, and Vicksburg were only a few in the holocaust. But battles had not divested him of daring, which he displayed when commanding thirteen men. He boarded a Union iron-clad (boat) out of coal which had run up the Yazoo River in Mississippi. He captured the boat and crew of 268 men, burned the vessel after appropriating its twelve Napoleon guns and about 1,000 small arms. Such a bold and reckless deed had brought him many assignments in the Secret Service and Signal Corps. After the news of Appomattox had filtered through to his camp near Tuscaloosa, Alabama, he had ridden to Fayette, Jefferson County, Missouri, to adjust himself to civilian life. Years later, George Washington Cable was to write a novel, *The Cavalier*, based on the war record of Paddock.

In the plantation town of Fayette, Paddock had studied law, had been admitted to the bar of Mississippi, and had married a daughter of a Mississippi planter. As a lawyer, Paddock had been successful in that state, but the humdrum of court and a country already made, had evoked his creative spirit to seek a frontier. In October, leaving his family, the former cavalry officer on a fine mount had traveled to Texas. On November 4, 1872, he had written his wife from Dallas:

> Dallas has about 4,000 inhabitants instead of 8,000 as reported. They claim 6,000 but they are not here. There appears to be a large amount of business done here, as far as I can judge in walking around two or three hours.
>
> Fort Worth is spoken of as the coming place—a man from there says it is quite a place now and destined to be a city. It is rough as anything you can think of. . . . It is going to be a fine country. It has rich soil and the people here all work for themselves.

Legend recounts that Paddock entering Fort Worth, did not see its frontier shabbiness—only the city to be. As all newcomers did, he walked across the square to the north edge of the bluff to see the tree-lined river, the panorama of the Trinity Valley. He foreglimpsed the coming of the railroad, magically transforming the village into a city. Thereupon he coined the phrase "Fort Worth, the Queen City of the Prairies," and "Fort Worth, the City of Beautiful Heights." These catchy figures of speech were to become Fort Worth's cognomens in the prosperous 1880s.

November's news was high voltage. Readers of the *Democrat* were made aware of the importance of the month—the time of the presidential, congressional, and state elections. It was the time of political liberation.

In October, disfranchised Fort Towners redeemed from political exile by the repeal of the "iron-clad oath" in 1871 and the passage of the Amnesty Act in 1872, hastened to comply in legal action for the coming election by taking an oath of allegiance to the Union. They had registered with Judge Barkley, Lorentz, and Rucker, the Negro member.

So old times came again to Fort Town's public square on November's election day. Laughter, wagers, and threats resounded around the hitching rails all about the square.

"The time has come to uproot them radicals," became the greeting of the day; and a glib politico who always sought Biblical guidance allegedly gave import of the event to unimaginative voters by remarking, "Didn't the Bible say, 'There's a time to plant, a time to pluck up, and a time to cast away'? Wal! the time has come to cast away them carpetbaggers!"

President Grant was running for reelection on the Republican ticket. Horace Greely, editor of the *New York Sun*, was the Democratic nominee for president, as well as the choice of the liberal Republicans. The majority of Fort Towners had decided upon Greely.

In a store on the square, they had been following the campaign in two newspapers, soiled from many readings: the *New York Sun* ("Downright good readin'," said one pioneer, "because Greely never lost an opportunity to roast Grant,"); and Brick Pomeroy's *Democrat* published at La Crosse, Wisconsin, which blasted the "bloated bond-holders" to whom the federal government paid the interest on the bonds in gold, while the common man could not obtain specie. There was plenty in America for everyone if it were not for the "bloated bond-holders," Pomeroy told his readers, and most Democrats believed him.

Therefore, with a desire for vengeance, Fort Worth males went to the polls. Passing through the file of Negro policemen, they voted with a stern calm born of their knowledge that again possessing the ballot and their inalienable right to hold office, they were once more masters of their own political fate.

C. B. Mitchell, who was one of the Fort Worth voters relates:

When we went to vote we had to pass between a row of Negro soldiers at the old stone courthouse, and they all glared at us. We voted them out that time. Davis was governor.

Dallas citizens also record that their election board had Negro members, and that they filed between Negro soldiers to vote.

At the ballot boxes, Tarrant County males thrashed the Republicans. Only 114 Republican votes were cast out of 1,700 votes registered in the county. Tarrant men elected Democrats to Congress, Democrats to the legislature, and voted to make Austin the permanent capital of Texas. Major Van Zandt was elected to represent Fort Worth in the House of

Representatives of the Thirteenth Legislature. Governor Davis remained in office, since the Constitution of 1869 provided a four-year term.

When returns of the November election for president of the United States were published, they revealed the ire of Texans; also the fact that the Democratic "solid South" was taking form. Although Grant was elected, Greely outran Grant in Texas by 20,000 votes—a ratio pleasing to Fort Worthians, as it somewhat soothed their anger aroused by the reality of another four years of President Grant in the White House.

Disappointment in politics, however, was not too damaging to their spirits, as economic progress was so evident in Fort Worth that a visiting editor felt compelled to write of its future prospects. The editor of the Lexington, Virginia, *Gazette* wrote in an editorial reprinted in the Kentucky *Tri-Weekly Gazette*, December 30, 1872:

> Fort Worth is a shabby village on a small river not over ankle deep . . . the country is sparsely settled, dwellings are five miles apart. But in two years it will be twice the size of Lexington. Fort Worth has a population of 2,000 inhabitants. It is having an unrivalled growth and ere long will surpass Richmond, Virginia in population and wealth.

"God makes the country, but man makes the town," were the words of Captain Paddock to be emblazoned in his newspaper early in 1873. And that was what had been happening in Fort Worth and Tarrant County since the mid-1840s. Frontiersmen had provided a mold in thought and had committed their ways to their desire. Now the power of their minds and spirit had given them the desire of their hearts. Standing on the threshold of a new era beginning in 1873, their thoughts in action would continue to power their village so that it would surge ever forward and upward even through the paralyzing "Panic of 1873." Their "little metropolis," as they lovingly saluted it, would through the outpouring of their creative energy become the "Queen City of the Prairies," the "City of Beautiful Heights." But this is another part of the drama of Fort Worth's history to be written by another author.

Epilogue

EVENTS molding affairs of the nation had reflected their influence over everyday existence in Fort Worth from 1853 to 1872. To these national currents Fort Worth men had wisely reacted. Through each national problem, they had carried their town, which held the total of their hope, to a new growth through overcoming. By their efforts the abandoned fort had been transformed into "a little metropolis." Some military posts in the "new West" were to become skeletons of yesterday. Not so with Fort Worth. It is now anchored on the prairies, an intense reality, formed by pioneer's belief in toil through tribulations.

A good town in a good land it was, even though an unfriendly Texas newspaper once described it as a "wicked, thriving, pushing little village." It had been a pushing village since men moved into the deserted quarters of the fort in 1853, and never would it cease to press forward.

In 1860, Fort Worth by advancing, was finally and legally made the county seat of Tarrant County. In 1866, through hospitality extended with unusual hearty vigor by its villagers, Fort Worth, not Dallas, had become the chief Trinity crossing on the McCoy-Chisholm Trail to Kansas. By 1872, the gates of fortune had been opened. Men were once again their own political masters. The town was burgeoning with activity. From the first days of spring until late summer, cattle was the heartbeat. Northern cattle buyers with ready cash, gathered in Fort Worth. Drovers with gold made it headquarters, while thousands of cattle from sunrise until late afternoon passed through in continuous procession. Herd bosses bought supplies in well-stocked stores for a drive of thirty or more days. Saddleries and bathhouses were appearing to serve for the welfare of cowmen. Keno parlors and saloons were rising to entice thirsty cowboys, which would give Fort Worth the appellation of "a wicked village."

Wagonyards were opening for immigrants. A transcontinental railroad was building toward the town. Businessmen, laborers and speculators were hurrying to get on the ground floor of the boom before the railroad arrived.

All this explosive expansion clamped the pattern of eternal progression upon Fort Worth. A pattern designed and nurtured by perceptive men whose energy powered in trials would ever continue, even in future distress, to steadfastly push the "little metropolis" into the splendor of "The Queen City of the Prairies."

Bibliography

Interviews, 1935–1971.

Calvert, Lucy Burton. Accounts of her father Noel Burton, Captain E. M.
  Daggett and Colonel M. T. Johnson, and his sons.
Chapman, Elizabeth Frances Terry. Daughter of Judge Terry supplied his-
  toric information of Reconstruction in Fort Worth and the events of the
  1870s.
Farmer, Sue. A sketch of the life of Press Farmer, as related by this great-
  great-granddaughter. Original materials supplied by Dorothy Burgess.
Isbell, Martha Elizabeth Ventioner. Accounts of the life of her father, Jim
  Ventioner, and of the daily life and Indian defense in the White Settle-
  ment in the 1850s and 1860s.
Isbell, Melvin. Information concerning conditions during the Civil War and
  the Reconstruction related in interviews with this son of Paul Isbell.
Keller, Mrs. E. H. Accounts of the life of her father, Captain Charles Turner,
  and events in Fort Worth from 1850 to 1870.
Lovejoy, Joe Barnard, Jr. Accounts from original material concerning his
  great-grandfather, Randolph Clark, and his great-great-uncle, Addison
  Clark.
Marshall, Mrs. Bert. An account of the "Peers House" (or Virginia Hotel),
  and early events in Fort Worth as related by the daughter of General
  J. M. Peers.
Meacham, W. A. An account of the activities of his grandfather during the
  Civil War in Tarrant County.

Minton, Mrs. Joseph J. Accounts of Julian Feild and William T. Ferguson as
    related from original material by their great-granddaughter, and a sketch
    of the life of Dr. Julian Theodore Feild, her grandfather.
Nash, Charles E. A sketch of the life of Z. E. B. Nash as related by his son.
Parker, Flora Arnold. Granddaughter of Major Ripley A. Arnold related
    human interest events about her grandfather and life at the military post.
Peak, Olive. Events occurring in the daily life of Fort Worthians during the
    1850s and 1860s related by the daughter of Dr. Carroll M. Peak in many
    interviews.
Pitner, Mrs. Guy R. Events concerning the life of Captain B. B. Paddock as
    related by this daughter from original manuscripts.
Rudmore, Mrs. Harry L. Events concerning the life of Professor Oscar J.
    Lawrence, as related by this daughter.
Thompson, Willis. Accounts regarding War Department photostats of the
    military record of his great-grandfather, Major Ripley A. Arnold.
Van Zandt, Sidney, and Sidney, Jr. Accounts of the life of Major K. M. Van
    Zandt as related by his son and grandson from original materials.

Manuscripts, Letters, Scrapbooks.

Dallas. Dallas Museum of History. Dr. Carroll M. Peak Papers. (Particular-
    ly for a political circular, "Bill to Permanently Locate the Seat of Justice
    in Tarrant County.")
Fort Worth. Library of Southwestern Baptist Theological Seminary. Record
    Book of the Lonesome Dove Baptist Church, Cross Timbers.
————. Fort Worth Public Library. Mary Daggett Lake Collection. Autobio-
    graphical sketches from the first pioneers, documents, deeds, photographs,
    miscellaneous manuscripts, newspaper clippings, scrapbooks.
————. Mrs. Chalmers W. Hutchison Collection. Letters. Captain B. B. Pad-
    dock to his wife, October through November, 1872.
————. Catherine Terrell McCartney Collection. Letters. Captain Joseph C.
    Terrell to his mother, Mrs. Susan Penn, 21 August 1861 to 2 February
    1871.
————. Jesse Boaz Gumm Collection. Scrapbooks containing notes, pam-
    phlets, excerpts from literary works, and clippings of historic events oc-
    curring in Fort Worth and Dallas from 1850 to 1870.
————. Lillian Randall Haltom Collection. Original materials and scrap-
    books of her grandmother, Mrs. C. J. Gambrell, whose husband owned a
    store in Fort Worth in 1869.
————. Rollins, Ruby Ola. Records of Pioneer Rest Cemetery Association.

Government Records.

U.S. War Department. Office of Adjutant General. Old Wars Division, Na-
    tional Archives, Washington, D.C.:
    Arnold, Brevet Major Ripley A. Letters to Major General Roger Jones,
        Adjutant General. June 15, July 30, 1849.
    Cooper, Col. Samuel. Report of an inspection of the 8th Military Dis-
        trict, 1851.

Johnson, Col. Middleton Tate. Service record of.
  Orders No. 13, 14 February 1849; No. 70, 17 October 1849; No. 50, 20
  August 1853. 8th Military District.
Starr, Lieut. Samuel. Report of buildings of Fort Worth on May 22,
  1851.
Whiting, Lieut. W. H. C. Report of tour of inspection, 1849–1851.

Typescripts, Microfilm.

Goerte, Anne Lenore. "Some Phases of the Development of the Fort Worth,
  Texas School System." Master's thesis, University of Colorado, 1934. Type-
  script, Fort Worth Public Library.
Texas Writers Project. "Research Data, Fort Worth and Tarrant County,
  1936–1941." 74 volumes. Typescript, Fort Worth Public Library.
Tidwell, Donovan Duncan. "A History of the West Fork Baptist Associa-
  tion." Ph.D. dissertation, Southwestern Baptist Theological Seminary,
  1940. Southwestern Baptist Theological Seminary Library.
U.S. Department of Commerce. Bureau of the Census. *Federal Population
  Schedule, Texas: Tarrant County, 1850.* Microfilm. Fort Worth Public
  Library.
————. *Tarrant County, 1860.* Microfilm. Fort Worth Public Library.
Wallace, Edward S. "General William Jenkins Worth, the American
  Murat." Ph.D. dissertation, Boston University, 1948. Typescript, Fort
  Worth Public Library.

Magazine Articles.

Bridges, C. A. "Knights of the Golden Circle, a Filibustering Fantasy."
  Southwestern Historical Quarterly, XLIV (January 1941): 287–302.
Crane, R. C. "Some Aspects of the History of West and Northwest Texas
  Since 1845." *Southwestern Historical Quarterly,* XXVI (July 1922):
  30–43.
Crimmins, M. L. "Report of Inspection of 8th Military Department Made by
  Bvt. Lt. Col. W. G. Freeman, Asst. Adjt. General, Pursuant to Instructions
  from Headquarters of Army, April 22, 1853." *Southwestern Historical
  Quarterly,* LIII (April 1950): 459–462.
————. "Fort Worth Was An Army Post." *Frontier Times,* XVI (January
  1939): 139–141.
Cummings, C. C. "Fort Worth's First Folks." *Bohemian,* I (November 1899):
  55–56.
————. "Trinity River—Origin of the Name." *Bohemian,* I (Easter Number
  1900): 81–82.
Elliott, Claude. "The Freedmen's Bureau in Texas." *Southwestern Historical
  Quarterly,* LVI (July 1952): 1–24.
Gage, Larry Jay. "The City of Austin on the Eve of the Civil War." *South-
  western Historical Quarterly,* LXIII (January 1960): 428–438.
Gard, Wayne. "Retracing the Chisholm Trail." *Southwestern Historical
  Quarterly,* LX (July 1946): 53–68.
Gibbens, V. E. "Lawrie's Trip to Northwest Texas, 1854–1855." *Southwest-*

ern Historical Quarterly, XLVIII (October 1944): 238–253.

Hall, Martin Hardwick. "The Formation of Sibley's Brigade and the March to New Mexico." *Southwestern Historical Quarterly*, LXI (January 1958): 383–405.

Haltom, Sallie. "My Life in Tarrant County and Other Parts of Texas." *Southwestern Historical Quarterly*, LX (July 1956): 100–105.

Maher, Edward R., Jr. "Sam Houston and Secession." *Southwestern Historical Quarterly*, LV (April 1952): 448–458.

Muckleroy, Anna. "The Indian Policy of the Republic of Texas." *Southwestern Historical Quarterly*, XXV (April 1922): 229–260; XXVI (July 1922): 1–29; (October 1922): 128–148; (January 1923): 184–206.

Neighbours, Kenneth F. "The Report of the Expedition of Major Robert S. Neighbors to El Paso in 1849." *Southwestern Historical Quarterly*, LX (April 1957): 527–532.

Norvell, James R. "The Reconstruction Courts of Texas, 1867–1873." *Southwestern Historical Quarterly*, LXII (October 1958): 141–163.

Richardson, Rupert N. "The Death of Nocona and Recovery of Cynthia Ann Parker." *Southwestern Historical Quarterly*, XLVI (July 1942): 15–21.

Singletary, Otis A. "The Texas Military During Reconstruction." *Southwestern Historical Quarterly*, LX (July 1956): 23–35.

Strickland, Rex Wallace. "History of Fannin County, 1836–1843." *Southwestern Historical Quarterly*, XXXIII (April 1930): 262–298; XXXIV (July 1930): 38–68.

Wallace, Edward S. "General William Jenkins Worth and Texas." *Southwestern Historical Quarterly*, LIV (October 1950): 159–168.

Webb, Walter Prescott. "The Last Treaty of the Republic of Texas." *Southwestern Historical Quarterly*, XXV (January 1922): 151–173.

Weems, Eddie. "Notes on Frontier Editors and Newspapers." *Southwestern Historical Quarterly*, LX (October 1956): 282–285.

White, William M. "The Texas Slave Insurrection of 1860." *Southwestern Historical Quarterly*, LII (January 1949): 259–285.

Williams, J. W. "Military Roads of the 1850s in Central West Texas." *West Texas Historical Year Book for 1942*, XVII (October 1942): 77–91.

————. "The Butterfield Overland Mail Road Across Texas." *Southwestern Historical Quarterly*, LXI (July 1957): 1–19.

————. "The National Road of the Republic of Texas." *Southwestern Historical Quarterly*, XLVII (January 1944): 208–224.

Winkler, E. W. "The Seat of Government of Texas." *Quarterly of the Texas State Historical Association*, X (October 1906): 140–171; (January 1907): 185–245.

Wooster, Ralph A. "An Analysis of the Membership of the Texas Secession Convention" (with a summary of data taken from the manuscript returns of Schedules 1, 2, and 4 of the U.S. Census of 1860). *Southwestern Historical Quarterly*, LXII (January 1959): 322–335.

Newspaper Articles.

Adair, W. S. "Once Plenty of Water in Trinity River." *Dallas News*, 25 May 1924.

————. "Texas Winter of 1866–1867, Mild All the Way." *Dallas News*, 24 February 1929.

"Baily Letter Genuine." *Dallas Herald*, 10 October 1860.

"Bird Fort Settlement." *Dallas Morning News*, 26 January 1902.

"Dallas Had Great Fire Back in 1860." *Dallas News*, 14 July 1929.

De Lorenzi, John. "Worth Dim Figure in His Home Town." *Fort Worth Star-Telegram*, 30 October 1949. Centennial Edition.

"Early Days in Fort Worth." *Dallas Herald*, 2 June 1866.

Elser, Max. "Looking Backward." *Fort Worth Record*, 28 September 1914.

"From Dallas via Birdville and Weatherford to Belknap, Young County." *Houston Tri-Weekly Telegraph*, 18 July 1856.

Kirch, Sam. "Slayer of Fort Worth Founder Becomes Prominent Citizen, State Official." *Fort Worth Star-Telegram*, 30 October 1949. Centennial Edition.

"Major General Worth Took Part in Three Campaigns." *Hudson* (New York) *Daily Star*. 18 December 1937.

"Major Van Zandt Helped Organize the First Church Here in 1870." *Fort Worth Star-Telegram*, 19 March 1930.

"Removal of County Seat from Birdville Caused Bitterness that Lasted a Generation." *Fort Worth Star-Telegram*, 15 December 1912.

"The Reunion." *Fort Worth Daily Gazette*, 6 September 1889.

Books.

Acheson, Sam. *35,000 Days in Texas*. New York: MacMillan Co., 1938.

Allen, William. *Captain John B. Denton*. Chicago: R. R. Donnelley and Sons Co., 1905.

Bailey, Thomas A. *The American Pageant: A History of the Republic*. 3d ed. Boston: D. C. Heath & Co., 1966.

Baillio, F. B. *History of the Texas Press Association: From its Organization in Houston in 1880 to its Annual Convention in San Antonio in 1913: To Which is also added A History of the Early Newspapers of Texas*, by the late Judge A. B. Norton. Dallas: Southwestern Printing Co., 1916.

Bolton, Herbert Eugene. *Athanase de Mézières and the Louisiana-Texas Frontier, 1768–1780*. 2 vols. Cleveland: Arthur H. Clark Co., 1914.

————. *Texas in the Middle Eighteenth Century*. Vol. 3. Berkeley: University of California Publications in History, 1915.

Brown, John Henry. *A History of Texas, 1685–1892*. St. Louis: L. E. Daniell, 1892.

————. *Indian Wars and Pioneers of Texas*. Austin: L. E. Daniell, 1890.

Clark, Ira G. *Then Came the Railroads*. Norman: University of Oklahoma Press, 1958.

Clark, Joseph L., and Garrett, Julia Kathryn. *A History of Texas: Land of Promise*. Rev. ed. Boston: D. C. Heath & Co., 1945.

Clark, Randolph. *Reminiscences*. Wichita Falls: Lee Clark, 1919.

Conkling, Roscoe P., and Conkling, Margaret. *The Butterfield Overland Mail, 1857–1869*. Glendale: Arthur H. Clark Co., 1947.

Considérant, Victor Prosper. *European Colonization in Texas: An Address to the American People*. New York: Baker, Godwin & Co., 1855.

————. *The Great West: A New Social and Industrial Life in Its Fertile Regions.* New York: DeWitt & Davenport, 1854.

Cox, James. *Historical and Biographical Record of the Cattle Industry and the Cattlemen of Texas.* St. Louis: Woodward and Tiernon Printing Co., 1895.

Crane, William Corey. *Life and Select Literary Remains of Sam Houston.* Philadelphia: J. B. Lippincott & Co., 1884.

de Cordova, J. *Texas: Her Resources and Her Public Men.* Philadelphia: E. Crozet, 1858.

de Shields, James T. *Border Wars of Texas.* Tioga, Texas: Herald Co., 1912.

————. *Cynthia Ann Parker: The Story of Her Capture.* St. Louis: Charles B. Woodward, 1886.

Dobie, J. Frank. *The Longhorns.* Boston: Little, Brown & Co., 1941.

du Bois, William Edward. *Black Reconstruction.* New York: Harcourt, Brace & Co., 1935.

Eby, Frederick, comp. *Education in Texas Source Materials.* Austin: University of Texas Bulletin No. 1824, April 25, 1918. Education Series No. 2. Austin: University of Texas [1919?].

Faulkner, Harold U. *American Political and Social History.* New York: Appleton-Century-Crofts, 1952.

Gammel, H. P. N. *The Laws of the Republic of Texas.* 10 vols. Austin: Gammels Bookstore, 1898.

Garrison, George P., ed. *Diplomatic Correspondence of the Republic of Texas.* Vol. 2. Washington: Annual Report of the American Historical Association, 1908.

Gulick, Charles Adams and Elliot, Katherine, eds. *Mirabeau Bonaparte Lamar.* 6 vols. Austin: A. C. Baldwin & Sons, 1921.

Hackett, Charles W., ed. and trans. *Pichardo's Treatise on the Limits of Louisiana and Texas.* 3 vols. Austin: University of Texas Press, 1931–1941.

Hall, Colby D. *Texas Disciples.* Fort Worth: Texas Christian University Press, 1953.

————. *History of the Texas Christian University.* Fort Worth: Texas Christian University Press, 1947.

Haney, J. H. *A Congressional History of Railroads in the U. S.* Madison: Democrat Printing Co., 1910.

Henderson, Harry McCorry. *Texas in the Confederacy.* San Antonio: Naylor Co., 1955.

History of Texas: Together with a Biographical History of Tarrant and Parker Counties. Chicago: Lewis Publishing Co., 1895.

Hodge, F. W., ed. *Handbook of American Indians North of Mexico.* 2 vols. Washington, D.C.: Government Printing Office, 1910.

Holden, William Curry. *Alkali Trails.* Dallas: Southwest Press, 1930.

Hunter, J. Marvin, comp. and ed. *The Trail Drivers of Texas.* 2 vols. Nashville: Cokesbury Press, 1925.

Jackson, George. *Sixty Years in Texas.* Dallas: Wilkinson Printing Co., 1908.

Kittrell, Norman G. *Governors Who Have Been and Other Public Men of Texas.* Houston: Dealy-Adey-Elgin Co., 1921.

Lindsly, Phillip. *A History of Greater Dallas and Vicinity.* 2 vols. Chicago: Lewis Publishing Co., 1909.

Maillard, Doran N. *The History of the Republic of Texas.* London: Smith, Elder and Co., 1842.

McConnell, Joseph Carroll. *The West Texas Frontier.* Jacksboro: Gazette Print Co., 1933.

McCoy, Joseph G. *Historic Sketches of the Cattle Trade of the West and Southwest.* Kansas City: Ramsey, Milleta and Hudson, 1874.

Moncrieff, A. R. Hope, ed. *Black's Guide to London and Its Environs.* 16th ed. London: Adams and Charles Black, 1911.

Morfi, Fray Juan Agustin. *History of Texas, 1673–1779.* Translated and edited by Carlos E. Castañeda. Vol. 6. Albuquerque: Quivira Society Publications, 1935.

Myers, Sandra L., ed. *Force Without Fanfare: The Autobiography of K. M. Van Zandt.* Fort Worth: Texas Christian University Press, 1968.

Norton, A. B. "A History of the Early Newspapers of Texas." In Baillio, *History of the Texas Press Association.* Dallas: Southwestern Printing Co., 1916.

Nunn, William C. *Escape from Reconstruction.* Fort Worth: Leo Potishman Foundation, 1956.

Paddock, B. B. *A Twentieth Century History and Biographical Record of North and West Texas.* 2 vols. Chicago: Lewis Publishing Co., 1906.

Peak, Howard. *The Story of Old Fort Worth.* San Antonio: Naylor Co., 1936.

Pray, R. F. *Battle of Sabine Pass.* San Antonio: Naylor Co., 1947.

Quaife, Milo Milton, ed. *The Border and the Buffalo.* Chicago: Lakeside Press, 1938.

Ramsdell, Charles William. *Reconstruction in Texas.* New York: Green and Co., 1910.

Rankin, Melinda. *Texas in 1850.* Boston: Damrell and Moore, 1850.

Reagan, John H. *Memoirs.* New York: Neale Publishing Co., 1906.

Reed, S. L. *A History of the Texas Railroads.* Houston: St. Clair Publishing Co., 1941.

Richardson, Rupert Norval. *Texas, the Lone Star State.* New York: Prentice Hall, 1943.

Spaight, A. E. *Resources, Soil, and Climate of Texas.* Galveston: A. H. Belo and Co., 1882.

Speer, William S., ed. *The Encyclopaedia of the New West.* Marshall: United States Biographical Publishing Co., 1881.

Terrell, Alexander W. *From Texas to Mexico and the Court of Maximilian in 1865.* Dallas: Book Club of Texas, 1933.

Terrell, J. C. *Reminiscences of the Early Days of Fort Worth.* Fort Worth: Fort Worth Texas Printing Co., 1906.

Texas Almanac (1860, 1864–1869) Galveston: Ward D. Richardson & Co., 1856–1871.

Texas Almanac (1945–1946). Dallas: A. H. Belo & Co., 1904–1949.

Texas and Pacific Railway. *From Ox-Teams to Eagles, a History of the Texas and Pacific Railway.* [n.p., n.d.]

Thrall, Homer S. *Pictorial History of Texas.* St. Louis: N. D. Thompson and Co., 1879.

U. S. Congress. *Annals of the Congress of the United States.* 31st Cong., 2d. Sess.; 1849–1883. Washington, D.C.: Government Printing Office.

Wallace, Ernest, ed. *Documents of Texas History*. Austin: Steck Co., 1960, 1963.

Webb, Walter Prescott. *The Great Plains*. Boston: Ginn and Co., 1931.

Wilbarger, J. W. *Indian Depredations in Texas*. Austin: Hutchings Printing House, 1890.

Williams, Amelia W., and Barker, Eugene C., eds. *The Writings of Sam Houston*. 8 vols. Austin: University of Texas Press, 1938–1943.

Winkler, E. W., ed. *Secret Journals of the Senate, Republic of Texas, 1836–1845*. Austin: Austin Printing Co., 1911.

Wooten, Dudley G. *A Comprehensive History, 1685–1897*. 2 vols. Dallas: William G. Scarff, 1898.

Wortham, Louis J. *A History of Texas*. 5 vols. Fort Worth: Wortham-Molyneaux Co., 1924.

Appendix

Appendix A

HEADRIGHTS IN TARRANT COUNTY

A list of early settlers who preempted land in Tarrant County will prove a valuable reference in tracing families of the present and future generations. Thomas William Ward was appointed commissioner to issue headright certificates to settlers, and the following were listed within the limits of Tarrant County:

Cornelius Connolly, 640 acres
Isaac Schoonover, 320 acres
J. W. Conner, 640 acres
Pete Schoonover, 320 acres
J. S. Ellis, 320 acres
W. D. Conner, 320 acres
J. P. Lusk, 320 acres
Thomas White, 320 acres
A. B. Conner, 320 acres
L. J. Edwards, 640 acres
A. Gaouhenaut, 320 acres
T. McCann, 320 acres
W. H. Hudson, 320 acres

R. Crowley, 320 acres
Isham Crowley, 320 acres
John Baugh, 320 acres
Michael Baugh, 320 acres
A. A. Robinson (three),
   160, 160, and 320 acres
Felix Mulligan, 640 acres
William J. Little, 320 acres
John Little, 320 acres
S. K. Smith, 320 acres
Isaac Thomas, 640 acres
Edward Little, 640 acres
John Bursey, 320 acres

S. Gilmore, 640 acres
J. B. York, 640 acres
Joel Walker, 640 acres
L. J. Tinsley, 640 acres
Sanders Elliott, 640 acres
John Akers, 320 acres
T. Akers, 640 acres
S. Akers, 320 acres
W. Morris, 640 acres
W. C. Trimble, 640 acres
H. Bennett, 640 acres
S. Pendleton, 320 acres
A. S. Trimble, 640 acres
J. W. Elliston, 640 acres
M. Elliston, 640 acres
W. Scruggs, 320 acres
H. F. Sargent, 640 acres
Mahulda Lynch (widow), 640 acres
A. G. Walker, 640 acres
S. Hayworth, 640 acres
W. A. Trimble, 320 acres
S. Sanger, 320 acres
John Condra, 640 acres
F. S. Carter, 320 acres
L. C. Walker, 640 acres
Parmela Allen (widow), 640 acres
R. F. Allen, 640 acres
R. Baker, 640 acres
J. A. Dunham, 640 acres
A. Barnes, 640 acres
Charles Medlin (part in Denton), 640 acres
H. Medlin, 640 acres
W. W. Hall, 640 acres
T. Mahon, 640 acres
Francis Thrope, 640 acres
A. Foster, 640 acres
D. Tannahill, 640 acres
James Cate, 640 acres
Charles Baker, 640 acres
H. Scruggs, 640 acres
William Bradford, 640 acres
V. J. Hutton, 640 acres
J. J. Goodwin, 640 acres
J. B. Barnett, 320 acres
George Burgoon, 320 acres
J. P. Alford, 640 acres
A. J. Huitt, 320 acres
J. J. Winfield, 640 acres

W. R. Loving, 640 acres
Ruth Brown (widow), 640 acres
Larkin Barnes, 640 acres
W. Underwood, 640 acres
J. J. Goodwin, 320 acres
M. K. Selvidge, 320 acres
J. R. Parker, 320 acres
John Brown, 640 acres
M. Goodwin, 640 acres
J. R. Baugh, 320 acres
David Bradshaw, 640 acres
M. Goodwin, 320 acres
William O'Neil, 640 acres
Mahulda Harris, 640 acres
J. Blackwell, 640 acres
H. Blackwell (son), 320 acres
Soloman Davis, 640 acres
C. C. Carter, 320 acres
L. Finger, 640 acres
J. Huitt, 640 acres
O. Medlin, 640 acres
J. Stephens, 640 acres
J. M. Stephens, 640 acres
E. M. Daggett, 640 acres
J. M. Brinson, 640 acres
J. Hyden, 640 acres
J. Degman, 320 acres
E. L. Harris, 320 acres
Hiram Blackwell, 640 acres
Anderson Newton (f), 640 acres
W. Mack, 640 acres
J. W. Lane, 640 acres
C. T. Lane, 320 acres
S. S. Lane, 320 acres
A. J. Stephenson, 320 acres
A. Stephens, 320 acres
J. L. Newton, 320 acres
H. G. Lynch, 320 acres
E. S. Terrell, 320 acres
D. C. Manning, 320 acres
Samuel Needham, 640 acres
Daniel Bracroft, 640 acres
I. Neace, 640 acres
Jesse Gallen, 640 acres
Jesse Gibson, 640 acres
T. M. Hood, 640 acres
J. A. Freeman, 640 acres
R. Eads, 320 acres
S. Freeman, 320 acres

Thomas Easten, 640 acres
A. F. Leonard, 640 acres

M. Hood, 320 acres

Appendix B

TARRANT COUNTY CITIZENS SUBJECT TO JURY DUTY—1855

Anderson, Wm.
Anderson, M. H.
Allen, J. G.
Allen, G. W.
Andrews, T. J.
Ayers, J. H.
Andrews, B. F.
Akers, John
Akers, Thos.
Allen, J. K.
Barnes, W. D.
Barnes, Larkin
Barnes, Anderson
Brown, D. V.
Boon, John
Booth, Ben
Bursey, John
Bosson, Wm.
Burgoon, Chas.
Brinson, M. J.
Bratton, Richard
Beall, W. M.
Byrd, J. A.
Burford, Wm.
Baker, Chas.
Bosmen, J. C.
Baker, Chas.
Burns, W. P.
Bennett, Hamilton
Brooks, Malone
Bates, E. A.
Cummings, J. M.
Crowley, B. F.
Crowley, Richard
Callaway, J. W.
Callaway, R. H.
Crow, G. W.
Crouch, L.
Cate, James
Curry, T.

Crocker, Thos.
Clark, J. W.
Chivers, A. M.
Chivers, Larkin
Clay, L. A.
Cohens, Lewis
Cromwell, W. C.
Conner, J. W.
Coleman, W. M.
Cross, Robt.
Cross, A. H.
Collins, W. W. R.
Conley, C.
Conner, W. D.
Chitwood, J. O.
Condra, John
Cotrell, Simon
Conn, Israel
Clifton, Lewis
Cloud, John
Clanton, W.
Drew, Smith
Dalton, Thos.
Dalton, Pat
Doss, Jesse
Dosier, Wm.
Duncan, Thos.
Dobkins, Alex
Dean, Silas
Daggett, H. C.
Davis, Sol
Danniels, J. M.
Durrett, J. M.
Daggett, E. M.
Daggett, C. B.
Brizentine, Wm.
Evans, J. M.
Evans, J. S.
Easter, Thos.
Elliott, R. M.

Elliott, Sanders
Elliott, J. W.
Eddy, Nath
Edwards, L. J.
Earles, Israel
Estes, Silas
Elliston, J. W.
Elliston, Mark
Evans, Wm.
Evans, James
Edwards, Sid
Feilds, Julien
Finger, Lewis
French, B. J. W.
Ferris, Walter
Farmer, G. P.
Farmer, J. B.
Farmer, D. V.
Freeman, A.
Freshour, John
Foster, J. B.
Foster, Harvey
Gilmore, Seburn
Grimsley, James
Giddens, W. M.
Godwin, M.
Goodwin, J. M.
Gibson, John
Gray, Thos. A.
Granbury, Hi
Gibson, Garrett
Hurst, J. A.
Holmes, T. P.
Harrison, T. J.
Harrison, John
Hazelwood, Wm.
Hazelwood, A.
Holland, W. J.
Hicks, Wm.
Howerton, F. M.
Holland, J. N.
Hood, J. A.
Harris, A. S.
Hughes, J. H.
Hutton, V. W.
Hall, A.
Harris, Abe
Howard, Jas.
Howerton, J. B.

Harrison, Jonas
Hendricks, G. B.
Hendricks, Green
Hurst, H.
Farrar, John
Hope, G. W.
Hudges, E. N.
Hope, G. W.
Harper, John
Inman, Jack
Johnson, M. T.
Johnson, J. R.
Jones, J. C.
Jasper, T.
Jones, J. F.
Johnson, J. B.
Jasper, J. H.
Jones, L. W.
Jones, J. B.
Jasper, A. J.
Johnson, A. D.
James, Ben
James, Enoch
Kinder, John
Kanaar, Francis
Kinder, George
Jones, Peter M.
Kirby, Joseph
Kelly, Jas. W.
Justice, Jesse
Lee, A. J.
Lockett, David
Sanderson, W. A.
Stone, Wm.
Stone, Green
Lynn, W.
Loving, S. P.
Lacey, C. C.
Loving, W. R.
Mason, Henry
Marchbanks, J.
Marchbanks, W.
Moody, Thos.
McKinney, J. N.
McKinney, T. N.
Moor, Elisha
Hayhall, T.
Mozier, J. K.
McKinney, R. C.

Moose, Berry
Smith, David
Slaughter, Robt.
Terry, Nat
Tannahill, D. K.
Turner, Wm.
Mooneyhan, J. J.
Moore, J. B.
Masten, W. K.
Mendy, Chas.
McKinney, T. J.
Mathis, Jas.
Owens, John
Popplewell, S.

Perry, Alford
Perry, N. B.
Pope, Pinckney
Richie, R. C.
Robinson, W. M.
Parker, I. D.
Parton, A. J.
Terry, Stephen
Torry, J. N.
Torry, Neal
Thompson, Milt
Turner, Carles
Walling, Vance

Appendix C

The following list of pioneers was made from several sources: a list made by Howard Peak and Merida Ellis to be found in the Tarrant County Scrapbook at Fort Worth Public Library, the secretary's book of the old Union Sunday School in the possession of Mrs. John S. Fort of Arlington, the tombstones of various old cemeteries throughout the county, and from documents and articles written on the history of Tarrant County. The list is not complete, for many of the stones were not legible and the documents could not furnish a complete list. It is possible that many on the list are duplications because of errors in initials and the use of familiar titles rather than the persons' actual names. Wherever possible, the spelling of the names has been carefully checked.

Adams, Bunt (Bunk)
Adams, Carter
Adams, Frank W.
Addington, S. S.
Addington, "Parson"
Addington, J. R.
Akers, Doc
Akers, George A.
Akers, John
Akers, Reasons L.
Akers, Thomas
Alford, B. M.
Alford, James P.
Allen, G. W.
Allen, J. G.
Allen, James K.
Allen, Robert G.
Allen, William Terry
Anderson, Abe

Anderson, Alex
Anderson, Burt
Anderson, Dart
Anderson, M. H.
Anderson, H. B.
Anderson, William
Andrews, A. T.
Andrews, Bolls
Andrews, J. B.
Andrews, T. H.
Andrews, T. J.
Archer, I. F.
Arnold, Major Ripley A.
Asbury, Jeremiah W.
Ayres, J. H.
Ayres, Benjamin P.
Back, Jacob
Bailey, Jim
Baker, Charles

Ball, F. W.
Bamberg, ...
Barcroft, Daniel
Barkeley, Dr. B. F.
Barkeley, Lon
Barnes, Larkin
Barnes, Josiah
Barnes, W. D.
Barr, John W.
Bates, F. A.
Beall, Warren
Beard, A. W.
Beard, J. J.
Beard, J. T.
Beckham, Robert F.
Bedford, Ben
Beeman, John
Bennett, Hamilton
Berliner, ...
Bird, Jonathan
Blackwell, Hiram
Blakeney, A.
Blount, Jerome
Boaz, David
Boaz, Richard
Boaz, W. J.
Bold, Lieutenant John
Bomford, Captain J. B.
Boone, George
Boone, John
Booth, Ten
Bosson, William
Bostwick, Charles Hanson
Bowlin, ...
Boyd, P. B.
Boyd, William L.
Bradner, James W.
Bradshaw, A. J.
Bratton, Richard
Brewer, William
Brinson, Fred
Brinson, Captain M. J.
Brinson, M. T.
Booke, Malone
Brown, M. F.
Brinson, T. A.
Bosman, J. C.
Brizentine, William
Brown, D. V.

Brown, Horatio
Brown, Lewis H.
Brown, Mrs. Ruth
Brown, T. E.
Burford, A. E.
Burford, C. J.
Burford, William
Burgoon, Charles
Burk, Francis
Burnett, Moses
Burns, W. P.
Bursey, John
Burton, Noel
Burts, Dr. W. T.
Byars, Nicholas
Byrd, J. A.
Caldron, John
Calloway, Hiram
Calloway, J. W.
Cambrell, John C.
Cameron, E. W.
Cameron, N. J.
Campbell, F. A.
Cannon, Carter
Cate, James
Cartwright, ...
Catlett, Harry B.
Chambers, A. J.
Chambers, Faribu
Chambers, J. K.
Chapman, John
Chapman, Sam
Chiles, A.
Chisum, B. L.
Chitwood, J. O.
Chivers, A. M.
Chivers, Larkin
Clanton, W.
Clark, J. W.
Clay, L. A.
Clifton, J. W.
Clifton, Lewie
Clifton, Theodore
Cloud, John F.
Cohen, Lewis
Cohn, Israel
Coker, N. M.
Coleman, K.
Coleman, A. C.

Coleman, James
Coleman, Madison
Coleman, P. E.
Coleman, Tom S.
Collier, Jack
Collier, John
Collins, Brit
Collins, W. W. R.
Condra, John
Conley, C.
Conner, Jess
Conner, A. H.
Conner, John
Conner, W. D.
Cook, Josiah
Copeland, A. H.
Copeland, T. B.
Cotrell, Simon
Courtney, John J.
Copeland, A. C.
Cowan, I. M.
Cowart, Charles
Crawford, W. C. E.
Creswell, Ambrose
Creswell, Cyrus
Creswell, Lytle
Creswell, R.
Crocker, Thomas
Cromwell, G. W.
Cromwell, W. C.
Cross, A. H.
Cross, Robert
Crouch, Avery
Crouch, L.
Crouch, W.
Crow, G. W.
Crow, Joe Boggs
Crowley, B. F.
Crowley, Hiram
Crowley, Richard
Cummings, John M.
Cummings, C. C.
Cummings, John
Cureton, Captain Jack
Curry, T.
Daggett, Ephriam Merrell
Daggett, Charles B.
Daggett, Henry
Daggett, Henry Clay

Dade, Dabney C.
Dalton, George
Dalton, Jasper
Dalton, Joe
Dalton, Pat
Dalton, Tom
Daniel, F. H.
Daniels, John
Darcey, Samuel J.
Darnell, Col. Nicholas
Daggett, E. B.
Darter, Francis
Darter, Mike
Darter, D. I. M.
Darter, W. A.
Davenport, C. G.
Davis, P. G.
Davis, Sol
Dean, M. T.
Dean, Ransom L.
Dean, Silas
Denton, A. N.
Dicks, Marcus
Dickson, E. A.
Dickson, Major John
Dietrick, Gesiene
Ditto, Lieutenant J. W.
Ditto, Mike
Ditto, Thomas B.
Dobkins, Alex
Dodson, Constant
Dodson, Jott
Donaldson, ...
Dorris, Dr. William E.
Dosier, William
Doss, Jesse
Drew, Smith
Duncan, Thomas
Dunn, Dr. J. C.
Dunn, W. W.
Durrett, Bob
Durrett, Dick
Durrett, Henry
Durrett, Jack
Earl, Arch
Earles, Israel
Easter, Thomas
Echols, W. B.
Eddy, Nathan

Edwards, Cass
Edwards, Lemuel J.
Edwards, Sid
Eggleston, Irving
Eggleston, Everett
Eggleston, J.
Elliott, J. W.
Elliott, John H.
Elliott, R. M.
Elliott, Sanders
Elliott, W. F.
Ellis, J. N.
Ellis, James
Ellis, M. G.
Elliston, Frank
Elliston, J. W.
Elliston, Mark
Elmore, A. M.
Eppler, Mrs. ....
Estis, Meredith
Estes, Silas
Evans, J. A. T.
Evans, J. M.
Evans, J. Sam
Evans, James
Evans, William
Ewing, Dr. ....
Farmer, Elijah
Farmer, D. V.
Farmer, G. P.
Farmer, Jake
Farmer, Joe B.
Farmer, Press
Farrar, John
Farrar, Simon
Ferguson, W. T.
Ferris, Walter
Field, D. R. A.
Field, Henry
Field, Dr. J. T.
Field, Jeff
Field, Joe
Field, Julian
Field, Dr. Sam
Field, Will
Finger, George
Finger, John
Finger, Lewis
Finger, Peter

Fletcher, Jasper
Ford, E. M.
Ford, P. H.
Ford, R. C.
Ford, R. Eli
Ford, Richard
Ford, W. M.
Ford, W. G.
Fort, John S.
Fort, L. T.
Foster, Allen
Foster, Harvey
Foster, J. B.
Fowler, A. Y.
Francis, N. B.
Freeman, Rev. A.
French, B. J. W.
Freshour, John
Gaither, Jerry
Gano, General Richard M.
Garathy, J.
Gardenhire, William
Gee, W. P.
Gibbins, R. C.
Gibson, Garrett
Gibson, John
Giddens, W. M.
Gilbert, Captain Mabel
Gilbow, E. H.
Gilliam, Will
Gilmore, Seburn
Givens, James
Goehenant, A.
Goodwin, Charley
Goodwin, Macajah
Granbury, Hi
Grant, James
Gray, Thomas A.
Green, Samuel Percival
Griffin, B. H.
Griffin, Colonel George
Grimsley, James
Griscomb, Lieutenant George
Hagood, Ben
Hagood, Tom
Halford, James P.
Hall, A. S.
Hall, Arch
Hall, Edward S.

Hall, John
Hall, W. C.
Hall, William D.
Hammond, P. K. S.
Hanks, A. M.
Hanks, E. D.
Hardesty, Charles
Hardesty, John
Harper, C. A.
Harper, John
Harris, A. H.
Harris, A. S.
Harris, Colonel Abe
Harris, R. M.
Harrison, John
Harrison, Jonas
Harrison, Joseph
Harrison, Thomas Jefferson
Harrison, William H.
Hart, Hardin
Hartman, Fortunate
Hartman, Sam
Haydon, James
Hayter, Rev. A. S.
Hayter, Fred
Hazlewood, A.
Hazlewood, William
Heath, Thomas Jefferson
Henderson, J. T.
Henderson, Joe M.
Henderson, W. A.
Hendricks, Green B.
Hendricks, H. G.
Hickey, Louis
Hicks, Lieutenant Watson
Hicks, William
Hilburn, Sebe
Hirschfield, John A.
Hodges, Dr. D. G.
Hoffman, G. G.
Holdman, Hardy
Holdman, John
Holland, J. N.
Holland, W. J.
Holloway, H. C.
Holly, William H.
Holman, J. G.
Holmes, T. P.
Holt, L. W.

Holt, Late
Holt, Dr. Pink
Holt, W. C.
Holt, W. C., Jr.
Hood, J. A.
Hope, G. W.
Hope, H. S.
Hosea, C. E.
House, P. M.
Hovenkamp, Edward
Howard, James
Howell, R. M.
Howerton, F. M.
Howerton, J. B.
Hudgens, Rev. E. N.
Hudgens, Philip D.
Hudson, Prof. John
Huffman, Phil
Hughes, J. H.
Huitt, John
Hurst, H.
Hurst, J. A.
Hust, John
Hutcheson, Alford
Hutcheson, Charles A.
Hutton, Vincent J.
Isbell, George Rufus
Isbell, Mel
Isbell, Paul
Ish, Rea M.
Ish, Rev. T. A.
Ish, William J.
Ingraham, John
Inman, Jack
Jackson, Dr. George
James, Ben
James, Enoch
James, Tom B.
James, William
Jasper, A. J.
Jasper, J. H.
Jasper, T.
Jenkins, E. M.
Jenkins, Zeb
Johnson, Alsford D.
John, Ben H.
Johnson, C. C.
Johnson, C. C.
Johnson, Coleman

Johnson, J. B.
Johnson, J. C.
Johnson, J. D.
Johnson, J. R.
Johnson, Colonel Middleton Tate
Johnson, M. T., Jr.
Johnson, Thomas J.
Johnson, Tobe
Johnson, W. J.
Jones, I. W.
Jones, J. B.
Jones, J. C.
Jones, J. F.
Jones, Jesse
Jones, L. W.
Jones, Peter M.
Jordan, Francis
Jopling, G. W.
Jopling, L. L.
Joyce, James
Justice, Jesse
Kane, Lewis
Kelley, James W.
Kemble, Henry
Kemper, David C.
Kennedy, M. D.
Kinder, George
Kinder, John
King, Richard
King, William
Kirby, Joseph
Kirkwood, ...
Kiser, John
Knaar, Francis
Lacey, C. C.
Lasater, O. R.
Law, P. J.
Lee, A. J.
Ledford, Silas
Leonard, William
Little, J. K.
Lockett, David
Loving, John S.
Loving, W. R.
Loving, Samuel P.
Loving, J. S.
Louchkx, Charles
Lowe, William
Loyd, Captain M. B.

Lusk, John P.
Lyles, John W.
Lytle, Minor
Lynn, Billy
Maben, N. M.
Maben, T.
Maclay, Robert P.
Maddox, Colonel W. A.
Majors, Tuck
Manley, J. S.
Mann, R. S.
Manning, ...
Marchbanks, J.
Marchbanks, Lafayette
Marchbanks, W.
Marshall, L. G.
Martin, C. W.
Martin, James D.
Martin, John H.
Mason, Henry
Masten, W. K.
Mathews, A. J.
Mathews, Thomas M.
Mathis, James
Matthews, Dr. Mansell
Mauk, David
Mayhall, T.
Mayo, W. R.
McClugn, Ashbel G.
McDonald, C. B.
McGinnis, John
McKee, William
McKinney, J. N.
McKinney, R. C.
McKinney, T. N.
McLamore, M. W.
McKinney, T. J.
McLemore, John
McLemore, William
Mendy, Charles
Melear, L. C.
Merrell, Major Hamilton
Milborn, Albert
Milborn, E. Z.
Middleton, Dr. A. K.
Millican, J. K.
Minter, Green M.
Mitchell, Ben C.
Milwee, Judge A. M.

Mitchell, Charles Ellis
Mitchell, Eli
Mitchell, John A.
Mitchell, Joseph E.
Mitchell, Matt
Mitchell, Richard
Mitchell, William L.
Mooneyham, J. J.
Montgomery, Lewis
Moodie, S. O.
Moody, Pleas
Moody, Rall
Moody, Thomas
Moor, Elisha
Moore, J. R.
Moore, Pleasant
Moorehead, Jacob
Moorehead, William
Moose, Berry
Morrison, Pat
Moseley, William
Mozier, J. K.
Mugg, John A.
Mulkey, George
Myers, Henry
Nance, Gideon
Nash, Z. E. B.
Netherly, Captain Alex
Neal, K.
Neice, Joel
Newton, Eli
Newton, Anderson
Norris, William
Norton, A. B.
Ogelsby, J. H.
O'Neal, Jim J.
O'Neill, William J.
Overton, A. W.
Overton, Lon
Overton, W. H.
Owens, John
Ozes, Jasper
Parker, Dan
Parker, Isaac Duke
Parker, Samuel
Parton, A. J.
Patton, William
Payne, C. G.
Peak, Dr. Carroll M.

Peak, Howard
Pearce, L. J.
Perkins, A. M.
Perkins, Lee
Perkins, Tom
Perry, Alford
Perry, Green
Perry, Melville
Perry, Napoleon B.
Petty, John
Petty, Sam A.
Petty, William
Pew, H. R.
Pew, John H.
Pickens, ...
Poe, Henderson
Poe, William
Pope, Pinckney
Popplewell, Sam
Powell, J. W.
Prather, C. D.
Purvis, Doug
Purvis, Joe
Purvis, John
Quaile, Amos
Quaile, William
Ragan, Stephen
Ragsdale, Smith
Ragland, D. J.
Ralston, A. S.
Ralston, John
Ramsey, John Seth
Ramsey, Merrick F.
Ramsey, Robert
Ramsey, S. S.
Randall, William
Randol, M. L.
Randol, A. J.
Rattan, Wade Hampton
Ray, Dr. J. D.
Reece, Bill
Reed, J. N.
Rice, William
Richie, R. C.
Richy, A. C.
Rintleman, A. C.
Roberson, W. A.
Robertson, Jeol
Robinson, Archibald
Robinson, Nathan

Robinson, Randol
Robinson, W. M.
Robinson, T. F.
Rodgers, Waling R.
Roy, John C.
Rudd, Sidney W.
Rudd, William H.
Ruddle, ⋯⋯⋯
Rumby, Eli
Russ, Bob
Rushing, J. L.
Russell, John
Russell, Stephen B.
Russell, W. C.
Samuels, Baldwin
Samuels, Jacob
Sanders, C. A.
Sanderson, William
Sawyer, W. F.
Scott, Jim
Scott, W. M.
Seaton, Sam
Sewell, Peter
Sharp, G. M.
Shelton, Dr. J. F.
Shippey, J. K.
Sigler, N.
Silkwood, Solomon
Slaughter, Robert
Smallwood, Porter
Smith, David
Smith, John Peter
Smith, Lieutenant Jim
Smith, Junius W.
Smith, N. A.
Snider, Robert
Snow, David
Spaight, Colonel A. W.
Solee, ⋯⋯⋯
Starr, R. West
Starr, S. C.
Starr, Samuel H.
Steele, I. M.
Steele, Lon
Steele, Lawrence
Stone, Green
Stone, William
Stockett, I. J.
Strahan, Dr. J. A.
Sublett, H. W.

Suggs, Henry
Swann, Fred
Swayne, John F.
Tandy, Roger
Tandy, William
Tannahill (Tannehill), D. K.
Tannahill, Robert
Taylor, Hugh
Taylor, Tom C.
Terrell, Dave
Terrell, Edmund S.
Terrell, George
Terrell, Joseph C.
Terry, J. N.
Terry, Nathaniel
Terry, Nathaniel, Jr.
Terry, Stephen
Terry, William
Thomas, George L.
Thomas, Hampton
Thomas, Martin V.
Thomas, T. A.
Thomas, William I.
Thompson, Milt
Thurmond, P. M.
Timberlake, Major J. E.
Tinsley, L. J.
Tolliver, Joseph
Torry, Neal
Trayler, Washington
Trice, J. T.
Tucker, Rowan
Tucker, W. B.
Turner, Charles
Turner, Jim
Turner, William
Tummins, S. N.
Tyler, Paul H.
Utley, Lieutenant Thomas
Veal, W. G.
Van Zandt, Major K. M.
Ventioner, Isaac
Ventioner, Jim
Wade, Reuben
Wade, Woodson
Walden, Legrande
Waldron, P.
Walker, A. G.
Walker, Jim
Waller, A. S.

Wallace, F. R.
Walling, Vance
Ward, Captain ....
Watson, James A.
Watson, Jason
Watson, John H.
Watson, John J.
Watson, Patrick A.
Watson, Patrick A., Jr.
Watson, R. L.
Watson, Thomas H.
Walters, William
Weaver, Harrison
Webb, Alex
Weems, John
West, C.
Wetmore, Louis

Wheeler, Cal
Wheeler, P. L.
Wiggins, David
Willis, Felix
Willis, Jacob
Witherington, John
Wilson, James
Wright, Albert
Wright, Dick
Wright, Jim
Wood, N. G.
Woods, James P.
Woods, M. L.
Wynne, William
Yandle, E. D.
Yantis, W. C.
York, John B.

Appendix D

LIST OF MEMBERS OF CAPTAIN WILLIAM QUAYLE'S COMPANY OF MOUNTED RIFLEMEN, STATE VOLUNTEERS, 1861

The following is a list of men who were members of Captain William Quayle's Company of Mounted Riflemen, State Volunteers, which was organized in June, 1861. It was the first company to leave Tarrant County, though it is doubtful if all the men were residents of the county. Quayle was later promoted to the rank of Colonel. His name is often found spelled Quayle.

Captain:
William Quayle
Lieutenants:
Robert R. Hunt
Joseph Calloway
A. B. Grant
Sergeants:
Thomas Berry
James E. Moore
Thomas Purcess
Joe H. Simmons
Isaac J. Curry
Corporals:
William R. Allen
William L. Boyd
David Mason
Lorenze Newton
Privates:
Reason L. Akers
George A. Akers

Doo Akers
I. F. Archer
Alex Anderson
Thomas Armstrong
William N. Allison
Peter M. Bush
Amos Burgoon
David Boaz
Richard Boaz
Cuinton Booth
Thomas L. Barcroft
D. J. Bradly
W. J. Barnhill
W. C. Carlton
David Cate
Smith Cummings
Gus Cread
Thomas H. Cox
William Cox
G. W. Cread

F. O. Clair
F. M. Dyer
John S. Dunn
Green Durham
Poke Dodson
Solon Dunn
Isaac P. Davis
J. N. Dodson
Ransom L. Dean
Mark Elliston
John S. Estill
Ed L. Eckardt
G. F. Ellis
John Friend
Robert W. Fisher
James M. Fregge
William Greenup
W. S. Gray
John Grimes
A. M. Hightower
Joe D. Henry
Hardy S. Homan
R. W. Harrison
John Hudgens
Richard Hayworth
J. W. Hutton
Waiter L. Jones
John King
Willia Lavender
Levi Leonard
Robert Lanham
Walter N. Leake
Robert Laney
Francis M. Lewis
John Lafoon

.... Lafoon
James McDaniel
W. D. McDaniel
M. McDaniels
J. L. Moorehead
.... Heil
Thomas Patton
C. C. Pearsell
G. W. Pointer
L. H. Pennington
John M. Parish
Addison Perry
J. J. Phillips
Reuben B. Rogers
George Roach
E. P. Richardson
Sylvester Record
Jesse Rogers
Ransom Russell
William M. Robinson
J. B. Sloan
E. A. Shults
J. R. Shaw
Alonzo Stevenson
Ed Syfert
John L. Tinsley
W. R. Trice
James Turner
James Thomas
William L. Tandy
N. W. Tolle
J. H. Tinsley
Terrell Woodson
Alexander White

Appendix E

MUSTER ROLL OF TARRANT COUNTY RIFLES 1862

The following is the Muster Roll of the Tarrant County Rifles. The company was organized in 1862 by Dr. Carroll M. Peak who was injured in a fall from his horse shortly before the company left for the war. Archives of Mary Daggett Lake.

Captain:
Dr. C. M. Peak
Lieutenants:
W. C. Yantis
J. Earl

Orderly Sergeant:
G. Boone
Corporals:
T. M. Matthews
P. G. Davis

J. Garathy
Surgeon:
Dr. W. P. Burts
Privates:
Thomas J. Johnson
S. A. Addington
J. W. Asbury
William Randall
H. G. Johnson
F. W. Adams
J. P. Alford
J. B. Andrews
J. Earle
A. S. Hall
W. C. Hall
H. C. Holloway
J. Johnson
Gideon Nance
J. B. Sanders
L. C. Jones
J. M. Murchison
W. M. McKee
Jacob Samuel
John W. Steinbeck
W. J. Terry
E. A. Dickson
A. N. Denton

J. Eggleston
C. G. Payne
H. B. Catlett
A. N. C. Lavender
James D. Martin
Lafayette Marchbanks
Leigh Oldham
Solomon D. Poer
John Peter Smith
C. A. Sanders
W. R. Loving
George Boone
M. D. Kennedy
Marcus Dicks
A. M. Harris
P. B. Boyd
G. C. Hoffman
N. M. Coker
Frank Wilcox
R. S. Wright
John R. Addington
David Snow
Nathaniel Terry, Jr.
R. Creswell
W. Crouch
.... McMillan

Ben M. Johnson was later made a first lieutenant of this company and H. B. Catlett was made second lieutenant. Both Thomas J. and Ben M. Johnson were made captains at a later date. Many of the members of this company sent substitutes to the war. Among these were Dr. W. P. Burts, P. C. David, John R. Garaghty, W. C. Yantis, George Boone, and Thomas M. Matthews.

Appendix F

MUSTER ROLL OF COMPANY F

Muster roll of Company F. Captain J. C. Terrell, Waller's battalion, cavalry Tom Green's First brigade, then Hardiman's brigade. Walker's division Texas troops, Trans-Mississippi department, enlisted at Fort Worth, Texas, March 1862. Archives.

Officers:
Captain:
J. C. Terrell
Lieutenants:
H. C. (Tobe) Johnson
J. W. Bradner

B. F. Arthur
J. F. Elliston
Sergeants:
W. T. Jones
W. L. Lee
J. W. Hutton

J. D. Jefferson

Corporal:

C. R. Matney

Privates:

W. T. Allen
H. T. Brown
W. M. Cross
C. C. Doss
H. W. Doss
P. G. Dalton
J. B. Edens
James Grant
Tom Geary
J. E. Hood
Sam Hood
J. M. Henderson
S. A. Hall
Tom Hardesty
J. R. Henry
B. Memam
T. B. James

Jack M. Johnston
C. D. Johnson
D. D. Jefferson
Sam Jefferson
J. B. Buckett
Dave R. Lakey
W. M. McKee
W. J. Mason
J. D. Prather
John D. Prather
Jim Prather
D. A. Price
T. B. Russell
J. W. Steinbeck
Jacob Samuels
E. H. Smith
R. P. Threlkeid
T. L. Utley
J. A. Walker
L. B. Walker
W. H. White

Appendix G

MUSTER ROLL OF COMPANY D, 9TH TEXAS CAVALRY
ROSS BRIGADE

The following is the Muster Roll of the second company that left Fort Worth for the Civil War in 1861. Captain Jack Brison commanding.
Roll of Company D, 9th Texas Cavalry, Ross Brigade:

Antone	Mexican who went through the war
Bunk Adams	
Dock Andrews	Slight Wounds
Carter Allen	Drew out at the end of 12 months
Dart Anderson	Drew out, over age, at end of 12 months
Burt Anderson	Drew out, under age, at end of 12 months
Capt. M. J. Brinson	Drew out, over age, at end of 12 months
Fred Brinson	Died at Corinth, Miss. 1862
Leroy Beavers	
Jim Bailey	
Bowlin	Lost in battle at Corinth, Miss. 1862
T. S. Coleman	Wounded at Vicksburg, Miss. 1863
Avery Crouch	Killed in 1864
Joe Boggs Crow	Killed. Indian Territory 1861
Lieut. J. W. Ditto	
Tom Dalton	Died at Corinth, Miss. 1862
Jasper Dalton	Died at Clarksville, Ark. 1862

Joe Dalton	Died at Corinth, Miss. 1862
Estis	Died at Headquarters 1861
Merideth Estis	Quit in a short time
Louis Finger	Quit at the end of the year
Jasper Fletcher	Quit
Lieut. Geo. Griscomb	
Charley Goodwin	Died at Corinth, Miss. 1862
Will Goodwin	Killed at Jonesburgh, Aug. 1864
Will Goin	Wagoner
Jerry Gaither	Deserted in 1863
Will Gilliam	
Lieut. Wilson P. Hicks	Killed at Thompson Sta., Tenn. 1863
Tom Hagood	
Pen Hagood	
Rev. T. A. Ish	Quit at the end of the year. Over age
Irishman	Quit in 1862
Lieut. & Capt. Jim Kelly	Killed at Corinth, Miss. 1862
Kirkwood	Quit
Kirkwood	Quit
Henry Kemble	Lost at Corinth, Miss. Died 1862
Kemble	Lost at Corinth, Miss. Died 1862
Jno. Kiser	Wagoner
Capt. Bill McLemore	Slight wounds
Jno. T. McLemore	
Manning	Lost at Corinth, Miss. Died 1862
Manning	Lost at Corinth, Miss. Died 1862
J. H. Martin	
Henry Myers	Quit in 1863
Jno. McGinnis	
Jim O'Neal	Killed in North Miss. 1863
A. M. Perkins	Slight wound. Came home.
Tom Perkins	Slight wound. Came home.
Lee Perkins	Slight wound. Came home.
Green Perry	Wounded at Corinth, Miss. Came home
Sam Petty	
Dan Parker	Quit at end of year. Over age.
Pickens	Quit at end of year. Over age.
Bill Reece	Slight wound. Came home.
Lieut. Jim Smith	
Solee	
Joe Tolliver	
Jim Turner	Slight wound. Came home.
Hugh Taylor	
Tom Taylor	Died at Vicksburg 1863
Lieut. Tom Utley	Quit at end of the year
Albert Wright	
Dick Wright	
Lieut. Jim Wright	
J. A. Watson	
J. H. Watson	Wounded twice. Came home.

Harrison Weaver	Wounded at Corinth, Miss. Came home.
James Wilson	Wounded at Elk Horn. Came home.
Jno. Witherington	Transferred to another Company.

Index

Note: Variant spellings and the use of initials versus full names may have resulted in duplicate entries for the same person.